America's Choice
The Election of 1992

America's Choice
The Election of 1992

William Crotty, Editor
Northwestern University

DPG

The Dushkin Publishing Group, Inc.

Credits

Page 16 Copyright © 1992 by The New York Times Company. Reprinted by permission.

Page 23 Reprinted by permission of Danby-Bangor Daily News.

Page 32 Reprinted by permission of Tribune Media Services.

Page 38 Copyright © 1992 by The New York Times Company. Reprinted by permission.

Page 56 Copyright 1992 Boston Globe, distributed by The Los Angeles Times Syndicate.

Page 66 Copyright © 1992 Dan Foote/Texas International Features.

Page 67 Reprinted by permission of *USA Today*.

Page 74 Reprinted by permission of Mike Luckovich and Creators Syndicate.

Page 84 Reprinted by permission of Don Wright, The Palm Beach Post.

Page 90 Reprinted by permission of Congressional Quarterly, Inc.

Page 92 Reprinted by permission of Congressional Quarterly, Inc.

Page 94 Reprinted by permission of Congressional Quarterly, Inc.

Page 95 Reprinted with special permission of King Features Syndicate.

Page 96 Copyright © 1992, *The American Enterprise*. Reprinted with permission from The New York Times/Special Features.

Page 97 Copyright © 1992, *The American Enterprise*. Reprinted with permission from The New York Times/Special Features.

Page 109 Copyright 1992 Boston Globe, distributed by The Los Angeles Times Syndicate.

Page 112 Reprinted by permission of The Center for the American Woman and Politics, Rutgers University.

Page 115 Reprinted with special permission of King Features Syndicate.

Page 125 Reprinted by permission of Mike Luckovich and Creators Syndicate.

Page 138 Reprinted by permission of Congressional Quarterly, Inc.

Page 140 Reprinted by permission of Don Wright, The Palm Beach Post.

Page 166 Reprinted by permission of Ed Gamble, The Florida Times-Union.

Pages 168–170 Reprinted by permission of the Associated Press.

Printed in the United States of America

Library of Congress Catalog Card Number: 92–76120

International Standard Book Number (ISBN) 1–56134–252–1

The Dushkin Publishing Group, Inc., Sluice Dock, Guilford, Connecticut 06437

Preface

The 1992 presidential election was a crucial, fascinating, and often quirky case study in American democracy at work, and this book is a series of 13 lively essays that dissect the election from every key point of view.

How did a little-known Democratic outsider with several vulnerabilities wrestle the nation's highest office from a Republican president whose popularity ratings had stood at 90 percent just a year earlier? Each contributor highlights a different aspect of the process, combining historical analysis, insights and anecdotes, and new research to draw conclusions about its significance.

Following my overview, John Tierney sets the scene, detailing the context in which voters halted a Republican dominance of the White House that had lasted for nearly a quarter of a century. Charles Hadley and Harold Stanley review the nomination process—the big-name Democrats who chose not to challenge Bush, the right-wing Republican who did, the winnowing out of Democratic contenders in the primaries, and the on-again, off-again insurgency of Ross Perot.

The general election campaign is illuminated from three points of view: Jerome Mileur focuses on how the two major parties deployed their strengths and support in the battle; John White details the issues and themes around which the three candidates built their appeals; and Jarol Manheim analyzes their attempts to harness the tremendous power of the media, from Perot's infomercials, through Clinton's town meeting approach, to the new role of TV talk shows.

The certainty of Bush's reelection faded as the campaign progressed, but who was responsible? Did Clinton and the Democrats forge their own victory, did Bush bring about his own demise, or did Ross Perot destroy Bush's chances? Frank Feigert examines the most successful third-party candidate since 1912, portraying the man, his campaign, and his impact on the election.

The spotlight of *America's Choice* moves from the presidency to the drama of congressional elections. John Jackson discusses why House members retired in record numbers and how voters reacted in apparent contradiction, urging limits on congressional terms while reelecting their favorite incumbents. Candace Nelson details how big spending fueled not only Ross Perot's race, but also those of scores of congressional candidates, as she traces the money trail—where it came from and where it went.

The variety of new faces in the 103rd Congress emphasize one of the most important outcomes of the 1992 election—the move to diversity on Capitol Hill. Janet Boles focuses on the role of women in this change—Anita Hill's allegations of sexual harassment, "the Hillary factor" in Clinton's race, the victories of such candidates as Carol Moseley Braun and Dianne Feinstein, and the strategies and financing of many other women's campaigns. John Kromkowski discusses the impact of ethnicity on American politics and the 1992 election.

Peter Miller exposes the inner workings of political public opinion polls, describing their uses and abuses in the critical election process. The final essay in *America's Choice* by Peter Nardulli and Jon Dalager poses the most significant question—how much change does this election augur, and how long might it last?—and offers some provocative answers.

The scholarship, analysis, and research of *America's Choice* are enlivened with humorous and colorful writing, incisive political cartoons, and a variety of illustrative charts, tables, and maps. This book will be an important and enjoyable adjunct to any study of the workings of American democracy.

I wish to thank two of my coauthors in particular, John K. White and Jerome M. Mileur, for their contributions in developing this book, and both Nan W. Crotty and Julie M. Crotty for help in researching and preparing the manuscript. I would especially like to express my thanks and those of my coauthors for the fine work of Irv Rockwood and all those at The Dushkin Publishing Group who directly contributed to the production of this book.

William Crotty

Table of Contents

Chapter One

Introduction:
A Most Unusual Election

William Crotty

It was an unusual election and a most exciting one. It was also a highly significant one. All presidential elections are important. Yet the 1992 election year derives added importance from the victory of a Democrat and the end to 12 years of Republican Party rule in presidential politics. Arguably, it could be the end of a conservative era that has stretched over a generation and the beginning of a new direction in American politics. If so, its importance will transcend that of most, placing it in a category with those of 1980, 1968, and 1960, all foreshadowing decisive changes in the national's political agenda.

Conservatives have controlled the White House since the election of 1968. The Republican Party has won five of the six presidential elections held between 1968 and 1988, a string broken only by the success of Jimmy Carter, a moderate to conservative Democrat in 1976, in the aftermath of the Watergate scandal. With the promise of giving new direction to America's government and a pledge to address the economic concerns that were paramount to the electorate, Bill Clinton and his vice-presidential running mate, Al Gore, won a potentially historic victory. How far they choose—or are able—to take the country in a new direction and how successful they are in addressing the nation's fundamental economic and social problems is yet to be determined. For the present, the significance is in the election results: another party is in power and a new team has taken office.

In addition, the election seemed to have a little something for everyone:

- the highest turnout in years, 55 percent, the best showing since 1972 and the reversal of progressive declines over the last three decades;[1]
- the failed efforts of an incumbent party to continue the conservative policies and dominance of the contemporary era and to keep intact its winning coalition;
- the attempts of the Democrats, in turn, to refashion and reshape their image and develop a new majority. They did this by running not one, but two, southern moderates, who directed their appeals to the white middle class that the Republicans, under both Richard Nixon and Ronald Reagan, had won over handily.

Family Income	Percentage of Voters		
	Clinton	Bush	Perot
$30–50,000	41	38	21
$15–30,000	45	35	20
Under $15,000	59	23	18

In effect, Clinton did succeed in putting together a more moderate coalition and in winning over the middle of the electorate, as he had set out to do (see the chapter by Peter V. Miller in this volume).[2]

It was also considered to be the "year of the woman," and 28 new female members were elected to the House and 4 to the Senate. The Senate contingent included Carol Moseley Braun of Illinois, an African American, the first black woman to serve in that body. In addition, both Senators elected from California were women, and Washington State sent first-time officeholder Patty Murray, the "mom in tennis shoes," as she billed herself during the campaign, to the Senate.[3]

Latinos did better than ever before in 1992, electing 17 members to the House (up from 10 in the last Congress), a number from new congressional districts intended specifically to increase Latino representation.[4] This trend should continue (see the chapter by John A. Kromkowski on ethnicity in this volume).

And finally, another first in this regard, a Native American, Ben Nighthorse Campbell, was elected to the Senate from Colorado.

And just to make sure things did not get too boring, there was H. Ross Perot. Responding, he said, to the wishes of the people, Perot dropped into the race, then out, and then in again, charging in the closing days of the campaign that Republican "dirty tricks" had driven him out originally.[5] Despite it all, he did unexpectedly well in the debates and with his television messages. He finished with 19 percent of the vote, an unusually good showing. In the postelection period, Perot was to say that his group, "United We Stand," would continue as a player on the national scene. While it would not become a political party, its organization would become more formalized and more financially self-sufficient.[6] He, or other independent, non–major party candidates, may well be a factor in presidential elections for years to come. To a large extent, their appeal to the electorate will depend on how well or how poorly a Clinton administration fares.

This chapter overviews the election year, looking in turn at the Republicans and then the Democrats in both the prenomination and general election stages of the campaign and then briefly at the Perot effort. It ends with an assessment of the potential short- and long-term significance of the election race and its outcome.

First, some observations on the Republicans, beginning with the context the presidency of George H. W. Bush provided for both the general election campaign and, earlier, the prenomination fight in the primaries. Especially important in this latter regard was the New Hampshire primary and the issues it raised and the challenges it presented to a Bush renomination.

THE REPUBLICANS AND THE BUSH PRESIDENCY

George Bush won the 1988 presidential election with what was perceived as, first, a decisive victory (52 percent to 45 percent over the Democratic candidate, Michael S. Dukakis) and, second, what was interpreted to be a mandate to continue the Reagan administration's policies and its electoral coalition.

During the 1988 campaign, Bush promised a "kinder, gentler nation," and at different points put himself forward as "the education president" and "the environmental president," self-characterizations that had little to do with his policies once in office (see the chapter by John T. Tierney in this volume). His most famous pronouncements, however—"Read my lips!" and "No new taxes!"—delivered to the Republican National Convention in the summer of 1988 and to a nationwide television audience in his speech accepting his party's presidential nomination, would come back to haunt him. The words played favorably with the Republican Party faithful who dominated the party's national convention, and they had appeal for the American electorate in general. However, they were also seen as something more. Bush's words were taken as a basic commitment to continue the tax, fiscal, and conservative economic policies of the Reagan years.

Bush broke this pledge with the budget compromise of the fall of 1990, worked out primarily between the White House and the Democratic leadership of the Congress, or so many of his more conservative supporters came to believe. The budget compromise did increase taxes as one aspect of a plan to reduce the staggering budget deficit, doubled during the Reagan presidency, and it put a cap on social and other spending.[7] The agreement to support these proposals was seen as the biggest single mistake of the Bush presidency—or, at least, candidate George Bush was to say this repeatedly during the campaign of 1992.

Basically, the Bush administration was dedicated to maintaining the status quo. It had *no* domestic agenda. And, in fact, in the fall of 1990 after the Americans With Disabilities Act and the amendments to the Clean Air Act were agreed to, John H. Sununu, the White House chief of staff, was quoted as saying that Congress could take the rest of the term off because "there's not a single piece of legislation that needs to be passed in the two years remaining."[8]

Going into the election, Bush in his four years as president had vetoed approximately 35 bills. In the post-election period he was to add vetoes of urban aid for America's cities and economic assistance to Los Angeles in its efforts to recover from the riots of April, 1992. In one sense, President Bush's vetoes (minimum wage increases; additional funding for programs in the Departments of Labor, Health and Human Services, and Education; mass transit authorizations; civil service, campaign finance and voter registration reform; civil rights bills; unemployment benefits; family planning and family leave bills), more than his policy initiatives, defined his presidency.

Two domestic decisions do stand out (in addition to the budget compromise of 1990). One was the veto of the family leave bill, seen as too expensive, and initially important primarily to a small but well-defined segment of the electorate. It was to be taken as a prime example of the Bush administration's insensitivity to the concerns of women.

The other was the appointment of Clarence Thomas to the Supreme Court. By any standard, Thomas, an African American, was a conservative Republican ideologue who had been a controversial figure during the Reagan years. Thomas had held several highly visible appointed positions in the Reagan administration—Assistant Secretary for Civil Rights in the Department of Education and later chair of the Equal Opportunity Commission, a post he used to oppose traditional, government-supported policies such as affirmative action. These positions, however, were not the lasting source of the controversy.

The need for Senate confirmation of the Thomas appointment, the hearings on his fitness for the nation's highest court, and, more specifically, the confrontation with Anita Hill, an African-American law school professor who had formerly worked with Thomas, provided explicit (and unusually graphic) charges of sexual harassment. The question was who to believe—Hill's accusations, which could not be verified, or Thomas's denials and countercharges of a "judicial lynching." The Senate panel, composed entirely of white males, was widely criticized for an intense and highly partisan cross-examination of Hill by its Republican members, and specifically by Senators Orrin Hatch of Utah, Arlen Specter of Pennsylvania, and Alan Simpson of Wyoming, and a seemingly cursory and unfocused questioning of Hill by its Democratic members. The panel chose to accept Thomas's version, and both it and the Senate voted to confirm him as a Supreme Court justice.[9]

By any gauge, it was a nasty business. The Thomas-Hill hearings were carried nationally on television. They transfixed a nation and, more importantly for the 1992 election, created a firestorm. The hearings, held in the fall of 1991, roughly one year before election and only months before the first of the primaries were to begin, did much to channel the anger and energies of women toward the election of 1992. One consequence was that more women ran and more were elected to Congress than ever before. Bush was also to lose the women's vote to Clinton (women: Clinton, 46 percent; Bush, 37 percent; Perot, 17 percent; men: Clinton, 41 percent; Bush, 38 percent; Perot, 21 percent). The "year of the woman," as it was called (not a new phenomenon for election years), is likely to mark the beginnings of a more assertive voice for women in American politics (see the chapter by Janet K. Boles in this volume).

"The "year of the woman," as it was called . . . , is likely to mark the beginnings of a more assertive voice for women in American politics."

George Bush's real interest lay in foreign policy and, appropriately, this area provided the defining moment for the Bush presidency and for Bush's 1992 campaign. The Cold War ended during Bush's watch, an extraordinary event that brought to a close a half-century of competition for dominance between the United States and its allies and the Soviet Union and its allies. In effect, the post–World War II period, with its conflicts in Eastern Europe, Korea, Berlin, Vietnam, Nicaragua, and other hot spots, drew to a peaceful conclusion—one that saw the embrace of democracy (tentative as it might be initially) and a commitment to various forms of free market economics in formerly communist countries. The Cold War had dominated American and international politics for over two generations. Its peaceful conclusion marked a major turning point in United States, and world, history.

One consequence was that the enormity of the event failed to sink in. Bizarre as it may seem, the ending of the Cold War and the decades-long balancing act between war, peace, and the potential for nuclear annihilation received little political attention. Beyond self-congratulatory statements and erratic efforts to pinpoint the immediate difficulties faced by the dominant Russian state and the newly created Commonwealth of Independent States and by the Eastern European former communist countries, opinion leaders did not quite know what to say or do.

A second consequence was that no one had begun to think through the ramifications of the changes—the pressure this put on political leaders to turn their attention to pressing domestic issues, and the likelihood that future international policy would revolve around questions of international economic competitiveness. There was no plan for the peace. The campaign, in its uncertain way, would begin to deal with some of these issues, but the main contributors to the debate were the Democratic candidates, Bill Clinton and Al Gore.

Third, and of the greatest immediate significance for the election, George Bush received little credit for the Cold War's end. True, it was a collaborative effort among a succession of administrations and between the major parties. It was also true that the policies of successive administrations differed in specifics and swung from being bellicose and hard-nosed to emphasizing more accommodation and cooperation between superpowers. Still, all administrations and both parties generally followed the same basic approach.

An event of the magnitude of the collapse of communism would appear to reflect most favorably on the presidency in which it occurred. Such was not to be the case. George Bush was to draw attention, rather ruefully, at different points during the campaign (and during the presidential debates) to the end of the Cold War and the belief that his administration should receive some (and on occasion he would argue, most) of the credit for such an outcome. Neither the Cold War, its end, nor the problems created

in its wake were the focus of much public concern during the campaign.

Rather, what defined the Bush presidency and more immediately, the campaign, was the war with Saddam Hussein and Iraq. Few knew or cared about Saddam prior to Iraq's invasion of Kuwait in August of 1990 and Bush's decision to answer the takeover with force. Through his rhetoric (the "liberation" of Kuwait was described as one objective), the president drew parallels to the United States' commitment to Europe in World War II.

The war began on January 17, 1991. It was quick, tough, and apparently decisive. Over in a matter of weeks, with minimal loss of American lives and ending in the complete rout of the Iraqi forces, it provided the high point of the Bush years. Less happily for the president and his advisers, it may have blinded them to the problems to come and, more specifically, the economic concerns of the voters that were to dominate the election year of 1992.

With the war successfully completed, Bush's popularity soared to over 90 percent. Such acclaim was virtually unparalleled in contemporary American history. His policies were considered a success, he had proven decisive as commander in chief, and a patriotic fervor gripped the land. Bush's re-election and another four years in office were conceded by both friend and foe. The president was believed to be unbeatable in an election.

The consequences of this were many. First, the major Democratic contenders abandoned the field. One after another, the Democratic Party's best-known and most formidable potential candidates announced their intention not to run for the presidency in 1992. Over time, the list would include Representative Richard A. Gebhardt, the Democratic Majority Leader in the House of Representatives and a candidate in 1988; the Rev. Jesse L. Jackson, spokesperson for African-American concerns and a presidential contender in both 1984 and 1988; Senator Bill Bradley of New Jersey, believed to be a coming star in the party but just surviving an uncomfortably close reelection race in New Jersey; Senator Sam Nunn of Georgia, a conservative and a respected and intelligent student of military affairs; Senator John D. (Jay) Rockefeller IV of West Virginia, whose concern with issues of health care almost propelled him into the race; and Governor Mario M. Cuomo of New York, the choice of most Democrats and the early front runner. Cuomo was believed to be the most formidable candidate the Democrats could field. He was the last to declare his intention not to enter the primaries (reportedly due to unresolved budget battles in his state).

In retrospect, perhaps the most notable noncandidate of all would be Senator Al Gore of Tennessee. A moderate, Gore had run unsuccessfully for the Democratic Party's presidential nomination as the southern candidate in 1988. Bill Clinton, governor of Tennessee's neighboring state of Arkansas, and also a moderate with basically the same appeal, position on issues, and constituency as Gore, was later to declare that if Gore had run, he would not have. Once Senator Gore decided he was out, Clinton quickly decided he was in.

The Democrats' "A" team had withdrawn from the field before the first primary vote was cast. The perception was that George Bush and the Republicans could not be beaten.

"[T]he president and his advisers never quite got beyond the euphoria of the war's aftermath."

A second consequence, mentioned earlier, of the overwhelming popular success of the Iraq War was that the president and his advisers never quite got beyond the euphoria of the war's aftermath. They were not able to redirect their attention to the domestic issues that concerned the voters or to shift gears as the electorate moved from pride in what had taken place in the Mideast to concerns with the serious economic conditions that faced them on the home front. Voters' memories are short. Their priorities had changed. The president and his advisers proved unable to remold their campaign, either in the primaries or in the general election, to respond effectively to the new public mood.

In September 1991, a month before a relatively unknown southern governor, Bill Clinton, was to declare his candidacy for the Democratic Party's presidential nomination, George Bush's popularity rating still stood at over 70 percent. Yet, and ominously for the Administration, in

the same poll, 75 percent of the respondents thought the country was "on the wrong track." The president and his advisers never appeared to take such warning signs seriously. They never did adjust to the intensity of discontent over economic conditions, and this failure was to cost them the election. In his presidential address at the beginning of the 1992 election year, the opening gun of his campaign, George Bush was still talking with pride about the successes in the war with Iraq. By this time, the public's attention had turned to other matters.

The New Hampshire Primary and the Pat Buchanan Challenge

The dimensions of the public's discontent began to become evident in the first of the primaries, New Hampshire, leading to a second major miscalculation—a mistake that would cost the Republicans severely. The primary served to determine the Bush campaign strategy throughout the remaining primaries and into the national convention (see the chapter by Charles D. Hadley and Harold W. Stanley in this volume). In many respects, it also helps explain Bush's determined espousal of an issue agenda during the general election campaign that appeared well out of tune with the dominant public concerns.

In New Hampshire, Patrick J. Buchanan, presenting himself as an advocate for the most conservative wing of the Republican Party, challenged Bush. Normally, a serious challenge within the party to an incumbent president's renomination is unthinkable (although it does happen on occasion, such as Senator Edward M. Kennedy's abortive challenge to President Jimmy Carter in the 1980 Democratic primaries). Buchanan was a right-wing columnist and media personality and a former aide in the Nixon, Ford, and Reagan White Houses. He is unabashedly conservative, outspoken, unrepentant, and aggressive—qualities that had served him and the Republican Party well when he was a crusader for the causes of the ideological right from within the White House. In an insurgent candidate, these same qualities were to hurt the Bush candidacy significantly and contribute to the president's defeat in November. Buchanan asserted that he challenged Bush in order to keep the president and his administration committed to conservative ideological goals. The right wing of the Republican Party never entirely trusted

5

George Bush, a problem he encountered throughout his political career.

Buchanan's New Hampshire challenge received extensive media attention. He had touched a nerve. In a normally Republican state, voters were angry, and they blamed the Administration. The economy was poor, many had lost their jobs, and they expected the government in Washington to do something about it. Buchanan served as the vehicle through which they could voice their anger. Bush won in New Hampshire (with 53 percent of the vote to Buchanan's 37 percent), but by a margin considerably below what was expected of an incumbent president.[10] The New Hampshire primary uncovered the intensity of the discontent over the economy and the Bush administration's failure to deal with it. Regrettably for the Republicans, and surprisingly, these were not issues Bush was to address effectively throughout the primaries or later in the general election campaign.

The Bush advisers misperceived the message. Whatever Bush had tried to do to prove his commitment to conservative Republicans (limits on abortion, the Clarence Thomas nomination, cutbacks in social programs, holding the line on taxes), it was not enough.[11] The Republican right wing did much, if not most, of the organizational and mobilization work of the Republican Party, both in the primaries and in the general elections. They were the party's activists, the party's ground troops, and their belief was that their concerns had to be addressed by any candidate seeking the party's nomination. Or so the Bush strategists believed. They were to concede much to the rightists in the prenomination period, attempting to mollify them, address their concerns, and deflect their anger, all in the name of renomination.

This was most evident at the Republican National Convention. Speaker after speaker reemphasized the watchwords of the right wing, from "family values" and "no new taxes" to support for private schools, a balanced budget, and tax and deficit reduction. Often the oratory was inflammatory, as most notably with Buchanan's speech and its call for a "cultural war."[12]

It was all unnecessary. George Bush had the nomination. He took 73 percent of the prenomination vote and 1,846 national convention delegates to Buchanan's 23 percent and 78 national convention delegates. Placating the right wing was not in his best interests. They had nowhere else to go, and their views did not reflect the concerns of the majority of the electorate who would vote in November. The Bush reelection team would have been better advised to set a tone of moderation and reason for the campaign in their national convention; develop acceptable positions on the issues most on the public's mind—jobs, the economy, national health care, education, the environment, and the deficit; highlight the candidates and maximize their appeal to a presidential (as against a party) electorate; and introduce the party's candidates for other offices—the U.S. Senate, governorships, the House of Representatives—much as the Democrats had done so effectively in their national convention. No issue of national concern was given substantial attention (with the possible exception of the deficit) at the Republican National Convention. This approach—placate the right wing, firm up your base—carried over into the general election.

To make matters worse, the Bush campaign was to start slowly. The president was not to begin serious campaigning until after Labor Day, while the Democratic ticket began with a well-received and now famous bus tour *immediately* after their national convention. Much of the summer was spent in efforts to convince a reluctant James A. Baker III, Bush's campaign manager in 1988 and a long-time close friend, to give up his position as secretary of state and take over as White House chief of staff and campaign director. The hope was that Baker could provide some direction and coherence to a forlorn effort. Baker did come aboard in August and some initial results were evident. As Election Day drew closer, however, Baker seemed to distance himself from a doomed effort.

President Bush did deliver a reasoned economic message in Detroit in mid-September, but it received little attention and he did not often refer to it again. Rather, he seemed much more comfortable in personally attacking his opponents—their character and trustworthiness; Clinton's ambiguity on a trade agreement with Mexico and other issues; Clinton's views on the Vietnam War and his efforts to avoid the draft; Clinton's visits to the Soviet Union while a student at Oxford and his participation in antiwar demonstrations while in England (there were even accusations that he was somehow disloyal and might have met in Moscow with the KGB, the USSR's secret police); and, stretching matters even further, Clinton's mother's travels abroad. The Bush campaign also had the State

Department search out Ross Perot's passport records, an act Perot called "a gross abuse of federal power."[13] The State Department official alleged to be in charge of the search, a political appointee, was dismissed in the post-election period, but the furor did not die down. Inquiries were threatened by the Congress, and a special prosecutor was appointed by the Bush administration's attorney general to investigate potential criminal misconduct. The allegations of misconduct reached into the White House. Baker, Bush's campaign manager, a potential future Republican candidate for the presidency, and those around him were rumored to be targets of the investigation.[14]

The tone of the Bush campaign was often shrill. It chose to attack Clinton's wife, Hillary, and her allegedly "unfeminine" and "anti-family" writings and activities. These charges were apparently efforts to appeal to a more traditional Republican constituency, and at one point Vice President Dan Quayle spoke out against "Murphy Brown," a fictional television character who became a single mother in the show. And Bush ended the campaign with attacks on the "ozone man" (Gore) and "environmental extremists" (Clinton and Gore) and with references to the two "bozos" he was running against.

Bush did not use the debates, with the possible exception of the last one, effectively. In one he was caught by the camera glancing at his watch, taken as a sign of boredom and a wish to be elsewhere, and in another instance, he could not immediately answer a question from the audience as to how the recession had affected him personally. His campaign not only did not forcefully address the issues of greatest concern to the majority of the public; it also appeared to lack focus, direction, and purpose. In fact, it even seemed, as captured by television and through pictures of an overstimulated candidate shouting accusations to rallies of the party faithful, to undercut his image of being presidential, one thing George Bush should have had as a strength.

In many respects, George Bush and the Republicans lost the election of 1992 as much as Bill Clinton and the Democrats won it. Yet in losing it, George Bush exacerbated tensions inherent in the Republican Party's coalition, problems that the party will have to deal with.

The Bush administration was old, seemingly out of ideas, and the conservative agenda, dating from the Reagan presidency back to the Nixon years, was exhausted. George Bush was not saying anything in 1992 that the Republicans had not been arguing since 1968. The difference was that the message was worn, overly familiar, and seemed irrelevant to the problems faced by the nation. The Republican Party appeared tired and its leaders out of touch. With an economy in recession, this time the voters were not buying. The party was not making contact with the majority of Americans, 61 percent of whom (the Clinton and Perot votes combined) voted for change.

The basic tensions in the Republican Party's coalition remain unresolved. The best-organized, most forceful, and most strident group in the party, the one that turns out in primaries and controls much of the party's machinery, is the party's most conservative and ideological wing. Yet the Republican right does not begin to represent the majority of the electorate's views. This is a problem that future Republican presidential candidates will have to contend with.[15]

This is not to write the Republicans off; far from it. After the Goldwater disaster of 1964, the Republicans rebounded to win the presidency just four short years later. They went on to hold the presidency for 20 of the next 24 years. Even in the aftermath of Watergate and the Nixon administration's abuses of office, the party rebuilt itself from the ground up between 1976 and 1980, resulting in the crushing wins of Ronald Reagan and 12 uninterrupted years of Republican rule. Nonetheless, the party has some fundamental divisions that will have to be addressed.

THE DEMOCRATS

December 20, 1991, was a pivotal point in the presidential elections. On that date, the last day to qualify for the New Hampshire primary, Mario M. Cuomo, the odds-on favorite of most Democrats, the strongest candidate the Democrats had to offer (and the one, not incidentally, the Republicans thought they would have to run against), declared he would *not* be a candidate in the New Hampshire primary. Effectively, this meant he would not be a contender for the Democratic Party's nomination for the presidency. The race became a free-for-all. The result was a hodgepodge field of virtual unknowns and oddballs, none with much to lose. The big boys, fearful of the Bush popularity and the Bush post-Iraq record, stayed home.

As it developed, the field included, in addition to Clinton, former senator Paul E. Tsongas of Massachusetts, the first candidate to declare in what appeared to be a long and lonely run by an outsider (Tsongas had left public office in 1984 for health reasons), yet one that would attract increasing attention. Tsongas emphasized fiscal responsibility and a planned reduction of the national debt, positions he felt the Democrats had to adopt in order both to meet the nation's economic ills and to compete effectively with the Republicans in the Reagan-Bush era. Tsongas was to win the first-in-the-nation New Hampshire primary (with 33 percent of the vote to Clinton's 25 percent). He was to finish well behind Clinton in both national convention delegates (551 to Clinton's 2,513) and percentage of the total primary vote (18 percent to Clinton's 52 percent).[16] Tsongas had suffered from cancer and went to great pains during the campaign to demonstrate his recovery and his physical fitness. In one notable "photo opportunity," he invited the media to a pool to watch him swim, and he ran television commercials showing him swimming competitively. He even had his personal physician issue a statement as to the state of his health. Unfortunately, his cancer reappeared in the post-election period, and he was readmitted to the hospital for treatment. He was to acknowledge that he had not been totally honest about his health and may, in fact, have misled the press and the public.[17] The question of a candidate's physical well-being and how best to assess it, given the demands of the office being sought, was again brought to the fore by the Tsongas situation.

Former governor Edmund G. (Jerry) Brown, Jr., of California had last run for his party's presidential nomination against Jimmy Carter in 1976. Brown was an advocate of renewable energy sources, term limits for public officeholders, and a $100 restriction on campaign contributions. He was a spokesperson for environmental concerns, and something of a "New Age" Democrat (at one point in his career he had been referred to as "Governor Moonbeam").[18] He was as unpredictable as ever in the 1992 campaign. His base of support was uncertain, but with occasional victories in primary states like Colorado and Connecticut and caucus states such as Maine, Nevada, and Vermont, and, most of all, with enormous stamina, he managed to stay in the race to the end, providing Clinton with his most persistent challenger. Brown finished with 20 percent of the vote and 608 national convention delegates. Along the way, he tirelessly promoted his 800 number for campaign contributions (a tactic at first ridiculed, then adopted, by other candidates, most notably Perot); a "flat tax" for all (of 13 to 14 percent on all income), a curious idea apparently adopted without much thought in the heat of the campaign and quickly forgotten soon after; and support for AIDS research.

Senator Joseph R. (Bob) Kerrey of Nebraska, war hero and former governor, had gained some attention earlier by dating Hollywood actress Debra Winger. Kerrey was considered to be an independent-minded moderate with a proven ability to attract votes from Republicans and Independents. He campaigned primarily on the issue of national health care. The potency of this issue had been shown a year earlier in a Pennsylvania special election for the Senate (the incumbent had died in office), when the favored Richard L. Thornburgh, a popular former governor and, more recently, Bush's attorney general, was outvoted by a relative unknown and undynamic newcomer to elective politics, Harris Wofford. The winner had run on the need for health-care reform. While Kerrey was expected to offer a serious challenge for the nomination, he was undone by poor organization and sketchy campaigning ("I don't know anything about how campaigns run and I don't intend to learn") and withdrew from the race in early March.[19]

Senator Thomas R. (Tom) Harkin of Iowa was a populist expected to do well (as was Kerrey) in the farm belt. Harkin was the most liberal of the candidates and saw himself as the heir to Franklin Roosevelt's New Deal. He saw himself as "the only true Democrat in the field" and his opponents as "warmed-over Republicans."[20] He had the support of organized labor, his principal asset, but (again like Kerrey) was undone by a weak campaign organization and an inability to get his message across to the liberal Democratic constituencies. He withdrew from the race immediately after Kerrey did and later campaigned for Clinton.

Governor L. Douglas Wilder of Virginia was the last of the candidates, a moderate black who had shown an ability in his public career to appeal across racial party lines. Wilder became involved in a controversy over the wiretapping of his car telephone that involved Virginia senator Charles Robb and several members of his staff. The Wilder campaign never took off, and he was the first to withdraw in early January, well before the opening of the primary season.[21]

Six guys named Moe, or the Six Dwarfs, as media pundits were to dub the field.

Once Wilder dropped out, followed in succession by Senators Kerrey and Harkin, the race was left to Clinton, Tsongas, and Brown. All things considered, the Bush campaign's overconfidence may have been understandable.

All of the candidates were controversial, and each had his liabilities.

Clinton, in addition to being the little-known governor of a small state (a point Ross Perot was to stress in the televised debates), suffered through accusations of marital infidelity—the Gennifer (with a "G," as the media would say) Flowers tapes were played and reported on extensively in the press. These accusations in New Hampshire, repeated throughout the primary season and in the fall campaign, and later charges that he avoided military duty in Vietnam and tried to enter a ROTC unit in efforts to avoid the draft (along with the curious release of a 1969 letter to the commandant of the University of Arkansas ROTC unit), and that he participated in, or perhaps organized and led demonstrations in England against the war while a Rhodes scholar at Oxford University, hurt his candidacy. His opponents were determined to focus public attention on his personal character and the "trust" issue. The charges were to dog him throughout the campaign and were the weak links in his otherwise smooth election effort.[22] Nonetheless, Clinton fought back in New Hampshire to come in second and went on from there to claim the nomination.

Even with the field reduced to three, and Clinton the clear favorite by the middle of nominating season, many in the party and the media were uncomfortable with his candidacy.[23] Many remained unconvinced that he could win and others refused to believe that he was the strongest candidate the Democrats could field. David Broder of the *Washington Post*, one of the nation's most respected and influential columnists, caught the mood of pessimism, writing in April: "The closer Bill Clinton gets to the Democratic presidential nomination, the more nervous—if not despairing—many of his fellow partisans become. To hear them talk, they're not sure whether their [national] convention will serve as a prelude to an election or a political execution."[24]

Clinton nevertheless went on to preside over a unified national convention that laid out the themes of the campaign, chose a like-minded southern moderate, Al Gore, as his running mate, and effectively began the general election campaign in mid-summer.

THE GENERAL ELECTION CAMPAIGN

"It's the economy, stupid!" a sign reportedly hung in Clinton's Arkansas campaign headquarters, pretty much tells it all. There were other issues, of course, but the economy was bad, and Clinton and the Democrats promised changes (see the chapter by John K. White in this volume). Median family income had actually decreased over the four years preceding the election, from $37,062 in 1988 to $35,939 in 1991, as stated in constant 1991 dollars. In addition, fully 44 percent of Americans expected conditions to worsen, with another 19 percent believing they could stay the same, as against only 26 percent who felt the economic situation would get better. Perhaps even more surprisingly, given the recent history of presidential races—Bush's pledge in 1988 not to raise taxes and the commonly accepted assessment that Democratic candidate Walter Mondale's publicly stated belief that taxes would have to be increased contributed to his overwhelming defeat by Ronald Reagan in 1984—almost two-thirds of survey respondents (62 percent to 32 percent) agreed that it would be necessary to raise taxes to redress the federal budget deficit.[25]

Until the end, the Bush campaign chose to emphasize, as it did through most of the election year, the trust and character issues.

> The fundamental strategy of the Bush campaign in the closing three weeks—to conduct a full-scale assault on Bill Clinton's character—is itself an implicit acknowledgement of an inability to revive the alliance that, by the late 1960s, had gained dominance. The [Democratic Party's] New Deal coalition had been overpowered by a new one: the affluent and the white working class; suburbanites and evangelical Christians; Americans of Eastern European descent and Protestants in the Republican Midwest heartland.[26]

This assessment was given by Thomas B. Edsall, a *Washington Post* reporter and author.[27]

He and others saw the Bush campaign as a study in desperation, one that failed to energize its previously dominant coalition and one that emphasized issues less relevant to the public's concern. He appeared to be right. In a *New York Times*/CBS news poll immediately prior to the election, the "trust" factor was not decisive enough to win an election: 4 percent trusted Bush "to deal with all the problems a president has to deal with" as against 40 percent for Clinton and 24 percent for Perot.[28]

"Bush was always more comfortable attacking Clinton and tearing him down than he was articulating his own vision," according to one Republican campaign official. "He never convinced voters he was going to do something here at home. He never offered a compelling picture of what he would do or how he would do it."[29] A "close friend" of former president Reagan commented after the defeat, "We're just kind of angry that Bush seemed to throw it all away and never seemed to get it all going."[30]

Voters' concerns repeatedly returned to the economy. A part-time worker in St. Louis: "I'm making half of what I made two years ago. . . . I don't have health insurance. Everything is so tight." A woman in Miami: "My godson is a lawyer and can't get work. A lawyer! . . . He's got a family. People are hurting." An auto worker in Michigan: "Honest to God, I think the working man gets it between the eyes no matter which way he turns. Nobody cares." A Perot sympathizer in Albuquerque: "We have to worry about the future. I have a couple of children. It's not fair that we're leaving this for our kids to clean up." And most starkly, a union official in Ypsilanti, Michigan: "They're going to have a revolution in this country one day. People have pride. They want jobs."[31] The *New York Times* reporter who recorded these remarks observed: "To tour the country is to be stunned by the pockets of Rust Belt devastation and the levels of blue-collar anger. Entire towns are gone—plants, main streets, schools." He concluded that "what the candidates seem not to be connecting with is that a way of life and self-respect are disappearing."[32]

Economic problems linked the blue-collar workers to the suburbanites and the middle class; this was the key. To the extent Clinton could keep the focus on the economy, and he largely did, he would win. The Republican coalition built on middle- and higher-income voters was split; Bush was not addressing their basic concerns ("I think the country needs to be brought together, not driven apart. It was so nasty," a former 1988 Bush supporter in Ohio said).[33] When all was said and done, it was not surprising that the people who felt their family's financial situation had improved (25 percent of the electorate) voted 62 percent for Bush, 24 percent for Clinton, and 14 percent for Perot. Those who felt they were worse off (one-third of the electorate) voted 61 percent for Clinton, 14 percent for Bush, and 25 percent for Perot. Those somewhere in the middle divided their votes between Clinton and Bush: 41 percent for each, with 18 percent for Perot). Pocketbook issues dominated the election discourse for the public.[34]

People were paying attention to the campaign in 1992 to an amazing degree, given the level of disinterest, cynicism, and alienation that marked the campaigns of 1988 and 1984 (76 percent found the 1992 campaign interesting, compared to 40 percent for 1988 and 56 percent for 1984).[35] In terms of what they heard, it was the Clinton message they liked and responded to on election day.

Beyond the message, the Clinton camp devised a tough-minded electoral strategy based mainly on previous party performance and current economic conditions (see the chapter by Jerome M. Mileur in this volume). As developed by David Wilhelm, a veteran of Chicago politics and a successful craftsman of much of Clinton's prenomination strategy, the intent was to begin the general election drive early, which was done well before the Bush campaign got into the field; develop largely insurmountable leads in a series of key states (this, too, was accomplished); and then to focus the remaining resources of the campaign on the carefully targeted states needed for an electoral college majority. By implication, states considered unwinnable were basically neglected, although no one was willing to concede this during the fall campaign.

The Clinton advisers divided the nation into three categories of states:[36]

- Category I, or "Top End" states—13 states and the District of Columbia:
  These were considered to be strong Democratic areas, to which the campaign devoted only the minimal resources needed to win. They included (in addition to the District of Columbia): Massachusetts, Rhode Island, West Virginia, Minnesota, and Hawaii, all heavily Democratic, and Califor-

nia, New York, Illinois, Washington, Oregon, Vermont, and Connecticut, all reasonably competitive and all (with California being the extreme example) facing difficult economic times. Clinton won each of these.

• Category II, or "Play Hard" states—18:

A full court press would be applied to these states, which were considered to be more competitive and less predictable than those in the other two categories. The election would be won or lost here. These states were the battleground. They included: Delaware, Georgia, Maryland, Missouri, Pennsylvania, Iowa, Kentucky, Louisiana, Maine, Michigan, Colorado, Montana, North Carolina, New Jersey, New Mexico, Ohio, Tennessee (Gore's home state), and Wisconsin. Clinton lost North Carolina by one percentage point; he won every other state.

• Category III, or "Big Challenge" states—19:

These were divided into 10 states in which minimal campaign effort, at best, was extended, and 9 others that were worth "watching." The latter received a slightly higher priority and more, although still severely limited, campaign attention and resources. In the first group were: Alaska, Virginia, Mississippi, Indiana, North Dakota, Nebraska, Oklahoma, Wyoming, Idaho, and Utah. The second included: Alabama, Arizona, Florida, Kansas, New Hampshire, Nevada, South Carolina, South Dakota, and Texas. Clinton did make occasional forays into some of these states (Florida and Texas are examples) to test the waters, to force the Bush campaign to focus more on their base, or in an effort to help a local candidate, but overall these were the orphans, essentially conceded by the Democrats to the Republicans. Still, Clinton managed to win close races in New Hampshire (39 percent to Bush's 38 percent and Perot's 23 percent) and Nevada (38 percent to Bush's 35 percent and Perot's 26 percent). He lost the rest.

Overall, the Clinton advisers focused on winning 376 electoral votes in 31 states and the District of Columbia. Clinton won 30 of the states, plus, unexpectedly, New Hampshire and Nevada, to give him 370 electoral votes, one hundred more than the majority needed for victory. The campaign was accurate in its con-

ception and unusually well executed in the field.

In turn, the Bush campaign began with significant advantages in the electoral college. Normally, the Republicans start a presidential campaign with a large, and in recent elections, decisive advantage. Before the 1992 campaign even began, the Republicans could expect to carry states totaling 202 electoral votes. These were states that had voted for the Republican Party's presidential nominee in each of the six previous elections, including the Plains, Mountain, Southwest, and Far West states. Another 13 states with an additional 152 electoral votes had supported the Republican candidate in all but one of the last six elections. The candidate's job is to hold this base and add to it, within the specific context of any given election year, the individual states needed to achieve the majority 270 electoral votes necessary for victory. Since 1968, Republicans have been spectacularly successful in this regard, capturing an average of 78 percent of the electoral votes (and 94 percent in the Reagan elections of the 1980s). The Democrats can count on a base of about 50 electoral votes.

Given its advantages and working from a position of incumbency, the Bush campaign understandably employed a more traditional approach than did the Clinton campaign. It did not begin to campaign until after Labor Day; it attempted to build on prior Republican successes in the South, Southwest, and Mountain states; and it chose as its principal battleground the larger industrial and urbanized states of the Midwest and Great Lakes region. Its most striking departure from previous Republican campaigns was in conceding California and its 54 electoral votes, the highest in the nation, to the Democrats. California had been one of the solid Republican states in the electoral college, voting for the Republican candidate in the six previous presidential elections. The state's economy was one of the hardest hit by the recession; the Bush campaign began there well behind that of Clinton and never recovered (Clinton, 47 percent; Bush, 36 percent; and Perot, 11 percent).

Overall, Bush won only 19 states with 168 electoral votes. While still losing, Bush did better in the popular vote than he did in California (Clinton, 43 percent; Bush, 38 percent; and Perot, 19 percent). But it is the cumulative advantage in the individual state contests that translates into electoral votes and decides presidential elections. In this regard, the Clinton

Figure 1.1

Electoral College Results for 1988

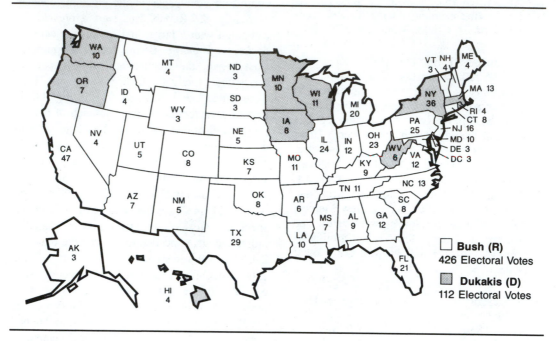

Figure 1.2

Republican Strength in the Electoral College: 1968–1984

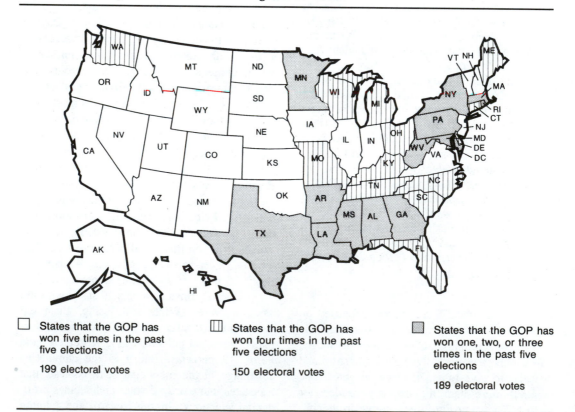

Figure 1.3

Electoral College Results for 1992

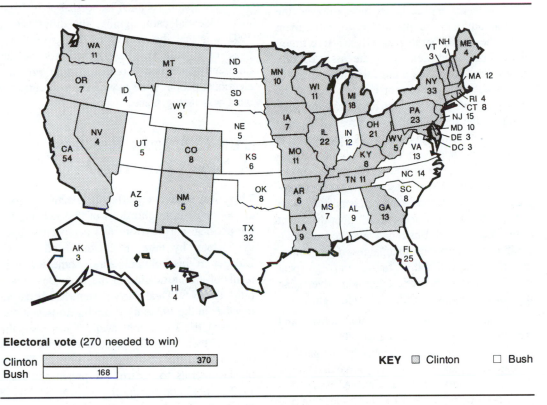

Electoral vote (270 needed to win)

Clinton 370
Bush 168

KEY ☒ Clinton ☐ Bush

strategy proved superior. Figures 1.1, 1.2, and 1.3 graphically illustrate its success.

THE MEDIA'S FEW NEW TWISTS

The Bush campaign again pursued a fairly traditional media strategy (see the chapter by Jarol B. Manheim in this volume). It emphasized the president's accomplishments in office and his personal qualities, coupled with attempts to cast doubt on his Democratic opponent's stature and ability to assume the office of the presidency. The Bush advisers also put more reliance on, and more funds into, national network advertising than did the Democratic ticket. None of this was unusual, and such an approach had proven widely successful in past elections.

The Clinton campaign was more innovative, opening up new paths of communication that both campaigns eventually used and that are likely to become staples of the campaign scene. One of the more interesting experiments of the campaign year was the imaginative use of previously neglected media outlets. Specifically, greater emphasis was placed on cable television and what George Bush had once referred to as those "weird talk shows." The approach was first explored in the Democratic primaries by Clinton and his fellow candidates, all badly in need of "free" television exposure. Once this approach was successful, and despite whatever early reservations he might have had, George Bush became an enthusiastic participant. Talk shows came into prominence as sources of viewer information: "Larry King Live" became a regular outlet for both Bush and Clinton, as did "Donahue," "Oprah," "The Today Show," and "Good Morning America," among others. Cable television also played a more important role in the campaign. In addition to the established CNN and C-SPAN serious news channels, such others as MTV, the Nashville Network, and even the Home Shopping Network took their place as hosts to the candidates and links to the audiences they wanted to reach.[37] The mood was set, perhaps, by Clinton's appearing on Arsenio Hall's late night television show to play his saxophone, sunglasses and all. It made for a more lively election year and an inventive use of a changing media scene.

Such an approach, in turn, allowed the Clinton advisers, in particular, to experiment with other media strategies. Given "free time" on national television from the assorted talk shows, the Clinton team allocated their funds in such a way as to put proportionately more of its television and radio budget into local and state media in the most competitive areas. This also allowed the campaign to tailor its message to its audience, an approach Richard Nixon had pioneered in his 1968 and 1972 races. As an example, Clinton was presented to southern audiences as "a different kind of Democrat," one not tied to the "tax and spend" liberalism that both Reagan and Bush had attacked so successfully in previous campaigns. One consequence also was that the Clinton campaign spent less on national network television advertising than any previous presidential campaign.[38]

Finally, the three presidential debates and the one vice-presidential debate drew unusual amounts of interest, a trademark of this particular campaign, and unexpectedly large audiences. People were interested; they wanted issues discussed—a point made especially clear in the second of the presidential debates when individual citizens, not representatives of the press, were allowed to directly question the candidates; and they were looking for answers to the everyday problems, and especially the economic worries, that they encountered.[39]

The experimentation with format and the unpredictability of the exchanges, given in particular the inclusion of Ross Perot, added to a sense of excitement and uncertainty, rare for presidential debates. The exposure that the debates gave the candidates added to the television "free time" they enjoyed in the campaign. This especially helped Clinton, by allowing his campaign to pursue their alternative media strategies, and Perot, who managed to build an audience for his half hour "infomercials." These also attracted an unexpectedly wide viewership. For some, it may have been nostalgia; Perot's use of basic note cards, crude (by today's standards) graphs, and a pointer while talking directly into the camera were reminiscent of television's early days in the 1950s. Whatever the appeal, the programs were effective. The only candidate who appeared to benefit minimally from the debates was George Bush, although his

performance in the last of the debates was generally assessed to be his strongest.

Television assumed its normal pivotal role in presidential campaigning; the difference in 1992 was that the campaigns (and specifically those of Clinton and Perot) used it somewhat differently and that, compared with previous elections, people were paying more attention to what was taking place.

THE ELECTION RESULTS: A NEW COALITION?

There was a tendency after the election to look at the long-run implications of the outcome for the political parties from two perspectives (see the chapter by Peter F. Nardulli and Jon K. Dalager in this volume). First, some saw it in terms of a reunification of the New Deal coalition. The New Deal party system had been put together in the 1930s by Franklin Roosevelt and it served the Democrats well; it has been the basis of their majority party dominance in the electorate in the contemporary era. It allowed the Democrats to control the presidency from 1932 to 1952 and during the periods 1960–1968 and 1976–1980. It continues to provide the core constituency for their virtually unbroken command of the Congress from 1932 to the present (although the Republicans had a majority in the House during the years 1952–1954 and in the Senate during the periods 1946–1948, 1952–1954, and 1980–1986).

There were grounds for believing in a renewed Democratic coalition. Clinton ran strongly among self-identified Democrats, stronger, in fact, than did such previous presidential nominees as Michael Dukakis, Walter Mondale, and Jimmy Carter in both 1976 and 1980. Since Democrats remain the majority party in terms of those identifying with it in the electorate, this in itself is important. Clinton also did well among lower-income groups, those with less formal education, Jewish and Catholic voters, liberals, African Americans, Latinos, and members of union households. Those were all core constituencies of the Democrats' New Deal alignment. He also took a plurality of votes in the South, another building block of the Roosevelt coalition.[40] While the results are not strictly comparable to earlier elections—there was a three-way split in this presidential vote—they were most encouraging. Many of the groups Clinton did best among are remnants of the Democratic Party's long-time constituency.

A second view is that Clinton has put together a new and somewhat different coalition that would serve as the basis for future Democratic success. He showed strength among young voters (a reversal for the Democrats from the Reagan years) and those with the highest level of educational achievement (an exception to the earlier trend indicated). In addition, compared to other recent Democratic candidates, Clinton fared better among the groups shown in Table 1.1. He also ran stronger than his party's recent predecessors among employed voters, Southerners, and single people. Some saw this as the potential introduction of a new era.[41]

The Democrats would be happy to accept either outcome—the revival of a dominant New Deal coalition or the fashioning of a new and somewhat modified party base. Such post-election analyses, however, tend to be overenthusiastic. The Republicans did not build the permanent electoral dominance many had predicted after the Eisenhower election in 1952, the Nixon elections of 1968 and, more importantly, 1972, or the Reagan landslides of the 1980s.

One implication of such analyses also is that the Republican Party's coalition has been permanently fragmented. Bush did well among Republican Party identifiers—conservatives, higher-income voters, white Protestants, homemakers, and born-again Christians—as do all Republican presidential candidates. Perot's support, and it is best to remember that Perot was a confounding factor in this election, proved to have the strongest appeal in relative terms (he did not win a plurality in any electoral group) to independent younger white males, Republican women (his 32 percent here virtually equalled Bush's 33 percent), Midwesterners, and those whose financial situation had worsened (a group Clinton took with a handsome 61 percent, to 25 percent for Perot and 14 percent for Bush). Where Perot's vote is likely to go in the future is anyone's guess, but it is fair to say that in 1992 it hurt the Republicans and their candidate, George Bush, more than it did the Democrats and their candidate, Bill Clinton. Clearly, it was to Clinton's advantage to have Perot in the race.

One election's results provide too little evidence on which to base much solid long-range speculation. Only future elections can show how permanent, or transitory, the 1992 voter coalitions are to be.

A Few Words on the Perot Factor

Ross Perot did better in the popular vote than any independent or third-party candidate since Teddy Roosevelt and his Bull Moose Party in 1912. However, unlike Roosevelt, he carried no states and received no electoral votes. He was not the splinter or factional candidate of major political party (such as were the independent or third-party candidacies of John Anderson, Eugene McCarthy, George Wallace, Henry Wallace, or Strom Thurmond). What then, does the Perot candidacy say about the politics of 1992?

First, Perot did not have a political party. In something of a stretch, he claimed that "the people" had asked him to run and so he did. "I'm Ross, you're the boss!" as he liked to say. His movement and his vote and certainly his rhetoric indicated a rejection of conventional parties and conventional politics (see the chapter by Frank B. Feigert in this volume). There is an independent, non-aligned group of potential voters in the electorate apparently fed up with and rejecting both parties. If so, the likelihood is that Perot, or other candidates like him, will be a factor in future elections. This movement in the electorate is not likely simply to disappear.

Perot also proved the value of having $60 to $100 million of his own money to spend on a campaign.[42] And he demonstrated the power of relying almost solely on television—his paid half-hour "infomercials" drew well (as did the debates), and the "free" television exposure of Larry King, Barbara Walters, "60 Minutes," and the talk shows proved important to Perot (as it did to all the candidates) throughout the campaign. This approach also is likely to be reemphasized in future campaigns.

Finally, Perot can be seen as a gauge of how really weak the parties' appeals can be and a barometer of the need for new ideas and new party coalitions. His strength is a direct measure of the problems the parties face and, at this early stage, a warning as to fundamental changes that yet might come.

Conclusion

Where does all this leave us?

This election could be seen as a reaffirmation of the power of television, although the ways television was used were more imaginative

Table 1.1

Percentage of Selected Groups Supporting Presidential Candidates, 1976–1992

	1992			1988		1984		1980			1976	
	Clinton	Bush	Perot	Dukakis	Bush	Mondale	Reagan	Carter	Reagan	Anderson	Carter	Ford
Women	46	37	17	49	50	44	56	45	47	7	50	48
Whites	39	41	20	40	59	35	64	36	56	7	47	52
60 years old and older	50	38	12	49	50	40	60	41	54	4	47	52
Westerners	44	34	22	46	52	38	61	34	53	10	46	51
Moderate Independents	42	28	30	47	51	42	57	30	53	14	45	53

Source: New York Times, November 5, 1992. 1992 data were collected by Voter Research and Surveys based on questionnaires completed by 15,490 voters leaving 300 polling places around the nation on election day. 1976 data were based on a survey conducted by CBS News with questionnaires from 15,300 voters. Data for other years were based on surveys of voters conducted by the *New York Times* and CBS News: 15,201 in 1980; 9,174 in 1984; and 11,645 in 1988.

than in previous campaigns and are more than likely precedent-setting.

The election was expensive, a little-needed reminder of the power, and necessity, of big money in American campaigns (see the chapter by Candice J. Nelson in this volume). The cost of the presidential election (for all candidates, prenomination and general election phases combined) came to an estimated $525 million to $550 million, slightly more than in 1988 and arguably the most expensive race in history.[43] Spending in House races was up 41 percent from 1990 ($313.7 million from $220 million), and the total included the most money ever used to win a House seat (a California Republican spent $5.4 million, against the previous record of $2.6 million). Expenditures in U.S. Senate races are difficult to compare across time because of the differences in constituencies, state sizes, and competitive patterns, but one thing was sure: a great deal of money was also invested in these races. Topping the list was the $10.2 million that California Democrat Barbara Boxer spent to move from the House to the Senate, and the $8.9 million and $8.7 million invested by Republican senators Alfonse D'Amato of New York and Arlen Specter of Pennsylvania respectively, in winning tough reelection fights.[44]

There is nothing in this election to modify the assumption of a candidate-centered politics based on the newer technologies of communication, substantial political funding, a short-term professional staff, for-hire political consultants,

and the immediate campaign needs of the candidate as crucial to elective politics in late-twentieth-century America.

At the same time, as a residue in particular of the Reagan years, there was a more policy-oriented political debate and more real choices offered the voters as to policy directions, both within and between the parties and (depending on how one characterizes Jerry Brown and the independent candidacy of Ross Perot) political movements, candidates, and the coalitions they represent.

Also, the Democrats were more active in the campaign—in effect, imitating the Republican Party and its national successes—in providing campaign resources and professional expertise, raising funds, and running national television advertisements. And even more unusual, the Democratic National chair, Ronald H. Brown, took an active role in determining the nomination field and then building a consensus behind the winning candidate, Bill Clinton. (Brown was later rewarded with an appointment to the cabinet as secretary of commerce).

A new Congress was elected, the most diverse in history. One hundred and ten new members were elected to the House of Representatives, including the greatest number of African Americans, Latinos, and women in history. The Senate experienced the election of four women senators, including the first black woman, to bring the total female membership to six—not a high number, but three times what it was prior to the election. It is a Congress likely to be impatient with the old ways of doing business.

For many, the encouraging aspect of the campaign was that the winning candidate ran on a ticket of change and the new Congress elected was also committed to change (see the chapter by John S. Jackson III in this volume). Expectations are high. Both the president and the Congress, and most especially the Democrats as the party in power, are going to have to produce. They will be held accountable. Excuses about "divided government" will no longer be enough to mask failures of leadership and vision. Every indication is that both the president and the Congress understand this and accept it. In the immediate post-election period, winning candidate Clinton indicated an intention to work with the Congress and early on made it a point to meet and consult with the congressional leadership. He also appointed a number of major congressional figures to his cabinet and to high administration posts (Senator Lloyd M. Bentsen of Texas, chair of the Senate Finance Committee, as secretary of the treasury; Representative Les Aspin of Wisconsin, chair of the House Armed Services Committee, as secretary of defense; Representative Mike Espy, the first black from Mississippi in Congress since Reconstruction, as secretary of agriculture; and Representative Leon E. Panetta of California, chair of the House Budget Committee, as director of the Office of Management and Budget). These appointments, plus the choice of Senator Al Gore of Tennessee as his running mate, indicate the intention of the new administration to cooperate with the Congress in developing a national policy agenda, rather than to perpetually run against it and blame it for the failure to address the nation's problems, much as the Carter, Reagan, and Bush presidencies chose to do.

Both Clinton and the media pronounced the end of an era of "gridlock." This stalemate between a Republican president and a Democrat-dominated Congress was blamed in campaigns and the press, rightly or wrongly, for past inability, unwillingness, or ineffectiveness in dealing with major national problems. The promise is for a period of action, policy innovativeness, and willingness by all involved to be judged by the consequences of their actions. The idea of policy accountability while in office is the best way to revive and strengthen the political parties, as well as faith in the entire political system, and provides an encouraging reaffirmation of the importance of campaigns and elections.

The most revolutionary thing to happen in the last 4 years, and more than likely the last 50, has been the end of the Cold War. As indicated, it was not an issue in the campaign, and its implications have yet to be grasped. For both parties, but especially for the Republicans, it is likely to result in a rethinking of electoral strategies and political commitments. It may even lead to something of a Republican realignment, a search for new issues and new appeals to keep its broad, and divided, coalition together. For 4 decades, foreign policy, and especially appeals to anticommunism and the related need for a strong national defense to combat, in Ronald Reagan's words, "the evil empire," have been staples of the Republican Party's appeal and one of its great strengths in the electorate. That rallying point is now gone and will have to be replaced, probably by some set of domestic issues and appeals. What they will be is difficult to say, but it is reasonable to expect the search will be a major preoccupation for a party seeking to reforge a winning coalition over the coming years.

And finally, the most important aspect of this election was the one most taken for granted by all concerned, as it should be. We in the United States take the peaceful transfer of power through elections to be a fact of political life. Yet, it is a most impressive exercise and one that has evolved through great cost over millennia. In the present case, and focusing on the post-election period, it was handled with grace and civility by all three parties and both candidates.

Despite its problems, the system does work, and it does so most impressively at times. This election is but the most recent example.

Chapter Two

The Election in Context: The Political and Institutional Setting

John T. Tierney

It's the economy, stupid!" These words, on a sign hanging behind the Little Rock desk of James Carville, chief political strategist for William J. Clinton's 1992 presidential campaign, probably appeared in every major American newspaper and newsweekly sometime in the weeks around the 1992 election. The sign was meant to be a constant reminder to the Clinton forces that their path to victory lay in remaining focused on a single, clear theme. The words also came to be viewed more widely by commentators and reporters (and through them, by millions of Americans) as a rebuke to President George H. W. Bush, who campaigned for re-election throughout most of 1992 with seemingly faint recognition that his presidency was in serious trouble, foundering, as it was, on the shoals of a rocky economy. There is no disputing that the nation's economic turmoil in the last couple of years of the Bush administration—and the president's apparent inability or unwillingness to move forward with any coherent agenda to deal with the problem—was the single most important factor in determining the outcome of the 1992 presidential election.

But to pin the election's outcome on the economy alone would be a mistake. George Bush may ultimately have been judged by the decline of middle-class prosperity and the length of the nation's unemployment lines, but the voters who sentenced him and his party to political exile were responding to lots of other factors as well. Part of what they responded to was the disciplined campaign waged by Bill Clinton, who presented himself to the voters as a

new-style Democrat, decidedly more moderate than the standard-bearers his party had anointed in recent elections. The voters also responded to the half-hearted, disengaged, and noticeably tired campaign effort mounted by George Bush. Later chapters will illuminate the ways in which the prenomination and general election campaigns affected the course of the election.

This chapter maps out the general political setting in the period leading up to the election year. In a sense, of course, this chapter has an overly ambitious goal, since the setting of the election is the broad sweep of historical and political forces over many decades that converged on November 3, 1992. Granting this, it is nevertheless instructive to consider some of the key events and circumstances of the few years leading up to 1992, in order that the election's outcome might be understood not just as a function of campaigns and candidates but in the context of the overall Reagan/Bush era, the record of the Bush administration in both foreign and domestic policy, and the political developments that affected the attitudes of the electorate as the presidential and congressional elections of 1992 drew near.

THE REPUBLICAN JUGGERNAUT OF THE 1980s

When Democrat Bill Clinton won the White House in 1992, he snatched that seat of power away from the Republican Party, which had occupied it for 20 of the previous 24 years. Indeed, 1600 Pennsylvania Avenue had come to be seen as a reliably Republican piece of real estate in the nation's capital, particularly in recent times, as Ronald W. Reagan succeeded in transforming the Republican strengths of the Nixon years into a formidable new electoral coalition that brought him to victory twice and then delivered again for George Bush, who had served as Reagan's vice president.

The political revolution wrought by Ronald Reagan is now a familiar story, told many places, and only its broad outlines need be reviewed here. At its core was the right wing of the Republican Party, which had not managed to capture the party's presidential nomination for one of its own since 1964, when Barry Goldwater challenged Lyndon B. Johnson, claiming to offer "a choice, not an echo." Reagan's campaign for the presidency in 1980 went well beyond that, promising unambiguous rejection of programmatic liberalism and unwavering support for the core tenets of conservative ideology: in foreign affairs, a vigorous anticommunism and support for a strong military establishment ready to be used in defense of America's interests; and in domestic affairs, a strong preference for private activity and bias against government authority, since in the conservative view, governmental attempts to act in domestic policy are likely to entail some restriction on people's freedom and are more likely to exacerbate a problem than to solve it.

Of course, by 1980, these ideas had support beyond the ranks of conservative Republicans. Many long-time Democrats had already left their party, which had been bleeding voters for years because of its association with policies that spoke to principles and interests that were not priorities to those who made up the party's traditional base. In the domestic sphere, these included policies such as affirmative action, occupational safety and health, and protection of endangered species—policies viewed by many working-class Democrats not as enlightened initiatives but as do-gooder notions that foster economic injustices in the form of restricted occupational advancement, lost jobs, closed factories, higher taxes, and general economic dislocation.[1]

In the foreign policy arena, Democratic candidates bore the burdensome legacy of the party's association with the antiwar demonstrations of the late 1960s and early 1970s and the

antiwar candidacy of Democratic senator George McGovern in 1972, all of which produced a backlash of nationalist sentiment from which the Republicans profited. Unfairly, the Democrats had come to be seen as lacking in patriotism and as weak on national defense, a perception that had hurt them in presidential politics in almost every race after 1964. (The exception was 1976, when Democratic candidate Jimmy Carter triumphed over incumbent president Gerald R. Ford, whose competence on issues of international affairs came into question after he asserted in a campaign debate that Poland was not under the sphere of influence of the Soviet Union.)

In 1980, the Republicans had in Ronald Reagan a candidate who knew how to appeal to disaffected Democrats, how to turn them into "Reagan Democrats." Of course, it did not hurt Reagan that his candidacy came at the end of a decade when the confidence of Americans in their political institutions and leaders had suffered an unprecedented series of shocks. After the loss of the Vietnam War, the Watergate scandal, severe shortages of oil, alarming rates of inflation, and the U.S. government's humiliating inability to secure the release of American hostages held by religious zealots in revolutionary Iran, it may not be so surprising that Americans in 1980 were less reluctant than they had been with Goldwater in 1964 to take a chance on a candidate who promised to change the basic course of American government.

What many Americans saw in their new president in the early 1980s seemed a fulfillment of their best hopes. Reagan committed his administration to cutting taxes, increasing defense spending, restricting the reach of meddlesome government, providing regulatory relief to the business community, and restoring the primacy of traditional moral values against the scourge of secular humanism. And the political value of those objectives was verified in the 1984 election when Reagan, hailing the return of "morning in America," overwhelmed Democratic candidate Walter F. Mondale, who was successfully portrayed as a traditional Democratic candidate, captive of the "special interests" (environmentalists, welfare advocates, feminists, peace activists, African Americans, senior citizens, Latinos, labor unions, and so on) that were said to be still calling the shots in the Democratic Party. George Bush was there with Reagan through it all.

When Bush took the mantle of Republican Party leadership from Ronald Reagan's shoulders in 1988, he was fortunate that all these forces of Republican political success were still aligned in his favor. There were also other factors working to his advantage. For one thing, Bush was essentially running on Ronald Reagan's record, which was still playing well with much of the electorate despite the Iran-Contra affair and the pervasive evidence that Reagan was a president who was largely detached from his job and uninformed about the activities of his own subordinates in the executive branch.

> *"With the help of this sophisticated campaign apparatus, Bush had managed to fashion for himself a likable and appealing image...."*

Moreover, Bush had access to the formidable campaign apparatus that the Republicans had established in earlier elections and refined during their years in the White House. Unlike the Democrats, who had to put together ad-hoc campaigns every few years to make a run at the White House, the Republicans had an institutionalized operation that benefited from continual practice and fine-tuning as they worked from within the White House to identify and mold the opinions of the national electorate and shape the news in ways that would be beneficial to the president. Additionally Bush had as the chief architect of his 1988 campaign James A. Baker III, who had honed his skills in media manipulation in three earlier presidential contests. The team also included Lee Atwater and Roger Ailes, whose go-for-the-jugular style of campaigning bespoke the continuing intensity of the Republican Party's desire to wield the power of the presidency. With the help of this sophisticated campaign apparatus, Bush had managed to fashion for himself a likable and appealing image.

With the help of this sophisticated campaign apparatus, Bush had managed to fashion for himself a likable and appealing image, some-

thing that, thanks to Ronald Reagan, now seemed to be a necessary feature for anyone hoping to succeed him. Bush's efforts in this regard were facilitated by the fact that in Michael S. Dukakis he had an opponent whose likable attributes, along with his passions and convictions, were allowed to be obscured by a stiff and reserved demeanor.

But Bush and his handlers knew that personality alone was not enough. In an appeal to those who found much that was harsh and distasteful about the Reagan administration's laissez-faire doctrines, Bush promised his would be a "kinder, gentler" presidency that would take on many of the domestic problems unheeded under Reagan's watch. Bush managed to convince voters that he would be not only an involved and engaged president (unlike his predecessor), but that his hands-on approach to governance would yield benefits in diverse policy areas. He spoke, for example, of his intention to be both "the education president," and "the environmental president." And in what may well be his best-remembered promise, made in his speech at the 1988 Republican Convention, Bush insisted that he also would be the protector of middle-class taxpayers: "The Congress will push me to raise taxes, and I'll say no, and they'll push, and I'll say no, and they'll push again. And I'll say to them, 'Read my lips: no new taxes.'" As anyone remotely alert to American national politics during the Bush administration knows, these words, while perhaps helpful in getting him into the White House, would also prove instrumental to his being shown back out of it.

George Bush's victory over Michael Dukakis in 1988 was an especially sweet one for Republicans, not only because Bush came from so far behind to win (he was down by 13 percentage points in the polls in May), but because it seemed to them an affirmation that the party's successes on the road to the White House were not in fact the consequence of one man's [Reagan's] attributes, but a function of the party's overwhelming skill and electoral solidarity. Although few were sufficiently perspicacious to see it at the time, when Bush took office in 1989 the seeds of political disaster for the Republicans were already sown. For along with the silver lining of a reinvigorated party, Ronald Reagan left Bush a legacy of storm clouds, including a changing global power structure, a crippling budget deficit, and high expectations on the part of the electoral constituency that the Republican Party had assembled.

FOREIGN POLICY

No other president in modern times has entered office with as much seasoning to the responsibilities of foreign policy as George Bush had. Formerly an ambassador to China, CIA director, ambassador to the United Nations, and vice president, George Bush had spent most of his political life in jobs that exposed him to and prepared him for the complexities of foreign affairs. Thus, when he finally moved into the Oval Office there was every reason to believe that foreign policy would be his strong suit as president. And clearly it was. Like his predecessors in modern times, Bush regarded foreign policy as the arena in which he would try to make his mark for the history books. Not only did the times seem especially right for this, but it fitted with his experience and inclinations, where domestic policy figured hardly at all. Adding to his strength in this area, Bush appointed the most able of his associates, James Baker, to be secretary of state, an assignment Baker

"[W]hen communism finally collapsed . . . the president and his supporters thought their record was unassailable."

coveted for the balance it would give to his own illustrious portfolio of policy experience. The combined talents of Bush and Baker, neither of them rigid ideologues, would be tested in different ways as they tried to chart a pragmatic approach for the United States through the changing labyrinth of foreign affairs.

Surely the greatest irony of the Bush administration's foreign policy record—one that was characterized by caution and included few noticeable missteps—is that its successes ultimately fueled George Bush's political downfall. The central point here is not as perverse as it sounds. In a sense, the Bush record in foreign policy can be separated into two categories: the

victory in the Cold War and the victory in the Gulf War. Each of these successes had much to commend it on its own terms, of course, but each carried political liabilities for the Bush administration that were appreciated too late by the President and those close to him.

As noted above, one of the things that attracted many elements of the electoral coalition that the Republicans assembled from 1980 through 1988 was Reagan's determination to restore American strength in the world. Americans wanted no longer to see other nations act with impunity against the interests of the United States, as, for example, Iran had throughout the last year of the Carter administration. So there was some gratification when the United States successfully exercised its power abroad, as it did under Reagan with the invasion of Grenada in 1983 and the air raid on Libya in 1986, and later under Bush, with the 1989 invasion of Panama aimed at ousting dictator Manuel Noriega. More important, however, was that these military excursions took place against a backdrop of sharp increases in defense spending that constituted the core element of Reagan's foreign policy, a kind of muscular anticommunism.

Thus, when communism finally collapsed in the Soviet Union and Eastern Europe under Bush's watch, the president and his supporters thought their record was unassailable. After all, by hewing to the uncompromising doctrines of his more ideological predecessor, Bush could claim to have helped hasten the end of Soviet communism, leaving the United States as the world's only military superpower. As Bush later said in a State of the Union speech, seeking to debunk the arguments of those who said he had done nothing other than be lucky enough to be president at the moment communism collapsed, the Cold War "didn't end; it was won" with the peace-through-strength policies that were the hallmark of the Reagan-Bush years.[2]

But winning the Cold War did not carry with it the kind of political benefits Bush and his partisans expected. First of all, many observers who were persuaded that the collapse of communism was indeed a victory saw it as more Reagan's than Bush's. And Bush got more than a little criticism for his restrained reaction to communism's last gasps. Whereas the Administration portrayed its cautious passivism as disciplined and purposeful (nothing was being done that might alarm Russian hardliners or lead to bloodier revolutions), critics saw the Administration's reticence as a sign of befuddlement. It was as if the Bush team "did not seem to grasp the magnitude of the changes overtaking Eastern Europe and the Soviet Union, and it played little part in them."[3]

Moreover, by the early 1990s many Americans were coming to the view that a military and political victory over the Soviets was hardly something to crow about if the Cold War had kept the United States fighting in the wrong trenches when it should have been paying more attention to its economic competition with Japan and the capitalist powers of Western Europe. Or, to put it in terms of a quip that circulated widely during the election year, "The Cold War is over, and Japan won." However sophisticated their understanding of international trade and competition, many American voters seemed to be paying enough attention to such matters to believe that the Bush administration had failed to protect the U.S. trade position by refusing to invest in the things that would matter in the long haul, such as education and investment incentives for energy technology. More generally, Bush was being taken to task for harming the nation's economic status by allowing its manufacturing base to deteriorate and by permitting trade rivals to exploit free access to U.S. markets without granting equal access to their own.

In short, the cessation of the Cold War, though clearly a historic and positive development, was not one that registered very intensely with many voters outside a relatively small circle of ideologues, its importance in the minds of other voters being overshadowed by growing problems at home. So Bush's efforts to capitalize on the Cold War victory yielded little political benefit.

But if it was real military adventure that Bush needed to burnish his brass as commander in chief, the opportunity presented itself in August 1990, when Iraq invaded Kuwait and the Bush administration responded by mobilizing a dazzling military campaign, in coalition with troops from other nations, that succeeded, once battle had begun, in forcing Iraq out of Kuwait in short order. Many of Bush's strengths were on display during the seven-month period the nation was consumed by preparation for the Persian Gulf War and then by the brief war itself. He dealt skillfully with Congress, building political support for the military initiative. He put his diplomatic skills to good use, drawing other nations into the effort to expel Iraq and rees-tablish Kuwaiti sovereignty. And he helped to orchestrate a startlingly successful military campaign that, with the aid of television, restored to Americans a sense of military superiority that had been absent for two full decades.

"[T]he blinding victory gave the White House a false sense of security and encouraged carelessness."

As impressive as it was in all these ways, the Bush administration's record in the Persian Gulf War entailed some negatives as well. Although accorded credit for the success of the military campaign, Bush earned scorn from many quarters for stopping it short of what many felt should have been its final objective, the removal of Iraqi president Saddam Hussein. Moreover, in the months following the war, the Administration was widely criticized for its failure to do more to ease the desperate plight of Kurdish refugees in Iraq, whose problems had been exacerbated by the war. But the greatest political negative stemming from the Gulf War was that it left Bush and those around him with a feeling of political invincibility that distorted their vision of the political landscape ahead. As Peggy Noonan, speechwriter for Reagan and on occasion for Bush, put it, "the blinding victory gave the White House a false sense of security and encouraged carelessness. The staff was too dazed by polls to see."[4]

Indeed, Bush's poll ratings were exceptionally high in the spring of 1991, as victorious American troops began to return home from the Gulf. His approval rating soared near 90 percent in many public opinion polls—a level unheard of for a president in the third year of his first term. Lulled into a sense of complacency by the afterglow of the Gulf War victory, Bush spent almost another half-year consolidating his gains in the foreign policy arena. In July 1991 he traveled to London for an economic summit of the major Western powers and then went on to Moscow for a meeting with then–Soviet president Mikhail S. Gorbachev. But while Bush tended to the luster on his foreign policy credentials, the economy of

BY DANBY FOR THE BANGOR DAILY NEWS, MAINE

the United States had worsened noticeably, and Bush's neglect of the domestic arena had already started to take a serious political toll, one the White House was still many months from recognizing.[5]

ECONOMIC AND DOMESTIC POLICY

It is one of the many ironies of the Bush presidency that this man who lavished so much of his time and attention on securing foreign policy accomplishments will probably be better known in the history books not for what he achieved abroad but for what he failed to do at home. It is a further irony that this president with a taste for diplomacy and a deftness for maintaining relationships would fail in the one task where both those attributes were needed—keeping faith with his own people. A large part of the reason George Bush lost the presidency is that he reneged on two promises he made to the American people—that he would be single-minded in

his commitment to "no new taxes," and that his would be a noticeably "kinder, gentler" presidency than Reagan's had been. The popular sense of betrayal voters ultimately felt was more than doubled by the fact that Bush seemed neither to understand nor to care that he had broken faith with the voters.

In truth, of course, the decision Bush made in 1990 to support a tax increase was not one he came to lightly; rather it was one pressed on him by a rapidly worsening budget deficit, which was by far the most troubling legacy Bush inherited from Reagan. The deficit's fantastic growth had been set in motion in the early 1980s largely by the combination of record peacetime defense spending and the tax cuts of Reagan's first year. The deficit's growth later was fueled both by intense partisan and ideological conflict and by Reagan's own "lack of realism" about fiscal policy, which kept Congress and the Reagan White House from reaching a policy accommodation to solve the problem.[6]

By 1990 the deficit seemed to be reeling out of control. As Congress deliberated on the

Bush administration's proposed budget for fiscal 1991, the President's Office of Management and Budget three times revised its estimate of the 1991 deficit, raising it from $100 billion in February 1990 to $138 billion in May and then up to $231 billion in July. In response to the worsening news, Bush made it clear that he was ready to drop his campaign promise and negotiate a budget package that included a tax increase. The immediate hailstorm of criticism from congressional Republicans was only the start of Bush's ensuing political problems, which got worse as summer turned to fall and Bush's indecision about what form the tax increase should take raised broader concerns about his capacity to lead the country through its domestic crises.[7]

However responsible and correct Bush's tax decision may have been from a policy standpoint, the president dealt himself a severe blow by reneging on the tax pledge, for it earned him the enmity of the Republican right, who had always been more than a little skeptical of the authenticity of George Bush's claim to the conservative mantle.[8] Bush's reversal on his tax stand also hollowed out his support among "Reagan Democrats," who had folded themselves into the Republican coalition in part because they saw in Reagan and Bush a commitment to keeping their taxes down. Moreover, while the tax hike would prevent the budget deficit from being even worse than if the increase were not allowed, the only thing voters could see was that the economy was worsening all the time and that the prosperity of the Reagan era, however artificial it may have been, was rapidly slipping away. The middle class was taking a beating.

The midterm elections of 1990 revealed this growing disarray in the Republican coalition, especially in the South, where white voters started returning to the Democratic fold. The Republicans' problem was that once Bush broke his promise not to raise taxes, the Democrats no longer had to stretch to portray the GOP as the party of the rich that wanted to provide tax cuts for the wealthy but stick it to everyone else. The "fairness" issue helped the Democrats across the country, as they won new seats in both houses of Congress for the third consecutive national election.

None of this jarred Bush from his preoccupation with foreign affairs, a fixation that was in many ways understandable in view of the scope of the Gulf War mobilization. But by the time Bush finally turned his attention back home in the fall of 1991, the high public approval ratings he had enjoyed in the spring were plummeting as the economy virtually ground to a halt—it was growing at a rate of less than 1.7 percent (the slowest period of growth since World War II).[9] Although unemployment rates actually had been higher in the recession of the early 1980s, the economy was still hemorrhaging tens of thousands of jobs each month, hurting Americans across the board, including many suburban voters who typically had been able to ride over rough economic waves in the past—computer engineers, mid-level managers, and professionals—people who had done quite well during the Reagan boom years and had been thanking the Republican Party with their votes. Many of these people had been forced, after long periods of unemployment, to take jobs with less pay and fewer benefits. For many, the loss of health insurance benefits was especially burdensome. In more and more families, two or three jobs were required to make ends meet. Noting these economic shocks, E.J. Dionne observed:

> This was more than an economic problem for conservatives. It became a moral problem as well. If the values conservatives espoused involved rewarding hard work, family stability and obedience to the law, what would conservatives say to those who lived by all those rules and found themselves slipping behind?[10]

The problem for Bush was not only that he had no answer but that by this time many Americans believed he had no comprehension of the travails they faced, and they had completely lost confidence in his willingness and ability to lead the way in addressing domestic problems.

"The kinder, gentler presidency Bush had promised was hard to discern. . . ."

The kinder, gentler presidency Bush had promised was hard to discern, since the occasional evidence of its existence (for example, his support for the Americans With Disabilities Act) was submerged under layers of what seemed to be presidential indifference. Bush turned a deaf ear to the chorus of voices calling on the White House to take the lead in forging a program to reform the nation's health-care system, which was plagued by rapidly escalating costs, high premium rates for the insured, and a growing uninsured population approaching 35 million Americans. He failed on his pledge to be the "education president," essentially doing nothing in that policy realm. As the election drew near, he vetoed the "family leave" bill, raising legitimate questions as to how much he cared about the problems of, for example, hard-pressed two-career families.

Moreover, this "environmental president" (another sobriquet sought by Bush) seemed to forget that large majorities of Americans consider environmental protection an important policy objective. Although Bush signed the landmark Clean Air Act of 1990, the president made little effort to claim credit for his role in pushing the bill and then allowed his administration (in the form of Vice President Dan Quayle's Competitiveness Council) to backpedal with regulatory and administrative interpretations that eroded the impact of the legislation. And although the president once promised "no net loss" of wetlands, in 1991 he pushed regulations that would open millions of acres of wetlands for development. The Bush administration also allowed the last vestiges of ancient domestic forest to be cut, opposed fuel-efficient automobiles, and dragged its feet on coming to terms with the problem of global warming.

VOTER DISENCHANTMENT

While the domestic policy positions Bush struck found support among some constituencies, he ended up alienating too many voters by his failure to live up to his own promises, by his unwillingness to develop a domestic policy agenda (preferring instead simply to react to circumstances and congressional initiatives), and by the rootless inconsistency that characterized his administration's approach to the concerns of the American people. Since early in his presidency, Bush had been plagued by the criticism that he lacked vision, that he had no ideological compass, no guiding philosophy, to help him negotiate the domestic policy terrain. Although

Bush derided such assertions with his dismissive references to "the vision thing," it was his lack of vision in two areas that would do him in—not just the absence of the kind of coherent political creed that had attracted and held people to Reagan, but his inability to see that his fellow Americans were no longer content with the status quo he seemed intent on maintaining.

Of course, different people had different reasons for their disappointment in Bush. Some had wanted him to be as conservative as Reagan. He wasn't. Others simply had wanted him to hold the line on taxes. He didn't. Still others had hoped he would come through on his rhetoric about improving education, protecting the environment, and helping families cope. He didn't. Thus, there was no particular ideological coherence to the disenchantment with Bush, no single cause for the gathering resentment that took on the character of a gathering storm by the end of 1991; rather, it cut across voters of different stripes and preferences.

"But one thing voters seemed increasingly to share in common was a desire for change."

But one thing voters seemed increasingly to share in common was a desire for change. In one way or another, they had grown tired of a president who promised one thing and delivered another. And as the recession ground on into the election year, too many voters found themselves weary of an era of Republican presidencies that had produced an America in which the rich got richer, the poor got poorer, and everyone in the middle struggled harder and harder just to make ends meet as real wages declined.[11] They were tired of watching the taxes of ordinary families reach record highs while the taxes of those at the top were cut. If during the election year Bush had been able to convince the voters that he would produce change in a second term (or even that he heard their call for it), he might have won. But it was a measure of how far out of touch the president was that he never seemed to recognize how much change already had occurred in the *minds* of Americans he long had served.

It's not as if Bush had no signals or messages that he was in trouble. One alarm sounded on November 5, 1991, when Democrat Harris Wofford beat Republican Richard L. Thornburgh, former U.S. attorney general and former governor, in a special election for a U.S. Senate seat from Pennsylvania. In his campaign, Wofford had criticized Bush for spending more time worrying about the problems of other countries than about those of his own, campaigned especially hard on the need for health-care reform, and taken the Bush administration to task for its failure to develop a health policy initiative. By the end of the month, a CBS/*New York Times* poll reported that Bush's overall job approval rating was in a free-fall, having dropped to 51 percent from 67 percent a month earlier and from its high of 80 in the spring. The president's support was undergoing a particularly striking erosion among middle-income voters, who were obviously unconvinced by the President's assertions that the recession was over—a claim that did not fit with their experience.[12]

While the generalized discontent with Bush was congealing by late 1991, more specific political opposition to his reelection would come from three different directions—from the Republican right-wing candidacy of Patrick J. Buchanan, from independent candidate H. Ross Perot, and from candidates for the Democratic nomination. Each represented changes taking place in the configuration of political competition for the presidency: in the Republican Party, a reopening of the inner ideological fault line that has always been the major source of tension within GOP ranks; among many independent-minded voters, a growing dissatisfaction with the two political parties that seem mired down by business-as-usual politics; and in the Democratic Party, an unmistakable shift away from the aggressive liberalism that had brought it defeat in the past and a shift toward a more disciplined, reasoned moderation, as represented by the party's two leading candidates throughout the primaries, Bill Clinton and Paul E. Tsongas. The next few chapters will elaborate on these challenges. For our purposes, what is important is that, different though they were in their particulars, what they all had in common was the argument that the status quo presidency of George Bush was no longer acceptable, that change was imperative.

Of course, however responsible Bush may have been for many of his problems, he could correctly point out to a restless citizenry that in the American system the president does not govern alone but shares power with Congress. And although Bush had started his presidency intent on being cooperative with Congress and trying to make the most of the voters' decision to retain a divided government (with the Democrats controlling Congress and the Republicans holding the White House), he ended up having more than his share of policy disputes with Congress. Bush vetoed more bills than any other president, and during his presidency partisan squabbling on Capitol Hill reached new heights, with the Democrats and Republicans more consistently at odds with one another than at any time in recent years.

One of the many consequences of all this was that Washington seemed more paralyzed than ever, the veto fights and Senate filibusters succeeding in derailing a wide range of bills,

> *"Congress is an institution held in chronically low regard by the American people. . . ."*

including improvement of public schools, job leave for family emergencies, fetal tissue research, easing of voter registration rules, gun control and other anti-crime initiatives, and an overhaul of campaign finance laws. Neither party did anything bold to attack the budget deficit. No subject received more talk—and less action—than overhaul of the nation's health-care system. And even though the president and Congress vowed to cooperate on an urban aid package after the Los Angeles riots in April 1992, their familiar habits of partisan sniping got the best of them, and the aid bill fell hostage to political gamesmanship over taxes. Thus, as the 1992 elections approached, American voters knew that the responsibility for the drift in governance rested not just with George Bush but with Congress as well.

CONGRESSIONAL POLITICS

Unlike presidential elections, congressional election races are decided largely on the basis of individual candidates and their campaigns, local problems and local issues.[13] But like presidential elections, the aggregate outcomes of congressional elections are affected by broad political trends, perceptions, movements, and events. Seldom is all this as evident as it was in 1992.

Congress is an institution held in chronically low regard by the American people, but its standing in the past several years has been diminished further, not just by its apparent inability to overcome its penchant for partisan squabbling, but by a steady stream of events that seemed to spell a new level of institutional disability. For example, despite the pervasive signs of a worsening economy and the costs of inaction on a host of domestic problems, Congress spent most of the first half-year after Bush's inauguration obsessing with three matters: the president's nomination of former senator John Tower to be secretary of defense (the nomination, eventually disapproved by the Senate, was complicated by charges that Tower was given to heavy drinking and philandering); a pay raise for members of Congress (that legislators finally turned down under pressure but then adopted later in the year when the spotlight was off them); and the ethics scandal engulfing House Speaker James C. Wright, Jr. (which eventually led to his resignation).

Things did not improve as 1989 wore on. As the press began to reveal the full dimensions of the financial crisis in the savings and loan industry, Washington was engulfed in one of its typical episodes of blame-shifting and finger-pointing. Democrats on Capitol Hill argued that the fiasco had its roots in the booming 1980s when Reagan administration officials, blinded by deregulatory zealotry, failed to supervise the thrift industry. Moreover, the Democrats insisted that as head of the Reagan administration's task force on deregulation and supervision of the banking and thrift industries, Bush must have known about the scope of the problem but failed to mention it during the campaign. For their part, the Republicans pointed to the efforts in 1987 by a Democrat-controlled Congress to forestall White House efforts to enact a bailout package of $15 billion, which was an amount inadequate to make much of a dent in the problem but which would have been better than

nothing. As the months went on, the Republicans were able to point to what they called the "sleaze factor" among Democratic legislators, many of whom had close ties to the lobbying machinery of the thrift industry (especially the U.S. League of Savings Institutions). In 1989 and 1990 there was a seemingly endless supply of news articles about the "Keating Five"—the five U.S. senators who collected nearly $1.4 million in campaign donations from Charles Keating of the bankrupt Lincoln Savings and Loan. The story fueled popular calls for campaign finance reform, which Congress ignored.

The widespread disgust with the politicians' handling of the savings and loan fiasco intensified as taxpayers came to realize the enormity of the price they were paying to bail out the thrift industry. Throughout 1990 the press gave lavish attention to OMB's changing estimates of the rapidly burgeoning budget deficit, which was fueled in part by the bailout. And Congress did little to help its low standing with the public when, in the month before the 1990 elections, the legislature fell into its worst deadlock with the president over the budget, leading to a well-publicized Columbus Day weekend shutdown of many federal facilities such as national parks.

Despite all this, there was surprisingly little voter retribution in the 1990 midterm elections. Even though more House members (15 of them) were defeated in November of that year than in 1986 and 1988 combined, the reelection rate for House incumbents was still extraordinarily high. And only one senator, Rudy Boschwitz, R-Minn., went down to defeat.

But the midterm elections were nevertheless filled with evidence of an anti-incumbent mood. Like Boschwitz, some of the defeated House members (for example, Representative Robert W. Kastenmeier, D-Wis., and Representative John W. Buechner, R-Mo.) were widely viewed as politically secure. Some others managed to win but had very close calls, including influential House members unaccustomed to close challenges, such as Majority Leader Richard A. Gephardt, D-Mo., and Representative Newt Gingrich, the minority whip from Georgia. Overall, although the crop of House challengers consisted mostly of poorly financed political newcomers, the winners' average margin of victory declined by several percentage points in both parties—an anomaly, since the usual trends is for the average share to increase for one party and drop for the other. And the

27

share of incumbents returned to office with at least 60 percent of the vote declined to 77 percent from 88 percent in 1988.[14]

Moreover, it was during the 1990 election that the "term limitation" movement first made noticeable waves, indicating a growing sentiment against long-term legislative incumbency and in favor of the notion that the political system would benefit from forced infusions of new blood. The typical term-limit proposal would limit House members to six two-year terms and senators to two six-year terms. Making no headway with the proposal as a legislative measure in Congress, advocates started getting the initiative on the ballot in the states. In 1990, three states adopted term-limit initiatives; going into the 1992 elections, the initiative was on the ballot in 15 states (where it eventually passed in 14 of them).

Even as the members of the 102nd Congress were taking their oaths of office in January of 1991, there was plenty of reason to believe that many of them would not be back to take another such oath in 1993—in other words, that the 1992 election would produce an unusually large number of departures from the House of Representatives. For one thing, many members of Congress felt exhausted by the realities of the congressional political environment—long work days with limited time for their families; the constant pressures of campaign fund-raising; the ceaseless haranguing and importuning by representatives of special interest groups; the relative joylessness of being a legislator during a time of fiscal austerity; and the growing public hostility toward incumbents. (On this last point, although members know that citizens tend to regard their own representatives more highly than they do Congress as a whole, legislative life holds fewer attractions in an era of pervasive electoral insecurity.)

Moreover, 1992 would be the first election following the decennial reapportionment and redistricting. The 1990 census triggered a reapportionment that shifted 19 seats from 13 states, mostly in the East and Midwest, to 8 other states, most of them in the South and West.[15] The redistricting attendant to such shifts tends to make legislators in affected states skittish, since it may mean, in the best case, that one will have a district with a new configuration and constituency or, in the worst case, that one will be forced to square off against a colleague when two districts have been melded into one. For many

members already stressed by the demands of electoral politics, any such change is simply more than they care to deal with, so voluntary retirements from the House tend to go up in election years following a census.[16]

Two developments in 1991 and early 1992 would virtually guarantee an unusually large exodus of members from the House. First, in October 1991, the nation went through one of its occasional spasms of collective obsession as tens of millions of Americans watched the televised hearings by the Senate Judiciary Committee of Anita Hill's stunning allegations of sexual harassment against Clarence Thomas, whom President Bush had nominated to a seat on the U.S. Supreme Court. Viewers taking either side in this case could (and did) find in the proceedings plenty of reason to censure the white male senators who handled the whole matter with extraordinary clumsiness and insensitivity—and to see those legislators as unfortunately typical of the whole sorry tangle of incumbents populating Capitol Hill.

Second, in early 1992, still reeling from the Hill-Thomas mess, Congress was rocked by another wave of institutional dishonor that caught over 300 members of the House in its undertow: an investigation by the Justice Department and the House Ethics Committee revealed that hundreds of members had been overdrawing on their checking accounts at the House bank, paying no penalties for the overdrafts (in some cases totaling hundreds of checks), sometimes running deficits, again without penalty, for long periods of time. Although the personal banking behavior itself may not have been all that reprehensible, what got voters angry was the symbolism of the whole thing. At a time when a badly sagging economy was leaving many in dire straits, voters were being reminded of the special treatment, the "perks," their representatives received for having been elected: free postage for official mail, free travel to certain foreign destinations, free medical care, free access to fancy athletic facilities, free parking at the Capitol and at National Airport, free fresh flowers, free income-tax assistance, and the like. It was simply further evidence, in the view of many Americans, that their elected representatives were arrogant and (like President Bush who, early in the campaign, visited a grocery store and was astonished by the barcode readers at the checkout counter) too insulated from the realities of everyday life in America.

Thus, as the general election races for Congress took shape in mid-1992, it was clear that the election would produce lots of new faces on Capitol Hill and that an unusually large number of those faces would belong to minorities and women. The number of minority members would go up because redistricting had created new districts with predominantly Latino and African-American populations. And in what was being called the "year of the woman," more women were running for congressional seats than ever before. Outraged by the Hill-Thomas hearings, and alarmed by the increasing fragility of abortion rights and the dearth of programs to aid struggling families, women offered themselves as candidates in record numbers, determined to fulfill the tee-shirt slogan, "A Woman's Place is in the House—And in the Senate."[17]

"[A] scornful public was sending an increasingly clear message that it was no longer in the mood to suffer fools gladly. . . ."

It also was clear that the members of the 103rd Congress assembling in January 1993 would be under heavy pressure from the public to produce change, both in the way Congress operates and in its approaches to public problems. Through their growing support for term limitation, a scornful public was sending an increasingly clear message that it was no longer in the mood to suffer fools gladly—especially on Capitol Hill, where there seemed such a high concentration of them.

CONCLUSION

In one of the television ads that made up part of her successful 1992 campaign for a U.S. Senate seat representing the state of Washington, Democrat Patty Murray—identified as "just a mom in tennis shoes"—looked into the camera and said, "I'm ready to roll up my sleeves, get this country moving again and offer the leadership real people deserve," as an announcer pronounced her "a voice for real change, finally." Citing this ad as typical of outsiders' promises in 1992 to shake things up if they got to Washington, one reporter noted that the word "change" was "being brandished like a talisman" in this election year.[18]

The mantra of change was central to Bill Clinton's campaign as well; it was a constant refrain in his public statements. Having aggressively presented himself to American voters as an agent of change, he could take from his victory (whether or not it constituted a "mandate") a sense that the people had spoken in favor of change. After all, the best means available to voters for bringing about changes in government policies and practices in a democratic society is to elect the candidate of the party not in power. And that's what they did, rejecting the Republican Party that no longer seemed to pay attention to them.

When he accepted his party's nomination for president in July of 1992, Clinton indicated quite clearly that he heard the anger and frustration of middle-class Americans, and he held out to them a promise that under his presidency attention would be paid: "In the name of all those who do the work, pay the taxes, raise the kids and play by the rules—in the name of the hard-working Americans who make up our forgotten middle class, I accept your nomination for president of the United States. I am a product of that middle class. And when I am president you will be forgotten no more."

But even those who felt most joyful and optimistic in the wake of Clinton's victory must have had mixed feelings as they considered the magnitude of the task before him. Bringing about real changes would not be easy under the best of circumstances, and the conditions Clinton inherited were certainly far from the best. However daunting the obstacles they face, the Clinton White House and Congress will have to work single-mindedly to put the nation on a new course with respect to its most persistent problems. How they do that—and how well—will provide the context for the presidential election of 1996.

On November 4, 1992, the day after the electorate turned him out of office, Vice President Dan Quayle, referring in part to the laser-like consistency of the Democrats' campaign, said of Bill Clinton and the future: "If he runs the country as well as he ran his campaign, we'll be in fine shape." Since presidents sometimes find that what served them well during the campaign also serves them well in office, and since Clinton's own victory over Bush may be read as a sign of the public's new willingness to hold its leaders accountable for what they promised they would do, perhaps Clinton should see to it that during his administration every executive office in Washington bears a poster reading "Change, stupid!"—or, alternatively, "Pay attention, stupid!"

Chapter Three

Surviving the 1992 Presidential Nomination Process

Charles D. Hadley and Harold W. Stanley

This chapter examines the presidential nomination process in 1992, a year in which the very value of a major party nomination was in question. Lesser-known Democratic candidates, struggling to focus attention on present dissatisfaction and future hopes rather than past indiscretions, each sought to separate themselves from the pack and emerge as a credible challenger to incumbent president George H. W. Bush. The emergence of an independent challenge by H. Ross Perot, a Texas billionaire businessman, midway through the nomination season, and his unanticipated departure during the Democratic National Convention, shaped the context within which the nomination contests unfolded. Challenges to both the Democratic front runner and the incumbent president persisted long after the party nominations were essentially determined. Rather than a nomination process that merely registered predetermined political preferences, the volatility of those preferences over the first eight months of 1992 serves to remind us that a dynamic nomination process helps shape the preferences it reflects. Those first eight months ran the gamut: public opinion backed Bush's reelection for the first four, favored Perot as president for most of the next two, then embraced Democratic nominee William J. Clinton in the final two (a choice with which it stayed through the general election).[1]

BACKGROUND

Those with serious intentions to challenge an incumbent president for reelection must, long in advance, lay the groundwork by establishing an organization capable of going the distance and a fundraising network to sustain that organization. In 1991 President Bush looked virtually invincible to Democrats considering such a challenge. Former senator Paul E. Tsongas (Massachusetts) announced his candidacy on April 30, 1991. Several more prominent Democrats did not follow in the footsteps of Tsongas. The next four Democratic announcements were of decisions not to run: former senator George McGovern (South Dakota, May 23), Representative Richard A. Gephardt (Missouri, July 17), Senator John D. Rockefeller IV (West Virginia, August 7), and Senator Al Gore (Tennessee, August 21). Three more withdrawals came later: Governor Mario M. Cuomo (New York, December 20), the Reverend Jesse L. Jackson (Washington, D.C., November 2), and Representative Dave McCurdy (Oklahoma, October 18). Ultimately, these seven withdrawals outnumbered the six decisions to run.

After Tsongas, the announcements of candidacy came from Governor L. Douglas Wilder (Virginia, September 13), Senator Thomas R. Harkin (Iowa, September 15), Senator J. R. (Bob) Kerrey (Nebraska, September 30), Gov-

BY LOWE FOR THE SUN-SENTINEL, FT. LAUDERDALE, FLA.

ernor Bill Clinton (Arkansas, October 3), and former governor Edmund G. (Jerry) Brown, Jr. (California, October 21).[2] Bush's political strength figured into calculations of candidacy, discouraging prominent Democrats. Not only had Bush put together a worldwide military and economic coalition to vanquish Iraqi president Saddam Hussein and his army, he had also garnered the overwhelming *bipartisan* support of Congress and the American public for the eventual military action that freed Kuwait and routed the Iraqi military with few allied casualties. With this military success, Bush not only obliterated the lingering national malaise related to the Vietnam War, he also became a national hero overnight. The president's popularity soared to an unprecedented height of 89 percent between February 28 and March 3, the highest approval rating ever recorded by the Gallup organization, surpassing the previous heights of Presidents Harry S. Truman (87 percent, 1945, after the surrender of Germany), Franklin Delano Roosevelt (84 percent, 1941, after the bombing of Pearl Harbor), and John F. Kennedy (83 percent, 1961, after the invasion of the Bay of Pigs in Cuba). The commander in chief later paraded down Wall Street with the returning troops to a heroes' welcome, the likes of which

was last seen almost a half-century earlier when American troops returned from World War II.[3]

> **"*Bush not only obliterated the lingering national malaise related to the Vietnam War, he also became a national hero overnight.*"**

Every silver lining has its touch of gray. Saddam Hussein remained in power. Signs of serious domestic discontent were pervasive among the U.S. public: between March 7 and March 10, 1991, only 27 percent approved of the way the president was handling the problems of poverty and the homeless; 28 percent, the savings and loan crisis; 31 percent, the federal budget deficit; 34 percent, the availability of health care; and, 37 percent, the economy. Approval was far lower among those who considered themselves Democrats or Independents.[4] In late 1990, prior to the Gulf War, Bush had broken an oft-repeated pledge from the 1988 campaign: "The Congress will push me to raise taxes, and I'll say no. And they'll push, and I'll say no. And they'll push again, and I'll say to them, 'Read my lips; no new taxes.' "[5] In the fall of 1990 Congress pushed new taxes and Bush said yes. In the same 1988 acceptance speech Bush had promised 30 million new jobs over the next eight years, a bold promise against which his record would be harshly measured.[6]

THE CANDIDATES

During November and December 1991, President Bush and six Democrats—former senator Tsongas, Governor Clinton, Senator Harkin, Senator Kerrey, Governor Wilder, and former governor Brown—raised the necessary $100,000 in 20 states ($5,000 per state) in amounts of $250 or less to qualify for public funding.

Though he sought to take advantage of the vacuum left by the Reverend Jackson among African-American voters, Wilder raised only enough to receive a meager $198,315 matching payment on January 2, 1992. He withdrew from the race on January 8, before it began, citing his need to attend to pressing state problems, leaving African-American Democratic voters to pick among five candidates, all white.[7] The absence of Jesse Jackson meant white presidential candidates would seriously court African-American Democratic primary voters for the first time since 1984, when Walter F. Mondale competed with Jackson for African-American votes.

Bush had challengers within his own party. Former Louisiana Republican state legislator David Duke, also a former Ku Klux Klan leader and neo-Nazi sympathizer, coming off a gubernatorial runoff campaign in which he garnered nearly 40 percent of the vote, announced his candidacy amidst widespread media interest. However, Duke never qualified for matching funds after exploring that option. Bush's other Republican challenger, conservative columnist Patrick J. Buchanan, did qualify for matching funds. The president, however, stood alone in his ability to raise such funds. Bush had certified and received $3,640,889 by February 4, an amount over twice that of his nearest Democratic challengers, Clinton ($1,400,599) and Harkin (1,327,120), who, in turn, received substantially more than Kerrey ($833,364), Tsongas ($556,445), and Brown ($393,048).[8]

THE CAUCUSES AND PRIMARIES: A PRELUDE OF FIREWORKS

Given the importance attached to the Iowa caucuses, New Hampshire primary, and Super Tuesday,[9] the nomination process appeared to favor Democrats Harkin from Iowa, Tsongas from northeastern Massachusetts near the New Hampshire border, and southerner Clinton. The two and a half weeks before the Iowa caucuses brought unexpected and potentially damaging surprises for front-runner Bill Clinton. The first broadside was fired by the tabloid *Star,* which purchased Gennifer Flowers's account of an alleged 1977–1989 extramarital affair with Clinton, a story prominently featured in its January 28th edition released on January 21. Clinton and his wife Hillary protested that their marriage should be judged by the fact that they were still together.[10] The second salvo was fired by the *Wall Street Journal* on February 6, when it reported that Clinton avoided the Vietnam War draft in 1969 by promising to enroll in an officer training program while attending the University of Arkansas Law School; he never did enroll in either; instead he chose to attend Yale Law School the following year.[11]

"[T]he widely reported Gennifer Flowers incident made Bill Clinton a household word. . . ."

Although a revelation of infidelity with Donna Rice sank Senator Gary Hart's 1988 presidential bid and political career, Governor Bill Clinton had several things in his favor. First, ground rules for the media appeared to have changed so that the accuser had the burden of proof. Second, prospects for the economy dominated the concerns of Democrats—particularly New Hampshire Democrats. The media reports of alleged marital infidelities and 25-year-old decisions over the draft were often seen as distractions from that dominant concern. As

Peter Jennings, ABC News anchor for "World News Tonight," recalled, "While we [the media] were trying to run Bill Clinton to the ground on the subject of Gennifer Flowers, the voters in New Hampshire wanted to know about the economy. And we were getting in their way."[12] Third, by the time of the Gennifer Flowers allegation, filing deadlines had already passed in 15 states having 28 percent of the national convention delegates. By the time of the draft evasion allegation that Clinton acknowledged on February 12, filing deadlines had passed in 18 states with 40 percent of the delegates.[13] Finally, the widely reported Gennifer Flowers incident made Bill Clinton a household word; his name recognition soared to 86 percent of all voters (89 percent among Democratic voters and those leaning Democratic), and his support among Democrats for the nomination rose over three weeks from 17 to 42 percent. This gave Clinton a commanding lead over his rivals among those who identified themselves as Democrats or who were leaning toward casting a Democratic vote in a January 31–February 2 Gallup poll (Brown had 16, Kerrey 10, Harkin 9, and Tsongas 9 percent). Equally important, 71 percent of all registered voters (73 percent of Democrats and Democratic leaners) reported that "the allegations about Bill Clinton's personal conduct and his handling of them" would not have much effect on their vote.[14]

The Iowa Caucuses Fizzle

Harkin's home-field advantage devalued the Democratic caucus in Iowa. With native son status, the popular Harkin was left alone to run against himself, spending scarce campaign dollars to best high-water marks established by past Democratic candidates such as the 59 percent received in 1980 by President Jimmy Carter against Senator Edward M. Kennedy. No other candidate except Jerry Brown even visited the state, necessitating treks to New Hampshire by the *Des Moines Register*'s famed David Yepsen in search of presidential campaign news to report. Ultimately, Harkin received 76.5 percent of the "delegate equivalents" in a contest where few Iowans bothered to participate—an estimated 30,000 in contrast to 125,000 in 1988. (Perhaps because the Iowa Republican establishment was so solidly behind President Bush, Buchanan and Duke chose not to participate.)[15]

The New Hampshire Primary

Democratic front-runner Clinton survived the Gennifer Flowers and draft evasion explosions well enough among economically depressed New Hampshire voters to be tagged—as Clinton proclaimed—the "Comeback Kid," garnering 25 percent of the vote in a record turnout and a second-place finish to New Hampshire neighbor Tsongas (33 percent). Tsongas had invested substantial campaign time rather than dollars to duplicate former Massachusetts governor Michael S. Dukakis's 1988 victory. By one count, Tsongas spent nearly twice as many campaign days there as either Clinton or Brown did (70 versus 43 and 40), with Kerrey and Harkin spending 57 and 52, respectively. Vietnam Medal of Honor winner Kerrey, emphasizing his combat experience, received 11 percent of the vote. Kerrey was reported to have outspent his rivals on television within the state with an estimated $800,000, only to come in a disappointing third in a clump with Harkin (10 percent) and Brown (8 percent). New York governor Cuomo, still flirting with an entry into the presidential fray, saw the well-publicized write-in campaign on his behalf fizzle with but 4 percent of the vote. Interestingly, House of Representatives Speaker Tom Foley publicly dismissed the Tsongas victory and declared Clinton the winner.[16]

On the Republican side, Buchanan, who was endorsed by the conservative *Manchester Union Leader,* seriously wounded President Bush. Bush received 53 percent of the vote to Buchanan's 37 percent, in large measure due to an ailing economy and Bush's breaking his "no new taxes" pledge. New Hampshire voters did more than send the president a message; they substantially dimmed his reelection chances in doing so. Since the 1940s, any sitting president who received less than 50 percent of the New Hampshire vote either withdrew from the race or was defeated in the general election; Bush came perilously close to falling below that level of support.[17]

Toward Super Tuesday

After the New Hampshire primary, the Democratic contests did not produce a clear front-runner. The Maine caucuses split between Tsongas (30 percent) and Brown (29 percent), with Clinton (16 percent) trailing in third place. The South Dakota primary was handily carried by Kerrey with 40 percent, followed by Harkin (25 percent) and Clinton (19 percent). The nomination calendar placed Maine and South Dakota immediately before the first of the southern primaries. With primaries coming up in Georgia, Maryland, and Colorado (March 3), South Carolina (March 7), and Super Tuesday (March 10), the calendar favored regional native son and political centrist Clinton. In Georgia and Maryland voters were free to participate in the primaries of their choice, with Colorado participants restricted to their party of registration and Independents free to choose between them. Campaigning in Georgia, Kerrey continued to play up the stark distinction between himself, a Medal of Honor war hero in Vietnam, and Clinton's draft avoidance. Kerrey voiced the fears of other Democrats when he stated that if Clinton were nominated, he "is going to be opened up like a soft peanut" by the Republicans in the general election.[18]

On March 3 the three primary contests produced three different winners. Colorado was a near three-way tie among Brown (29 percent), Clinton (27 percent), and Tsongas (26 percent). Maryland proved to be a two-way contest between Tsongas with 41 percent and Clinton with 34 percent, with the other candidates each gaining only single-digit support. Georgia, on the other hand, was a Clinton rout of Tsongas by 57 to 24 percent, the next closest competitor being Brown with but 8 percent. The clear loser was Kerrey, who folded his tent two days later, withdrawing from the race on March 5.[19] Clinton widened his victory margin in South Carolina, gaining 63 percent to 19 percent for Tsongas. Harkin, endorsed by 15 labor unions with 7.7 million members, had not fared well. His union endorsements had not translated to his benefit, given their predominant location in the "rust belt" states holding later primaries. Harkin withdrew from his campaign on March 9.[20]

Super Tuesday

Only Tsongas and Brown remained to challenge Clinton for the nomination. On Super Tuesday, Clinton registered impressive victories in the southern states, victories ranging from 52 percent in Florida, where Tsongas, banking on a win, took only 34 percent of the vote, to 65 percent in Texas (versus Tsongas's 19 percent), to a high of 73 percent in Mississippi, with the remaining challengers in single digits. As expected, Massachusetts and Rhode Island belonged to Tsongas, who trounced Clinton and Brown by 67 to 11 and 21 in Massachusetts and by 53 to 21 and 19 in Rhode Island. With the Super Tuesday votes aggregated, Clinton was the clear winner with 54 percent, followed by Tsongas (28 percent), and distantly by Brown (11 percent).[21] The designers of Super Tuesday had hoped to rally the southern states behind a moderate Democrat who could win the presidency in 1988. What they failed to accomplish in 1988 did not elude them in 1992.

Bush solidified his hold on the Republican nomination with Super Tuesday. Having voluntarily yielded to Buchanan the role of major challenger to Bush, and having been kept off the Republican ballot by many determined state Republican parties, David Duke was about as invisible as his former Invisible Empire. Unable to raise campaign funds, let alone sustain even a region-wide campaign organization, Duke remained in single digits on Super Tuesday, even in his home state of Louisiana (9 percent). Only in Mississippi did Duke amass 11 percent. Pat Buchanan had assumed the role of legitimate conservative opposition or "thorn," continuing to consistently take from 25 to 30 percent of the vote away from President Bush. The president, on the other hand, continued to gain disproportionate shares of delegates in "winner-take-all" contests. In stark contrast to Super Tuesday 1988, after which Bush had the Republican nomination sewn up with nearly 74 percent of the national convention delegates in his column, he had just over a quarter of the total delegates for 1992, in part due to the election calendar.[22]

"The Democratic race narrowed further following Super Tuesday."

The Democratic race narrowed further following Super Tuesday. After a second-place

Table 3.1

Cumulative Percentages of Presidential Primary Votes Cast and Committed Delegates: Major Democratic and Republican Candidates, 1992

Date	Clinton		Tsongas		Brown		Bush		Buchanan	
	Votes	Delegates	Votes	Delegates	Votes	Delegates	Votes	Delegates	Votes	Delegates
March 4	38.1	4.6	30.9	2.6	11.3	0.8	64.5	6.7	32.3	0.9
March 11	50.4	16.5	28.6	8.1	19.9	1.9	67.5	25.4	28.3	2.1
March 18	50.6	22.1	27.3	10.0	12.6	3.0	68.8	32.2	27.1	2.1
March 25	50.3	23.1	27.1	10.2	13.1	3.5	68.9	34.0	27.0	2.1
April 8	48.5	29.5	26.5	12.6	16.1	6.2	70.4	43.6	24.8	2.4
April 30	49.2	37.0	25.1	12.5	17.1	7.5	71.2	49.4	24.5	2.5
May 6	50.6	40.0	23.8	12.5	16.9	8.0	71.7	54.8	24.1	3.1
May 13	51.1	41.6	23.2	12.5	16.8	8.2	72.1	56.8	23.7	3.2
May 20	51.0	43.4	22.9	12.9	17.3	9.2	72.2	61.1	23.5	3.3
May 27	51.7	46.1	21.6	12.8	16.9	9.2	72.2	64.0	23.0	3.4
June 3	51.9	58.6	18.1	12.9	19.9	14.2	73.0	83.6	22.4	3.5
Total Votes	(10,471,965)		(3,644,543)		(4,023,373)		(9,512,142)		(2,912,142)	
Total Delegates	(2,511.75)		(551.00)		(608.25)		(1,846)		(78)	

Note: Delegate count is from the Associated Press. The total delegate counts are 4,287 (Democratic) and 2,209 (Republican). Tsongas dropped out of the presidential race on March 19, 1992, but continued to accumulate votes and delegates. For individual primary results, see the *Congressional Quarterly Weekly Reports* for July and August in the sources below.

Sources: Compiled from "The National Tally," *Congressional Quarterly Weekly Reports* of March 7, March 14, March 21, March 28, April 11, May 2, May 9, May 16, May 23, May 30, and June 6, 1992; "Primary Recap: The Aggregate Vote," *Congressional Quarterly Weekly Report: Guide to the 1992 Democratic National Convention,* July 4, 1992, and *Congressional Quarterly Weekly Report: Guide to the 1992 Republican National Convention,* August 8, 1992.

showing in Illinois with 26 percent of the vote and a third-place showing in Michigan with 17 percent, former senator Paul Tsongas suspended his quest for the Democratic Party presidential nomination. Front-runner Clinton posted convincing wins in both states, with 52 percent in Illinois and 51 percent in Michigan.[23] Jerry Brown, just as Buchanan did among the Republicans, assumed the role of spoiler and remained in the race until the very end in spite of the futility of the quest (Table 3.1). Clinton's Connecticut loss to Brown gave Brown enhanced credibility for filling the vacuum left by Tsongas. In an unusual move, Harkin endorsed Clinton and came to his defense by tearing apart Brown's flat tax plan. Said Harkin, "Things I see happening in the Brown campaign lead me to believe something destructive is happening."[24] Attempts to downplay the Democratic infighting were given a powerful reinforcement by the Democratic Party chairman, Ron Brown, who stated that some of Brown's criticisms of Clinton "crossed the line."[25]

Clinton continued to garner a cumulative total of 50 percent of the votes cast, even though the media continued to dog him with the "character" issue. His percentage of the delegates moved steadily higher. Clinton gained the majority needed in the last week of primaries in Alabama, California, Montana, New Jersey, and New Mexico. He weathered a long, grueling process, made all the more demanding under Democratic proportional representation rules.

President Bush, on the other hand, started with nearly two-thirds of the votes, a cumulative percentage that increased to 70 by the April Republican contests and ended with 73 by the end of the June 2 primary elections. By the end of April he had clinched renomination, holding Pat Buchanan to about a quarter of the votes cast and but 2.5 percent of the delegates, given his party's "winner-take-all" rules. By the end of the primaries, the president had 83.6 percent of the delegates to Buchanan's 3.5 percent. David Duke, with but 1 percent of the votes, was shut out of the allocation of delegates.

Primary Turnout and Shares of the Vote

Clinton ran in 39 primary elections, some of which were "beauty contests" not used to select delegates. Exit polls in 29 of these states provide, when combined, an overview of his voter support patterns (Table 3.2). Despite his youth and position as an activist centrist, Clinton secured greater support among Democrats among the elderly, minorities, those with less education, and the less affluent. Clinton's ability to put together strong support in the primaries from less well-off whites and African Americans augured well for Democrats in the fall. Clinton received disproportionate support from African Americans, the middle-aged and older, Protestants, those with a high school education or less, and moderate to low family incomes. Clinton's support spanned the ideological spectrum: liberals (47 percent), moderates (54 percent), and conservatives (48 percent).

Glee in the Clinton camp over these support patterns was tempered by a realization that participation had declined in the 1992 primaries. In 1992 nearly 20 million voters took part in the 40 Democratic primaries; in 1988 more than 23 million participated in 37 primaries. In the 21 states that held Democratic primaries in 1988 and 1992, voter turnout was down by more than 2.6 million voters, from 14.9 to 12.3 million (a 17 percent decline). Some states had increased turnout in 1992—states in which Tsongas fared best. New Hampshire voters turned out in record numbers, posting a 35.9 percent increase; neighboring Massachusetts increased by 11 percent; followed by Maryland (7 percent) and Rhode Island (3 percent). Tsongas won all of them. The only states with increased primary turnout that favored Clinton were Oklahoma (6 percent), Illinois (0.2 percent), and North Carolina (0.2 percent). The remaining 15 states registered double-digit voter turnout declines ranging from 11 percent (West Virginia) to 47 percent (Mississippi).[26] The Democratic primary voter turnout decline was less drastic when comparing 1992 with a 1972–1988 average in the 18 states holding primaries over the entire period.[27] African-American turnout was off, in part because the mobilizing effect of Jesse Jackson's candidacy was absent. The suspicion loomed on the Democratic side that perhaps a relatively lackluster field of candidates had not connected with the voters. Clinton's emergence as the presumptive nominee in the face of such competition was not invigorating.[28]

Republican turnout also was down. Republican primaries were held in 14 states in both 1992 and 1988. Voter turnout increased in Maryland (20 percent), Georgia (13 percent), Massachusetts (12 percent), New Hampshire (10 percent), and Oklahoma (4 percent). The steep declines registered in South Dakota (52 percent), South Carolina (24 percent), and Texas (21 percent) were uncharacteristic of the remaining states posting voter turnout declines, which ranged from 1 percent in Florida to 7 percent in Louisiana.[29]

CANDIDATE ENDORSEMENTS

The systematic accumulation of the necessary votes and delegates is but part of the story of Clinton's ultimate success. As he moved from state to state and region to region after New Hampshire, he had the active support of sitting governors and lieutenant governors, former governors, members of Congress, and big-city mayors through his leadership roles in the centrist Democratic Leadership Conference (DLC) and National Governors' Association, (e.g., Kurt Schmoke of Maryland and Richard Daley of Chicago). Among others, Clinton was actively supported by Governors Zell Miller of Georgia, Richard Riley of South Carolina, Edwin W. Edwards of Louisiana, Ned McWherter of Tennessee, David Walters of Oklahoma, Brereton C. Jones of Kentucky, Bruce Sundlun of Rhode Island, Howard B. Dean of Vermont, Booth Gardner of Washington, Bruce King of New Mexico, Bob Miller of Nevada, Roy Romer of Colorado, George Sinner of North Dakota, John Waihee III of Hawaii, Mike J. Sullivan of Wyoming, Lieutenant Governors Buddy MacKay of Florida and Mel Carnahan of Missouri, and former governors Richard D. Lamm of Colorado and William Winter of Mississippi. Texas governor Ann Richards did little to hide her partiality to Clinton, though she made no official endorsement. With these big-name endorsements came those from a host of statewide elected officials, massive support from state legislators, as well as solid support from members of Congress and big-city mayors.[30]

Clinton's campaign was not embraced by Democratic elected officials to the extent it would be once his winning ways emerged in the

37

Table 3.2

The 1992 Democratic Primaries: Patterns of Voter Support

Group	Percentage of Vote			Percentage of Primary Voters
	Clinton	Brown	Tsongas	
Sex				
Men	50	22	20	47
Women	51	20	21	53
Race/ethnicity				
Whites	47	23	25	78
African Americans	70	15	8	14
Latinos	51	30	15	4
Age				
18–29 years	47	24	19	12
30–44 years	45	26	22	33
45–59 years	51	19	20	25
60 and older	59	15	18	30
Religion				
Protestant	55	14	21	50
Catholic	44	24	24	30
Jewish	45	15	33	6
Education				
No high school diploma	67	14	10	8
High school graduates	61	17	15	27
Some college	48	23	18	27
College graduates	42	24	26	20
Some postgraduate education	38	23	28	18
Family income				
Less than $15,000	62	17	13	15
$15,000 to $29,999	55	19	18	25
$30,000 to $49,999	48	23	21	30
$50,000 to $74,999	45	23	25	18
$75,000 and over	38	23	29	11
Partisanship				
Democrats	57	19	17	67
Independents	36	25	27	29
Republicans	34	18	32	4
Ideology				
Liberals	47	26	20	35
Moderates	54	18	19	45
Conservatives	48	17	23	20
Family's financial situation, compared to four years ago				
Better today	44	24	22	14
Same today	50	20	20	39
Worse today	53	20	18	45
Total, all 29 states	50	21	20	100
Total votes (millions)	9.0	3.8	3.5	18.0

Note: This table, which constructs a Democratic primary electorate for the nation, combines vote totals and results from exit polls conducted in 29 Democratic primary states from February to June. Vote totals are from secretaries of state. Exit polls were conducted by Voter Research and Surveys. Each state influences the total table according to its share of all votes cast. Other candidates, who received 1.7 million votes combined or 9 percent of the total, are not shown.

Source: New York Times, July 12, 1992, p. A18.

summer. The Democratic governor of Pennsylvania, Robert P. Casey, greeted Clinton before the Pennsylvania primary with an appeal for an open convention: "We have to recognize reality. The primary process is not producing someone who has a good crack at winning in November. . . . We've got a tiny minority of Democrats voting for Bill Clinton, and he's winning every race without generating any sparks, any enthusiasm, any momentum. . . . People have a tremendous unease about him. . . . He has to address the character issue in some way. Maybe he can turn this around. I hope he can."[31] Although harsh, Casey's assessment was not out of line with similar readings of the public by Clinton's own campaign. As discussed later, they worked to turn the situation around and succeeded.[32]

Though he continued to gather endorsements from congressional "super delegates" throughout the nomination phase of the presidential selection process, Clinton and members of Congress were uneasy with each other. The House banking scandal contributed to an anti-incumbency mood. Both Clinton and congressmen had their own "character" problems that they worked hard to leave behind, so they danced at a distance rather than embraced. By late February, for example, Clinton had endorsements from 8 U.S. senators and 44 U.S. representatives from 18 states, his nearest rival being Kerrey with 5 senators and 7 House members from 9 states. Jerry Brown, the lone challenger at the end, had but 1 endorsement, U.S. representative John Conyers, Jr. (D-Mich.). By late April, Clinton was endorsed by 17 senators and 75 House members, twice the numbers posted by former governor Dukakis at the same point in his 1988 nomination bid.[33]

After meetings with uncommitted super delegates in the offices of Senator Dennis DeConcini (D-Ariz.) and Representative Don Edwards (D-Calif.), DeConcini noted that "Many of us question his electability. The reality is he's got a lot of problems." This concern was echoed by Representative Leon E. Panetta (D-Calif.): "Some members are obviously very nervous. [They] are concerned about what ultimately will be used against him in November." On the other hand, there was the feeling expressed by Representative Charles W. Stenholm (D-Tex.) that "The governor has won it the old-fashioned way. It's time for us to get on with the job of electing him president." Reservations aside, both Ed-

wards and DeConcini worked with the Clinton campaign for an April 29 meeting with Clinton that was well received by House and Senate members, though over half the super delegates in each chamber remained uncommitted.[34]

> **"Perot redefined the way candidates campaigned for the presidency. . . ."**

Clinton, too, sought endorsements away from the state capitals and Congress. Using his endorsements from the teacher and public employee unions, Clinton successfully blocked an early AFL-CIO endorsement of Harkin. When Harkin bowed out of the race on March 9, Clinton expected to pick up Harkin's union support. While a number of Michigan union leaders moved to Clinton, Brown picked up the endorsement of the United Auto Workers and some of the other union leaders. Finally in mid-April, with all of the candidates except Brown out of the race, Clinton received the endorsement of the AFL-CIO Executive Council, the AFL-CIO representing 33 members unions with some 14 million members.[35]

POPULAR SUPPORT FOR THE PEROT INSURGENCY

As Clinton continued to struggle to put the "character" issue behind him, and as President Bush was forced to campaign actively to ward off the Buchanan challenge, folksy populist billionaire H. Ross Perot appeared on the scene, sensing that the public considered both Clinton and Bush flawed and vulnerable. Perot redefined the way candidates campaigned for the presidency by appearing on CNN's "Larry King Live," "Donahue," and other such shows. Clinton followed suit, appearing on the network morning shows, "Larry King Live," MTV, and on Arsenio Hall's late-night show, where he played "Heartbreak Hotel" on the saxophone.[36] President Bush held back, deeming such campaigning "not presidential." Eventually he joined the circuit. The public found Perot refreshingly plain-spoken. For example, Perot told Phil Donahue that "Anybody intelligent enough to do this job wouldn't want it." (Apparently, later, Perot wanted it.) When asked by Larry King if he would run for president, the cagey Texan indicated, "I might, if people in all 50 states asked me to." At another point, Perot indicated he would spend $100 million "or whatever it takes" to run a world-class campaign.[37] (George Bush, who told David Frost he would do "whatever it takes" to be reelected president, had apparently met his match in Perot, a man who had not only the will but also the wallet.)

Perot supporters, with his behind-the-scenes financial support, enthusiastically set about the task of getting him on the ballot in all 50 states. In effect, he set about building a grassroots political organization. In doing so, he refused to take campaign contributions greater than $5, he said, "so they can have some skin in the game."

In May and June, Perot and Bush were vying for the lead in public opinion polls, with the edge to Perot (Figure 3.1). Perot became the first independent candidate in the history of polling to surpass a sitting president. Perot not only led in most national polls, but also registered strong support even among Republican and Democratic primary voters who had just voted for Clinton or Bush. In California, Ohio, and New Jersey, one-quarter to nearly one-half of each party's primary voters told exit pollsters they would have voted for Perot had he been on the ballot.[38]

Although Clinton had made impressive gains, winning 22 straight primary elections since the close loss to Jerry Brown in Connecticut, and being the first Democratic candidate ever to win the primary elections in the 10 most populous states, Perot's meteoric rise stole the show at the close of the nomination season.[39] Perot's independent campaign obscured Clinton, relegating Clinton's national support to third place, far behind Bush and Perot. Perot had never declared his candidacy nor entered a single primary or caucus. Pundits anticipated that Perot's support would wither with time: the public knew little about Perot,[40] and learning more might mean liking him less. But the novelty of Perot's campaign, that he was doing as well as he was, and the deep-seated public desire for change gave pundits pause.

AFTER THE PRIMARIES AND CAUCUSES

In ads for the Comedy Channel's coverage of the Democratic National Convention, Al Franken admitted that he was a Democrat, recognizing that as the Comedy Channel's national political reporter, he probably should not say so. But he was "excited" about 1992. While the names of McGovern, Mondale, and Dukakis reminded him of big losers, 1992 would be different: this time the Democrats might come in third!

Most national polls did indeed show Clinton a distant third in May and June. The Democratic nomination would be his, but general election prospects were not pleasant. In June, Mervin Field, veteran pollster and political analyst, reviewed state poll results throughout the nation and concluded that Clinton's support was so minimal that he was not a factor in the electoral college predictions.[41] Yet at summer's end, after the two national party conventions and prior to the traditional Labor Day kickoff for the general election campaign, Clinton enjoyed a wide lead over Bush in national polls, most state polls, and electoral college projections (Figure 3.2).

> "*If anybody tells you they knew what was going to happen, they're lying.*"

What led to the turnaround? Looking back on the summer months from the perspective of early September, Clinton pollster Stanley Greenberg noted, "If anybody tells you they knew what was going to happen, they're lying."[42] The Democrats succeeded in framing the voters' choices. The contest, which in early June amounted to an embrace of Perot's newness, did not turn into a collective judgment on Clinton's character but rather into a referendum on the Bush presidency.[43] The Bush presidency was found to be lacking: the economy and Bush's job approval rating not only failed to recover and rise; both actually worsened over the summer. In June and early July, Bush forces and Perot had verbally duked it out over Perot's tendency to

Figure 3.1

Presidential Public Opinion Poll Trial Heats, 1992: Bush, Clinton, and Perot

Percent of voters

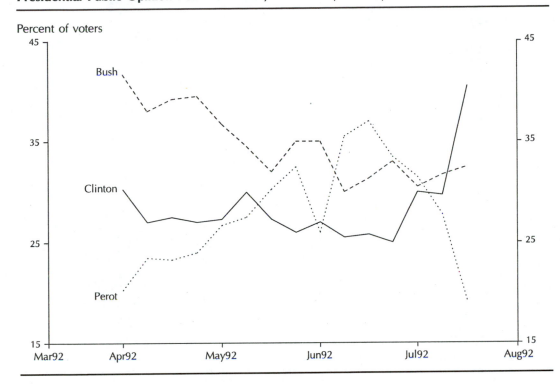

Note: The candidate support shown is a weekly average from the 42 available national polls that were in the field between March 26 and July 15. Most polls are of registered voters.

Source: Polling data from *American Enterprise,* July–August and September–October, 1992; *Public Perspective,* September–October, 1992; compilations provided by Jen Baggette, American Enterprise Institute; and various issues of the *New York Times* and the *Gallup Poll Monthly.*

hire private investigators. Perot's sudden decision to withdraw (never having declared) his presidential candidacy benefited Clinton, as he became the sole alternative to Bush's reelection.

Perot's withdrawal on July 16, the day of Clinton's acceptance speech, put Clinton even more in the spotlight. Clinton had remained relatively detached from the Bush-Perot bickering, working to become better and more favorably known. Overall, the Democratic Convention boosted Clinton more than the Republican Convention did Bush. Clinton's selection of Senator Al Gore as his running mate contrasted favorably with news stories of prominent (mostly unnamed) Republicans who were urging Bush to dump Vice President Dan Quayle from the ticket. Bush's campaign had difficulty pushing consistent themes, largely because the ones they tried were not working. Family values, Hillary-bashing, Jim Baker as domestic policy czar, tassel-shoed lawyers, linking Clinton to the Democratic Congress, portraying Clinton as yet

another tax-and-spend Democrat, Clinton as subversive because he protested the Vietnam War in London and took a college tour of the Soviet Union, gay-bashing—these were some of the Republican themes that failed to resonate with the public to Bush's advantage. Incumbents presiding over tough economic times must persuade the public the challenger would be even worse. At this, Bush failed. Clinton showed himself to be a skilled, sure-footed, energetic campaigner. After the Convention, the Democratic campaign team did not slack off; the Clinton and Gore families actively campaigned, resorting to bus tours of America's heartland to help solidify the gains in public support.

Clinton ended the primary and caucus season with a majority of delegates and one of the most impressive Democratic vote-getting showings[44] since 1968, but he was bruised and battered. The nomination was assured, but sewing up the nomination provided neither greater, more favorable media coverage nor a band-

41

Figure 3.2

Presidential Public Opinion Poll Trial Heats: Bush and Clinton

Percent of voters

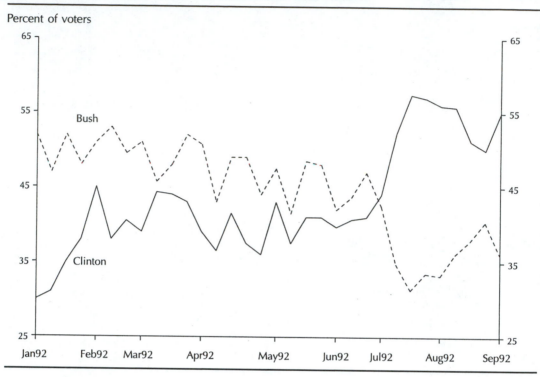

Note: The candidate support shown is a weekly average from the available 101 national polls that were in the field between January 2 and August 27. Most polls are of registered voters.

Source: Polling data from *American Enterprise,* July–August and September–October, 1992; *Public Perspective,* September–October, 1992; compilations provided by Jen Baggette, American Enterprise Institute; and various issues of the *New York Times* and the *Gallup Poll Monthly.*

wagon psychology that some previous nominees had enjoyed. Perot's rise ruined that.

Clinton had some grounds for optimism about Perot's candidacy, but the immediate reality was not rewarding in May and June. One highly speculative point was that Perot's candidacy might mean that no candidate would secure an electoral college majority, thus throwing the election into the Democratic House of Representatives, where Clinton would hold an advantage.[45] Less speculative was that Perot's candidacy seemed to be fueled largely by a dislike for Bush. If Perot could be counted on to bash Bush, Clinton could take a higher road. Both Bush and Clinton had much to gain from walking a fine line, likening and lightly contrasting themselves with Perot, hoping to secure Perot supporters once Perot's candidacy lost its luster.

With Perot's strong rise, political advisers to Bush and Clinton were pondering how to wage a three-way bid for an electoral college majority. One line of thought held that Bush and Clinton should each shore up the political party base, since about one-third of the vote could suffice in a three-way race.[46] Clinton advisers disavowed such a strategy.[47] Clinton, in widely publicized moves, confronted labor leaders and Jesse Jackson (over Sister Souljah's comment in the wake of the Los Angeles riots that blacks should take a week off from killing one another to concentrate on whites). Such "counter-scheduling" moves signaled that this Democratic nominee would not be a captive of powerful Democratic constituent groups.[48]

Bush forces did the heavy lifting when it came to Perot-bashing. During June and early July, bickering between Perot and Bush surrogates provided opportunities for Clinton to campaign in a mode that suggested he was above such squabbling. Bush forces made much of Perot's tendency to resort to private investigators to check on employees, opponents, and Bush's own children—"un-American," Bush called it. Republican focus groups had discovered public discomfort with Perot's authoritarian streak, and the issue of private investigators gave legs and substance to this discomfort.[49]

> ## "Bush forces did the heavy lifting when it came to Perot-bashing."

Perot's withdrawal from a race he never entered rebounded to Clinton's benefit. Clinton became the sole alternative to Bush's reelection in a year marked by voters who desired change, convinced that Bush could not deliver—no matter what the voters meant by "change." Perot's withdrawal statement contained a reference to the "revitalization of the Democratic Party," suggesting what he later denied, that he took some comfort in Clinton's improving political prospects.[50] Clinton had remained detached from the Bush-Perot bickering, working prior to the Democratic Convention on becoming more favorably known by highlighting his less-than-privileged past and his family.[51]

One rap at Clinton, the "slick Willie" label, echoed concerns that he was too eager to try to please all of the people all of the time. Clinton's responses to questions about his draft record, accusations of marital infidelity, and drug use (to which he responded that he had smoked marijuana but didn't inhale) gave another dimension to "slick Willie." Such personal issues might have destroyed lesser candidates and campaigns. To respond, the campaign emphasized images of Clinton as a family man and as an individual who had worked his way up from less fortunate circumstances.[52] Focus groups helped shape those responses. Prior to the Democratic Convention, "researchers discovered that voters had no idea where Clinton came from. Because of the rich-kid schools he had attended—Georgetown, Oxford, and Yale—they assumed he was a Bush-style blue blood. At the convention, the campaign made sure voters found out that Clinton had lost his father before he was born and had worked his way through school. . . . Focus-group members . . . found the family melodrama of the alcoholic stepfather, who occasionally beat up Clinton's mother, to be an alternative and equally compelling explanation for the candidate's dislike of confrontation" and his eagerness to please.[53]

Image refurbishing paid off for Clinton. In May and June only about 15 percent of the public viewed Clinton favorably, 40 percent unfavorably, and 45 percent undecided or not knowing enough about him to say. Dramatically, this turned around to 36, 24, and 40 during the Democratic Convention, ratings that persisted into the second week of August. The Republican Convention dented those favorable ratings a bit, but the ratings reverted to 36, 28, 36 later in August. The public's view of Clinton had improved, while the view of Bush had not.[54]

By muting concerns about his character, Clinton forces were better able to frame the voters' choice to their liking: "A stark choice in economically troubled times: change versus the status quo, a Democratic presidency chock-full of domestic policy proposals or a Republican presidency with little to say about the problems at home." Republicans desired a different frame: "A second Bush administration hot off its successes abroad, now ready to 'target America' with a host of moderate to conservative reforms, or a return to the tired, failed, bureaucratic solutions of Democratic orthodoxy."[55] Voters' strong concern with domestic problems devalued the strongest points of the Bush approach. As one Bush strategist put it, "Here's a good and decent man who believes he has flat nailed it, long term, in terms of preserving the peace, and his political fortunes have declined at the same time."[56]

Bush's general election campaign started late. He remained in presidential rather than campaign mode for too long. By the time he shifted to campaign mode at the Republican Convention, it was too late to do very much about some of the major problems pressing upon his campaign, problems that Democrats had been stressing for months.[57] As one prominent southern Republican said in August about the Bush campaign, "They have to give people a reason to be for [Bush]. We've spent seven months now, and there are a lot of reasons to be for him, but they haven't focused the public's attention on those reasons."[58] One Bush aide, reflecting on focus groups held prior to the Republican Convention, complained, "People haven't heard of anything that he's proposed or done. And if you tell them about something, they don't believe it, because they've never heard of it before."[59] Bush's desire to pull Secretary of State James A. Baker III back to head up the reelection campaign underscored Bush's troubling political situation.

The public thought the country was on the wrong track, the economy was not picking up, and the president's approval ratings were anemic and not improving over the summer—hardly auspicious circumstances in which to mount a come-from-behind akin to the one Bush managed in 1988 against Dukakis. Republican pollsters were finding that almost 8 in 10 Americans said the country was on the wrong track (up from 5 in 10 in 1988).[60] Neil Newhouse, a Republican pollster, explained the need to raise Clinton's negatives: "[H]ow do you move a President who's sitting at 35 percent approval rating up to 50 percent in the polls? And part of the answer is, you have to get voters to vote for him who don't approve of the job he's doing, by making Clinton less palatable to some of your swing voters than George Bush is."[61] Clinton's improved favorability ratings in July and August showed the short-run failure of this approach. Another possibility—raising Bush's approval ratings—also came to grief. Before the Republican Convention, Bush's rating was 35 percent, down from the range of 37 to 41 that had prevailed in May and June and the 1992 peak of 47 percent in January. At the end of August the rating had only climbed back to 40 percent.[62]

Running mates do not decide presidential election outcomes, but the selection of Senator Gore gave the Democratic ticket a lift and a helpful contrast with the Republican ticket. Media coverage of Republican presidential politics contained frequent discussion of whether Bush should dump Quayle from the ticket, a move that might have gratified some Bush critics but one that would have suggested the initial selection was a mistake, hardly reassuring for those wondering about Bush's judgment. The all–Southern Baptist Democratic ticket made southern states more competitive, making Republicans commit

time and resources to keep this recently acquired base of support.[63] Clinton's pick of Gore was not a conventional ticket-balancing move, but an astute response to the predicament of the campaign. Clinton pollster Greenberg explained it this way: "Gore was reinforcing. If you assume that the primary process did not allow Bill Clinton to be known, the vice-president process, rather than to balance him, needed to reinforce him." The addition of Gore and his family proved politically rewarding. Joint appearances of the Clintons and Gores proved particularly so, and such appearances were frequent.[64]

CONCLUSION

The nomination campaign sorely tested Clinton. He survived, but arrived at the end of the primary and caucus contests trailing both Bush and Perot in the national opinion polls. The summer months and the national conventions provided opportunities for Clinton to reintroduce himself to the American people. Clinton's success in doing so mirrored Bush's failure.

The general election campaign loomed ahead, Democratic leads had been lost before, and 1992 was proving to be a topsy-turvy year for political prognostications. The volatility of public opinion in 1992 and recent campaign history provided little comfort to those hoping Clinton's large leads in July and August would persist through the general election. Four years earlier, beginning in the late spring, Michael Dukakis enjoyed a lead over Bush in the polls (17 percentage points after the Democratic Convention), a lead that melted in the heat of August's Republican Convention. Even the last elected Democratic president, Jimmy Carter, barely squeaked by after losing almost all of a 30-point post-convention lead to Gerald R. Ford in 1976. The political gains of the summer would have to be secured in the general election campaign.

Chapter Four

The General Election Campaign: Strategy and Support

Jerome M. Mileur

George Bush liked to picture his 1992 candidacy as a reprise of Democrat Harry S. Truman's 1948 "give 'em hell" run against a "do-nothing" Congress. In many ways, the 1992 presidential election held more surprises than any since 1948, though none as dramatic as Truman's come-from-behind upset of Republican Thomas E. Dewey. One of the surprises was the comparative ease with which Arkansas governor William J. Clinton won both his party's nomination and the fall election, the first settled by early April and the latter effectively over by early October. Another surprise was the on-off-on-again candidacy of H. Ross Perot, whose 19 percent share of the November vote was the best showing of a third-party candidate since 1912, when Theodore Roosevelt won 27 percent. But a bigger surprise was how far and fast President Bush fell from favor with the American electorate. Seemingly unbeatable in the spring of 1991, he went on to become only the fourth sitting president to be defeated for reelection in this century—his popular vote down 22 percent (more than ten million ballots) from 1988, a drop half again as large as that of Jimmy Carter in 1980 and close to that of Herbert Hoover in 1932.[1] In effect, George Bush did turn out to be like Harry Truman, but it was the *mirror* image.

In retrospect, the biggest surprise in the 1992 elections may be that there were not more surprises, for the year began with an electorate restive with anger and frustration. Public cynicism toward government and politics was high, as was public pessimism about the ability of the political system to deal with the nation's prob-

lems. No single event had provoked this popular disillusionment with government; rather it was, as Dan Balz and Richard Morin described it, "disillusionment by a thousand cuts."[2] One set of problems was economic—a declining industrial base, an aging infrastructure, foreign competition, growing joblessness. Another set was societal—skyrocketing health-care costs, decaying cities rife with homelessness and violence, families in distress, schools in torment. A third set was governmental—gridlocked nationally by divided party control, dominated by special interests and big money, staffed by politicians more interested in attacking one another than the nation's problems. And underlying it all was a federal budget deficit out of control.

More than anything, however, Americans worried about the economy and what it held for their futures. The end of the Cold War signaled cuts in defense spending that threatened dislocation or worse for hundreds of thousands of Americans—and for middle-aged, college-educated engineers and other professionals, as well as blue-collar workers. It signaled, too, the closing of military bases, which threatened thousands more jobs in commercial, financial, and service industries that had grown up around these bases. Foreign competition in the automobile, electronics, and other industries threatened additional numbers of American jobs. As suburbia, the homeplace of the American Dream, became also the homeplace of most Americans, the fear grew that the dream was becoming a nightmare. The middle- and upper-middle class Americans who populated the suburbs were

45

haunted more and more by the fear that the "new world order" meant radically diminished circumstances for themselves and by the guilt that their children would be the first generation of Americans who could not hope to dream of having a better life than their parents.

▬▬▬▬▬▬▬▬▬▬▬▬

"In February 1991, about 40 percent of Americans thought the country was headed in the wrong direction; by January 1992, almost 80 percent did."

▬▬▬▬▬▬▬▬▬▬▬▬

The suburbs, the new American nation, seethed with a new politics of discontent.[3] The euphoria that swept the country ten months earlier in the aftermath of the stunning military success in the Gulf War had long since been replaced by growing fears that the country was on the wrong track. In February 1991, about 40 percent of Americans thought the country was headed in the wrong direction; by January 1992, almost 80 percent did. Fears about the economy were the reason. As the election year arrived, 45 percent of Americans said that improving the economy was the single most important issue, and most thought that things would get worse before they got better.[4]

As Republicans surveyed 1992, it was clear that the economy posed a threat to the reelection of President Bush, whose approval ratings for his handling of the presidency had dropped by almost half since the previous spring. But the White House was unimpressed by the field of Democratic challengers and also believed that recovery was on its way, that the economy as a campaign issue would take care of itself. The party focused instead on how to capitalize on voter disgust with incumbents, hoping to make gains in the Congress at the expense of large Democratic majorities in both houses. For Democrats, the popular mood posed threats as well as opportunities. Many saw the economy as a natural issue for the party of Roosevelt. Polls reinforced this, reporting that Democrats were generally viewed as the party more likely to deal effectively with the nation's hard times. But the growing national gloom, with its antipa-

thy toward incumbents, also raised fears among congressional Democrats that their party might be unable to hold onto what power it had in Washington.

A REPUBLICAN NATION

The Republicans entered the 1992 election year on the most impressive winning streak in the history of presidential politics since the Virginia Dynasty in the first quarter of the nineteenth century. Winning seemed automatic. The GOP had prevailed in five of the last six presidential contests, two of them landslides, and, in these elections, they had captured 55 percent of the two-party vote and 79 percent of the electoral votes. This bettered the Democratic Party's performance in the six elections from 1932 through 1952, when the party of FDR won the presidency five times, twice by landslides, but failed to match the Republicans otherwise—winning just 54 percent of the two-party vote and but 70 percent of the electoral vote.

Republican success had been driven by a political philosophy that joined the party's traditional anticommunism and opposition to big government to a new social conservatism that decried both liberal laxity on crime and liberal indifference to traditional American values of family, work, neighborhood, peace, and freedom.[5] This conservatism enabled the GOP to capitalize on a partisan realignment that had been underway in the South since the end of World War II, as the issue of race drove increasing numbers of white southerners (especially males) away from their historic loyalty to the Democratic Party.[6] In its opposition to abortion, the GOP philosophy also found support among both conservative Catholic voters in the urban North, many of whom had been lured from the Democrats by the independent candidacy of George Wallace in 1968, and Protestant evangelical and fundamentalist voters from the lower Midwest to Dixie.

Born of Barry Goldwater in 1964, nurtured by Richard Nixon in the 1970s, and consummated by Ronald Reagan in the 1980s, this new Republican Party was a political powerhouse. Its national and congressional party committees raised unprecedented amounts of money, offered a full plate of campaign services and professionals to GOP candidates, and devised campaign strategies that made artful use of new

Figure 4.1

The Republican "Lock" on the Electoral Vote: 1968–1988

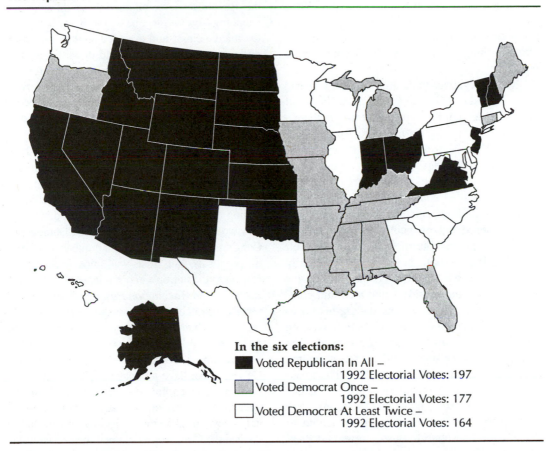

In the six elections:

- ■ Voted Republican In All –
  1992 Electorial Votes: 197
- ▨ Voted Democrat Once –
  1992 Electorial Votes: 177
- □ Voted Democrat At Least Twice –
  1992 Electorial Votes: 164

Source: Congressional Quarterly's *Guide to U.S. Elections,* 2nd ed., for 1968–1984 elections; *Congressional Quarterly Weekly Report,* November 12, 1988, for 1988 election.

campaign technologies and techniques.[7] This political capacity reinforced the party's conservative philosophy to produce a much-celebrated Republican "lock" on the electoral college. From 1968 through 1988, as Figure 4.1 shows, the GOP won repeatedly in all sections of the country save the Northeast and upper Midwest, but even in those regions they won more often than not in Pennsylvania and Wisconsin. In short, the party had a geopolitical base of 21 unfailingly Republican states with 197 electoral votes, a near-perfect set of 16 states with 177 electoral votes (most of which had strayed from the Republican reservation only for Georgian Jimmy Carter in 1976), and 5 other states with 90 electoral votes in which the GOP had a clear advantage. Together, these states gave the Republicans more than two-thirds again the number of electoral votes needed to win the Oval Office.

George Bush inherited this Republican Party and rode it to victory in 1988, wrapping himself in the conservative successes of Reagan and making the liberalism of Michael Dukakis *the* issue in the campaign. Dukakis was portrayed as philosophically wrong-headed (Willie Horton, the Pledge of Allegiance) and as lacking the character (values) required for the presidency. The Democrats failed to counter the visceral assaults of the GOP and lost an election that had seemed theirs to win only a few months earlier. But the outcome left Bush with the White House and little else. Unlike Franklin Roosevelt, whose New Deal left Democrats with an unfulfilled liberal agenda that organized national party politics for two decades after his death, Ronald Reagan left the Republicans with no conservative agenda and little more than vaguely good feelings about his presidency, the latter

47

undercut by the Iran-Contra affair. Bush did nothing to fill this void in 1988. By campaigning on the Dukakis negatives, he won the White House without having to define the purpose of his presidency. It was a strategy devoid of the "vision thing," and it would haunt him as president.

Conservatives in the Republican ranks had long doubted that George Bush was really one of them, and his failure as president to articulate a clear philosophy of government fueled their suspicions. When he broke his 1988 "no new taxes" pledge in a budget deal with congressional Democrats, it seemed proof to many that Bush was a man of no settled convictions. But in the early months of 1991, grumblings on the party right were drowned out by public applause for the success of Desert Storm. The Gulf War left President Bush basking in the approval of nearly 90 percent of the American people. This seems to have lulled the president into a certain complacency about his reelection, dulling his sensitivity to disquiet on the party right and diverting attention from plans for the 1992 campaign. The White House even shut down its political polling during the summer and fall of 1991.[8] The awakening came in November in a special Senate election in Pennsylvania when Democratic long shot Harris Wofford came from far behind to defeat Dick Thornburgh, Bush's former attorney general.

"[T]he economy was the issue and would stay that way throughout 1992."

By December, as the president's men rushed to put his reelection campaign in order, the bloom of spring had wilted, and fears about the economy had sprouted everywhere. The president's overall performance ratings had dropped 40 points. More ominous, 70 percent of Americans now disapproved of Bush's handling of the economy; two in three believed the nation should set a new course; and more (46 to 36 percent) thought the Congress was doing a better job on the economy than the president was.

When pollsters asked which party was more trustworthy on various issues, the Democrats led the Republicans on all having to do with the economy—by two to one as the party better for the middle class, and even led slightly on which party was more likely to hold down taxes. The Republicans held leads of two to one on foreign affairs and national defense, as well as a five-point lead on morals and values, but the economy was the issue and would stay that way throughout 1992.[9]

In January, President Bush led a trade mission to Japan that ended in failure and embarrassment. He came home for a State of the Union address in which he claimed credit for ending the Cold War, announced the dawn of a new world order, and challenged the Democratic Congress to act promptly on a number of domestic proposals, but Bush was unpersuasive with respect to the nation's economic woes. As David Broder of the *Washington Post* noted, he patched together an economic message geared more to reelection than to recovery and thus failed to rally voter confidence behind his presidency.[10] It was a defining moment missed by the president. He would not have another until the Republican National Convention seven months later. In the meantime, public opinion grew harsher in its judgment: in December, as many Americans blamed the Congress as blamed the president for the state of the nation's economy; by April, 29 percent blamed Bush, 13 percent fingered the Congress.[11]

But the president was challenged by more than the economy in early 1992; he also faced a palace revolt, as a long-threatened challenge from the party's right wing materialized in the person of former Richard Nixon speechwriter, now political commentator, Patrick J. Buchanan. Securing the GOP's conservative base was fundamental to Bush's reelection, yet through 1991 the White House had for the most part been unmoved by conservative complaints. In New Hampshire, Buchanan attacked the president on a range of issues, but saved his most searing and sneering assaults for the Administration's management of the economy. Buchanan went on to win 37 percent of the GOP vote in the Granite State and, in the end, forced the president to campaign actively there. Buchanan challenged Bush through the remaining primaries and, while no threat to the president's renomination, he made himself a factor in the party's electoral equation.

In the spring, a pint-sized prairie storm, H. Ross Perot, blew onto the national scene to challenge the likely nominees of the two major parties. Perot mounted a campaign centered on the economy in general and on the national debt in particular, which seemed also driven by a personal distaste for the president as a leader. The Perot appeal, advanced with colorful pie charts and simple solutions for complex problems, tapped into the anger and frustration of voters, and when he moved to the top of the presidential polls in early June the Bush forces shifted their fire from Clinton to Perot. The Bush campaign seems to have seen both Buchanan and Perot as conservative challenges to the president's renomination and reelection, but, in fact, more than simply conservative unrest, both measured the breadth and depth of public unhappiness with the Bush presidency for its inattention (seen increasingly as indifference) to the nation's sluggish economy. This misread of Buchanan and Perot disoriented the Bush forces, diverting them from the Democrats as the real challenge and from the economy as the real issue. Where Republican campaigns in the 1980s had been models of strategic planning and efficient execution, with tactics to match party and public sentiments, the Bush campaign in this critical period in the spring of 1992 seemed muddled as to both aim and conduct.

DEMOCRATS IN A POLITICAL WILDERNESS

Republican success in presidential elections since the late 1960s mirrored Democratic failure. The party of Franklin Roosevelt had not only lost five of the last six contests for the White House, but since Harry Truman's win in 1948, it had lost seven of ten presidential elections. And of its three wins, two were by the narrowest of margins: Jimmy Carter in 1976 with a bare majority of the popular vote (50.1 percent) and John F. Kennedy in 1960 with less (49.7 percent). Indeed, in the ten presidential contests from 1952 through 1988, the Democrats had won only 45.3 percent of the total vote (the Republicans 51.7 percent), and in the last six they had won just 42.9 percent. Yet the Democrats had controlled Congress almost continuously over the 40 years from 1953 through 1992, winning the House of Representatives in every election since 1954 and controlling the Senate in all but eight of these years.

> "*Divided government . . . had become a way of life in American national politics.*"

Divided government—one party in charge of the executive, the other in control of the legislature—had become a way of life in American national politics. There had been no period in the nation's history like that from 1955 through 1992. In this institutional setting, the Republicans were seen as the party of national purpose—the presidential party—and the Democrats the party of special interests—the congressional party. Public opinion polls at once reflected and reinforced this reality. Americans saw the GOP as best able to manage the great issues of state (defense, foreign relations, and prosperity) and the Democrats as best able to represent narrower interests over a broad range of domestic issues (environment, education, civil rights, welfare, and so on). This dichotomy had repeatedly misled Democratic presidential candidates, never more than in the 1980s, into adopting essentially legislative strategies in their bids for the White House. They tried to build a national majority from the varied interests that supported the party on particular issues, but the sum was always less than the total of the parts, because presidential politics, unlike that in Congress, is not a discrete and additive process. The Democrats failed regularly on the "vision thing," as George Bush was to do in 1992.

For many Democrats, the outcome of 1992 seemed settled by mid-1991, 15 months before any ballots were counted. President Bush continued to enjoy popular approval for his Gulf War win, and over the summer all of the leading Democratic contenders for the party's 1992 nomination dropped out of the race—save one, New York governor Mario M. Cuomo, who once again anguished in Albany. With the party's first string on the sidelines (Cuomo joined them in December), the Republican "lock" on the electoral college seemed one that not even Houdini could pick. Moreover, congressional Democrats were faced with the twin terrors of reapportionment and an anti-incumbent mood abroad in the country, which together imperiled

49

their party's "lock" on the Congress.[12] The president sought to reinforce these fears by making government "gridlock" an issue in his reelection bid. In his State of the Union address, Bush announced an agenda for the Congress, demanded that it be acted upon by March 20, and declared that "the day after that, if it must be, the battle is joined."[13] But the battle was not joined. In the fall, when the president revived his attack on gridlock, the critique argued as much for a Democrat in the White House (unified government with one party in control of and accountable for the federal government) as it did for returning Bush to the Oval Office (a check on the liberal excesses of a Democratic Congress, that is, gridlock).

Arkansas governor Bill Clinton emerged early as the best of a modest Democratic field. In New Hampshire, he survived an assault upon his character, deflecting charges of womanizing prompted by Republican apparatchiks. He finished second in the nation's first primary, losing to former U.S. senator Paul E. Tsongas from neighboring Massachusetts. Learning from the mistakes of Michael S. Dukakis four years earlier, Clinton responded promptly to personal attacks with rebuttal and counterattack, a tactic that was to be a hallmark of his campaign. This also enabled Clinton to make a preemptive strike, to remind voters of the Republicans' negative campaign four years earlier and to warn the public to be on guard against more of the same in 1992. "Slick Willie," as Clinton came to be labeled by the GOP, proved slick indeed, but more in the teflon tradition of Ronald Reagan than in the manipulative media style of the 1988 Bush campaign. Nothing stuck to Clinton, in part, because 1992 was an issues election, but also because his preemptive strike tainted all Bush criticisms as negative campaigning. For Republicans, it was a case of being hoisted on their own petard, and the GOP was slow to get the point.

By early April, after wins in the Super Tuesday, Illinois, and New York primaries, Bill Clinton had the Democratic nomination wrapped up, and indeed went on to capture all of the remaining primaries. This early win afforded the Clinton campaign a luxury unknown to any Democrat since Lyndon B. Johnson in 1964: the time to plan for the fall campaign—to refine its message, define its candidate, adjust its organization, budget its resources, plan the national convention, and hone a strategy for the general election. Ironically, the surge of Ross Perot in May and June gave the Clinton forces even more time to plan, as the Bush campaign changed tactics in these weeks, shifting its focus—and that of the news media—from Clinton to Perot. The Clinton team used this respite from intraparty and news media pressure well.

The Clinton organization was restructured in these weeks, as more national figures were brought onto the staff, working relations with state party organizations were strengthened, and control of the campaign was located clearly in Little Rock.[14] These weeks were also used to dress Clinton, the prospective president, as a different kind of Democrat—a pragmatist in the tradition of Roosevelt and Kennedy, sympathetic to liberal concerns but constrained by the reality of the possible.[15] It was a delicate strategy that courted all of the party's special interests—including women, minorities, labor, and environmentalists—but did so by embracing elected officials from or identified with those groups while distancing Clinton from unelected activists.[16] At the same time, Clinton kept faith with his moderate (economic liberal, fiscal conservative) roots in the Democratic Leadership Council, of which he had been a founder and leader; the council became the base, philosophically, for his national candidacy.

Among the important decisions in this period was the generally unexpected selection of Tennessee senator Al Gore as Clinton's running mate, the geographically tightest ticket since 1948, when Missourian Harry Truman tapped Kentucky Senator Alben Barkley as VP. It was an unconventional pick, which did little to balance the ticket but did a lot to redefine the image of the national Democratic Party.[17] Both were political moderates, and they were the first all-southern Democratic ticket since 1828. This worried some liberals, who feared that it foreshadowed a switch in party strategy from one focused on the northern tier of old Progressive states from New England to the Pacific West to one aimed at restoring the historic Democratic loyalties of Dixie. It was, however, a "bait and switch" strategy that led the GOP to commit time and resources to hold its deep south base while the Democrats ran a northern campaign concentrated in the nation's midsection, not in Dixie.

The redefinition of the party was complete in mid-July at the Democratic National Convention, whose orderliness, moderation, and unity of purpose stood in sharp contrast to those that had gone before it for a quarter-century. More than redefinition, the convention also marked a reconstruction of the party, its calm masking, as Thomas Edsall notes, an intraparty "factional struggle between center and left" that was "won by the center."[18] The party platform called for greater individual responsibility—a "new covenant" that promised a government that would ensure opportunity—and sought to unite the party constituencies around a different understanding of their interests, arguing that:

> The most important family policy, urban policy, labor policy, minority policy and foreign policy America can have is an expanding entrepreneurial economy of high-wage, high-skill jobs.

Similarly, Clinton accepted his party's nomination in the name of "those who do the work, pay the taxes, raise the kids and play by the rules, in the name of the hard-working Americans who make up our forgotten middle class."[19]

"The convention made Clinton a national figure, a leader, head of a born-again Democratic Party whose new appeal was to moderate, middle-class suburbanites as well as to liberals."

The convention made Clinton a national figure, a leader, head of a born-again Democratic Party whose new appeal was to moderate, middle-class suburbanites as well as to liberals. With FDR and JFK as models, Clinton had taken his party back to the future. He had gone into the convention with very low approval ratings—16 percent in late June—but emerged with extraordinary public support (30-point leads over President Bush in some polls). This convention "bump" was due in part to the fact that Americans had come once again to see the Democrats as a party that could govern effectively, but it was due also to the abrupt withdrawal from the presidential race of Ross Perot, who quit on the

day after Clinton's nomination and the day of his acceptance speech. Perot's departure no doubt added to the audience for the Clinton speech, but, more importantly, it left the Democrat as the only candidate of change.

GEOGRAPHY AS DESTINY

After 70 years as the nation's also-ran party, the Democrats had come to power in 1932 with Franklin Roosevelt riding a coalition of middle- and working-class voters centered geographically in the urban North. For Roosevelt and his heirs, the party strategy for taking the presidency was simple: win the big urban industrial states in the Northeast and Midwest, rich in electoral votes, then pick up whatever else was needed in the South or West. With big-city machines cranking out the "ethnics," and with industrial unions, greatly strengthened by New Deal policies, mobilizing blue-collar workers, the strategy was well designed for its time and place. Democrats occupied the White House for 28 of the 36 years that followed FDR's 1932 win, a reign interrupted only by World War II hero Dwight Eisenhower's eight years in the Oval Office.

The 1960 election of John Kennedy was the last hurrah for the Roosevelt coalition, a reality concealed by Lyndon Johnson's landslide win four years later. In 1932, winning the seven largest northeastern and midwestern states meant 190 electoral votes, over 70 percent of the number required for the presidency—and in his four presidential bids, FDR had won 25 out of 28 combinations (seven states × 4 elections). But the great population movements that followed World War II eroded this electoral base. In 1972, when Richard M. Nixon pummeled George S. McGovern, these seven states cast 171 electoral votes, ten percent less than in 1932. By 1984, when Ronald W. Reagan routed Walter F. Mondale, they cast 157 electoral votes, 17 percent less than in 1932; and by 1992, they had only 144 electoral votes, a quarter less than in 1932 and barely more than half the total required to win the White House.

The party of Roosevelt had undergone other changes. The big-city machines were gone, and labor unions were weakened by changes in the nation's industrial sector. Moreover, the once-solid South, the Democrats' political base from the 1820s to the 1930s, had become increas-

Figure 4.2

The Two Democratic Parties

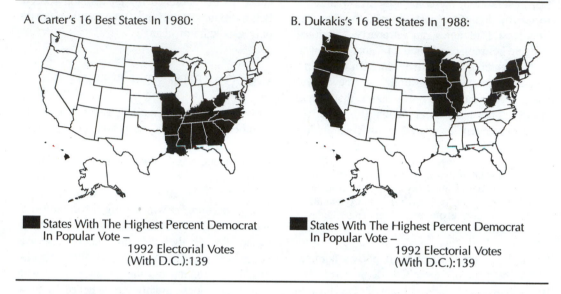

A. Carter's 16 Best States In 1980:

B. Dukakis's 16 Best States In 1988:

■ States With The Highest Percent Democrat In Popular Vote –
1992 Electoral Votes (With D.C.):139

■ States With The Highest Percent Democrat In Popular Vote –
1992 Electoral Votes (With D.C.):139

Source: Congressional Quarterly's *Guide to U.S. Elections,* 2nd ed, for 1980; *Congressional Quarterly Weekly Report,* November 12, 1988, for 1988.

ingly disloyal. Beginning in 1948, there were third-party insurgencies in the South, as well as defections to the GOP, culminating in the 1968 presidential candidacy of Alabama governor George Wallace. His racist-tinged, anti-Washington, "send the pointy-headed liberals a message" campaign played well in parts of the urban North as well as in the Deep South. The Republicans learned the political lesson.[20] Capitalizing on race as a wedge issue, but without the overt racism of Wallace, the GOP appealed to both the blue-collar ethnic voter in the North and the racially polarized white voter in the South, thereby hitting the Democrats simultaneously in their northern urban base and among their traditional southern backers.

The measure of Republican success is that, in the six presidential elections after 1964, the seven big northern states that had been bedrock Democratic from FDR to JFK voted Republican in 31 of 42 contests. Twice, in 1980 and 1984, all of these states voted Republican, and two of them (Illinois and New Jersey) voted for the GOP in every election after 1964. In addition, all of the six Deep South states, from South Carolina west to Louisiana, including Florida, voted against the Democratic presidential nominee in 29 of the 36 contests from 1968 through 1988, breaking ranks only for Georgian Jimmy

Carter and then (except for his home state) only in 1976. The Deep South had joined the Plains and Mountain West as the political base for Republican presidential candidates.

By the late 1970s, the Democrats had their own two-party system—one a party of liberal activists, the other a party of moderate pragmatists; one more northern, the other more southern. In an era of party reform, a fight for control of the national party, the competition between these factions seemed more often a civil war than a family affair.[21] By 1992, this intramural struggle was evident in two geographical bases within the party, shown in Figure 4.2: a southern core, manifest in the 1980 candidacy of Jimmy Carter, and a northern tier, clear in the 1988 candidacy of Michael Dukakis. In nominating Clinton and Gore, it appeared that the Democrats had decided to fight for the South. The party's all-southern ticket, however, only skirmished in Dixie, and instead marched north to victory.

In 1992, choosing between these two political bases was, in some respects, easy for the Democrats: the southern core had only 136 electoral votes, barely half the number needed to win, whereas the northern tier commanded 224, only 46 short of the 270 required for the White House. Moreover, the northern tier seemed a more easily expandable base, as it was united by public policy concerns that were more compatible nationally than were those that organized the politics of Dixie.[22] At the same time, the party's northern tier had not been charmed by the southern moderation of Jimmy Carter. These states, including those of the West Coast, had been more attracted to Yankee liberals like Walter Mondale and Michael Dukakis, who were in turn a big chill to Democrats in the South.

Geographically, the logical expansion of the Democrats' northern base was into the central East and lower Midwest, that is, the states that border the Ohio River. With the nomination in hand, Bill Clinton and Al Gore moved dramatically in precisely that direction. Boarding a bus in New Jersey the day after the convention, the "new" Democratic team—Bill and Hillary Clinton, Al and Tipper Gore—set out on a week's journey that took them from New Jersey through Pennsylvania, West Virginia, Ohio, Indiana, Illinois, and into Missouri at St. Louis. A tactical stroke of genius, the bus tour, which became a staple of the campaign, not only played to large and enthusiastic crowds all along the way, but also filled the political vacuum between the Democratic and Republican National Conventions, the period in which Michael Dukakis's 16-point lead had vanished four years earlier. Except for Indiana, the home state of Vice President Dan Quayle, the Clinton-Gore ticket swept these states in the fall, along with Kentucky on the south side of the Ohio River. They added 44 of the 46 electoral votes needed for a successful northern strategy; Arkansas *or* Tennessee could do the rest.

The post-convention bus trip was the first piece in a carefully crafted general election strategy that mapped the political terrain, defined issue priorities, shaped grass-roots organization, and provided for quick response to Republican attacks. Geographically, the campaign targeted 31 states and the District of Columbia on which to concentrate its resources. Fourteen of these states, plus the District of Columbia, were seen as the "top-end" states, the foundation upon which the campaign would be built. Eighteen were identified as "play-hard" states, the battlegrounds on which the election would be won or lost. The base included the three pillars of the northern strategy (California, Illinois, and New York), where poor state economies had given the Democrats seemingly insurmountable leads. The Clinton campaign

allocated some, but not full resources to its top-end or "safe" states. It devoted full resources to the play-hard battleground states, which were concentrated in the central East and Midwest but included some in the South and Mountain West.[23] The remaining 18 "big-challenge" states were essentially conceded to the GOP, with few or no resources expended upon them. For the Democrats, the top-end states held 186 electoral votes, the play-hard states 194, and the throwaways 158.

> **"*The Clinton campaign stuck to its plan with a remarkable discipline.*"**

The Clinton campaign stuck to its plan with a remarkable discipline. Table 4.1 reports the campaign days that were spent in different states and illustrates both the strategy and the discipline of the Clinton forces. The campaign spent little time in the category #1 base states won by Dukakis in 1988, except for Wisconsin (a play-hard state). It gave little time to the category #4 Bush states, except for North Carolina (another play-hard state) and Florida, at which the Democrats made a run in October. The Clinton campaign clearly stayed focused on states in categories #2 and #3, which included 16 of the play-hard battleground states to which it devoted maximum resources.[24] In November, the Democrats prevailed in all of the top-end states, in all but one of the play-hard states (North Carolina), and even won one big-challenge state (Nevada).

The careful management of campaign resources only partially explains Clinton's territorial triumph. His geographical plan was backed up importantly with a message that spoke to voter concerns in the targeted states, a street-level organization that turned out the vote in critical states, and a capacity for prompt counterattacks to blunt Republican thrusts at the Democratic standard-bearers. The state of the economy was *the* issue in 1992. It overwhelmed all others. Twice as many Americans said it was their major concern as identified any other issue, and those issues which came closest to it—the national debt

Table 4.1

Clinton–Gore Campaign Days Spent in the 50 States*

1. *States won by Democrats in 1992 and 1988* (10)

Three or fewer days	—	8 states	(60 electoral votes)
Four to eight days	—	1 state	(33 electoral votes)
More than eight days	—	1 state	(11 electoral votes)

(Total days = 23; average 2.3 per state)

2. *States won by Democrats in 1992; lost in 1988 by less than 2.5%* (6)

Three or fewer days	—	1 state	(3 electoral votes)
Four to eight days	—	4 states	(109 electoral votes)
More than eight days	—	1 state	(11 electoral votes)

(Total days = 36; average 6.0 per state)

3. *States won by Democrats in 1992; lost in 1988 by more than 2.5%* (16)

Three or fewer days	—	5 states	(18 electoral votes)
Four to eight days	—	6 states	(56 electoral votes)
More than eight days	—	5 states	(66 electoral votes)

(Total days = 108; average 6.8 per state)

4. *States lost by Democrats in 1992 and 1988* (18)

Three or fewer days	—	14 states	(84 electoral votes)
Four to eight days	—	2 states	(45 electoral votes)
More than eight days	—	2 states	(39 electoral votes)

Total days = 52; average 2.9 per state)

---

* Any part of a day spent campaigning in a state is treated as a "day" in that state. Thus, candidates could spend a "day" in several states on a single calendar day.

Source: Compiled from reports of the Presidential Campaign Hotline (Falls Church, VA: American Political Network), August 31–November 2, 1992.

and health-care costs—were essentially economic issues as well.[25] The Clinton campaign sank its teeth into the economic issue and clung to it with the tenacity of a pit bull—faulting the Bush presidency for its indifference to stagnation and joblessness, calling for change, and advancing a recovery plan to "grow" the economy through an "investments" strategy. Economic liberalism had been the glue of the New Deal coalition, and Clinton used it to overcome the racial and social issues that agitated the so-called Reagan Democrats who populated the suburbs that were key to winning the battleground states in the central East and Midwest.

The message was critical, but it was brought home with impressive grass-roots organizations in the key states. The campaign worked closely with Democratic state party organizations through ties Clinton had been building for a decade, prompting a former national party official to declare, "Clinton made better use of party personnel and apparatus than anyone in history."[26] Ohio was typical, where the state coordinator, John Eade, delighted in their efforts:

We'd put together a phone operation, made over a million calls Election Day to move the vote. We had a minimum of two people per precinct in over 1,500 precincts across Ohio. In Cleveland, we had a fleet of 40 rented taxis, we had six buses and about 35 sound trucks on the street, plus over 100 cars. We had fleets of rented cabs in Cincinnati, in Columbus, to have transport to move people.[27]

The Ohio organization was replicated in Illinois and elsewhere. Win or lose, these ground wars were important because they forced the GOP to fight for turf it had been used to winning with a mere show of the party flag. Eade again: "We pinned them down in Ohio, so they couldn't move over to Pennsylvania, New Jersey, other places we needed."[28]

Finally, the Democratic campaign was calibrated for quick response to Republican attacks. Unlike Dukakis four years earlier, these "new" Democrats proved able to deliver a punch as well as to take one. James Carville, commander of the Clinton forces, took special post-election pleasure in this war of the fax machines:

We reacted and responded to his [Bush's] attacks very early and very aggressively. . . . It's just like in a boxing match, if they keep throwing punches and you keep fighting them off . . . they didn't have the same pop. His [Bush's] hands were heavy in the last 10 days.[29]

From New Hampshire in January to Arkansas in October, the Clinton camp had to defend itself against attacks on the character of its candidate, from womanizing to draft dodging, and, as is so often the case in sports, a good defense protected the offense.

BUSHWHACKED REPUBLICANS

As the nominating season ended in early June, Ross Perot had become a major threat to both parties, but especially to the GOP. In late May, the Gallup poll reported Perot tied with Bush; in early June, it found him slightly ahead.[30] Polls in a number of reliably Republican states west of the Mississippi River also had Perot leading, and, in the final round of primaries, exit polls in California, New Jersey, and Ohio showed Perot the candidate of choice among large numbers of both Bush and Clinton voters.[31] Bled in the primaries by the Buchanan challenge, the Bush campaign feared that the Perot insurgency would mean a hemorrhage of support.[32] More immediately, it presented a different, albeit related problem: caught in the crossfire of two opponents, the Bush campaign was unable to plan.

In late June, the Bush forces went after Perot. Branding him a "temperamental tycoon" with a "scorn for the Constitution," they painted him as by nature unsuited for the presidency. It is not clear that the Republicans wanted to knock Perot out of the race, as he seemed in some ways to be hurting Clinton more than Bush, but they certainly wanted to stall his momentum, and they did. Perot's standing in the polls began to fall. The GOP and press offensives against Perot came at a time of growing turmoil within his campaign, as tensions mounted between its handful of professionals and its determined amateurs. Never comfortable with the trappings of modern campaigns and stung by the attacks on his person, Perot dramatically quit the race.[33] Coinciding with Clinton's nomination, Perot's withdrawal fed a firestorm of support for the "new" Democrats, who got the biggest post-convention "bounce" ever.

> **"Adding insult to injury, Bush was booed at baseball's annual midsummer All-Star game."**

While the Democrats capitalized on the moment and took their campaign aggressively to the Republicans, President Bush, like Democrat Dukakis four years earlier, stayed in his office attending to his job. He did try to repair his campaign organization by bringing back the Mr. Goodwrench of American politics, James A. Baker III, to fix the president's reelection machine. But the Democrats kept up the pressure and maintained their advantage in the weeks between the two party conventions. In 23 national polls from mid-July to mid-August, Clinton led in all with at least 52 percent support and an average lead of 22½ points over the president.[34] Adding insult to injury, Bush was booed at baseball's annual midsummer All-Star game. As the Republicans gathered to renominate George Bush, his was an embattled presidency. The problems were many. There was, of course, the economy—nearly one in two Americans thought it was getting worse; over 70 percent thought the country was headed in the wrong direction—and both Clinton and Perot had been relentless in their concentration on it as *the* issue. Polls suggested that nothing was so damaging to the president as his reticence—the White House called it "prudence"—in dealing with the economy. Then, there was the "vision thing." Bush had declared himself "the "education president," "the environmental president," and more, but there were no programs to equal the rhetoric. He had declared "a new world order," but there was no program to match the slogan. But worst of all, there was no plan for the economy.[35]

The president was beset as well by party problems. Some were coalitional: abortion and the broken tax pledge had made the GOP a house divided, and the end of the Cold War had removed the glue that had held warring party factions together since the 1950s. Indeed, some conservatives had begun to speculate publicly that the party's right wing might be better off if Bush lost to Clinton.[36] Other problems were tactical: constituencies essential to Republican

BY WASSERMAN FOR THE BOSTON GLOBE

polls between the GOP assemblage and Labor Day, Clinton continued to lead, but fell under 50 percent support in 7 and on average was ahead of Bush by only 10 points.[38] But in many ways, the convention exacerbated the president's re-election problems. It had been planned in late spring, when securing the party's conservative base was of first importance, and it gave prime time on opening night to spokesmen from the Republican right. The convention adopted a platform with "family values" as its center-piece, joining Nixon's "social issues" (abortion, race) with Reagan's "cultural values" (the nuclear family, work, patriotism) and making feminists and homosexuals special targets of often harsh and exclusionary rhetoric. The convention "clearly spoke its mind," conservative columnist George Will wrote, and showed that "there can indeed be indecent exposure of the mind as well as the body."[39]

The acceptance speeches of George Bush and Dan Quayle framed the issues of the fall campaign. Embracing family values, the vice president renewed the "us versus them" appeal to middle- and working-class voters, declaring the gap between the two parties to be a "cultural divide." "It is not just a difference between conservative and liberal," Quayle asserted, "it is a difference between fighting for what is right and refusing to see what is wrong."[40] The president recalled foreign policy successes from the Berlin Wall to the Gulf War and promised to bring the same proven and trustworthy leadership to domestic matters in his second term. He promised to cut both taxes and spending, blamed the Congress for blocking his recovery program, and attacked his opponent as a taxer, a spender, a man of little experience and of less character. But Bush failed once again, as he had in his State of the Union address, to set forth a clear plan to restore the nation's economic health. In early September, before the Detroit Economic Club, the president at last unveiled an agenda for economic recovery, but the speech was not seen by a national prime-time audience, and by then Clinton's lead in the polls had inched back up to 15 points.

When President Bush finally got into his "campaign mode," he found himself in a game of catch-up ball, the inning late, and his team trailing badly. Unlike Clinton, who had left the Democratic convention to invade states needed to expand his party's electoral base, Bush moved from the GOP convention to campaign across

hegemony in the 1970s and 1980s were breaking ranks with the GOP. None were more critical than the socially conservative, working- and middle-class Reagan Republicans—mainly sub-urban Catholics in the North and churchgoing white Baptists in the South—who found themselves faced with a choice between their values and their jobs. As they had felt abandoned in the 1960s by the Democrats' preoccupation with society's victims, they now felt betrayed by Republican attention to the rich at their expense. They were among those most worried about the nation's economic future and among those most unhappy with Bush.[37] They were also a primary target of the Clinton and Perot campaigns.

The president's camp hoped for a bounce from the Republican National Convention to cut into Clinton's lead, and it got one. In 15 national

Table 4.2

Bush-Quayle Campaign Days Spent in the 50 States*

1. *States won by Republicans in 88 by 59% of two-party vote* (15)

Three or fewer days	—	12 states	(73 electoral votes)
Four to eight days	—	3 states	(50 electoral votes)
More than eight days	—	0 states	(0 electoral votes)

    (Total days = 36; average 2.4 per state)

2. *States won by Republicans in 1988 by 55–58.9% of two-party vote* (13)

Three or fewer days	—	5 states	(22 electoral votes)
Four to eight days	—	6 states	(65 electoral votes)
More than eight days	—	2 states	(53 electoral votes)

    (Total days = 55; average 4.2 per state)

3. *States won by Republicans in 1988 by 50– 54.9% of two-party vote* (12)

Three or fewer days	—	7 states	(40 electoral votes)
Four to eight days	—	3 states	(99 electoral votes)
More than eight days	—	2 states	(29 electoral votes)

    (Total days = 49; average 4.1 per state)

4. *States won by Democrats in 1988* (10)

Three or fewer days	—	9 states	(93 electoral votes)
Four to eight days	—	1 state	(11 electoral votes)
More than eight days	—	0 states	(0 electoral votes)

    Total days = 16; average 1.6 per state)

* Any part of a day spent campaigning in a state is treated as a "day" in that state. Thus, candidates could spend a "day" in several states on a single calendar day.

Source: Compiled from reports of the Presidential Campaign Hotline (Falls Church, VA: American Political Network), August 31–November 2, 1992.

the South to secure his party's base in that region. This preoccupation with the president's electoral base was to be characteristic of the Bush campaign. Where the Democrats adopted an offensive geopolitical strategy aimed at *adding* states to their northern base, including the plan to play hard in a number of traditionally Republican states if only to make the GOP expend resources on them, the Republicans chose a defensive strategy aimed at *holding* the states Bush had won four years earlier and, with the exception of Wisconsin, giving the Democrats a free ride in their base states.

Table 4.2 illustrates the Republican strategy. The Bush forces were clearly concentrated on states in categories #2 and #3, which the president had won in 1988 with 50 to 59 percent of the two-party vote. Few resources were spent on states in category #1, which seemed almost certainly Republican, and few also on states in category #4 that seemed almost surely Democratic. Bush had beaten Dukakis with 156 electoral votes to spare, a sizeable margin for error that made circling the White House wagons a

reasonable strategy as 1992 began. But by the time the president hit the campaign trail in September, this margin had eroded significantly. Polls in California and Illinois, with 76 electoral votes between them, showed Bush behind by more than 20 points, and their loss would cut his 1988 margin in half. There were other dark clouds in what had already been a stormy year for the president: Reagan Democrats in key states like Michigan and New Jersey, faced with the choice between values and jobs, were opting for the latter; younger voters, once thought to be the rock of a Republican realignment, were moving away from the GOP; and the party's evangelical right continued to have doubts about Bush.[41] Yet the Republican game plan did not change.

The Bush and Clinton campaigns differed in other ways. For one, the Democrats fought a guerrilla war in which the strategy was to contest the election state by state. The Bush forces fought a national campaign. This difference is clearest in their respective ad campaigns. The Democrats limited their spending to about 20 states and, through computerized evaluations, targeted their message to particular groups in those states. The Republicans, on the other hand, spent heavily on national network programs that scattered their message to voters in states they expected to lose as well as those they sought to win.[42] The Democratic lead in September may account for the Bush strategy, as the president's immediate problem was to raise both his positives *and* Clinton's negatives so as to create a sense of momentum for his candidacy. A week after the president's Detroit speech, for example, in which he set forth a positive plan for the economy, his campaign went negative, attacking Clinton for evading the draft and for anti–Vietnam War activities abroad.

"In 1992, the monetary playing field was level, and, if anything, tilted somewhat in favor of the Democrats."

A second difference was in the comparative vigor of the two campaigns. President Bush had been slow to undertake his run for reelection, leaving it to Vice President Quayle to carry the administration banner through the primaries. A comparison of Tables 4.1 and 4.2 suggests that the Bush campaign continued to be less energetic in prosecuting the general election. The Clinton-Gore ticket made half again as many visits to its battleground states as the Republicans did to theirs (categories #2 and #3 in both tables). As the "out" party, the Democrats had to work harder to offset the GOP advantage of incumbency, and they appear to have done just that.[43] A final difference was that, for once, the Democrats held their own with the Republicans in fundraising. From the mid-1970s through the 1980s, the GOP raised far more party money in presidential years than did the Democrats. In 1992, the monetary playing field was level, and, if anything, tilted somewhat in favor of the Democrats. This enhanced the capacity of the Democrats to fight a guerrilla war.

But the decisive flaw in the Bush campaign was that it lacked a message in a political year when Americans were deeply worried about

their futures and were asking what the federal government might do to ameliorate their condition. Bill Clinton and Ross Perot understood this and stuck tenaciously to the economy as the issue of greatest concern to voters. Each offered detailed plans to revive the economy and restore growth. The Bush campaign searched frantically and frenetically for an alternative. It found none: not gridlock in Washington, nor family values, nor Clinton's character, nor Democratic liberalism. The October reentry of Ross Perot into the race only compounded the president's problem, as he became but one voice in three, caught once again in the crossfire of two opponents, denied the chance to go one-on-one with Clinton in the debates, and assured that the economy would remain center stage. It was only after the last debate that Bush, as Dukakis had four years earlier, freed from the constraints of campaign calculation, found his voice and went aggressively after Clinton, attacking his record as governor of Arkansas and arguing that the issue was trust. It narrowed the gap between them, but, as with Dukakis, it was too little, too late.

CONCLUSION

On November 3, Bill Clinton won the presidency. He was the first Democrat in 16 years to do so. In a three-way race, he won almost 44 million votes, 2 million more than Dukakis had, in a year in which the national vote topped 100 million for the first time. In the electoral college, Clinton bested Bush by a 100 votes more than the number needed to win. The economy was the issue. Those who thought it good voted overwhelmingly for George Bush, but were only 20 percent of the electorate; whereas those who thought it not so good or worse, 80 percent of Americans, went decisively to Clinton.[44] Demographically, the "new" Democrats ran strongest among those racial, gender, religious, education, and income groups that are the traditional constituencies of the party, but the baby-boomer ticket, in a clear generational appeal, did reclaim the youth vote for the Democrats, their message of change and hope capturing almost half of both first-time voters and those under 25.[45] But geography was the key. As Figure 4.3 shows, the Democrats won by building upon the northern tier of states that had been most favorable to Dukakis in 1988. The Democrats designed a campaign strategy to fit the geopolitical impera-

Figure 4.3

Comparison of 1988 Dukakis and 1992 Clinton Vote by State

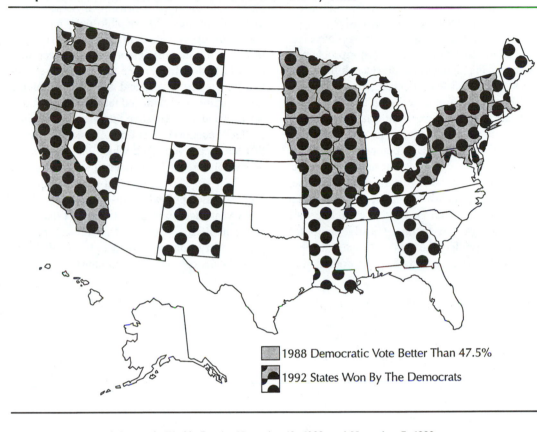

1988 Democratic Vote Better Than 47.5%

1992 States Won By The Democrats

Source: Congressional Quarterly Weekly Report, November 12, 1988, and November 7, 1992.

tives of this electoral alignment and executed their plan with remarkable discipline. Clinton had strength in all parts of the country, but it was in the central East and Midwest, in those states along the Ohio River, that the election was fought and won.

Ross Perot was the wild card in the 1992 election, but in the end, his candidacy had no marked effect on the outcome.[46] He ran best in New England and in the old Populist and Progressive states of the West. In the battleground states of the Midwest and central East, Perot drew support about equally from both parties, except in Michigan, where he cut sharply into the Clinton vote. The most successful insurgent candidate since Theodore Roosevelt, Perot's greatest impact upon the nation's politics may not yet have been seen. His strong performance in states west of the Mississippi River (he scored over 25 percent of the vote in eight and topped 23 percent in six others) did what third parties have done so often: it shook the political moorings in

those states and put them up for grabs. This presents a problem for both parties: the West Coast is critical to the Democrats, the Plains and Mountain West essential to the Republicans. One party's problem is, of course, the other's opportunity, and with the presidency, Clinton and the Democrats now hold the initiative.

George Bush might well have been reelected in 1992, and many saw the campaign as the culprit. Vice President Quayle and GOP National Chairman Richard Bond agreed that the Democrats had done better, while former Reagan campaign operative Ed Rollins called the Bush campaign "the worst in presidential history."[47] The White House had been slow to assemble the president's reelection team and, once in place, it seemed forever in cruise control, unable to shift gears to meet the changing contours of the campaign trail. Whereas the Clinton forces had clearly learned from the Dukakis mistakes four years earlier and had adjusted their strategy and tactics accordingly,

59

the Republicans were content to replay the 1988 campaign. Their effort seemed mechanical, predictable, and not framed to fit the politics of 1992. The Bush team chose a defensive strategy at the outset, and it never got off the defensive.

In the end, however, the major problem of the Bush campaign was the president himself. As one of his associates observed, commenting on Bush's reelection bid, he "didn't seem to have his heart in it."[48] Never comfortable with politics, never able to conquer the "vision thing," and never able to escape comparison with his predecessor, George Bush was in many ways the wrong man, in the wrong job, at the wrong time. He came of age in World War II, he had prepped for the presidency on the Cold War, and he was, some said, its last victim. Clearly engrossed with foreign policy, he was confronted in 1992 with an America consumed by its condition at home. As Bush faced this dilemma, he was as well a man without a party, or at least one whose party had embraced a principled conservatism that made his *laissez-faire* philosophy look tepid and, in the eyes of some on the Republican right, unworthy of support. George Bush never won the affection of his party's younger, more doctrinaire conservatives, and the collapse of the "evil empire" had removed the stitching that had sewn various conservative interests together into the GOP coalition. It is one of history's ironies that the great event with which the Bush presidency will forever be associated—the end of the Cold War—is also the one that greatly undid the political base upon which his presidency rested. Forty years ago, explaining the loss of the presidency in 1952, a Democrat concluded that his party had run out of poor people. In 1992, the Republicans ran out of Communists.

Chapter Five

The General Campaign:
Issues and Themes

John Kenneth White

Presidential contests often raise important issues on which voters can render judgments, but the American electorate brings much more to the voting booths than issue preferences. Voting is not a dispassionate act; it is an act of passion inspired by a country where ideas count and adherence to the tenets of classical liberalism (especially individual freedom and equality of opportunity) are articles of faith. The election of 1992 proved to be no exception. The economy, and a gnawing concern that the next generation would be worse off than their parents, were major factors in determining the outcome. But the election of Bill Clinton and Al Gore, who are, in Gore's words, the "children of modern America,"[1] signaled a generational shift that brought into focus (and perhaps some resolution) the arguments surrounding the cultural liberalism of the 1960s.

Sixty-six years ago, in a book aptly titled *The Phantom Public,* Walter Lippmann wrote: "We call an election an expression of the popular will. But is it? We go into a polling booth and mark a cross on a piece of paper for one of two, or perhaps three or four names. Have we expressed our thoughts on the public policy of the United States? Presumably we have a number of thoughts on this and that with many buts and ifs and ors. Surely the cross on a piece of paper does not express them."[2] In the decades since Lippmann penned those words, presidential contests have been reduced to a few simple questions posed by the candidates and emphatic answers from the voters. For example, in 1980 Ronald Reagan asked a disgruntled electorate,

"Are you better off than you were four years ago?" Americans shouted a resounding "NO!" and made the ex-movie star and former California governor their president. Four years later Reagan repeated his query, and by landslide margins voters answered positively by giving him another term.[3] George Bush asked voters in 1988 to read his lips, which mimed the words "no new taxes." Not liking taxes much and believing the Democrats were prone to "tax and spend, tax and spend," a majority backed Bush—making him the first incumbent vice president to win the White House on his own since Martin Van Buren did so in 1836.

Four years later Bush suffered a stunning defeat, losing 16 percentage points in the popular vote from his 1988 totals. Not since 1968, when Hubert H. Humphrey saw his support plummet by 18 points from Lyndon B. Johnson's 1964 vote, has a political party suffered such a steep decline. Americans rendered harsh judgments about Bush's stewardship: 58 percent thought they were "worse off" than four years before, and just 38 percent said they were doing better; moreover, 69 percent said the country was "worse off" as a result of Bush's economic policies.[4] These dismal poll results were reflected in the shrinking Republican totals. Bush's 38 percent of the popular vote equalled that posted by Republican Barry Goldwater in 1964, and was *worse* than the percentages given incumbent presidents Jimmy Carter in 1980 and Herbert Hoover in 1932. Not since William Howard Taft finished third in 1912 has a standing chief executive fared so poorly. The reason? A large sign taped to a wall in the Clinton headquarters said it all: "IT'S THE ECONOMY, STUPID!"

Exit polls showed how potent an issue the economy had become. Of those leaving the polls on election day, one-quarter said they were "better off" than they were four years earlier, and Bush defeated Clinton among these voters by a two-to-one margin. Two-fifths put their financial situation at "about the same," and they split their votes evenly between Bush and Clinton. But one-third of the electorate, a plurality, described their plight as "worse," and they divided their ballots as follows: Clinton, 61 percent; Perot, 25 percent; Bush, 14 percent.[5] Many blue-collar workers, once a mainstay of the Reagan and Bush coalitions, found layoff notices attached to their time cards and abandoned the Republican presidential ticket in droves. Clinton won heavily blue-collar cities like Gadsden, Alabama, and Waterbury, Connecticut—both of which had previously supported Reagan and Bush. Of the 1988 "Bush Democrats," many of them blue-collar workers, 54 percent returned to the Democratic fold.[6] Even New Hampshire, which had not supported a Democrat for president since 1964, fell into the Clinton column thanks to the recession which had ravaged that rock-ribbed Republican state. Forty-six percent of New Hampshire voters said the economy was "poor"; and 62 percent of them sided with Clinton, 23 percent backed Perot, and a mere 15 percent stayed with Bush.[7]

> **"During the 1980s, Ronald W. Reagan built an impenetrable economic fortress around the Republican Party."**

During the 1980s, Ronald W. Reagan built an impenetrable economic fortress around the Republican Party. Surveys following the 1980 campaign showed the Republicans with a 61 percent to 20 percent advantage over the Democrats as the party more likely to reduce unemployment. Those margins ebbed in 1984 and 1988, but the economic issue still worked for the GOP. By 1992 the Republican economic defenses were in ruins, and the Democrats enjoyed a 66 percent to 25 percent lead on the jobs question. Reagan poll-taker Richard B. Wirthlin exclaimed, "I've never seen a change of that magnitude—a gross shift of 82 points."[8]

While the economy was mentioned as the "top concern" by supporters of the three presidential contenders, exit polls found that voters had very different opinions as to the remedy for recovery (see Table 5.1). Fifty-three percent thought the next president should reduce the budget deficit, 22 percent said expand federal programs, and 14 percent said cut taxes. Deficit reduction had a special resonance with H. Ross Perot's followers: 42 percent said it was a priority—just 18 percent of Clinton voters and 15 percent of Bush backers agreed. Thirty percent of Clinton voters cited health care as their number-one concern, and 22 percent of Bush voters thought keeping taxes low mattered most.[9] A smattering of Bush backers listed education and the environment as their chief worries. So much, then, for "the education president" and "the environmental president."[10]

THE NEW PESSIMISM

In nearly every campaign, voters urge candidates and tell pollsters that they want the candidates to talk about "the issues." In 1992 voters were no longer compliant—they demanded that the presidential contenders stick to the issues. During the second presidential debate, a member of the audience berated the candidates for "trashing their opponent's character and their programs," noting that the time spent on these matters was "depressingly large." This voter chastised the candidates, asking: "Why can't your discussions and proposals reflect the genuine complexity and the difficulty of the issues to try to build a consensus around the best aspects of all proposals?"[11] Bush, Clinton, and Perot each promised, to varying degrees, to do a better job.

But as Walter Lippmann implied in *The Phantom Public,* elections are not decided by issues per se. In fact, presidential contests rarely formulate public policy. Rather they are ongoing referendums about who we are and what we believe. The American polity is not a structure of government so much as it is a contract between the government and its citizens whose clauses contain shared values. Visiting the

Table 5.1

Issue, Concerns, and Candidate Preferences—1992 (in percentages)

One of the top issues is:	Clinton Voters	Bush Voters	Perot Voters
. . . the economy and jobs	**50**	**28**	**52**
. . . the federal deficit	**18**	15	**42**
. . . health care	**30**	10	**14**
. . . taxes	8	**22**	13
. . . education	17	8	10
. . . family values	7	**27**	9
. . . abortion	10	18	5
. . . environment	9	2	4
. . . foreign policy	1	18	2
Government should:			
. . . provide more services	55	20*	26
. . . cost less	36	72	66

* Some voters chose not to answer the question.

Note: The top three issues cited by each candidate's supporters are in boldface.

Source: Voter Research and Surveys, exit poll, November 3, 1992.

United States in the 1920s, Gilbert K. Chesterton concluded, "America is the only nation in the world founded on a creed."[12] That creed includes many inherent "rights" that accompany American citizenship—particularly "God-given rights" such as individual freedom and equality of opportunity. Americans devoutly express their devotion to these tenets of classical liberalism, especially at election time.

Classical liberalism is an ideology with special appeal to an upwardly mobile, optimistic middle class. From the Pilgrims to today's new immigrants, Americans have believed in the malleability of the future by the individual. So prevalent is this belief that our language is littered with such emotive phrases as "the American Dream," which presuppose that with hard work each generation can do better than the one before. A steelworker captured these sentiments beautifully: "If my kid wants to work in a factory, I'm gonna kick the hell out of him. I want my kid to be an effete snot. I want him to be able to quote Walt Whitman, to be proud of it. If you can't improve yourself, you improve your posterity. Otherwise, life isn't worth nothing."[13]

Garry Wills once wrote that in the United States one must adopt the American Dream "wholeheartedly, proclaim it, prove one's devotion to it."[14] During the 1980s, the Republican Party led by Ronald Reagan proclaimed it was the repository of the hopes and aspirations embodied in the promise of the American Dream.

Accepting the GOP nomination in 1980, Reagan promised "to build a consensus with all those across the land who share a community of values embodied in these words: family, work, neighborhood, peace and freedom."[15]

Reagan's values mantra of family, work, neighborhood, peace, and freedom was a powerful elixir. Richard Wirthlin called it "a strategy of values," and claimed it was the key to Reagan's success in 1980.[16] But what gave the values strategy its power was the economic recovery that began in 1983 and continued throughout Reagan's tenure as president. Americans are of two minds when it comes to core values: they are predisposed to believe in the tenets of classical liberalism, yet they seek constant reassurance and yearn for examples from their own life experiences (and those of other role models) that the old values have not lost their meaning. Ronald Reagan understood this yearning. George Bush did not.

Bush apparently thought it was enough to assert his faith in traditional values, often repeating them in mantra-like fashion, but without the accompanying policies that would help make those values an enduring reality. This worked so well in the Willie Horton negative-style campaign of 1988 that Bush adviser Deborah Steelman acknowledged that if her candidate were to declare himself on a few big issues, "We'd have less of a chance to win than we do."[17] Bush's distinction between his "campaign mode" and his "governing mode" resulted in his incapacity to make the necessary connections between values and public policy—a problem Bush derisively dismissed as "the vision thing." In 1988, the media were frustrated with Bush's mangled syntax and awkward allusions to "the vision thing." Four years later, facing tough economic times, voters echoed the media's frustrations with Bush. Orville Mitchell, a Kansas farmer, spoke for many:

"You can talk about family values and military service and all that stuff. But when it gets down to the bottom line, it's how the economy is going."

You can talk about family values and military service and all that stuff. But when it gets down to the bottom line, it's how the economy is going. The economy is in trouble. We had a heck of a time getting Bush to even admit it was in trouble. Now he knows it's in trouble because he's in trouble.[18]

To Bush, aspiring to be president was a plausible reason to seek the post in 1980 and 1988, and to ask for another term in 1992. This fundamental misunderstanding of the linkage between values and governing transformed Reagan's "values strategy" from a sharp-edged rhetorical thrust into a dull sword. Acting out of habit, and believing that mere repetition of the words was enough, Bush pursued his own "values strategy" in 1992. But as Richard Wirthlin noted, the Democrats "cleaned our clocks"[19] on the values argument, adding:

The words, "family values," have almost become an icon in this election. In some ways it's a fairly empty icon. Simply saying that "we believe in the family," doesn't gain the candidate much at all. It may even lose votes. . . . We found that if you attempt to tap into something that is as closely, sensitively and personally held as a basic value, you can quickly get a backlash if you treat it too blatantly or too explosively.[20]

The backlash hit the Republican Party full force. When Los Angeles exploded in flames,

Vice President Dan Quayle declared that the problem in the inner cities was a deviation from traditional family structures. Quayle criticized television's "Murphy Brown" for "mocking the importance of fathers by bearing a child alone and calling it just another life-style choice."[21] In a fiery speech at the Republican National Convention, Patrick J. Buchanan expanded on Quayle's theme. Buchanan argued that the nation was in the throes of a "cultural war" whose protagonists were the duo of "Clinton & Clinton"—a reference to the Democratic nominee and his wife, Hillary:

The agenda Clinton & Clinton would impose on America—abortion on demand, a litmus test for the Supreme Court, homosexual rights, discrimination against religious schools, women in combat—that's change, all right. But it is not the change America wants. . . . It is not the kind of change we can tolerate in a nation that we still call God's country.[22]

In an infamous close, Buchanan harkened back to the Los Angeles riots. Recalling the National Guardsmen who were "ready to lay down their lives to stop a mob from molesting old people they did not even know," Buchanan drew this moral imperative: "As they took back the streets of Los Angeles, block by block, so we must take back our cities, and take back our culture, and take back our country."[23]

Buchanan's and Quayle's attacks on the "cultural elite" missed their marks. Granted, most Americans were not ready to subscribe to alternative family life-styles or deviant sexual practices. Asked whether government should "encourage traditional family values" or "encourage tolerance of nontraditional families," 68 percent opted for the former and just 26 percent said the latter.[24] The Reagan values consensus remained in place. But what really bothered voters was a new pessimism that the next generation would be poorer than their parents. Polls showed that respondents were unimpressed by GOP arguments that Democrats lacked fealty to traditional American values. Sixty-eight percent in an NBC News survey said the economy was the most important factor in casting their presidential ballots; only 19 percent mentioned family values.[25] Polls showed many were unimpressed by the Republican values rhetoric. In fact, 34 percent actually said the Democrats were "better at upholding traditional family values," while just 32 percent named the Republicans as better on this issue.[26]

This statistical dead heat was remarkable. Back in 1972 Republican Richard Nixon dubbed Democrat George McGovern the "amnesty, acid, and abortion" candidate. By successfully depicting McGovern as the representative of the 1960s "hippies"—more concerned with making love, not war; challenging conventions; and all-too-tolerant of drug use—Nixon tarred the Democrats as out of step with traditional mainstream values. Bush tried to reprise Nixon's campaign by pinning the "hippie" label on Clinton. He caricatured his opponent as a Rhodes scholar who travelled to the Soviet Union as a student (with whom and what Clinton did there Bush ominously left to the imagination); a draft dodger who shirked his responsibilities while protesting the Vietnam War; a drug user who, although he didn't inhale, tolerated its use; and a womanizer who mocked family values by too often straying from the marriage bed. But voters were not buying. A September CBS News/*New York Times* survey found that 79 percent said that Clinton's manipulation of his draft status would have "no effect" on their electoral decision.[27]

What *was* an issue was a surprising lack of faith in the future. From Massachusetts Puritan John Winthrop's invocation that the new nation must be a "city on a hill," to the "manifest destiny" that dominated the nineteenth century, Americans have exhibited supreme confidence in the national "mission"—not to colonize the world, but to spread the tenets of classical liberalism to all parts of it. Americans came to believe that theirs was a special land, a nation set apart from all others. This belief is known as "American exceptionalism." In a turn-of-the-century book entitled *Success among the Nations,* Emil Reich captured the essence of American exceptionalism, writing that Americans were "filled with such an implicit and absolute confidence in their Union and in their future success, that any remark other than laudatory is unacceptable to the majority of them."[28] Reich added that "It has never been our fortune to catch the slightest whisper of doubt, the slightest want of faith, in the chief God of America— unlimited belief in the future of America."[29] In a famous February 1941 editorial in *Life* magazine, Henry Luce coined the phrase "The American Century" to rally his countrymen on what the nation's role would be in the post–World War II era:

America as the dynamic center of ever-widening spheres of enterprise, America as the training center of the skillful servants of mankind, America as the Good Samaritan, really believing that it is more blessed to give than to receive, and America as the powerhouse of the ideals of Freedom and Justice—out of these elements surely can be fashioned a vision of the 20th century. . . .[30]

By 1992, Americans were no longer so self-assured. The American Century seemed over, and American exceptionalism was under siege. Ironically, the doubts occurred after one of the greatest successes in American political and diplomatic history: the end of the Cold War. Nothing should have provoked more breast-beating about the righteousness of the American cause than the successful conclusion of a 40-year struggle against communism. George Bush certainly thought it important to use the end of the Cold War as yet another demonstration of "American exceptionalism." In a June television interview, Bush took pride in the Cold War's conclusion and his own role in making it happen: "I hope every Mother and Dad out there says, 'Hey, we ought to give this president a little credit out there for the fact that our little kids don't worry so much about nuclear war.' Isn't that important?"[31]

> **"We won the Cold War, and now they're saying here's a pink slip."**

It was important. But the Cold War's rapid close caused many economic dislocations that added to public worries about the future. Companies that once formed the heart of the "military-industrial complex" dispensed "involuntary separation" notices to their workers. One of them, Charlie Witt, Jr., from the Groton, Connecticut, Electric Boat shipyard, told a reporter: "We won the Cold War, and now they're saying here's a pink slip."[32] Electric Boat planned to lay off 4,000 employees by December 1992, and estimates are that the defense industry will lose one million jobs by 1996.

This "structural unemployment" gave rise to a widespread belief that "something differ-

ent" was needed to cope with the burgeoning post–Cold War challenges. This feeling transcended partisanship, and spawned the independent candidacy of H. Ross Perot. In a televised "town meeting," Perot told viewers: "If we let our economy continue to deteriorate, we, like Russia, will no longer be a superpower. And Russia is living proof that if you're broke you're not a superpower. We almost went broke in the Cold War. . . . We've got to turn that around now with the highest priority. We've got to reorganize our government from the top down. That's going to take hard-minded thinking and action. Talk won't do it."[33] Perot's "can-do" rhetoric and self-characterization as a modern-day Horatio Alger got him 19 percent of the ballots—the best third-party showing since Theodore Roosevelt headed the Bull Moose Party ticket in 1912.

Bush's failures and Perot's appeal were not enough to make Bill Clinton president. The Democrats had to relearn how, in David Kusnet's apt phrase, to "speak American."[34] This was a major task. In 1988, Democratic presidential candidate Gary Hart lamented: "I don't want to be president of a country that thinks like Ronald Reagan."[35] Four years later Bill Clinton sought to design his campaign and

his first 100 days as president on the Reagan model. Clinton understood the misgivings that voters had about the Democratic Party's adherence to traditional values. In his acceptance speech, Clinton exhorted his listeners: "We offer our people a new choice based on old values. We offer opportunity. And we demand responsibility. The choice we offer is not conservative or liberal, Democratic or Republican. It is different. It is new. And it will work."[36]

Clinton used the value-laden phrase "New Covenant" to package his approach to governing. That label was deliberate, and it carried a powerful punch. Ralph Whitehead once described the United States as "the only country on earth dedicated to the ideas of building a new Jerusalem. . . ."[37] Clinton's term "New Covenant" captured these sentiments—arguing that a brighter future could be had if it was centered on the values of opportunity, responsibility, and community: "In the end, the New Covenant simply asks us all to be Americans again. Old-fashioned Americans for a new time. Opportunity. Responsibility. Community. When we pull together, America will pull ahead."[38] Clinton offered his humble beginnings in a small Arkansas town as an illustration of how these values still worked. Accepting the Democratic

Table 5.2

Expectations for the Clinton Administration (in percentages)

Issue	Clinton Will	Clinton Will Not	No Opinion
Improve education	69	25	6
Improve conditions for minorities and the poor	68	27	5
Improve the health-care system	64	30	6
Improve the quality of the environment	64	29	7
Keep the nation out of war	60	27	13
Improve the economy	59	35	6
Reduce unemployment	58	37	5
Increase respect for the United States abroad	50	40	10
Control federal spending	40	54	6
Reduce the federal budget deficit	38	54	8
Avoid raising your taxes	20	74	6

Source: Gallup/CNN/*USA Today* poll, November 10–11, 1992. Text of question: "Next, I have some questions about the Clinton administration, which will take office in January. Regardless of which presidential candidate you preferred, do you think the Clinton administration will or will not be able to do each of the following?"

nomination, Clinton recalled how his father died before he was born, how his mother went to work as a nurse, how with manic determination he was awarded entry into the nation's prestigious universities, and how as governor of Arkansas he used the values of opportunity, community, and responsibility to make a better life for his constituents. Born in Hope, Arkansas, Clinton ended his peroration with these words: "I still believe in a place called Hope."[39]

Clinton's call for a restoration of confidence struck a responsive chord. One of the criteria in the job description for a presidential candidate is that he or she appeal to the voter's highest aspirations. Franklin Roosevelt met this test by being jauntily optimistic—one of the secrets of his enormous political success. But his "heirs"—Jimmy Carter in 1980, Walter F. Mondale in 1984, and Michael S. Dukakis in 1988—had a dour mien. Ronald Reagan, a former New Deal Democrat, had FDR's flair for inspiration. David Kusnet wrote of the Reagan years: "For the past decade, Republicans have been more at home with (and more adept at) the rhetoric of American exceptionalism."[40] Bush ceded much of that rhetoric to his Democratic opponent, preoccupied as he was with questioning Clinton's character and raising doubts about the future under a Clinton administration. Clinton was hopeful about what lay ahead, but he also exhorted Americans to do their part:

I want to be your president. But you have to be Americans again—not just getting, but giving. Not placing blame, but taking responsibility. Not just looking out for yourselves, but looking out for each other, too. I believe America is a nation of boundless hopes and endless dreams. And the only limit to what we can do is what our leaders ask of us, and what we are willing to ask of ourselves. I believe in America. . . . Together we can do it.[41]

"To the Best of My Ability"

Throughout 1992 it was the American voter—to an extent unprecedented in any recent campaign—who forced the candidates to respond to their concerns and deepest fears about the future. On election night, the television networks quickly made viewers aware that something important—something they had collectively wrought—had occurred. The immediate impact was an infusion of some desperately needed cautious optimism. Forty-seven percent said Clinton's victory made them feel "more hopeful" about their economic future. A Gallup/CNN/*USA Today* survey taken after the election showed significant majorities thought Clinton would improve education, create better conditions for minorities and the poor, improve health care, enhance the quality of the environment, keep the nation out of war, provide a growing economy, reduce unemployment, and increase respect for the United States overseas. Only when it came to controlling federal spending, reducing the deficit, and taxes were respon-

"[1992] was not a typical, run-of-the-mill election."

dents less optimistic (see Table 5.2).[42] The shibboleth that the Democrats were the party that taxes and spends too much still had resonance.

But 1992 was not a typical, run-of-the-mill election. Its meaning will be fully revealed in the mists of history long after the Clinton presidency becomes a dim memory. But already this much is clear: Americans responded to Clinton's call to have the "courage to change,"[43] and supported him—not for his detailed issue positions, but because he believed in the values of opportunity, community, and responsibility, and for his confidence that we can do better as a people and a country. Our nation is at a political crossroads, and voters seem willing to support a leader who strikes the correct moral or reaffirming tone. When Bill Clinton took the oath of office on January 20, 1993, he pledged, as did his 41 predecessors, to execute the duties of the presidency "to the best of my ability." The next four years will test just how well President Bill Clinton does in performing the part he auditioned for in what promises to be a great American drama.

Chapter Six

Media Strategies in the 1992 Campaign

Jarol B. Manheim

It's morning in America. There's a bear in the woods. Willie Horton. Lee Greenwood. The tank ride. Boston Harbor. The handlers.

Ever since Lyndon B. Johnson's extraordinarily negative campaign against Barry Goldwater in 1964—best remembered for the "Daisy" spot, which proved that a single nuclear explosion, even a figurative one, can etch itself indelibly into the political psyche—Americans, and their media, have come to view campaign commercials as the defining elements of a presidential contest. Tens of millions of dollars have been poured into producing dozens of memorable political spots in the last 30 years, and hundreds of millions into purchasing time on television networks and local stations to air them. The styles have varied from year to year, party to party, and candidate to candidate. The themes have rolled from issue to issue, personality to personality, image to image. The only constant has been the advertisements themselves—their accepted centrality to the defining of candidates and building of electoral support.

But not in 1992.

In 1992, political spots, though numerous, were an afterthought in the general election campaign, an item in the toolbox of the tactician rather than that of the strategist. With the exception of H. Ross Perot's so-called "infomercials," a series of 30- and 60-minute broadcasts highlighting the candidate and his economic policies, political advertising in this campaign was neither strategically significant nor artistically interesting. There were ads, to be sure, but they were neither influential nor memorable.

This is not to say, however, that the media played a less important role in the campaign than they had in recent years. To the contrary, the media—or more correctly, the media strategies of the respective campaign organizations—were more central than ever. But they were central in different ways, ways that were logical extensions of the campaigns of 1964 through 1988, but that point to a future of ever more sophisticated efforts by campaign professionals to manage—one could easily say "manipulate"—the media for political advantage. Let us take a step back to examine the context in which political journalists functioned, and in which political campaigners made their strategic decisions coming into the 1992 contest. Then we will examine the conduct of the media campaign in 1992. And finally, we will consider the implications of the most recent campaign for the role of mediated discourse in the American politics of 1996 and beyond.

THE NEWS DOCTORS

Back in the 1960s, television was just beginning to emerge as the medium of choice for news and public affairs information among the American people. Indeed, it was not until that decade that television sets were sufficiently widely distributed among the population that the medium could be seen as potentially influential. Television journalism was still strongly influenced by the values and styles of print journalism. Indeed, virtually all of the medium's journalists came to their respective newsrooms from previous employment with one or another newspaper or magazine, or from television's electronic cousin, radio.

▬▬▬▬▬

"[I]n the 1960s, television was just beginning to emerge as the medium of choice for news and public affairs information among the American people."

▬▬▬▬▬

The differences between television and these other media are of two principal types. The first is psychological. Research has shown that, when they watch television, people tend to let the medium set the pace of communication and define the content and context of the message. In fact, because television messages go by so quickly and cannot be recalled (leaving aside the more recent advent of in-home video recording), the medium controls the interpretation of the message to a degree much greater than print. And because television messages are so complete, providing no opportunity for individual viewers to fill in blanks in the images the medium creates, television messages are much more likely than those of radio—which requires the listener to paint a picture in his or her own mind—to produce a relatively uniform understanding of the message across a large and diverse population, like that of the voting public.

And there is one more important psychological difference. Precisely because of the pacing and comprehensiveness of the television image and the fact that it is received without stimulating the viewer to do any individual thinking about the message, television is far more effective at conveying emotions and very simple messages than it is at conveying rational arguments and complex ideas.

The second set of differences between television and other mass media is economic. Put most simply, by comparison to radio or print media, television production is extraordinarily expensive. It requires a great deal of complex equipment, consumes vast amounts of electrical power, and employs entire classes of technicians whose jobs have no parallel in the other media.

In the American economy, this high cost of production is covered by the sale of advertising (or its public-television equivalent, corporate and foundation underwriting). This in turn means that television programs are expected to attract sizable audiences so that the sales staffs can sell advertising time to corporations at a rate that covers costs and produces a profit. As a general rule, the bigger the audience for a given program, the higher the rates that can be collected for advertising aired during that program, and the higher those rates, the more profitable the enterprise. There is pressure, then, on the producers of television programs to design those programs to have a maximal appeal to the prospective audience, pressure that is not unique to television, but that is, nevertheless, much more intense in this medium.

The newsroom is not immune to that pressure. And in fact, news is very profitable. All of the major networks have historically made money on their news reporting, and for many local stations, the local evening news program is the single largest profit center of the entire operation. But not all newsrooms are equally profitable, and therein lies the tale.

Beginning around the time that Lyndon Johnson launched the "Daisy" ad, there emerged a group of media consultants—they came to be known as "news doctors"—whose expertise was grounded in what was then emerging as a substantial body of research-based knowledge about how people process information from the mass media and about other related aspects of human psychology, and whose sensitivities were principally economic. In other words, these consultants understood the importance of a client station's gaining a competitive edge in the race for advertising dollars, and they had a plan for using the newly emerging knowledge of television's influence on its viewers to help their clients.

Hired first by several local stations affiliated with the ABC network and Westinghouse Broadcasting, stations that had in common their last-place standing in their respective local news markets, the news doctors devised a new form of television news—some might say the first form of news that was designed expressly for the medium, which came to be known as the "eyewitness" format. It is the style of presentation that we see today on nearly every channel—heavy on graphics, live-action film or video, human drama, personalities, and interplay among a cast of several anchorpersons. But what is commonplace today was innovative in an era when the national news lasted 15 minutes, and local news perhaps twice that, all read in great seriousness from printed text or teleprompter by one (or in the case of NBC's groundbreaking "Huntley-Brinkley Report," two) white male talking heads. And its effect was galvanizing. In virtually every instance, the station with the new eyewitness style of news leaped from last to first in its market.

"[M]any people in the audience have come to view Phil Donahue or Oprah Winfrey as journalists, and "Inside Story" or "Unsolved Mysteries" as news."

Success like that does not go unnoticed, and it was not long before station after station, and eventually network after network, learned the lessons of the new format. Hard news was softened by bringing to the fore the effects of events on *people* ("Your parents have been kidnapped and brutally killed. Your three-month-old daughter has been thrown from a train and maimed. Tell me . . . how does it feel?"), and story selection was changed to increase the emphasis on human rather than institutional news. Dramatic video became more important than solid background reporting. A pretty face and a reassuring voice came to outweigh journalistic experience. Even Dan Rather took to wearing sweaters rather than those formal old coats and ties. And anchormen and *women* all across America laughed and joked their way through the nightly horrors to communicate one simple message to their audiences: The world is a nasty place, but we still like each other and we still like you. So tune in tomorrow.[1]

And tune in people did, and still do. The success of defining news in television's own terms has continued. And as the broadcasting industry has gone through changes of ownership that have typically placed in control corporate executives devoted much more to economic values than to news values, the pressure on newsrooms to produce programming that em-

phasizes entertaining the audience more than informing it has moved television journalism much more toward good television, and much less toward good journalism in the traditional sense. So it is that many people in the audience have come to view Phil Donahue or Oprah Winfrey as journalists, and "Inside Story" or "Unsolved Mysteries" as news. Keep that thought.

THE SPIN DOCTORS

At the same time that these news doctors were initiating changes in the style and substance of television news, a similar group of political consultants, whom we'll call "spin doctors" even though that term actually has a more specialized meaning, using the very same body of developing research on media use and effects, began to play a central role in determining strategy for the conduct of political campaigns, first at the presidential level, then in more and more state and local races. But where the news doctors' goal was to maximize the audience for a given station or network news program and thereby increase profits, the spin doctors set out to *build electoral coalitions* by using their specialized knowledge of the media to develop campaign messages that would appeal to particular segments of the voting public, then targeting those messages to maximize their desired effects and to minimize the collateral damage that would come from the wrong message reaching the wrong voter. Like the news doctors, they came to rely more and more on symbolic and emotional messages, less and less on detail and reason.

It's morning in America. I feel good. Willie Horton. That could happen to me. The tank ride. That clown could be running the national defense. The message is there, but it is a message of a particular kind, one that conveys feelings, but not one that engages the mind of the viewer. It is, in effect, eyewitness campaigning.

Though there are many things one could point to in characterizing the trends in political advertising—and campaign messages in general—over the last several election cycles, the one that attracted the most attention from scholars and journalists alike was the rise of negativity.

It is an enduring trait of human nature that we are prone to exaggerate the significance of our own times and experiences precisely because they are our own. The emergent concern about negative campaigning is a case in point. Historically, candidates for public office in the United States have been charged with remarkable regularity since the earliest days of the republic with sexual misconduct, lack of patriotism, physical ugliness, and sheer stupidity. If even half of these charges had validity, it is a wonder we have managed to muddle through all these years. Still, by more recent standards there was, in elections through 1988, a sharp upswing in the attention to such themes, and that upswing caught the eyes of journalists and voters alike.

Post-Watergate journalism, with its tendency toward distrust of all public figures and their policies, contributed significantly to this trend, if in no other way than generating a context of public expectations that emphasized the negative. And journalistic "feeding frenzies" focused on such intrigues as Joe Biden's plagiarism or Gary Hart's heartthrobs—the 1992 equivalent was Bill Clinton's alleged dalliance with Gennifer Flowers—surely enriched the mix.[2] But in the electoral arena, a primary moving force toward negativism was the theme selection for the ever more invasive campaign advertising.

There are several reasons that campaigns have employed such messages. For one thing, negative ads are fun to do and fun to view. They add an element of entertainment to an otherwise dreary exercise. For another, they are excellent vehicles for energizing voters who are already committed to a candidate. They get people revved up. Third, they can sometimes force the opponent onto the defensive and give the campaign momentum and control of the agenda for a period of time. But perhaps most important of all, they make news.[3]

Essentially, there are two classes of media in a political campaign: paid and free. Paid media include such things as advertisements or bumper strips. Free media—some consultants use the term "earned" media—take the form of news coverage or other media appearances. From the perspective of the campaigners, the advantage of paid media is the amount of control they exercise over the shape, timing, and placement of the message. The disadvantage is that such messages are generally recognized by prospective voters as nothing more than campaign propaganda. As a result, paid media have low credibility and limited persuasive effect. In contrast, free media have high credibility—the mes-

sages assume the credibility of the deliverer, typically a more or less respected journalist, and of the showcase, a news or other program or journal that the voter has independently chosen to read, hear, or view—but are controlled by persons outside the direct influence of the campaign. In other words, the campaigners have the most effective control over the least effective media, and the least effective control over the most effective media.[4]

As a result, much of the increase in sophistication of political campaigns in recent years has taken the form of evolving strategies for "managing" free media messages by manipulating journalists and news organizations. And negative advertising has played a central role in that for a reason that we have already seen: Negative advertising meets the criteria of "newsworthiness" established by the news doctors. It is inherently dramatic, personal, conflict-driven, and interesting. It is news.

The model that is uppermost in the minds of consultants "going negative" is the "Daisy" spot, in which a young girl's counting up of daisy petals faded into a countdown and a nuclear explosion, while the voice of Lyndon Johnson offered voters a choice: either they must love each other or they must die. That ad was placed only once, but was then repeated many times in news accounts and analyses until almost everyone saw it, and almost everyone had a chance to attach to it the credibility of a favorite journalist. It did not matter that the ad was decried; it mattered that it was repeated. The lesson was straightforward: negative advertising has a multiplier effect to the extent that it is sufficiently outrageous to make news.[5] By 1988, when much of the news coverage of the campaign centered on various controversial television advertisements, this ethic had come to define not only political advertising, but the general strategies of political campaigning. Early indications were that 1992 would see nothing but more of the same.

CONTRAINDICATIONS

Two things happened after the 1988 election that altered this trend, though only on the margins so far. First, journalists began to give more than lip service to their contributory negligence in the drive toward negativity. Second, more and more members of the public, whose tolerance for inane messages was being tested, reached the saturation point. The first countertrend was instigated largely by influential journalist David Broder, who undertook a personal campaign to encourage his colleagues to be more responsible in their election coverage.[6] The second became the basis for the most broadly based challenge to the two-party dominance of presidential elections in contemporary U.S. history, the challenge mounted by H. Ross Perot.

> *"[T]hough campaign journalism may not have gotten much better in 1992 than in 1988, at the least it appeared to have halted its decline."*

For his part, Broder challenged the news media not merely to repeat negative advertising, but to explicate it. His newspaper, the *Washington Post*, for example, was one of several in 1992 that regularly dissected campaign messages to identify underlying facts and strategies. *USA Today* published a weekly "People's Press Conference" in which the campaigners responded to questions from readers, while the *Los Angeles Times* set its film critic to analyzing the campaign as a theatrical performance. And even the television network newscasts gave at least lip service—though at times little more—to reducing their reliance on soundbites and increasing their substantive analysis of the candidates and their programs. In the words of ABC News anchor Peter Jennings, "We'll only devote time to a candidate's daily routine if it is more than routine. There will be less attention to staged appearances and soundbites designed exclusively for television."[7] Perhaps befitting a political campaign, the performance was somewhat less than the promise. But though campaign journalism may not have gotten much better in 1992 than in 1988, at the least it appeared to have halted its decline. For their part, the public all but gave up on meaningful choice, and that may have proven a saving grace. For out of the popular frustration and disillusionment that began the year, there emerged a populist candidate with a focused—albeit not detailed—message

that attracted sufficient support to force candidates George Bush and Bill Clinton back from the brink of gloss and negativity. That candidate was H. Ross Perot, and the message was that people wanted responsible action from their politicians. Clinton got the message sooner, and stuck to his one-issue approach, which was captured in a sign near the door of his campaign headquarters that said: "It's the Economy, Stupid." It was a reminder to stay focused on his dominant affirmative message. Bush got the message much later—probably in the second presidential debate, in which citizens were selected to ask the questions. Pundits at the time expected Bush to use the debate to attack Clinton in a last-ditch effort to save his presidency. An early questioner, however, to much applause, instructed the candidates to stick to the issues and stop attacking one another. Bush seemed to be thrown off his stride, and never recovered the initiative. Ross Perot, in effect, simply nodded and said "Amen."

But Perot was not the simple populist he claimed to be. He was, of course, a billionaire who spent nearly $60 million of his own money on the campaign, more than the 55 million dollars allotted from public funds to either Bush or Clinton. But that is not really the point. In the present context, Perot's populism is best understood as a product of his media savvy. Here, again, context contributes to understanding.

One of the strategies (besides negative advertising) that spin doctors have devised to aid their candidates is avoidance of the national press. National-level reporters are among the most-feared individuals in all of politics. That is because they know how to ask tough questions, and they are doggedly persistent in doing so. And as we have seen, in 1992 they were in a mood to do battle. To defend against the threat implicit in such questions, campaigners have developed an evolving series of techniques that keep their candidates out of harm's way, yet at the same time provide a defense against the charge that they are avoiding the media. When Richard M. Nixon campaigned in 1972, for example, he regularly invited to Washington the *publishers* of newspapers from around the country for "press conferences." The public did not distinguish between journalists and publishers, but Nixon and his advisers knew that the latter came from the business side of the news organization, that they had a natural antagonism for their journalist employees arising from their

73

My guests today are Bill Clinton, H. Ross Perot, George Bush and Donna, a transexual with amnesia...

DONAHUE

BY MIKE LUCKOVICH FOR THE ATLANTA CONSTITUTION

focus on the bottom line rather than the written word, and that they were relatively more likely to be Republicans. They were, in short, a friendly audience that nevertheless provided "cover" from charges of avoiding the press. In the years since, candidates have employed a variety of other means for the same purpose—an end run around the national media.

In 1992, this strategy took two innovative forms. The first, and probably most significant, was the move from news to talk shows and the so-called "infotainment" circuit as a forum for "serious" political discourse. Why talk to Dan Rather—who had attempted pointedly to hoist then-candidate George Bush on the petard of the Iran-Contra scandal in the last go-round—or to a reinvigorated Peter Jennings, when Larry King or Phil Donahue could lob softball questions to an ooing and ahhhing audience of just plain folks? Candidates of the people on the people's programs. It was a natural, once someone had the insight to do it.

Clinton started early with his town meeting format, but it was Ross Perot who, in stage-managing a "Draft Ross" movement on "Larry King Live," had the real vision of the potential of this forum. It was in response to his initiative that Clinton went on to play the saxophone with

Arsenio Hall and to meet and greet the MTV audience, and that Bush, who early in the year had declined to appear on what he described as "weird talk shows" because doing so was not "presidential," showed up in the space of about one week toward the end of the campaign with Larry King, Bryant Gumbel, Katie Couric, Charlie Gibson, Harry Smith and Paula Zahn, Sam Donaldson, and David Frost, appeared on ESPN and the Nashville Network, and even submitted himself to the fawning attention of emergent right-wing talkster Rush Limbaugh.[8] The effect here—and the reason that these appearances represented an advance in image management strategy—was to place the candidate in a setting that gave the appearance of meeting the people, yet one where journalistic challenges were unlikely and where the opportunities for message control were manifest. Indeed, the interviewers actually cooperated in exercising such control by prescreening questions from the public. They, too, after all, had an image to maintain.

The second new form—and perhaps the definitive act of the Clinton campaign—was the bus ride. The intercity bus, like the talk show, is widely regarded as a people's medium, though of transportation rather than communication. By riding the bus early and often, even to his inauguration, Clinton was able to communicate symbolically the ties he felt with his constituents. But the real genius of the bus rides was their effect on news coverage. Not only did they assure Clinton of headlines at each stop, but they made "natural" the emphasis the campaign gave to local rather than national journalists. It is the case that local journalists, especially television journalists, are more popular and better known among their audiences than their national counterparts, and that local angles always enhance the play a story will receive. These journalists are also, however, less experienced, less knowledgeable in national political affairs, and more easily overawed by the presidential presence. The bus tours guaranteed that Clinton would benefit from the credibility and interest attendant on the local coverage, and at the same time provided a safe cover against charges that he avoided the press—even, of course, as he did precisely that.

THE PRESCRIPTION

With the stakes so high, the spin doctors leave little to chance. Every word, every move, every expression is carefully planned. And though spontaneous actions do sometimes intrude unwanted into the campaign, every effort is bent toward following the doctors' prescription. Given its success, let us take as our example the Clinton campaign.

> *"We know from long experience that campaigners will do whatever they think will win them votes."*

Bill Clinton's campaign began using focus groups—small groups of citizens who are used to test various campaign messages—to chart its path as much as a year before the then-governor of Arkansas announced his candidacy, and everything from his hair style and his smile to his aggressive responses to negative news or attacks was pretested, tested, and retested.[9] Still, in

April 1992, things were not going well. The only spring Flowers on voters' minds was named Gennifer, and the draft that Clinton felt was not a gentle spring breeze, but an old national war wound. The candidate was seen as slick and untrustworthy, his wife Hillary as cold and ambitious. The prognosis was poor.

But then Clinton's spin doctors—pollster Stan Greenberg, strategist James Carville, and media adviser Frank Greer—pulled out their prescription pad and penned a confidential memo to the candidate, setting out a plan to establish the Clintons as "an honest, plain-folks idealist and his warm and loving wife." The *outline* of the plan ran fourteen single-spaced pages. Among its elements, Clinton was advised to play his saxophone on a television talk show and to poke fun at himself for his claim to having tried marijuana but "not inhaled." Beyond that, it reported the results of campaign research based on surveys and focus groups, identified points of vulnerability to Republican attacks, and set forth the themes and strategies that Clinton ultimately employed to redefine himself and to hold off the Bush challenge.[10]

THE FUTURE HEALTH OF THE BODY POLITIC

With all these news doctors and spin doctors, you'd think the body politic would be healing. But the fact is that the patients served by these doctors are the media and the candidates, not the voters. The only thing the public has going for it here is not that it is a patient, but that it is *im*patient. We know from long experience that campaigners will do whatever they think will win them votes. And we know that, at least until 1992, the conventional wisdom among political professionals has been that voters would accept—would *respond to*—the most trivial, meaningless, negative, and demeaning messages in campaign media. So that is what they provided.

But in 1992, voters expressed their anger and frustration. To the extent that turnout increased, it increased in support of Ross Perot. When the public had a real chance to express itself, what it expressed was a general, systemic outrage at the state of political dialogue. Some candidates adjusted and did well. One did not, and he lost the presidency.

If 1992 was a turning point in the conduct of presidential campaigns, that is not likely to be reflected in a turning away from sophisticated media-driven strategies. After all, the media are essential devices for reaching the vast and widely dispersed pools of electoral support in the United States. Rather, it will be reflected in a turning of those strategies to formats and tech- niques that convey a popular touch for the candidate without surrendering control of the message. That is the challenge for campaign strategists in 1996—and it is also the challenge that will confront the citizenry.

Chapter Seven

The Ross Perot Candidacy and Its Significance

Frank B. Feigert

It can be argued that the Ross Perot candidacy of 1992 was quite unlike any other we have ever had. Certainly, we never before had a billionaire, self-made or otherwise, run an independent campaign for president. Unrestricted by federal laws regulating campaign finance, he was able to spend as much as did the major-party candidates. And the fact that he had never held or sought elective office also set him apart from what one thinks of in terms of either third-party or independent candidacies. Furthermore, how often does a candidate for president bow out and then reenter? Yet, as will be made clear, there are historical antecedents to Perot, and he fits into a long tradition of unusual challenges to two-party domination of American electoral politics. Granting this, we also deal with his effects on the election, those feared and those realized. Finally, we hazard a guess or two as to his future role.

First, a disclaimer is necessary. Far too much of little value or substance has been written about Perot's motivations in this election. Why did he enter the race in the first place? Did he want to ensure that George Bush could not win reelection? Did he ever seriously believe that he could win? There are hundreds of questions such as these that have been and could be raised, but to little end. What H. Ross Perot thought or believed may be of interest to gossips, but it would have little significance as compared to the simple electoral fact that he received 19 percent of the popular vote, and what this might say about the American political system in 1992. In short, in this chapter we will not attempt to ascribe motivations to Perot.

THE HISTORICAL CONTEXT

Perot's candidacy can be considered as part of a long tradition of independent and third-party candidacies. Rossiter has described several types of such challenges, and it appears that Perot can be described, with qualifications, as having headed a "dissident hero" effort.[1] These are normally personalistic in nature, crystallizing around a well-known figure from a major party, who may be unhappy at having been overlooked for the nomination himself, or perhaps at the issue positions taken by the party from which he has bolted.

Several twentieth-century examples of this phenomenon come to mind. These include the Progressive Parties of Theodore Roosevelt (1912, also known as the "Bull Moose" Party), Robert La Follette (1924), and Henry Wallace (1948). George Wallace's American Independent Party of 1968 fits this mold, and John Anderson's independent candidacy of 1980 does as well.

Several questions arise here in terms of Perot. Since he had never held public office, how could he have bolted from one party or the other? Yet, from his close relationships with several Republican presidents, including Bush up to the point where they publicly broke, it could be inferred that Perot was a disaffected Republican. Also, given his distaste with "politics as usual," he can be seen as dissenting from the two-party system. Regardless, there is one point about his nominal predecessors that cannot be denied. Each was temporary, a single-year candidacy, melting away, having left no organization or base to carry on the good fight, especially at lower office levels, where the work to build a lasting organization must start. These campaigns represent "trickle down" politics, in which little is left to take root for future campaigns. Yet, as this is written, Perot has announced that he will continue to fund United We Stand, as a "watchdog" group. Whether this can serve as the basis for a revived candidacy in 1996 is something to which we will return. But, before proceeding, it is helpful to get something of a perspective on Perot's campaign, from the time it first became news.

Chronology

A common complaint about American presidential campaigns is that they last far too long. No sooner were the results in for the 1992 election than we began to ask questions about who was or would be organizing for 1996. Patrick J. Buchanan? Dan Quayle? Jack Kemp? Phil Gramm? James A. Baker III? From this viewpoint alone, the Perot campaign was refreshingly short, even if one considers it all of a piece, ignoring his exit and reentry. Table 7.1 sets out some of the principal aspects of his campaign.

"[I]t can be argued with some conviction that Perot's candidacy did not suddenly emerge with his appearance on "Larry King Live.""

Of course, it can be argued with some conviction that Perot's candidacy did not suddenly emerge with his appearance on "Larry King Live." It had been discussed in various media at least as far back as the previous November. Thus, the "aw shucks, if they want me" aspect is somewhat disingenuous. Certainly, it seems that Perot had probably given the matter some consideration before making his CNN appearance. However, for those who had not been paying attention earlier, the media and popular response to Perot's seemingly casual willingness to allow himself to be drafted by volunteers must have seemed refreshing indeed.

Not indicated in the table is the extent to which Perot emerged almost instantaneously as a media star. Early polls showed him ahead of George Bush, with Bill Clinton trailing badly. Some polls also showed him potentially capable of carrying several states, including the electoral heavyweights of California and Texas. Yet, all this came to naught when he dropped out of the campaign, less than five months after his CNN appearance. The reasons he gave are indicated in the table, and we will take them at face value.

However, after reentering the campaign and shortly before the election, Perot himself cast doubt on his own motivations. Earlier reports had circulated about "Inspector Perot," a thinly disguised attempt by GOP operatives to compare him to the comic Inspector Clouseau character immortalized in the "Pink Panther" movies. Allegedly, Perot had authorized investigations of his employees, some of his campaign staff, and perhaps even President Bush's children. This was the so-called "dark side" of Perot, an image carefully cultivated by those who wanted him out of the campaign. Perot later charged that the *real* reason he had bowed out was that he had received reliable reports that the GOP had planned to disrupt his daughter's wedding, and publish faked photographs of her in compromising situations. Thus, an image of Perot as a paranoid, justifiable or not, emerged at a critical time, when he was ostensibly trying to discuss real issues. Whether he could have done any better in the election than he did, had he not withdrawn only to reenter, and had he not been associated with such matters as this, can never be known. But these factors are indeed part of the historical record.

CANDIDATE PEROT: PERSONAL TRAITS

How does anyone get into the position of running for president? Conventionally, this involves a long time in politics, building a career at the local, state, and perhaps national level. In recent years this has been somewhat shortened, as we have twice elected individuals who each had a total of only eight years experience in state politics. Jimmy Carter, prior to his 1976 election, had been in the Georgia legislature for four years and was governor for another four. Ronald Reagan, on succeeding him in 1980, had twice been California governor.

Table 7.1

Major Event Chronology in the 1992 Campaign of Ross Perot

Date	Event
February 20	On "Larry King Live," CNN national broadcast, says he will run for president if he can get on the ballot in all 50 states, through a grass-roots petition drive.
March 15	Dallas headquarters established with 100 telephone lines and an 800 number.
April 15	Petition drive organization is headed by Tom Luce, an old friend, employee, and adviser.
May 26	Resigns as head of Perot Systems; hires Buchanan's campaign pollster.
June 3	Announces the hiring of Ed Rollins and Hamilton Jordan, former insiders in Republican and Democratic campaigns.
June 21	On the ballot in 15 states, another 18 pending certification.
July 11	In address to NAACP, makes reference to "you people," offending African Americans and others.
July 15	Ed Rollins resigns over differences in strategy.
July 16	Perot announces he will not run, since he cannot win and his presence would cause the absence of a majority in the electoral college, throwing the election to the House of Representatives. Also expresses approval of Democrats' economic plans.
July 20	Meets with leaders from state campaigns, pledging to keep the movement alive.
July 22	Warns of coming economic catastrophe, announces that his own economic plan will soon be released.
September 22	FEC report shows Perot spent $4 million in August, the most he had spent in any month. On "CBS This Morning," discussing his withdrawal, says "I think I made a mistake, because they [the major parties] did not really address the issues."
September 27	Receives high-level delegations from the major parties, to hear presentations on their economic plans to reduce the national deficit.
September 28	Announces, on "Larry King Live," an 800 number for voters to call if they want him to run.
October 1	Announces his reentry into the campaign. Accepted as debate participant by Bush and Clinton.
October 11	First debate. Some polls show him the "winner."
October 13	Vice-presidential debate.
October 15	Second debate.
October 20	Third debate.
October 25	Charges that the real reason he had earlier left the campaign was to protect his daughter from a GOP plan to disrupt her wedding.
November 3	Winning no electoral college votes, receives 19 percent of popular vote.

Each party in 1988 had had an amateur unsuccessfully seek its nomination. Pat Robertson entered the GOP primaries, losing to Bush in the end. The Rev. Jesse L. Jackson lost the Democratic nomination to Michael S. Dukakis. But neither had shown the ability to generate as much support as Perot did. What made Perot such a popular figure?

The obvious answer is his wealth. Having been an IBM salesman, he left the company to form Electronic Data Systems in 1960, borrowing $1,000 from his wife to pay for incorporating the new business. From this point on it seems a reliving of Horatio Alger stories. With pluck, luck, a lot of hard work, and that $1,000 from his wife, Perot had, by the time of his campaign, amassed a personal fortune estimated at better than $3 billion. He had, as he was fond of saying, "lived the American dream." From this background as a businessman he claimed an ability to offer common-sense solutions to the problems of deficit management and reduction. As a non–major party candidate, the fact that he was able to meet the petition requirements of 50

79

states was something of a political miracle. Only George Wallace in 1968 and John Anderson in 1980 had been able to meet these.

He also ran as an "outsider," a claim that was applauded as well as regarded skeptically. In one sense, he was another of the political amateurs to whom we have referred. Yet his ability to gain large government contracts and funding for various projects, such as Alliance Airport in Fort Worth, demonstrate the abilities of the ultimate lobbyist insider. Certainly few outsiders have ever enjoyed the White House access he had under Richard Nixon, Reagan, and Bush.

Less obvious were some of his personal traits. His intense loyalty to his subordinates was revealed when he mounted a successful rescue mission of EDS employees from Tehran in 1980, whereas U.S. embassy personnel were held hostage for a year.[2] This was consistent with his image as the man who had financed an abortive mission to Vietnam in 1969 to bring Christmas gifts to American prisoners of war. He championed the cause of MIAs, insisting on a proper accounting of U.S. losses in Vietnam.

Among his traits were his personal appearance and his rhetoric. Clearly not a "blow-dried" candidate of the image-makers, he could make fun of his large ears and suggest that "what you see is what you get." His speech, too, was full of homilies that suggested he was a common man, his great wealth notwithstanding. However, some of his metaphors were perhaps too macho, including such phrases as getting "down in the trenches," and "getting under the hood and fixing it." As we shall see, his electoral support was considerably more from men than from women, and this may have been a factor in his lack of electoral success.

The Media Candidate

It is widely conceded that Presidents Franklin D. Roosevelt and Ronald W. Reagan were masters at using the media. In Ross Perot we have a candidate who was made both for and by the media. Given his near-mythical status as a self-made billionaire, his (relatively) humble origins, and a speaking style that was direct and unpolished, he was able to attract large audiences from the outset. It is difficult to envision anyone else, for instance, who could so readily captivate the media (and the hours of free air time that

followed) on the basis of a seemingly casual admission that he might be willing to run. From this time until only a few days before the election, Perot ran a campaign almost exclusively in the media, rarely venturing out onto the campaign trail for personal appearances. In short, the campaign took place largely in television studios.

> **"***It will be some time before anyone computes the number of hours of "free" media that accrued to Perot, especially on television.***"**

The Free Media It will be some time before anyone computes the number of hours of "free" media that accrued to Perot, especially on television. However, it seems fair to say that he was the willing subject of and guest on the morning talk shows for all the major networks,[3] and may even have had more time than did Bush[4] and Clinton. Television specials, such as an ABC "National Town Meeting," had higher viewer ratings than some regularly broadcast shows, including a major league baseball playoff game.

There were numerous potential benefits to his campaign from so much free exposure, in which he could portray himself as a folksy savior of the nation ("I'm here as the cleanup man. I'm just a guy showing up after the party with a shovel and a broom to clean it up.").[5] However, or perhaps because there is substantial evidence of voter discontent with the media, he also ran *against* those in the media, while using them to get his own message across that they were out of touch with the concerns of ordinary people. Speaking to Bryant Gumbel on the "Today" Show, he said,

I suggest that all you folks up there in the anchor rooms spend more time in Wal-Mart and Home Depot. . . . Get out there where the rubber meets the road. They'll all recognize you. And just listen to what the people are saying. And I believe that you're out of touch, with all due respect.[6]

The print media were not spared, either.

> I think you'll do anything for a "gotcha" story. . . . That just means anything that'll get you a headline, get you a bonus. You get among your peers and you high five and say: "O.K., now I'm a big man. I got a story on the front page."[7]

For such remarks, as with any other candidate, he came to be the object of serious media criticism. Where once Johnny Carson had recognized that he could not be overly critical of Perot in the spring phase of the campaign, Jay Leno, Dana Carvey and others could make him the butt of their humor in the fall. And in the print media, none said it stronger than the *New York Times* in their pre-Election Day lead editorial.

> For all his homespun honesty on economic issues, his day-to-day behavior bespeaks a smart, manipulative, imperious and impatient man . . . a man poorly versed in the arts of compromise and negotiation on which effective leadership depends. . . . One way or another, Mr. Perot has already seized the attention of the country and the candidates. That is sufficient reward for one who would make an insufficient President.[8]

Among Perot's free media appearances was his inclusion in the debates with President Bush and Governor Clinton. How did this affect his candidacy? Given his inclusion in the debates on reentering the race, his campaign recovered some of the legitimacy it had lost when he dropped out. And while his performances were credible enough, they could not close the gap that had been created by his leaving, when so many of his supporters apparently drifted principally to Clinton. We will never know what would have happened had he stayed in. However, it is also fair to say that his debate appearances helped reinforce his supporters. Nonetheless, the staunchest of these must have winced at one point. The quixotic nature of the campaign was illustrated when his running mate, Vice Admiral James B. Stockdale, asked the now-famous and oft-parodied question, "Why am I here?" in his own debate with Vice President Dan Quayle and Senator Al Gore. The net effect of the debates for Perot is indicated by his change from 8 percent in the ABC News poll before the first debate, to 12 percent before the second, and 15 percent immediately after the third.[9]

The Paid Media Uninhibited by Federal Election Commission (FEC) restrictions on Clinton and Bush because they were using limited public financing, Perot was able to use television to an even greater extent than did they, spending an estimated $60 million, most of it his own money. Clinton and Bush, by contrast, could spend only 60 percent of the $55.2 million each received from the FEC. However, in evaluating this, the most striking thing is not the sheer amount of money Perot spent, but the way in which he used it. Conventional wisdom holds that 30- to 60-second spot commercials are most effective, given the audience's short attention span. It must also be conceded that a good deal of television advertising in recent years has been superficial, dwelling as it has on a candidate's image rather than on his or her achievements.

Admittedly, Perot ran some superficial advertising, of the sort that stressed his "world-class family" and their virtues. But his more serious half-hour "infomercials" drew unexpectedly large audiences. In these, Perot would sit at a desk, pointing at graphs and charts, discussing issues such as the budget, the deficit, and his approaches to solving these and related problems. In a very real sense, he was paying for the American public to sit through a series of civics lessons. Was this why he was able to win 19 percent? Or, was he preaching to the converted? It may be some time before we know, if we ever do.

The Campaign Organization

It has long been a staple of American campaigns that candidates can work with two organizations, the party and their own. Indeed, in the pre-nomination contest, it has been inevitable that candidates develop their own staffs who then must integrate their efforts with those of the party.[10] A principal aspect of the Perot campaign is that it was decidedly nonparty, if not wholly antiparty. No primaries had to be entered, no opponents had to be contended with, critical media could be ignored; the staff could center its energies on the single initial task of getting Perot on the ballot in all 50 states. This accomplished, they then had to devote themselves to whatever tasks were handed to them by the candidate himself.

Herein lies the essential nature of the Perot campaign. A major operating principle is that the candidate should never be his or her own manager. Buffers are needed so that the candidate, at best, can make choices between options provided by the manager. More typically, the manager has a staff who specialize in such aspects of the campaign as speechwriting, scheduling, public relations, party relations and coordination, and the like. This often gives the appearance that the candidate is the product of "handlers," including a staff of "spin doctors" who give the most favorable interpretation of their candidate's performance. Yet it can be argued readily that, despite a large staff of "volunteers," some genuine and some paid, Perot was his own manager in every respect. As he was fond of saying, "What you see is what you get."

"[T]he net effect was that Perot made all the major decisions and left the staff to fill in the details."

Recall that, in our chronology, we listed Perot's hiring of Ed Rollins and Hamilton Jordan, familiar figures on the national campaign scene for the Republicans and Democrats, respectively. Jordan had been an unknown when he managed Jimmy Carter's winning campaign in 1976, and had been rewarded with the position of White House Chief of Staff. Their hirings by Perot, at reported figures in excess of $1 million, seemed to signal his seriousness of purpose, and perhaps his willingness to play conventional campaign politics, albeit without the benefits or hindrances of party label. While we may never know exactly what led Rollins to quit shortly before Perot stepped out of the race in July, he nevertheless emerged as one of Perot's most scathing critics. ("Little did I know no one could make him look more kooky than he has himself."[11]) Was this because Perot was unwilling to take and follow advice? Because he never anticipated the extent to which he might have given up control of his own campaign? Was there a clash because Perot was used to making his decisions? Doubtless, there will be many versions of what happened, but the net effect was that Perot made all the major decisions and left the staff to fill in the details. Much has been made of the volunteer

basis of Perot's campaign. Few of his staff achieved any public recognition except for Orson Swindle, director of United We Stand, Perot's nominal organization. Swindle himself was the object of public criticism from Perot. Having suggested that "Bush would be a preferred second choice to Mr. Perot," Swindle was castigated for suggesting that *any* second choice was discussable.[12]

Some aspects of the organization have come out. We know, for instance, that, Perot's insistence to the contrary, it was not really developed from the grass roots. Having given impetus to the campaign through his "I will if they want me" statement on "Larry King Live," it seems dubious that Perot simply sat back and watched thousands of volunteers develop and pay for a phone bank in order to receive calls with offers of support. Rather, a headquarters was established with some volunteers and some paid staff. As the petition requirements were learned for each state, and they had to be met, state directors emerged, some, if not all, paid, and these provided the basis not only for securing signatures, but also for running each state's campaign once the petitions were accepted.

It must be stressed that, for all his disdain for conventional party politics, Perot's United We Stand was not at all unlike the way in which political parties necessarily operate, organized at the national, state, and local levels. What *was* unusual was that, protestations to the contrary, this was an organization essentially run from the top down. When Perot was "considering" his reentry, he provided an 800 number for voters to call if they wanted him to run again. The fact that each call was recorded as a "yes," and that some voters may have felt misled when they called, is essentially irrelevant. This effort was mandated at the top, and one would have to be rather gullible to accept the appearance of a voters' draft to which the hero reluctantly responded. The use of paid advertising in August and September, when he was nominally not a candidate, strongly suggests that the reentry was a foregone conclusion. Only one person could have made that decision, and it seems that it was made quite early.

Of special interest was Perot's ability to have delegations from the two major campaigns appear in Dallas to make presentations on their economic programs, even though it then appeared that Perot was on the verge of announcing his renewed candidacy. While some may see this as a cynical ploy on the part of Perot, it is also understandable that neither party was willing to risk alienating Perot's supporters, should he choose not to enter the race again.

PEROT AS CRITIC

Perot played several roles in the 1992 campaign, and they can be summarized by one word—critic. We have already mentioned two of these, as critic of the media and of conventional party politics. But his criticisms went further than this.

Critic of the Process

Fundamentally, Perot was a critic of the entire political process as it has developed. A common buzzword in the 1992 campaign was "gridlock," suggesting that Washington was unable to operate effectively, given the presence of lobbyists for "special interests." We have mentioned that he ran as an "outsider," although he had for years enjoyed ready access to the White House and Congress. Perot was quick to suggest at every turn that the U.S. government had plans for everything (for example, health care, deficit reduction, job creation), but that nothing was being done about them in a meaningful way. Further, he dwelt at some length on the problem of former members of our government acting as lobbyists for foreign governments and interests, and some of these serving as members of the Bush campaign team.

Perot also emerged as a critic of our electoral process. Tying together his complaints that the media focus on personalities instead of issues, he suggested various reforms of the process. One of his suggestions at a broadcast of the National Press Club was that exit polling be banned. When asked if this would not present problems with the First Amendment, his suggestion was to "change it." One of his suggestions, along these lines, was far from original, but might yet be adopted. Basically, he suggested a national election day on which polls would open and close at the same time in all 50 states.

While deploring soundbite politics, a seeming tendency of politicians to offer simplistic solutions to complex problems with slogans or quick responses that could make the evening news in a quote of a few seconds, Perot himself was a master of it. His quick wit and ability to use seemingly homely phrases made good print and electronic news, and gained him even more free media coverage. Seemingly, a day never passed in the campaign without another pithy Perot quote. And, in doing so, he appeared evermore to be a critic of President Bush and his administration. For instance, in the first debate he said, "I don't have any experience in running up a $4 trillion debt."

Critic of Bush

A frequently asked question about Perot's campaign was why he was running, and one of the more common responses was that he was doing so in order to deny Bush reelection. Whether this was true or not, he did little to discourage such speculation. As the above quote shows, he was never short on disdain for the president. In the first debate, he was only mildly critical of Clinton, while criticizing Bush on at least three counts (the deficit, Bush's criticism of Clinton's record as a Vietnam War protestor while in England, and failing to stop those who were "preaching hate" at the GOP convention).[13] Other Perot criticisms of Bush involved the Vietnam MIA issue and how the Administration had held up support for Alliance Airport as a political reprisal.

For the most part, it can be said that what criticism Perot had of either of his two opponents was largely directed at Bush. Not until the third debate did he show his disdain for Clinton (then leading well in the polls), by suggesting that being governor of a small state scarcely qualified Clinton for the presidency. Compared to his evident scorn for Bush, this seemed mild, indeed.

"Whatever his motivation, it seems that Perot did Clinton no harm by dropping out."

At this point, it is worth noting that, when Perot dropped out of the race in July, the prevailing question was where his supporters would go. Each side, of course, expressed the wish, if not

BY WRIGHT FOR THE PALM BEACH POST

expectation, that Perot's voters would be welcome. Since Perot left the race in the middle of the Democratic Convention, and he apparently had words of praise for the Democrats, it seemed to some that Perot had acted in a Machiavellian fashion, deliberately hurting Bush. Given the reasons that Perot offered at the time, and the fact that he later entered the race again, and that he subsequently said that the *real* reason he had dropped out was to protect his daughter and her wedding from a Republican "dirty tricks" operation, this scarcely seems reasonable. Yet it is a fact that Clinton led from the moment Perot dropped out. It might have been the boost that normally accrues to a candidate coming out of a convention. Whatever his motivation, it seems that Perot did Clinton no harm by dropping out. Whether or not Perot's candidacy, initial or ultimate, hurt Bush on Election Day, is a point to which we return shortly.

Critic of Parties

Perot's candidacy can be taken as an implicit criticism of the two-party system. Forgoing the usual paraphernalia of parties and their processes, he was self-nominated, avoiding primaries and a national convention. In this way, he

could claim that he was the agent of good citizens across the country who wanted him to clean up that proverbial "mess in Washington." Implicit in his criticisms of the entire electoral and political processes was blame ascribed to the parties for the gridlock he and others saw in Washington.

Interestingly, he was somewhat paralleled in this by both Bush and Clinton. The president pointed to the unwillingness of the Democrats in Congress to work with him and accept his plans. Clinton could not overly criticize congressional Democrats, with whom he would have to work. But by running his campaign from Little Rock, and keeping Congress at arm's length, Clinton, too, could speak of gridlock, while claiming that he was a legitimate outsider as far as Washington was concerned.

IMPACT AND SIGNIFICANCE: DID PEROT COST BUSH THE ELECTION?

In the search for reasons why a president who had been so popular 18 months before the election could lose, there may be a tendency to search for factors that have nothing to do with the candidate or his campaign. Surely, the argument goes, there must have been *some* negative impact from the Perot campaign. Perhaps this is so.

In this context, it can be argued with some conviction that dissident heroes, Perot included, can have a decisive impact on the outcomes of presidential elections. Figure 7.1 shows the four instances in this century where third-party candidates have received 10 percent or more of the vote. It also shows the net change in popular vote for the incumbent party. From this analysis it might very well seem that significant dissident hero candidacies (and these were the only ones to break the 10 percent barrier) have hurt the incumbent party badly. In three of the four elections (1924 excepted), the party from which they were dissenting lost not only the election but the presidency as well (William H. Taft, Hubert H. Humphrey, George H. W. Bush).

However, it is also important to point out that the so-called dissident hero serves to crystallize dissent for any number of reasons with the incumbent regime among those who are not going to mount the barricades for their nominal leader. A dissident party and its leader provide a vehicle for the discontented. Thus there is little reason to believe that Perot cost Bush his reelection. It is probable that, in the absence of a Perot candidacy, many might very well have either not voted at all or else have supported Clinton.

Perot and Turnout

With a 55 percent reported turnout rate, and more than 100 million voters, the 1992 elections reversed a slide in eligible voter participation. From the 1960 election of President John F. Kennedy onward, seven straight presidential elections showed a declining turnout, to the point where, in the 1988 election, scarcely more than 50 percent of eligibles participated. This trend was the subject of innumerable analyses, popular and scholarly, and seemed to bode ill for the future of a democratic country. As compared to other, especially Western, industrialized democracies, the United States ranked at the bottom of the list in voter participation.

Was Perot's candidacy the reason for this jump of 5 percent? The easy answer would seem to be yes, since his was such a striking candidacy in so many respects. But it must also be pointed out that the decline had taken place in 1968 as well, when George Wallace's third-party can-

didacy had received more than 13 percent of the vote. There is another way to look at this. As Rhodes Cook saw it, "[A]bout 15 percent of Perot's voters would have stayed home if Perot had not been on the ballot."[14] There is some support for this position when we examine the 1988 and 1992 turnout figures for each state. The Perot vote can account for roughly 40 percent of the variance in turnout between the states, and for about 8 percent of the difference in turnout as compared to 1988.[15] Hence, Perot's presence in the election was partially, but not wholly, responsible for the increased turnout.

Sources of Perot's Support

Was this a broad-based popular campaign, appealing across the spectrum? First, in the electoral college sense, Perot carried no states at all, although he did finish second in Utah, and came close to second in a few others. He also finished third with 22 percent in Texas, his native state, where early polls had shown him the clear leader, before he dropped out. The states where he received 25 percent or more of the vote were Alaska (28 percent), Idaho (28 percent), Kansas (27 percent), Maine (30 percent), Montana (26 percent), Nevada (27 percent), Oregon (25 percent), Utah (29 percent), and Wyoming (26 percent). For the most part, he did marginally better in the thinly settled states of the West. Did Perot's plain-spokenness and patriotism appeal more in these areas? It seems likely, although we cannot be certain at this time.[16]

In terms of the demographic bases of his support, there is some indication that he drew support from all social groups, if we can split enough hairs among the 19 percent who eventually supported him. Although his support varied widely throughout the campaign, there are some signs to suggest that a typical Perot supporter was likely to be a suburban or rural young white male. In this there *may* be some indication that Perot cost Bush votes, since recent Republican strategy had been targeted at younger voters, the presumed economic "beneficiaries" of the Reagan-Bush years. If this is the case, it may not bode well for the short-term future of the GOP, if they lost a base that had been carefully cultivated. For the most part, however, it seems that Clinton and Bush were harmed equally by the Perot candidacy in the end.[17]

Figure 7.1

Third-Party Votes Above 10% and Net Vote Losses for Incumbent Parties: 1900–1992

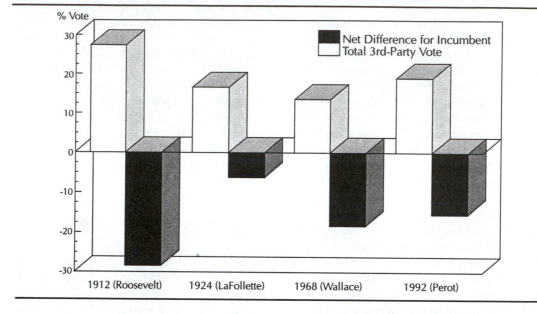

Impact on the Process

It is far too early to determine whether Perot will have any lasting impact on the political and electoral processes. There are many instances of proposed reforms having been offered in the past by established politicians. These have either been ignored, or enacted into law with substantial changes. Their ultimate success has hinged on a series of factors totally beyond the control of any politician, elected or otherwise.

> *"If the economy improves, Perot will be able to engage in the time-honored tradition of credit-claiming. And, if it falls short of any of his goals, particularly job creation, he can emerge again as a critic."*

There is only one thing that can be said with certainty, and for which Perot will doubtless claim credit. Since Perot brought the budget deficit and our crushing national debt forcefully to our attention, President Clinton and the Congress will have to address these problems with some alacrity. Whether or not the solutions they offer approach those suggested by Perot is essentially immaterial. What *is* important is that something be done about these problems, and soon. Related to this is the problem of a faltering economy. Whether or not one wants to believe President Bush that an upswing was already in progress by the time of the election, the effects of a drawn-out recession doubtless had a role to play in Bush's defeat, and in support for both Clinton and Perot. If the economy improves, Perot will be able to engage in the time-honored tradition of credit-claiming. And, if it falls short of any of his goals, particularly job creation, he can emerge again as a critic.

Will there be reforms of the electoral process? Perhaps, but these are seldom the kinds of issues that make or break a candidate, since most voters would not place them high on their wish lists. More likely is a series of reforms dealing with lobbying activities, especially by former government officials. As the Clinton transition was taking place, a premium was placed on tough new ethical standards for public servants, and Perot will likely claim credit for these as well. Doubtless, he will find that these efforts will be less than effective, and he will be able to maintain a critical posture on these and similar issues, as well.

Finally, recent events suggest that we can probably expect little by way of media reform. After having been excoriated throughout the campaign by Perot, television crews came close to hindering Navy Seals and U.S. Marines during a night landing on the beaches of Somalia. If such behavior by members of the media continues—and it will—Perot, along with others, will continue to criticize the electronic and print media. And the media will publicize the criticisms of themselves!

Perot's Future in Politics

Will Perot run again in 1996? At this stage, as throughout 1992, it is difficult enough to predict his intentions with any degree of certainty. Clearly, so much depends on how well President Clinton's administration addresses the problems of the economy, our budget deficits, and the national debt. Perot has indicated that he will continue to fund United We Stand, as a watchdog group. In Britain, the "loyal opposition" is often regarded as providing a "shadow government," ready to take the reins of office. For this to succeed in the public mind, United We Stand will have to develop a public perception of something more than a single maverick candidate. Whether or not this happens, Perot could have an organizational basis for one of his apparent favorite roles, that of critic-at-large. He may very well be aided in this by reports that he is being courted to host his own talk show, making of him the kind of media personality he has so often criticized.

If he does run again, there is some question as to whether or not he could gain any greater success than he's already shown as a third-party candidate. As discussed above, "dissident hero" candidacies lack a base other than those who are attracted in the short term by the image of the candidate. Previous efforts of this sort have not been revived, but there is nothing, including Perot's own vast wealth, that says that he must go with precedent. A significant body of opinion in the United States holds that we need a viable third party, and Perot could conceivably fund this effort over the next several elections.

Alternatively, consider the possibility if Perot were to enter the 1996 Republican primaries, as Wallace entered the Democratic contest in 1972. Operating within the party, he would not be restrained by the financial limitations other candidates face. If, as some believe, there will be a significant battle among the religious right, economic conservatives, and moderates of the GOP, to whom would he appeal? His willingness to accept abortion would alienate the religious right, who might be expected to divide their support between such candidates as Dan Quayle and Pat Buchanan, who are already making precampaign noises. The economic conservatives would most likely be attracted to such candidates as Jack Kemp and Phil Gramm, but Ross Perot could lay claim to a conservative position of his own. He could conceivably bring to the primaries the support of some of those who backed him in 1992. It is not an impossible scenario.

It does seem likely that Perot will not simply go away. His influence in 1992 was relatively minimal, other than serving as a critic and gadfly, and bringing some people out to vote who might otherwise have stayed away. As always, Perot is the only one who knows what he will do next; Americans will doubtless follow his moves with great interest, if not with the great support he once enjoyed.

Chapter Eight

The Congressional Races

John S. Jackson III

The year 1992 was a very bad one for Illinois' senior senator, Alan Dixon. In the March Illinois primary he lost his bid for a third term in the U.S. Senate to a young African-American woman, Carol Moseley Braun, who before that race was largely unknown outside Cook County, where she was Recorder of Deeds. In the preliminary campaign before the primary, Senator Dixon saw his record and reputation bashed repeatedly in television and newspaper advertisements by the third candidate in the race, Al Holfeld, a wealthy Chicago trial lawyer, who spent several million dollars of his personal fortune to try and unseat Senator Dixon.

While Dixon and Holfeld cut each other up in the very public bloodletting before the primary, Carol Moseley Braun was quietly benefiting from their high-profile quarrel. She won the Democratic primary with 38 percent compared to 35 percent for Dixon and 27 percent for Holfeld. Braun then went on to win the general election in November with a 55 percent to 45 percent victory over the Republican nominee, Rich Williamson. In January of 1993 Carol Moseley Braun took her seat in the U.S. Senate, becoming the first African-American woman to join the world's most exclusive club, a club which until the 1992 elections had been largely white and largely male throughout the 204-year history of the republic.

Carol Moseley Braun initially decided to enter the Illinois primary against Senator Dixon at the urging of friends and supporters who were upset with Senator Dixon's vote in the summer of 1991 in favor of ratifying President Bush's nomination of Clarence Thomas to be a United States Supreme Court justice. Various women's groups looked for candidates to run against those who had voted for Justice Thomas. Carol Moseley Braun decided to challenge Senator Dixon on the basis of that vote.

At the filing deadline in December 1991, Senator Dixon did not appear to be at all vulnerable. His first two Senate victories had been by very large statewide margins. In 1986 he beat Republican Judy Koehler by almost 1 million votes, gaining 65 percent of the total vote cast. He had been a statewide officeholder, both secretary of state and state treasurer for 10 years in Illinois before winning the U.S. Senate seat in 1980, in spite of the Reagan landslide. He had a record of 44 years in public office in Illinois, never having lost a single race since he ran for the first time at age 21. He was known as a middle-of-the-road moderate Democrat with a lifetime of friendships and IOUs built up in the regular Democratic Party in Cook County and in downstate Illinois, and who had many friends among the Republican establishment. In fact, the Republican Party had difficulty recruiting big-name Republican candidates to run against Senator Dixon in 1992, since few wanted to be a sacrificial lamb. That image of Dixon's invulnerability came crashing to the hard political earth in the March Democratic primary, when Alan Dixon became the only U.S. senator running for reelection in 1992 to be beaten in a primary. He was then joined in defeat by four other colleagues, two Democrats and two Republicans, who lost in the general election.

Dixon's startling upset defeat in the Illinois primary is emblematic of the subjective fear all members of Congress carry with them—an unwary vote, a series of bad decisions, and the result may be the loss of a job and career. The fears of defeat far outweigh the accolades of winning a reelection and enjoying the many political advantages an incumbent member of Congress may enjoy. And 1992 was not an ordinary year in congressional elections, just as it was not business as usual in the presidential race. Senator Carol Moseley Braun's unexpected victory in both the primary and the general

> **"1992 was not an ordinary year in congressional elections, just as it was not business as usual in the presidential race."**

election is indicative of the most notable trend in the 1992 congressional elections—the remarkable diversification of the Congress, which accelerated through a relatively high turnover rate that year. The 103rd Congress, which took office in January 1993, was the most demographically diverse Congress in American history. Senator Carol Moseley Braun was one of 124 new faces elected to the House and Senate in 1992. This chapter presents the twin themes of the historic advantages incumbents have enjoyed in seeking reelection to the U.S. Congress and the dramatic increase in diversity in the U.S. Congress produced by the 1992 election results. It also explores the very closely related term-limits movement that reached full flower at the state level in 1992. It concludes with an analysis of the public policy implications of the 1992 congressional elections coupled with Bill Clinton's victory.

INCUMBENTS AND TURNOVER

One of the well-documented generalizations in the legislative studies field is that incumbents who seek reelection have a high probability of success.[1] In addition, it is easy to demonstrate that incumbent legislators have a long list of advantages over challengers. Probably the most tangible and most crucial advantage is that incumbents almost always are able to raise more campaign funds than are challengers. While raising and spending the most money is not an absolute guarantee of victory, as the Carol Moseley Braun defeat of Alan Dixon in 1992 indicates, it is nevertheless true that there is a high correlation between spending the most money and winning.[2]

In addition, the incumbent has many other political advantages. The incumbent, by definition, has won at least one prior election to that office, and often it is many prior elections. Incumbent legislators have the advantage over their challengers of having name recognition by their constituents, and name identification alone is about half the battle, especially if the name identification is not accompanied by a negative image. Gary Jacobson summarized the equation in the following words:

> Incumbents are better liked—by a wide margin—as well as better known than are challengers. At any level of familiarity, voters are more inclined to mention something they like about the incumbent than about the challenger; negative responses are rather evenly divided, so the net benefit is clearly to the incumbent.[3]

The incumbent has the great advantage of having served the constituency, of bringing home the bacon in terms of federal projects and jobs in the state or district. In addition, the incumbent can act as a go-between with the federal bureaucracy. Doing casework, getting good things done for individual constituents, has become a major commitment for members and their staffs. The successful members are those who do the casework assiduously and who use those local contacts and favors as a part of their claims for reelection.[4] Careful casework is one of the reasons incumbent reelection rates are ordinarily so high, especially in the House.

Table 8.1 presents the incumbent reelection rates and the turnover for the U.S. House between 1946 and 1992. As is evident from this table, the reelection rate in the House ranged from a low of 88 percent in 1992 to a high of 98 percent achieved in both 1986 and 1988. In addition, 1990 was not far behind at 96 percent. In 1992 the 110 new members elected to the House is second only to the 118 new members who went to the House in 1948 and exceeded the post-Watergate shake-up of 92 new members in

Table 8.1

House Turnover, 1946–1992

Year	Retirements†	Defeated in Primary	Defeated in General Election	Total Turnover*
1946	32	18	57	107
1948	29	15	68	118
1950	29	6	32	73
1952	42	9	26	81
1954	24	6	22	56
1956	21	6	16	46
1958	33	3	37	79
1960	26	5	25	60
1962	24	12	22	68
1964	33	8	45	91
1966	22	8	41	73
1968	23	4	9	39
1970	29	10	12	56
1972	40	12	13	70
1974	43	8	40	92
1976	47	3	13	67
1978	49	5	19	77
1980	34	6	31	74
1982	40	10	29	81
1984	22	3	16	45
1986	38	2	6	50
1988	23	1	6	34
1990	27	1	15	45
1992	65	19	24	110

†Includes retirees and those running for other office
*Also includes open seats due to deaths and resignations

Source: Congressional Quarterly Weekly Report: Special Report, "The New Class: More Diverse, Less Lawyers, Younger" (Washington, DC: November 7, 1992), 23.

1974 and Lyndon B. Johnson's remarkable Great Society class of 1964. So 1992 was very hard on House incumbents when one considers those defeated in primaries (19), those defeated in the general election (24), and those who decided not to run or who ran for higher office (65)—at least some of whom were already politically wounded.

Undoubtedly, the House banking and post office scandals had something to do with setting this record. Several members of Congress decided not to run in the wake of having a long list of overdrafts on the House bank that were made public; others who were tainted lost in the primaries or the general election; and virtually every single incumbent found himself under attack for the sins of the Congress—both real and imagined.

The possibility that the House bank and post office scandals were a sort of last straw is supported by the fact that 1992 turnover rates in the Senate were not particularly high by histori-

cal standards. Political scientists have long pointed out that it is usually more difficult for incumbents to get reelected to the Senate than to the House.[5] The 89 percent reelected in the Senate in 1992 was actually reasonably high by historic standards, and the 97 percent reelected in 1990 (only one incumbent was defeated) was unprecedented. Generally the Senate reelection rates were in the 55–85 percent range during the 1970s and 1980s. In addition, more senators were elected below the 60 percent "safe seat" margin than was true in the House in those decades. (See also Figure 8.1 for House and Senate reelection rates from 1946 through 1992.)

There are many reasons for the greater competitiveness of the Senate seats. Senators, of course, represent an entire state, which is true for only seven House members from the very least populated states. This ordinarily means that senators represent a much larger and more heterogeneous population than any House mem-

Table 8.2

Senate Turnover, 1946–1992

Year	Retirements	Defeated in Primary	Defeated in General Election	Total Turnover
1946	9	6	7	22
1948	8	2	8	18
1950	4	5	5	14
1952	4	2	9	15
1954	6	2	6	14
1956	6	0	4	10
1958	6	0	10	16
1960	5	0	1	6
1962	4	1	5	10
1964	2	1	4	7
1966	3	3	1	7
1968	6	4	4	14
1970	4	1	6	11
1972	6	2	5	13
1974	7	2	2	11
1976	8	0	9	17
1978	10	3	7	20
1980	5	4	9	18
1982	3	0	2	5
1984	4	0	3	7
1986	6	0	7	13
1988	6	0	4	10
1990	3	0	1	4
1992	10	1	3	14

Source: Data compiled from Norman Ornstein, Thomas Mann, and Michael Malbin, *Vital Statistics on Congress: 1987–88, Congressional Quarterly,* 1987, and from *Congressional Quarterly Weekly Reports* for 1988, 1990, 1992, Washington, DC.

ber. The senators usually represent one or two big cities in many states, plus small cities, small towns, and rural populations. The average House member represents approximately 575,000 people, and those districts can be much more compact and homogeneous than the average state. Since a Senate seat is a higher-profile political office, it usually attracts an experienced and well-financed challenger. Neither party can afford to leave a Senate seat without opposition, while many House incumbents are practically or literally unchallenged. For all these reasons, the reversal of fortune in the 1992 House defeats of incumbents, coupled with their voluntary retirements, is unusual. In fact, if this trend were to continue, the House could once again become the more sensitive barometer of public opinion the Constitutional Framers intended it to be. It clearly has not been playing that role very directly in an era when well above 90 percent of incumbents were routinely reelected. The fact that House retirements and defeats for the in-

cumbents were substantially greater than those for the Senate may be the most important outcome of the 1992 congressional elections.

THE DEMOGRAPHIC DIVERSITY OF THE CONGRESS

Holding a seat in the U.S. House or Senate is by definition an elite position in society. There are only 100 senators and 435 voting members of the House, and those offices are highly coveted. Social science research has consistently demonstrated that historically the people elected to high-level political office in this country have been predominantly from upper-middle-class status.[6] While occasionally the offspring of clerks, laborers, and small farmers have found their way to success in the U.S. Congress, a working-class background has not usually been the norm for most members. The members themselves are usually upwardly mobile, with considerably more education and more personal income than the people they represent. In addition, up until recent elections the members of Congress have been overwhelmingly white and male.

That situation had been changing gradually in the decades of the 1970s and 1980s as more minorities and more women were elected to Congress. This trend toward diversity accelerated dramatically as a result of the 1992 elections.[7] Table 8.3 provides the overview of the demographic diversity attained in the U.S. Congress as a result of both the 1990 and 1992 elections.

> *"Holding a seat in the U.S. House or Senate is by definition an elite position in society."*

As is quite evident from Table 8.3, the one category with the greatest change was in the women members of the House and Senate. At least partially because of the backlash against the Clarence Thomas hearings, a record number of women ran for the House and Senate. This was the source of the Carol Moseley Braun candidacy introduced at the beginning of this chapter. In addition, as is evident from this table, the number of women elected to the Senate in 1992 was three times the number in 1990 (up from 2 to 6), and the number elected to the House almost doubled. In an election popularly dubbed "the year of the woman," these results represented real progress for the women in Congress; however, their 10.8 percent of the total House membership in the 103rd Congress still fell far short of their percentage (52 percent) of the total national population. Obviously, there are many criteria by which representative bodies can be judged as to how "representative" they actually are, and straightforward demographic representation is only one such standard. Nevertheless, it is a standard that has the virtue of simplicity, and it is the one most often adopted by advocates of various group interests.

By that demographic standard the number of African-American members in the House is where group representation comes nearest the

Figure 8.1

Incumbent Reelection Rates, 1946–1992

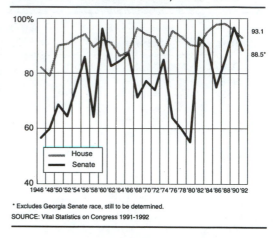

* Excludes Georgia Senate race, still to be determined.
SOURCE: Vital Statistics on Congress 1991-1992

Source: Dave Kaplan and Charles Mahteslan, "Election's Wave of Diversity Spares Many Incumbents," *Congressional Quarterly Weekly Report* (Washington, DC: November 7, 1992), p. 3576.

norm. There were 25 African-American members of the House (5.7 percent) after the 1990 elections and 38 voting members (8.7 percent) after the 1992 elections. Since African Americans make up approximately 12 percent of the total population, it is evident that they have come closest to this particular norm of demographic representation. On the other hand, Carol Moseley Braun in the Senate represents only 1 percent of the total, and she joins 5 other female members of the U.S. Senate. Also, the number of Latino members in the House increased from 11 to 17 in 1992. Latinos make up 8 percent of the U.S. population, and they constitute 3.9 percent of the House in the 103rd Congress.

None of this is intended to suggest that groups necessarily have inadequate representation if their demographic composition in the Congress is not an exact mirror of the total U.S. population.[8] It does suggest, however, that this symbolic normative goal also has some political substance. The more deeply committed and activist members of various women's and minority groups claim that their interests cannot be adequately represented by members of other groups. Thus, their drive has been to increase the representation of their groups in Congress, and the natural corollary is a decrease in the number and percentage of white males. This trend is clearly in evidence in the results from the 1992 elections; the 103rd Congress is the most diverse demographically in the nation's history. Women's

Table 8.3

Demographic Characteristics of Congress Resulting from the 1990 and 1992 Elections

Congress:		102nd	103rd
Women:	House	28	47
	Senate	2 [1]	6
African Americans:	House	25	38 [2]
	Senate	0	1
Latinos	House	11	17
	Senate	0	0
Native Americans	House	1	0
	Senate	0	1

[1] Refers to members elected in the 102nd Congress. Mrs. Quentin Burdick was appointed to the Senate from North Dakota to fill her late husband's unexpired term.
[2] Refers to voting members.

Sources: Various news reports and *Congressional Quarterly Weekly Report: Special Report* (Washington, DC: November 7, 1992), 7–10.

groups and other minority groups will try to ensure that this trend continues in subsequent elections.

The occupational backgrounds of the members of the 103rd Congress also became more diverse. Lawyers have always predominated as the number-one category in the U.S. Congress. This makes sense—Congress does make our laws, and lawyers are drawn from a "brokering" occupation, one which fits the skills needed in the legislative process. As can be seen in Table 8.4, lawyers are still the largest occupational category in the 103rd Congress at 239 members (almost half); however, this is down slightly from the 244 lawyers in the 102nd Congress and down dramatically from the 288 lawyers in the Watergate class of 1974. The second largest occupational category is business and banking, which is probably indicative of upper-middle- or least middle-class status. This is followed by "public service" at a total of 97, undoubtedly indicative of the career politicians who get elected to Congress. Education at number four is growing, and farming, with only 27 members, is declining.[9] Again, these results for the 103rd Congress, when linked to what is known from other studies of earlier Congresses, indicate an increasing diversity in the membership.

Bill Clinton promised that his first cabinet would look more like the American people than earlier cabinets had, and he took care to appoint more women and minorities than previous presidents had. The results of the 1992 elections indicate that the Congress has moved more in that same direction than any previous Congress. Whether they also mirror the basic values and policy preferences of the American people is more difficult to discern. However, if they do not mirror those values and preferences, the presumption of democratic theory is that the voters will throw them out in the next election. That threat to incumbents has not had a lot of objective weight behind it in election years when more than 90 percent of the House and Senate incumbents were reelected; however, the aggregate turnover rates in the 1992 elections show that the process can work that way. In addition, it only takes the defeat of one popular and well-entrenched incumbent like Alan Dixon to strike fear into the hearts of the other colleagues in the Congress. Indeed, many scholars maintain that it is the desire for reelection and this subjective fear of defeat, much more than the objective turnover data, which really provide for accountability in our legislative bodies.[10]

THE TERM-LIMITS MOVEMENT

Certainly one recent political phenomenon well designed to strike fear into the hearts of incumbents in Congress and the state legislatures is the *term-limits movement*. In 1990 three states passed some form of term limits, mostly aimed at their state legislatures; however, the referendum in Colorado also included the U.S. Congress. The new Colorado law was quickly

Table 8.4

Members' Occupations

	House			Senate			Congress
	Democrats	Republicans	Total	Democrats	Republicans	Total	Total
Acting/ Entertainment	0	1	1	0	0	0	1
Aeronautics	0	2	2	1	0	1	3
Agriculture	7	12	19	3	5	8	27
Business or Banking	56	75	131	12	12	24	155
Clergy	1	1	2	0	1	1	3
Education	45	20	66 †	6	5	11	77 †
Engineering	2	3	5	0	0	0	5
Homemaking	0	1	1	0	0	0	1
Journalism	11	12	24 †	7	2	9	33 †
Labor Officials	2	0	2	0	0	0	2
Law	122	59	181	33	25	58	239
Law Enforcement	8	2	10	0	0	0	10
Medicine	4	2	6	0	0	0	6
Military	0	0	0	0	1	1	1
Professional Sports	0	1	1	1	0	1	2
Public Service	51	36	87	8	2	10	97
Real Estate	9	17	26	2	3	5	31

*Statistics based on apparent winners as of Nov. 6, 1992.

*Because some members have more than one occupation, totals are higher than total membership.

†Includes Sanders, I-Vt.

Source: Congressional Quarterly Weekly Report: Special Report, "The New Class: More Diverse, Less Lawyers, Younger" (Washington, DC: November 7, 1992), p. 23.

challenged in federal court, since the Constitution provided that each House shall be the judge of the qualifications of its own members. Nevertheless, a major national campaign was launched

> "*[O]ne recent political phenomenon well designed to strike fear into the hearts of incumbents in Congress and the state legislatures is the* term-limits movement."

on behalf of the term-limits movement at both state and national levels. It was well funded by a variety of people who professed to be fed up with Congress, with the state legislatures, and

with "business as usual" in politics. It also took on partisan overtones as many Republicans latched onto this movement as providing hope for changing the Democratic majorities that had dominated most Congresses since the end of World War II. President Bush endorsed the movement in December 1990, and he and Vice President Dan Quayle campaigned heavily against the Congress in general and in favor of the term-limits movement in 1992. The public opinion polls showed that voters favored the idea by 2:1 margins.[11]

Indeed, as the data in Figure 8.2 indicate, support for term limits increased significantly between 1964 and 1990. There was one setback in 1991, when the voters in the state of Washington narrowly defeated a term-limits proposal.

The Washington congressional delegation, under the leadership of Speaker of the House Tom Foley, campaigned heavily against the proposition. In spite of that setback, by 1992 the term-limits movement was widespread, and it appeared to be an idea whose time had come

News Item: WOMEN'S POWDER ROOM INSTALLED IN SENATE CHAMBERS.

with the American people. It also probably reflected some of the same Populist spirit and anti-establishment backlash that fueled the Perot presidential campaign in 1992. A total of 14 states voted on some kind of term-limits provision in 1992, and it passed in every one. Those states were Arizona, Arkansas, California, Florida, Michigan, Missouri, Montana, Nebraska, North Dakota, Ohio, Oregon, South Dakota, Washington, and Wyoming. Most of these propositions limited senators to two terms, or 12 years, while House limits ranged from 6 to 12 years. For example, California voters adopted Proposition 164, which would limit House members to only three terms and Senate members to two terms.

The House and Senate results in Bill Clinton's home state of Arkansas are illustrative of all these somewhat anomalous trends in 1992. As President Bush repeatedly stressed in his attacks on Clinton in the presidential campaign, Arkansas is a small state. It has a population of 2.3 million people, giving it only four House seats. Going into the 1992 election, Arkansas was represented by three Democrats: Bill Alexander from the 1st District with 24 years of seniority, Beryl Anthony from the 4th District with 14 years of seniority, and Ray Thornton of the 2nd District with 8 years of seniority (having served two different districts in divided terms). The

fourth member was Republican John Paul Hammerschmidt from the 3rd District with 26 years of seniority. Both Anthony and Alexander were beaten by challengers in the Democratic primary. Alexander from the very rural and conservative Mississippi Delta of east Arkansas was defeated by a 32-year-old woman, Blanche Lambert, who had never before run for public office. In fact, her first experience in Washington was as a receptionist in Congressman Alexander's office. Lambert went on to win the general election as well. Anthony was defeated in the Democratic primary by the secretary of state of Arkansas, who, in turn, lost to a Republican, Jay Dickey, also a newcomer to public office, in the November election. Alexander had written 487 overdrafts and had other prior personal problems; however, Anthony had no such liabilities and had been a leader in Congress, having chaired the Democratic Congressional Campaign Committee from 1986 to 1990. Anthony was plagued by the general "throw the rascals out" syndrome, a vote in favor of the "Brady Bill" that brought down the wrath of the National Rifle Association in a rural, sportsman-oriented district, and a belated recognition of his electoral danger. In the 3rd District, Hammerschmidt, the 13-term veteran, was replaced by Tim Hutchinson, a young Republican state legislator. Ray Thornton in the 2nd District in

Figure 8.2

Support for Congressional Term Limits, 1964–1990

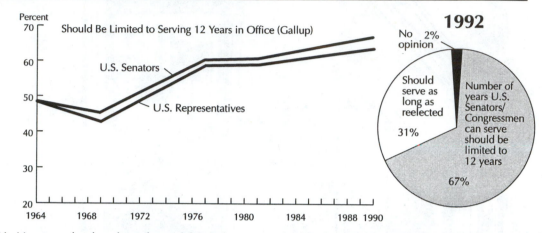

Limiting terms has long been favored, but today support for the idea is stronger than ever. In 1964, nearly half supported the idea; today nearly 7 in 10 do.

Source: Karlyn H. Keene and Everett Carll Ladd, eds., "How Different Groups View Congress Term Limits," *The American Enterprise* (Washington, DC: November/December, 1992), p. 89.

central Arkansas remained as the only surviving incumbent. In summary, in the year when Arkansas sent Bill Clinton to Washington, they also sent 3 freshmen out of 4 seats to Congress from a state that took pride in the seniority of its congressional delegation, and for the first time in history elected 2 Republicans to the 4-person House delegation.[12] In addition, Blanche Lambert became the only woman from Arkansas elected in her own right since Hattie Caraway was elected to the U.S. Senate in 1932.

On the Senate side the Democratic veteran Dale Bumpers was running for a fourth term. He was unchallenged in the Democratic primary and was faced in the general election by an articulate young Baptist minister, Republican Mike Huckabee. Huckabee had been president of the Arkansas Baptist State Convention, a position of some importance in a Bible Belt state, and he generally ran a competent campaign; however, he was swamped by Bumpers, who garnered over 60 percent of the vote in November.

At the same time, Arkansas voters were also passing a referendum to limit Senate and House terms to 12 years. This referendum passed by a wide margin. Obviously many Arkansans voted for their favorite senator, Dale Bumpers, while also voting to make it impossible for future electorates to have the same choice.[13] This somewhat anomalous result was duplicated in many of the 16 states which had approved the term-limits proposal in either 1990 or 1992. Academic research has demonstrated repeatedly that many voters do not exhibit a great deal of internal consistency, or "constraint" in their belief systems.[14] On the one hand, there are grounds for questioning the philosophical consistency that produced these split-ticket results, at least at the aggregate levels.

On the other hand, there may be some sense which can be made of this paradox. That is, it is well known that the voters display a very low level of approval for Congress *as an institution.* Indeed, as Figure 8.3 indicates, that level of disapproval reached record highs in 1990–92.[15] As we saw earlier, this high level of institutional disapproval was coupled with an even higher propensity to vote in favor of one's own member of Congress—especially in the House. Obviously, the individual and institutional calculuses were distinct. That distinction may have declined somewhat in 1992 as the incumbents found themselves in trouble with the voters and as the margins of even the victorious incumbents declined significantly.[16] In addition, 13 percent of those elected to the House in 1992 won by less than 52 percent of the vote, compared to only 2.7 of the House members elected in 1988. Only 58.3 percent of the House members in 1992 enjoyed 60 percent or greater

Figure 8.3

Congressional Job Approval Ratings: Individuals v. The Institution

Question: **Do you approve or disapprove of the way the U.S. Congress is handling its job? Do you approve or disapprove of the way the representative from your own congressional district is handling his or her job?**

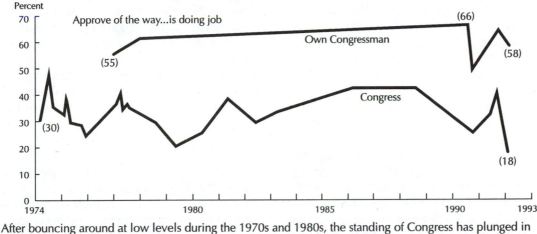

After bouncing around at low levels during the 1970s and 1980s, the standing of Congress has plunged in the 1990s. Individual members have always fared better than the institution.

Source: Karlyn H. Keene and Everett Carll Ladd, eds., "How Different Groups View Congress Term Limits," *The American Enterprise* (Washington, DC: November/December, 1992), p. 89.

margins, down from 84.6 percent in 1988.[17] These results may indicate that there has been a reappearance of the marginal districts once thought to have vanished.[18] The term-limits movement was undoubtedly viewed through the prism of the voters' evaluations of Congress *as an institution*, more than through the prism of their evaluations of their own incumbents. From this perspective the 1990 and 1992 results seem somewhat less anomalous.

PUBLIC POLICY IMPLICATIONS

The results of presidential and congressional elections are always mined carefully to see what predictions they can yield about the possible shape of public policy in the next administration. The results of the 1992 elections were particularly interesting because this was the first election since 1976 when one party would control both houses of Congress as well as the presidency. In addition, any time there is a change of administration and party control in the White House, there is a heightened sense of anticipation of new people, new policies, and renewed vigor in the executive branch. Bill Clinton's campaign, with its emphasis on the "time for a

change" theme and his victory for a new post–World War II generation of presidential leadership, certainly intensified the expectations for public policy change.

"[A]ny time there is a change of administration and party control in the White House, there is a heightened sense of anticipation of new people, new policies, and renewed vigor in the executive branch."

The question of what sort of public policy "mandate" is produced by the presidential results is always problematic, and 1992 was no exception. Critics such as Republican senator Robert Dole, the Senate Minority Leader, pointed out that Clinton had received only 43 percent of the popular vote. Clinton supporters retorted that many other presidents in this century, including Woodrow Wilson, Harry S. Truman, John F. Kennedy, and Richard M. Nixon, had received less than a majority, and a plurality outcome is almost guaranteed if there is a substantial third-party or independent candidate in the race. H. Ross Perot, who received 19 percent of the popular vote, ranked as second only to Theodore Roosevelt in the 1912 election as the strongest independent candidate of the twentieth century. Clinton supporters also retorted that 62 percent of the voters (Clinton's plus Perot's totals) voted for "the candidates of change" and against the status quo.

It is widely recognized that a candidate wins the American presidency by winning a majority of the electoral college vote rather than a majority of the popular votes. This means that a presidential candidate, to be successful, must concentrate on building a coalition of the states equal to 270 votes. By this standard, Bill Clinton did very well, since he got 370 electoral votes compared to 168 for George Bush. (Perot did not carry a single state, so he received no electoral votes.) In fact, the 1992 results show the electoral college working as it usually does, that is, a relatively close popular vote plurality is translated into a much larger electoral majority. Supporters of the electoral college contend that this electoral-college-majority enhancing effect adds to the legitimacy and political strength of the incoming president. Thus, the sizable electoral majority in 1992 could be interpreted as magnifying the Clinton mandate, and Clinton and his supporters stressed this interpretation.

The other aspect of any policy mandate results from the aggregate congressional election outcomes. By this standard, the most important fact was that the Democrats controlled a substantial majority in both Houses. They won 259 seats in the House, down from 268 in 1990–92, and 57 seats in the Senate, equal to their previous number. Like most political conflicts, these results are subject to two different partisan interpretations. The Republicans stressed that they had actually gained votes in the House (an increase of 9) in the face of a Clinton electoral landslide. The Democrats retorted that they still controlled close to a 100-vote majority in the House and a 14-vote majority in the Senate, in spite of its being a postredistricting year; this fact was originally expected to favor the Republicans because of their sunbelt and suburban population gains. Political calculations always color what-

ever spin the interpreters of congressional elections will place on the aggregate outcomes.

At the very minimum, one would have to conclude that the policy gridlock that had clogged the legislative and executive branches since the 1980 elections had been broken by the 1992 results. Under divided government there had been deep policy and ideological disagreements between the Republican presidents and the Democrat-controlled Congress. Although the empirical support for this proposition is mixed in the academic literature, it was often asserted in the popular press and by the politicians that divided government led to stalemate, to policy gridlock on big issues like the deficit, taxes, health care, industrial policy, and trade policy during the Reagan-Bush years. Indeed, both President Bush and Vice President Quayle campaigned vigorously against the "gridlocked Congress" and, of course, they advocated breaking the gridlock by electing a Republican president and a Republican majority in both houses of Congress. The voters partially followed their advice by putting both branches under the control of one party for the first time since the Carter administration. As Democratic senator Daniel Patrick Moynihan of New York exclaimed after the election, "It's our deficit now!" Others suggested that the Democratic Party no longer had any excuses for failing to address the country's major problems and that they would be held accountable in the next election. Although we do not really have responsible party government in the U.S., there was certainly a strong public expectation that the Democrats in Congress and the White House should begin addressing a backlog of accumulated problems. At the minimum, the possibilities of partisan buck-passing were reduced, and this put the onus on Congress to cooperate with the Clinton administration to show some positive results.

There was a near-consensus in the country over the nation's number-one public problem, and the voters and political elites agreed that "It's the Economy!" Public opinion polls consistently showed that consumer confidence was very low and fears of unemployment very high during the 1992 campaign. More than any other issue, this one was President Bush's political undoing. The Clinton team clearly recognized this fact throughout the campaign, and they shrewdly kept their message focused primarily on the economic and job themes throughout the fall. If there was a single-issue mandate in the Clinton victory, it had to be the injunction to do something to heal the economy.

Clinton was both lucky and unlucky in the aftermath of his victory. Very soon after the election a variety of both subjective and objective economic indicators improved—at least somewhat. The subjective indicators could be interpreted as a favorable reaction to the Clinton victory and an expression of confidence in him. The objective indicators, such as increased housing sales, somewhat reduced unemployment rates, and an upturn in third-quarter productivity, had been in the pipeline, and the president's supporters claimed them as the "Bush recovery."

It was against this somewhat uncertain backdrop that Clinton convened his economic summit or economic seminar in Little Rock in December 1992. Clinton faced the arguments of some in the press as well as political critics, who claimed that the economy did not need any short-term stimulus and only needed to be left alone. Clinton and his forces countered that the nation needed to concentrate on long-term and structural economic problems, regardless of the need for a short-term stimulus. While that was undoubtedly an accurate diagnosis, it still provided something of an uncertain trumpet on the economic front for the Clinton program in Congress during the crucial first days. Political scientist Elaine Kamarck of the Progressive Policy Institute, a long-time adviser to Bill Clinton, estimated that he would have, at the most, a six-month honeymoon period with the Congress and that it was very important to get his major legislative initiatives underway in that period.[19] Certainly that estimation squares with the experience of most recent presidents. It was clear during the transition period before Clinton took office that he planned to use his period of maximum leverage with Congress to good advantage in advancing his policy agenda. His advisers also urged him to keep the agenda relatively short and manageable.

Beyond the economy, it was evident that Clinton would also focus on a national health care plan. Indeed, it was interesting to note that he merged the national health care package into the larger economic recovery theme in his Little Rock Economic Summit. Also on the policy short list was Clinton's campaign proposal to create a national college loan program and to couple it with a national service corps option as

a way for students to repay their loans. That proposal was also consistent with his overall "investment in people" theme.

Naturally the members of Congress could be expected to have their own ideas about all these plans. They are elected from their more limited constituencies, and they have their own political calculations embedded in different electoral timetables. Nevertheless, at least the Democrats and some of the Republicans had been elected on the "time for a change" theme, with much emphasis on fixing the economy. In addition, many of these members of Congress also ran on pledges to do something about health-care costs. Indeed, it was the 1991 Pennsylvania election of Democratic senator Harris Wofford over Attorney General Richard L. Thornburgh that started the downslide of the Republicans in 1992. It seemed abundantly clear that legislators from both parties and a wide variety of interest groups expected to join the new Clinton administration in shaping some sort of national health care policy fairly early in Clinton's term.

There were many other potential issues on the public agenda; however, the short list for Clinton and the 103rd Congress certainly stressed long-term economic questions, deficit and tax policy, training programs, and health-care reform. Also, almost all of the new women candidates elected to Congress in 1992, and many of the men, had run on pro-choice platforms. This seemed to be one specific issue area where Clinton could expect very widespread support among the newcomers for his policy preferences. On pro-life and pro-choice, one of the most intractable political debates of two decades, the issue was finally devolving to one of waiting periods, parental consent, use of federal money, and other restrictions, and not to the fundamental question of legal abortions.

CONCLUSION

American presidential and congressional elections provide some fairly broad, but not detailed, policy mandates, some endorsement of symbolic direction, that is, either "stay the course," or "time for a change," and occasionally endorsement for specific policies such as the pro-choice position in 1992. Beyond that, what they provide is mostly a license for one set of political elites to control public power. These elites can be the well-entrenched incumbents in either the Congress or the presidency who get a license to continue, or they can include a large contingent of challengers and newcomers who get to take

> "*While high-level officeholders will always be political elites, . . . they may more and more come to reflect the tremendous and growing demographic diversification of America.*"

power. The 1992 elections featured more of the latter, with 124 new members of Congress and the new Clinton administration in the White House. These newcomers were not just more of the same in American politics. They were the most diverse lot of political leaders ever elected to high-level office in the nation's history. They included women, African Americans, and Latinos in unprecedented numbers in both the legislative and executive branches.

These new members of the House and Senate, along with the new faces in the Clinton administration, could be the vanguard in a sexual, racial, and ethnic sea change in American politics. While high-level officeholders will always be political elites, by definition, they may more and more come to reflect the tremendous and growing demographic diversification of America. Social scientists are already documenting the trends that will lead the schools and workplaces of the early twenty-first century to be the most racially, ethnically, and sexually diverse we have ever known in this country. The 1990 and 1992 elections seemed to accelerate those same trends in American politics. We may never see an era again when the political process and the high-level offices are so thoroughly dominated by white males as they were in the eighteenth, nineteenth, and twentieth centuries in the United States. Politics is about both continuity and change, but the emphasis was certainly on change in 1992.

Chapter Nine

Money and Its Role in the Election

Candice J. Nelson

The 1992 election was the most expensive in American history. More money was raised and spent by presidential and congressional candidates than ever before. Estimates are that close to $400 million was spent in the presidential election, and close to $500 million was spent to elect candidates to the House and Senate. Many more millions of dollars were spent by candidates for state and local offices, and on state ballot initiatives.

For all candidates, whether they are running for president of the United States or the city council, money is necessary to run a campaign. Money enables candidates to build a campaign organization, hire staff, and, most importantly, get the candidate's message, his or her reason for running, to the voters. In 1992 H. Ross Perot used money, his own money, to pay for a series of "infomercials" to tell potential supporters why he was running for president and what he saw as the problems with the United States economy. There were other third-party candidates who ran for president in 1992, but they lacked sufficient resources to become household words. How many people knew, much less remember, Lenora Fulani or John Hagelin?

The 1992 election was the most expensive race in history for several reasons. First, in the presidential election there was a third-party candidate who happened to be a billionaire and who was willing to spend "whatever it takes" to be elected president. Historically, third-party candidates have been underfunded compared to the major-party candidates.

Second, the congressional districts had been changed as a result of redistricting. The new districts meant many incumbents were running in districts at least partially unfamiliar to them, which meant incumbents spent more money to get their campaign message to their new constituents. Also, redistricting, coupled with the House bank scandal, in which 303 House incumbents were found to have overdrawn their checking accounts,[1] led 53 incumbents to retire, rather than seek an uncertain reelection outcome.[2] As a result, there was a larger than normal number of open-seat and competitive House races, and it is in competitive races that the most money is often spent.

Third, the amount of money spent in Senate races often depends on which states have seats up in any one election year; more money is spent in large states than in small states. In 1992 the two largest states, Texas and California, had, between them, three Senate seats being contested. Ross Perot's candidacy, congressional redistricting and scandal, and an expensive mix of contested Senate seats all contributed to the costs of the 1992 elections.

HISTORY

The campaign finance system under which presidential and congressional candidates ran for office in 1992 has only existed for the last two decades. Prior to 1972 candidates for federal offices could raise and spend unlimited amounts of money, and the sources of the money did not have to be reported. In fact, it was the excesses in fund-raising of the Committee to Reelect the President, or CREEP, President Richard M. Nixon's reelection committee, that led to the passage of the Federal Election Campaign Act of 1971.

The Federal Election Campaign Act of 1971, or FECA, and the Revenue Act of 1971, which accompanied it, were passed to remove large campaign contributions from presidential elections and to require disclosure of all campaign contributions. The FECA has been amended three times, in 1974, 1976, and 1979. The 1974 amendments established contribution limits for individuals, political action committees, and political parties in federal elections, established spending limits, and created the Federal Election Commission (FEC) to administer the law. In January of 1976 the Supreme Court, in *Buckley v. Valeo,* held that some parts of the 1974 law were unconstitutional. Congress subsequently passed the 1976 amendments to bring the FECA into compliance with the Supreme Court's decision. In 1979 the act was once again amended to allow large individual, corporate, and labor union contributions to be made to the political parties for certain party-building activities, such as voter registration and get-out-the-vote drives.

> **"The campaign finance system under which presidential and congressional candidates ran for office in 1992 has only existed for the last two decades."**

The Federal Election Campaign Act allowed us to know, for the first time, how much money was being raised and spent by candidates for federal office, as well as how much money was being contributed to candidates by special interests through political action committees. While the costs of presidential campaigns are somewhat controlled by public funding, the costs of congressional campaigns have risen dramatically over the last 20 years. Campaign spending in congressional general elections rose from $66 million in 1972 to $445 million in 1990.[3] Cam-

paign contributions to congressional candidates from political action committees rose from $8.5 million in 1972 to $105.6 million in 1990.[4]

CAMPAIGN FINANCE LAWS

The Federal Election Campaign Act of 1971 and the amendments to the Act in 1974, along with the Revenue Act of 1971, provided for public funding of presidential general elections and partial public funding for presidential candidates in the prenomination period. In order to qualify for public funds in the prenomination phase of the campaign, candidates for president must raise $5,000 in each of twenty states in amounts of $250 or less. Once candidates qualify for federal funds, contributions to their campaigns from individuals in amounts of $250 or less are "matched" with federal funds. Candidates who accept public funds must agree to accept a limit on both the overall amount of money they spend in the prenomination period and their spending in each state. In 1992 the overall spending limit for the prenomination period was $33.1 million, while the state spending limits ranged from $552,400 in the smallest states to $9.8 million in California.[5] In 1992, 11 candidates qualified for and received federal matching funds, including 2 third-party candidates, Lenora Fulani and John Hagelin. Fulani received $1.9 million in federal funds and Hagelin received $100,000.[6] Since 1976, when public funding first became available in presidential elections, only two candidates have not accepted public funds: John Connally in 1980 and Ross Perot in 1992.

Once the Democratic and Republican candidates receive their party's nomination, they are eligible for a federal grant for their general election campaigns. In 1992 President George Bush and William J. Clinton each received $55.24 million to run their general election campaigns.[7] In accepting public money for the general election, candidates must agree to spend no more than the amount of money they receive from the federal treasury, and they cannot accept any private contributions to their campaigns. In addition to the money given to candidates for the prenomination and general election campaigns, the Democratic and Republican parties each receive money from the federal treasury for their nominating conventions. In 1992 each party received a little over $11 million for their conventions.[8]

Unlike presidential elections, there is no public funding in congressional elections. The 1974 amendments to the FECA established both contribution and spending limits for congressional elections, but the Supreme Court, in *Buckley v. Valeo,* struck down spending limits unless they were accompanied by public funding, as in the presidential election. However, the Court did uphold the contribution limits. The limits apply to all candidates for federal office.

Individuals may contribute up to $1,000 per candidate per election, up to $20,000 to a national party committee, and up to $5,000 to any other political committee, such as a political action committee, but an individual's total political contributions in any calendar year may not exceed $25,000. Political action committees (PACs) may contribute up to $5,000 per candidate per election, but there is no limit on the total amount of money PACs may contribute to candidates. Party committees, such as the Democratic and Republican National Committees and the Democratic and Republican House and Senate campaign committees, may contribute money to candidates in two ways: through direct contributions and through indirect, or coordinated, contributions. House candidates may receive up to $10,000 from each of the three party committees, while Senate candidates may receive up to $17,500 from both the national committee and the Senate campaign committee, and another $10,000 from the House campaign committee. Coordinated contributions are expenditures made by the party committees on behalf of candidates, but they are not given directly to a candidate. For example, the party committee could pay for a poll for a candidate. The coordinated contribution limit for House candidates is $10,000, set in 1974, but indexed for inflation. In 1992 the amount party committees could spend on House candidates was $27,620, except in states with only one congressional district, where the limit was $55,240. For Senate candidates, the amount the party committees may spend on behalf of candidates is $.02 multiplied by the state's voting-age population, and then indexed for inflation, or $20,000, whichever is greater. In 1992 the coordinated expenditure limit was $55,240 for the smallest states and slightly over $1.2 million for California, the most populous state.[9]

In addition to the public funding provisions for presidential elections and contribution limits for congressional elections, there are a few other campaign finance law provisions that are particularly important. There is no limit on the amount of money a candidate can spend on his or her own election, unless, in a presidential election, the candidate accepts public funding. In 1988 Herbert Kohl spent $7 million in his successful run in Wisconsin for the United States Senate.[10] In 1992 Michael Huffington, running for Congress in California, spent over $4 million of his own money in his successful bid for a House seat.[11] However, the most dramatic example of a candidate's ability to spend his or her own money in a campaign was Ross Perot's unsuccessful 1992 presidential campaign, in which he spent almost $60 million of his own money.[12]

Another important provision of the campaign finance laws is that there is no limit on the amount of money individuals and groups can spend on independent expenditures. Independent expenditures are those made in support of or in opposition to a candidate, but no contact is permitted between the individual or group making the expenditure and the candidate or campaign. While few individuals make large independent expenditures, trade and professional associations such as the National Association of Realtors, the American Medical Association, and the Auto Dealers do use independent expenditures to try to influence the outcome of elections. In 1988 $21.1 million dollars was spent on independent expenditures, two-thirds of which was spent in the presidential election.[13]

Independent expenditures in 1988 were lower than in 1984, and the decline in independent expenditures continued in 1992. For example, the Auto Dealers and Drivers for Free Trade PAC spent $1.4 million on independent expenditures in 1988, $750,000 in 1990, and only about $100,000 in 1992.[14]

While federal election law prohibits corporations and labor unions from contributing corporate or union funds to candidates for federal office, there is no prohibition on organizations collecting voluntary contributions from individuals within the organization and giving those contributions to candidates or political parties in one package. This practice is called bundling, and was commonly used by some corporations during the 1992 election cycle.

Finally, perhaps the most interesting provision of the FECA for the 1992 elections is the provision enacted in 1979 to allow unrestricted contributions to party committees for party-

103

building activities. In addition to the $20,000 individuals can give to the party committees, individuals can also give unlimited amounts of money to the party committees for party-building activities, such as voter registration and get-out-the-vote activities. In states which allow political contributions from corporations and labor unions, corporate and union treasury funds also can be contributed to state party committees. These unrestricted contributions are called soft money, and they played a large role in the 1992 elections. Until 1992 soft money contributions did not have to be disclosed by the political parties, but FEC regulations enacted in January of 1992 required the party committees to disclose their large donations.

THE PRESIDENTIAL ELECTION: CANDIDATE FUND-RAISING

In 1992 11 candidates—7 Democrats, 2 Republicans, and 2 third-party candidates—qualified for federal matching funds during the primaries and caucuses. The 2 nominees, Bill Clinton and George Bush, received the largest amount of federal money, with Bill Clinton receiving slightly more than George Bush. Clinton received $12.5 million in federal matching funds for his prenomination campaign; George Bush

"The most interesting aspect of money in the presidential election was not the public money that was raised and spent by the candidates, but the private money . . . ."

received $10.1 million. Among the unsuccessful candidates for president, Patrick J. Buchanan and Edmund G. (Jerry) Brown, Jr., received the most money from the federal treasury: Buchanan received $4.6 million in federal matching funds and Brown received $4.2 million. The other 4 Democratic contenders fared far less well in their fund-raising. Thomas R. Harkin received just under $2 million in federal matching funds, Joseph R. (Bob)

Kerrey received just over $2 million, and Paul E. Tsongas received $2.9 million in federal matching funds, while both Larry Agran and L. Douglas Wilder received less than $300,000 in federal matching funds. Of the third-party candidates, Lenora Fulani received far more in federal money than did John Hagelin; Fulani received $1.9 million to Hagelin's $100,000.[15]

Party Fund-raising and Soft Money

The most interesting aspect of money in the presidential election was not the public money that was raised and spent by the candidates, but the private money, particularly the soft money, that was raised. Despite the fact that the Federal Election Campaign Act was passed to prevent wealthy individuals from making large campaign contributions to presidential and congressional candidates, large campaign contributions were the rule in the 1992 presidential election.

Both the Democratic and Republican Parties gave special recognition to wealthy contributors. Democrats who contributed $100,000 or more to the Democratic Party were called "trustees," and those who gave $200,000 or more were invited to be "managing trustees."[16] Individuals who gave the Republican Party $100,000 or more were invited to be members of "Team 100." Team 100 members received special briefings from high Bush administration officials, and some even traveled overseas with members of the Bush administration.[17]

Team 100 was started during the 1988 presidential campaign. In 1988 249 individuals and corporations gave at least $100,000 to the Republican Party; the number of Team 100 members was up slightly in 1992.[18] However, in October, as the election loomed closer, some members of Team 100 found reasons to also contribute to the Democratic Party. Edgar Bronfman, chairman of Joseph Seagram and Sons, had contributed $450,000 to the Republican Party during the 1992 election cycle, but both he and his son gave $100,000 to the Democratic Party in October.[19]

Similarly, corporations whose bundled contributions had heavily favored the Republican Party found themselves making October contributions to the Democratic Party as well. The Revlon Group, whose owner, Ronald Perelman, is a Team 100 member, contributed $120,000 in checks to the Democratic National

Committee in October, and Merrill Lynch and Co., whose president, William Schreyer, is also a Team 100 member, gave $50,000 to the Democratic Party in October. Prior to their October contributions, the Revlon Group had contributed $140,000 to the Republican Party during the 1992 election cycle and only $21,700 to the Democratic Party, while Merrill Lynch had contributed $377,000 to the Republican Party and only $47,300 to the Democrats.[20] It appears that as the election drew closer, and the election of a Democrat seemed likely, individuals and corporations who had previously supported the Republican Party decided to make contributions to the Democratic Party as well, in order to improve their access to a Democratic administration.

The record for soft-money contributions to a presidential campaign occurred during the prenomination phase of the campaign, when the Republican Party raised an estimated $9 million at a fund-raising event called The President's Dinner. Individual contributors gave as much as $400,000 to pose for pictures with the president or sit with a member of the cabinet, while corporations were encouraged to bundle as much as $1,500 in contributions from their employees.[21] The dinner proved an embarrassment for at least one contributor. Michael Kojima, a California businessman, contributed $500,000 to the Republican Party during the 1992 election cycle, even though his two ex-wives had thought he was bankrupt. The Republican Senate–House Dinner Committee and Kojima's ex-wives entered into a legal battle over who had claim to Kojima's contribution to the dinner.[22]

Following the 1988 presidential election, President Bush nominated 11 members of Team 100 to ambassadorships in his administration.[23] Managing trustees in the Clinton campaign may find themselves similarly rewarded. One of President Clinton's first cabinet-level appointees was Robert Rubin, cochairman of Goldman Sachs, a privately held investment banking firm. Rubin was nominated to be assistant to the president for economic policy and, as such, to head a new National Economic Council within the White House, modeled after the National Security Council.[24] Rubin raised millions of dollars for the Democratic Party Convention in 1992, and he and his partners helped to raise $4.2 million for a Democratic Party fund-raiser in September 1992. Goldman Sachs employees and their spouses contributed more money to the Clinton campaign than any other group in the country. About $100,000 was donated to the campaign, and estimates are that as much as $1 million was raised by Goldman Sachs's partners for the Democratic presidential ticket.[25]

A Comparison of Democratic and Republican Party Contributions

While the Republican Party exceeds the Democratic Party in the amount of federally limited funds or "hard money" they are able to raise and spend, the parties are much more on a par when it comes to raising soft money. In 1988 the Democratic Party raised $23 million in soft money; the Republican Party raised $22 million.[26] In 1992 both parties exceeded their 1988 soft-money totals. By mid-October the Democratic Party had raised approximately $31 million in soft money, and the Republican Party $47 million.[27]

The Republican Party raised more money than the Democratic Party in 1992, just as it did in previous election cycles. As of mid-October the Republican Party had raised $164.4 million in hard money, while the Democratic Party had raised $85 million.[28] However, the flow of money to the two parties' campaign committees shifted dramatically during the election cycle. In 1991 the Republican National Committee (RNC) raised over three times the amount of money that the Democratic National Committee (DNC) raised. That pattern continued during the first three months of 1992, and the RNC continued to have a slight fund-raising lead during the spring and early summer. However, from July until shortly before election day, DNC receipts exceeded those of the RNC by approximately $14 million.[29]

When hard- and soft-money contributions are combined, the Democratic Party's success in fund-raising in the late summer and fall is evident. In August the DNC raised $17 million, yet the RNC raised only $7 million, despite the fact that the Republican National Convention was in August, providing the party with fund-raising opportunities. In September the DNC raised $15.6 million, $11.2 million in hard money and $4.4 million in soft money, while the RNC raised $11 million, $9 million in hard money and $2 million in soft money.[30] Now that the Democrats control both the White House and the Congress, the Republican Party may find that it no longer enjoys a fund-raising advantage, and fund-raising parity between the two parties may well be achieved.

Ross Perot

If the full-scale return of large contributions to presidential elections was one story in the 1992 presidential elections, the other was the ability and willingness of a third-party candidate to spend millions of dollars of his own money, first to get on the ballot in all 50 states, and then to get 19 percent of the popular vote in the general election.

The last third-party candidate to make a serious bid for the presidency was John Anderson in 1980. Anderson raised $17.1 million, including $4.2 million in federal election funds, which he received after the election. Of the $17.1 million raised, Anderson had to spend $5.4 million, more than one-third of the campaign's revenue, on the costs of raising money and getting on the ballot in all 50 states.[31] In contrast, the two major-party candidates, Jimmy Carter and Ronald W. Reagan, each received $29.4 million from the federal treasury, almost twice what Anderson raised and almost three times what he actually had to spend on his campaign.[32]

In contrast to Anderson, Ross Perot spent almost $60 million of his own money on his election effort.[33] During the last week of the campaign, Ross Perot contributed $1.2 million to his campaign.[34] While total spending on behalf of the Clinton and Bush campaigns exceeded Perot's expenditures, Perot, unlike John Anderson in 1980, was able to spend more money on his presidential campaign than the two major-party candidates were allocated from the federal government for their general election campaigns.

"The biggest money story of the 1992 presidential election was the return of large contributions to American politics."

The biggest money story of the 1992 presidential election was the return of large contribu-

tions to American politics. Be it through soft-money contributions from individuals, corporations, or labor unions, or through wealthy, self-financed candidates for the presidency and Congress, the large contributions removed from American elections in 1974 returned full-blown in 1992.

THE CONGRESSIONAL ELECTIONS

Redistricting, retirements, and Senate elections in both New York and California combined to make 1992 the most expensive congressional elections in history. Eight Senators and 53 House members chose not to seek reelection.[35] When combined with the number of incumbents who lost in their primaries, chose to run for another office, or died in office, there were 96 open House seats in 1992.[36] Many House members who did run for reelection found themselves in competitive elections for the first time in years. Dan Rostenkowski, the Chairman of the House Ways and Means Committee, who comfortably won reelection in 1990 with 79 percent of the vote,[37] spent close to a million dollars in 1992 and barely squeaked through the primary with 57 percent of the vote.[38] Among the top 10 spenders going into the final weeks of the election were Richard A. Gephardt, the House Majority Leader, Newt Gingrich, the House Minority Whip, and Vic Fazio, chairman of the Democratic Congressional Campaign Committee.[39] In 1992 Gephardt spent twice what he did in 1990 to win reelection.

Spending by House and Senate general election candidates increased 25 percent over 1990 spending. When all congressional candidates, including those who lost in primaries, are included, spending increased 45 percent over 1990. Comparing spending in Senate elections from one election cycle to the next is not very useful because of differences in the states holding elections in each cycle. However, spending in House elections increased 39 percent over the 1990 election cycle.[40]

The average winning Senate candidate spent $2.7 million in 1992, while losing Senate candidates spent, on average, $1.5 million. The average winning candidate in House elections spent almost $402,000, whereas losing House candidates spent only about $140,000.[41] Michael Huffington's congressional race in the 22nd con-

Table 9.1

Average 1992 Campaign Expenditures by House and Senate Candidates (in thousands of dollars)

	Senate	House
Incumbents	$2,800	$428
Challengers	1,500	118
Open Seats	2,000	270

Source: Calculated from "FEC Finds Congressional Campaign Spending Up $75 Million as 1992 General Election Approaches," FEC press release, October 30, 1992.

Table 9.2

Congressional 1992 Campaign Spending by Party and Type of Race (in thousands of dollars)

	Senate	
	Democrats	Republicans
Incumbents	$2,060	$3,750
Challengers	2,190	920
Open Seats	2,040	2,040
	House	
	Democrats	Republicans
Incumbents	451	392
Challengers	101	129
Open Seats	305	234

Source: Calculated from "FEC Finds Congressional Campaign Spending Up $75 Million as 1992 General Elections Approaches," FEC press release, October 30, 1992.

gressional district was the most expensive House race. Huffington spent over $4 million, or about $37 per voter. In contrast, William Natcher spent only $6,600 in the 2nd district in Kentucky, about 5 cents per voter.[42]

In 1992, as in previous elections, incumbents had the fund-raising advantage. While not all incumbents outspent their opponents, many did. In 175 House races, of which 154 had an incumbent running for reelection, the winner outspent the loser by 10 to 1.[43] In 1990 only 6 incumbents spent more than $1 million; in 1992 almost three times that many spent over $1 million.[44]

Table 9.1 compares spending by House and Senate incumbents, challengers, and open-seat candidates. In both the House and Senate, the average expenditures of incumbents exceeded the average spending of both challengers and open-seat candidates. However, the differences among incumbent, challenger, and open-seat candidate spending are far greater for House candidates than for Senate candidates. Senate incumbents outspent challengers by almost two to one, and outspent open-seat candidates by almost one-third. In the House, incumbents spent almost four times as much money as challengers, and spent slightly more than 50 percent of what open-seat candidates spent. Senate incumbents spent, on average, $2.8 million, while Senate challengers spent on average $1.5 million, and Senate open-seat candidates spent on average $2 million. The average spending by a House incumbent was $426,000, compared to only $118,000 by House challengers and $270,000 by House open-seat candidates.

The disparity between spending of House incumbents and challengers has been growing steadily since 1984. In each election cycle since 1984, average incumbent expenditures have increased over the previous election, while average challenger expenditures have decreased.[45] However, what distinguishes 1992 from other election cycles is that average incumbent expenditures were greater than the average expenditures of open-seat candidates. Because of concerns over redistricting and fallout from the House bank scandal, incumbents in 1992 outspent both challengers and open-seat candidates. In contrast, the differences in expenditures among Senate incumbents, challengers, and open-seat candidates were similar in 1992 to differences in previous election cycles.

Table 9.2 looks at spending by House and Senate incumbents, challengers, and open-seat candidates, but also compares spending by Democrats and Republicans. Senate Democratic incumbents outspent their Republican challengers by an average of two to one. The average expenditure of Senate incumbents was $2.06 million, while Republican challengers spent on average $.9 million. Republican incumbents outspent their Democratic challengers by 60 percent. The average Senate Republican incumbent expenditure was $3.7 million, while the average Democratic Senate challenger spent almost $2.2 million. Spending by Senate Democratic and Republican open-seat candidates was virtually the same.

In the House, incumbents of both parties outspent challengers by approximately four to

107

one. The average expenditure by Democratic incumbents was $451,000, compared to $129,000 for Republican challengers. Republican incumbents spent on average $392,000, slightly less than Democratic incumbents, but Democratic challengers spent on average just over $100,000, less than Republican challengers. Democratic open-seat candidates outspent Republican open-seat candidates by about $70,000, with Democrats spending on average $305,000, compared to $234,000 for Republican open-seat candidates.

───────

"The most controversial source of funds for congressional candidates are political action committees, or PACs."

───────

Special Interests

The most controversial source of funds for congressional candidates are political action committees, or PACs. House candidates are more dependent on PAC contributions than are Senate candidates. In 1992 House incumbents received 47 percent of their campaign contributions from PACs, whereas Senate incumbents received 32 percent of their contributions from PACs. Challengers receive far less support from PACs; for House challengers in 1992, 15 percent of their campaign contributions came from PACs, while Senate challengers received just 12 percent of their campaign contributions from PACs. House open-seat candidates got one-fourth of their campaign contributions from PACs, while open-seat candidates in the Senate received almost one-fifth of their contributions from PACs.[46]

Table 9.3 compares the percent of their campaign contributions Democratic and Republican incumbents, challengers, and open-seat candidates in the House and Senate received from PACs. As Table 9.3 shows, Democrats are more dependent on PAC contributions than Republicans, and House Democrats are more dependent on PAC contributions than Senate Democrats. Over half of all contributions to

Table 9.3

Percentage of 1992 Campaign Contributions from PACs by Party and Type of Candidate

	Senate	
	Democrats	**Republicans**
Incumbents	38	27
Challengers	13	9
Open Seats	21	16
	House	
	Democrats	**Republicans**
Incumbents	52	39
Challengers	27	9
Open Seats	29	20

Source: Calculated from "FEC Finds Congressional Campaign Spending Up $75 Million as 1992 General Elections Approaches," FEC press release, October 30, 1992.

House Democratic incumbents came from PACs, whereas Senate Democratic incumbents received slightly more than one-third of their contributions from PACs. House Republican incumbents received almost 40 percent of their contributions from PACs, while Senate Republican incumbents received slightly more than one-quarter of their contributions from PACs. Democratic and Republican House and Senate challengers were the least likely recipients of PAC contributions. Both Republican House and Senate challengers received just under 10 percent of their contributions from PACs, while Democratic Senate challengers received 13 percent of their contributions from PACs, and Democratic House challengers received just over one-quarter of their contributions from PACs. Open seat candidates received less than one-third of their campaign contributions from PACs, irrespective of partisanship or office.

While Democratic congressional candidates were more often the recipients of PAC contributions than were Republicans, George Bush and the Republican Party received substantial support from special interest groups. A number of industries gave money to Democrats in Congress but also heavily supported George Bush and the Republican Party. For example, the securities industry supported congressional Democrats by two to one, but individuals with ties to the securities industry gave more money to George Bush than to Bill Clinton and collectively contributed $5 million to the Republican Party, but only $1.8 million to the Democratic

BY WASSERMAN FOR THE BOSTON GLOBE

Party.[47] The alcoholic beverage, waste management, air transport, crop production, electric utility, and health professional industries all gave 60 percent or more of their PAC money to Democrats in Congress, but more than two-thirds of the money contributed to political parties and presidential candidates went to the Republican Party and George Bush.[48] Some organizations were equally supportive of both Republicans and Democrats. Atlantic Richfield, Archer Daniels Midland, RJR Nabisco, Philip Morris, and the Tobacco Institute all gave at least $100,000 to Democrats and Republicans, and Atlantic Richfield gave both the Democratic and Republican National Committees $100,000 on the same day.[49]

The patterns of congressional campaign financing that existed during the 1980s continued in the 1992 elections. Incumbents were far better funded that challengers, and the gap between the two continued to widen. Special interests, through their political action committees, continued to be pragmatic in their giving. Forty-two percent of all contributions to incumbents were from PACs, while challengers received only 13 percent of their contributions from PACs.[50]

PROSPECTS FOR CAMPAIGN FINANCE REFORM

Campaign finance reform has been debated in each of the last three Congresses. In the 100th Congress a campaign finance bill was drafted by Senate Democrats, but a Republican filibuster, which a record eight cloture votes could not stop, prevented the bill from being debated on the Senate floor.[51] In the 101st Congress campaign finance bills passed both the House and Senate, but differences between the House and Senate bills were never resolved.[52] The campaign finance bill passed by the 102nd Congress was vetoed by President Bush, and Congress failed to override the veto.[53]

The campaign finance bill passed by Congress in 1992 would have established voluntary spending limits for House and Senate candidates, provided public funding for congressional candidates, further restricted the amount of money candidates could accept from PACs, and limited soft-money expenditures by party committees. The bill limited spending in House races to $600,000, with no more than $500,000 to be spent in the general election. The spending limit in Senate elections varied from $950,000 to $5.5 million in the general election, depending on a state's population, and candidates could spend up to two-thirds of the general election spending limit in the primaries. House candidates who agreed to spending limits could receive up to $200,000 in public matching funds, while Senate candidates who agreed to spending limits would receive government vouchers equal to 20 percent of the state spending limit to purchase television time. Senate candidates could accept no more than $2,500 from a PAC, while House candidates could accept no more than $5,000. Total PAC contributions to a House candidate could not exceed $200,000, while Senate candidates could accept no more than 20 percent of their general election spending limit from PACs.[54]

Some observers believe campaign finance reform passed the 102nd Congress because no one expected the bill to become law.[55] President Bush had promised to veto any campaign finance bill that contained spending limits or public funding.[56] However, President Clinton supports campaign finance reform, so drafters of campaign finance reform legislation in the 103rd Congress need to craft a bill that members of Congress can live with. If a campaign finance bill passes the 103rd Congress, there is every reason to believe it will become law.

CONCLUSIONS

Congressional redistricting, the House bank scandal, Senate races in California and Texas, and Ross Perot's presidential campaign all contributed to the most expensive election in American history. Wealthy contributors again participated in elections in record numbers, and special interests continued to pour millions of dollars into campaign and party coffers. The costs of campaigns, the role of PACs, and the soft-money "loophole" in campaign finance laws all led to demands for campaign finance reform in the last three Congresses. The same issues were again present in the 1992 elections. The question is how a new president and a new Congress will address those issues.

Chapter Ten

The Year of the Woman

Janet K. Boles

It really was the year of the woman in 1992—the year of the woman candidate, the woman voter, the woman contributor, and the women's agenda. It was also a year when gender-conscious voting appeared as a factor in several contests. And the wife of a presidential challenger received scrutiny from the media and voters that formerly was reserved for incumbent "first ladies."

Female political spin doctors, fearing that this year's media predictions of a major breakthrough for women in elected office were setting unrealistic expectations, emphasized that no single year is the year of the woman. Past experience justified such caution. Beginning in 1972, many election cycles had been touted as "the year of the woman." The first appearance of large numbers of female delegates at the presidential nominating conventions that year sent a positive message. In 1974, the Watergate scandal (and the lack of female involvement) served to make women candidates especially attractive. The vice-presidential candidacy of Geraldine Ferraro and the discovery of a "gender gap" in presidential voting marked 1984 as another year of the woman. And in 1990, eight women (including three incumbent members of the House) ran for the U.S. Senate, only to see the Gulf crisis increase the saliency of national defense and foreign policy, two areas in which women candidates traditionally are perceived as weaker than men. Only incumbent Nancy Kassebaum (R-Kan.) was elected that year.

The increase in female office-holding at all levels over the past three decades has been steady and incremental. From 1975 to 1992, the percentage of women serving in statewide elective office increased from 10 percent to 18 percent, including three current governors. Similarly, female representation in state legislatures increased from 8 percent to 18 percent. However, the pattern of national-level office-holding is not one of two-fold growth; instead, the glass ceiling metaphor is most appropriate. From 1975 to 1992, the percentage of women serving in the U.S. Congress barely increased, from 4 percent to 6 percent.[1] Figure 10.1 shows the gradual changes in the ratios of women and men officeholders over the last two decades.

There were, however, some indications that 1992 could be different. First of all, the combined impact of redistricting, retirements, and an anti-incumbency mood presented an opportunity to which women responded. A record 11 women received their party's nomination for the U.S. Senate; 106 women, up from the previous record of 69 in 1990, were nominated for the U.S. House, and 2,373 women won nomination for state legislatures, an increase of 309 over 1990.[2] The view of women as political outsiders and their sheer numbers on the ballot promised real change if enough could be elected. The end of the Cold War and the new interest in domestic issues had the potential to neutralize a perceived weakness of women in elected office, while maximizing their strengths on "people" issues.

Politically experienced women and women's groups had turned to electoral politics after the ratification campaign for the Equal Rights Amendment ended in failure in 1982. This had swelled the eligible pool of female candidates; the number of professional women with their own money to contribute to political campaigns had also increased. Renewed abortion rights activism and outrage over the Anita Hill–Clarence Thomas hearings were expected to help women candidates.

Figure 10.1

Percentage of Female and Male Officeholders

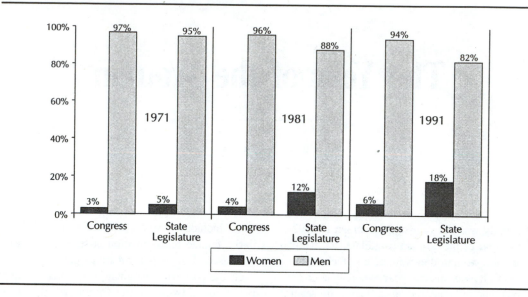

Source: Center for the American Woman and Politics (CAWP), Eagleton Institute of Politics, Rutgers University, New Brunswick, NJ.

On November 3, women in elected office scored at least a minor breakthrough. In the U.S. Senate, 5 women (with 1 incumbent, 6 percent of the body) were elected. Among them was Cook County official Carol Moseley Braun (D-Ill.), the first African-American female senator. Former representative Barbara Boxer and former San Francisco mayor Dianne Feinstein, both Democrats, made California the first state to be represented only by women. The 47 women who were chosen for the new House (11 percent) included 8 African Americans, 3 Latinas (and the first of Puerto Rican and Mexican-American heritages) and 1 Asian-Pacific woman. Virginia sent its first woman to Congress. A record 1,374 women won seats in state legislatures (with holdovers, 20 percent). Twenty-one women were elected to statewide offices (with holdovers, 22 percent), although none of the 3 women running for governor won.[3]

THE ANITA HILL FACTOR

The year of the woman really began on October 11, 1991, with the reopening of nationally televised confirmation hearings on the nomination of Clarence Thomas to the U.S. Supreme Court. For three days the all-male Senate Judiciary

Committee heard testimony concerning allegations of sexual harassment brought by University of Oklahoma law professor Anita Hill against Judge Thomas. The committee sharply questioned the credibility of Professor Hill without reaching a conclusion about whether her charges were true. On October 16, the Senate voted, 52–48, to confirm.

"The year of the woman really began on October 11, 1991, with the reopening of nationally televised confirmation hearings on the nomination of Clarence Thomas to the U.S. Supreme Court."

Over the course of the next year, public opinion on the relative truthfulness of Hill and Thomas underwent a complete reversal. Whereas polls taken immediately after the hearings showed those who believed Thomas outnumbered those believing Hill, 2 to 1 or even 3 to 1, those taken 12 months later found that Hill's version of events was either equally accepted or was believed by margins of 10 percentage points.[4]

This same period included the two highly publicized rape trials of William Kennedy Smith and boxer Mike Tyson and the Navy Tailhook sexual harassment scandal. Accusations of sexual assault and harassment were also brought against Senators Brock Adams (D-Wash.) and Daniel Inouye (D-Hawaii) by women citing incidents dating back to the 1970s, a lag in reporting that exceeded that of Anita Hill. Furthermore, Thomas proved to be far more conservative on the bench than some of his supporters had expected. In *Planned Parenthood v. Casey* (1992), he aligned himself with the bloc seeking to overturn *Roe v. Wade* (1973).

The Women's Campaign Fund, in a direct mailing, described the Hill-Thomas hearings as a "sickening spectacle" and urged contributions with the statement, "This one's for Anita." Unlike male candidates in 1992, female candidates were very successful with direct mail appeals; Anita Hill served as a rallying figure for female donors.

Several women cited the hearings as a factor in their decision to run for the U.S. Senate. Boxer, a leader in the march of seven congresswomen up the great steps of the Senate to demand that Anita Hill's charges be investigated, only to be denied entrance as "a stranger," vowed to "open the doors" of the Senate to women. In her last television ad, Lynn Yeakel, the challenger of Hill's interrogator Arlen Specter (R-Penn.), recounted a number of his "wrong" (economic) votes, then concluded: "But in the end, he'll only be remembered for one thing."

The picture of that all-male committee was a dramatic image and certainly brought wide awareness of the underrepresentation of women. As Dianne Feinstein put it: "Two percent may be o.k. for milk, but it isn't for the U.S. Senate."[5] However, it is difficult to determine what impact, if any, the hearings had on voters' decisions. Exit polls in the Illinois Democratic primary showed that Braun beat Senator Alan Dixon 6 to 1 among white suburban women dissatisfied with his vote to confirm Thomas, enough to cost him renomination. Likewise, those in Illinois, Pennsylvania, and California opposing Thomas's confirmation overwhelmingly (by margins of 65 to 71 percent) supported Democratic female candidates in the general

election. But without some measure of the relationship between Democratic Party identification and opposition to Thomas, these figures should be cautiously interpreted.

WOMEN'S ISSUES IN THE ELECTION

From the first polls measuring the issues of greatest concern to the 1992 electorate to the exit polls taken on November 3, the distinctive concerns of women were dominant. These included women's rights issues such as abortion and policies dealing with women's traditional areas of interest, such as health care, children and the family, education, unemployment, and the environment. As Dianne Feinstein observed: "The women's agenda is the agenda of the nation. Who knows families better than women?"[6]

Family Values

At one point in the Democratic National Convention, convention chair Ann Richards introduced Senator Barbara Mikulski (D-Md.) to present six female Senate candidates for brief remarks. At the same point in the Republican Convention, Patrick J. Buchanan attacked the impact of radical feminism on the Democratic Party. Although Barbara Bush, wife of the president, tried to be inclusive in her address in her definition of family, the message from the Republican Convention was very different in a nation where only 20 percent of labor-force-age families consist of a breadwinner and a full-time homemaker.

Over 68 percent of voters agreed that political candidates should talk about family values, and by September the Democratic Party was viewed as slightly better (34 percent) than the Republicans (32 percent) at upholding traditional family values.[7] According to exit polls, however, "family values" was the second most important issue (behind jobs and the economy) for Bush voters. Bush was supported by 65 percent of those mentioning "family values."

Abortion

Early in the campaign, Democratic focus groups indicated that women's issues were breaking the party's way; in particular, pro-choice voters had become *the* single-issue voters. Until the Court's *Webster* decision in 1989 gave the states new authority to restrict abortion, the sizes of the "pro-choice" (abortion should be legal in all cases) and the "pro-life" (illegal in all cases) groups differed only slightly. After the decision, the percentage of those holding a pro-choice stance expanded to twice that of the pro-life sector. In the November exit polls, pro-choice Americans exceeded their pro-life counterparts, 34 percent to 8 percent.[8]

The 1992 party platforms reaffirmed long-standing positions (Democrats, pro-choice; Republicans, pro-life). However, a poll taken in June seemed to indicate that rank-and-file party members might be lining up in a different direction. Republicans were strongly supportive of the pro-choice movement (63 percent to 29 percent), while Democrats were split 50 percent (pro-choice) to 43 percent (pro-life).[9]

Democrat Bill Clinton framed his stance as pro-choice, but with exceptions for parental notification and a ban on some government funding. Pro-life George Bush, too, appeared to move, with Vice President Dan Quayle, toward a more moderate position when both said they would support female relatives in their choice of an abortion. Barbara Bush was even clearer, saying that abortion is a personal choice and should not appear in party platforms.

In the general election, the pro-choice movement was, on balance, victorious. Maryland voters, 62 percent to 38 percent, enacted *Roe* into state law; Arizona defeated, 69 percent to 31 percent, a referendum prohibiting most abortions. Fifteen to 20 more pro-choice votes were picked up in a House already pro-choice by a small majority; 1 vote was lost in the Senate, leaving some 59 pro-choice senators, depending on the issue. But once again, single-issue voting appeared to favor the pro-life presidential candidate. In November exit polls, 13 percent of voters mentioned abortion as a salient issue; of these, 54 percent supported Bush, with Clinton attracting 38 percent and Perot, 8 percent.

THE HILLARY FACTOR

The woman candidate who received the greatest media coverage in 1992 appeared on no ballot. Hillary Rodham Clinton, as wife of the Democratic candidate, was in the running for a posi-

tion that produced four of the nation's ten most admired women in the world, according to a 1991 poll, including the top-ranked Barbara Bush, a popular symbol of the traditional woman.[10]

"In a nation still uncertain about role change for women, 'the Hillary factor' tapped into a deep cultural division."

Hillary Clinton promised to be a very different role model for the nation. Not only would she be the first college graduate since Pat Nixon, she was also a nationally acclaimed practicing attorney, who had always been her husband's policy-partner. In a nation still uncertain about role change for women, "the Hillary factor" tapped into a deep cultural division. There were few aspects of Hillary Clinton's life that escaped criticism. She was portrayed as the over-doting yuppie mother of an only child (in contrast to Mrs. Bush, mother of six); a radical feminist ("I suppose I could have stayed home and baked cookies"); a careerist of dubious ethics; and a power-hungry spouse ("I'm not some little woman standing by her man") that one critic dubbed "the Winnie Mandela of American politics."[11] Her scholarly writings and speeches on children's rights, some dating back to 1973, were analyzed by the political right.[12]

After post-convention polls showed a backlash against Hillary-bashing, the Republican campaign announced that it would discourage further attacks. But what could not be ignored was that Democratic focus groups in the spring believed that Hillary Clinton was "running the show." Candidates have been "handled," at least since the selling of Richard Nixon in 1968; likewise, Hillary Clinton's role in the campaign underwent changes. She was now presented as the wife of the candidate and a good mother, with a special interest in children. Daughter Chelsea became more visible. *Family Circle* magazine invited the wives of the two major-

BY BORGMAN FOR THE CINCINNATI ENQUIRER

party candidates to submit chocolate-chip-cookie recipes for readers to rank by ballot. Hillary Clinton cheerfully distributed bags of her cookies, urged a vote for her recipe, and won the contest. Her black velvet headband gave way to a softer hairstyle, her business suits to soft pastels. Media interviews were restricted, and "my husband" and "he" replaced "us" and "we" in her statements.[13]

The perceived "silencing" of Hillary Clinton resonated with professional women who, like her, had learned to suppress their thoughts in the workplace. For others, it was probably reassuring that the old rules about presidents' wives had been restored. Opinion polls indicated that the public was both inattentive (by July, only 2 percent could recall her controversial statements and between one-half and one-third had no opinion of her, favorable or unfavorable, throughout the campaign) and open to a First Lady who continued to practice law. The critical comments, like negative campaigning generally, did progressively reduce her "favorable impressions" in Gallup polls in March (65 percent), July (55 percent), and December (49 percent).[14] But did she lose votes for Bill Clinton? In an election in which vice-presidential candidates rarely have a measurable impact, not to mention candidates' wives, the answer is almost certainly no.

WOMEN CANDIDATES AND THEIR CAMPAIGNS

As in all competitions, "the year of the woman" was actually the year of many women's campaigns, each with unique strengths and problems. The gender of the candidate was only one characteristic shaping each contest.

Running as an Outsider

In a year in which voters were disgusted with congressional perks, pay raises, and policy gridlock, women candidates, as outsiders, were expected to be especially attractive. A *Times-Mirror* poll taken in December 1991 found that 77 percent of those surveyed agreed that it was "time for politicians to step aside and make room for new leaders," up from 62 percent in 1987.[15]

Many women explicitly ran as "outsiders" who understood the concerns of average working people. Carol Moseley Braun filmed a spot ad from her kitchen counter; state senator Patty Murray of Washington ran as "just a mom in tennis shoes." Women's fundraiser Lynn Yeakel's ads boasted of her "proven record of helping people that all the politicians can only

115

dream about" and asked, "Where does it say that our senators have to be career politicians like Arlen Specter?" The "outsider" label has its downside as well; terms such as "novice," "inexperienced," "political unknown," "naive," and "ill-informed" were used by the press and opponents to describe all three women. Murray saw a poll lead of 24 percentage points in October fall to 5 points shortly before the election when her opponent, five-term representative Rod Chandler (R-Wash.), called her a political novice who wouldn't be able to protect the state's industries from coming defense cuts.

Although female incumbents also benefit from a general perception that women are more honest, Representatives Barbara Boxer and Mary Rose Oakar (D-Ohio) were portrayed as "insiders" who abused the perks of office (including 143 and 213 overdrafts, respectively, at the House bank). Of 27 congresswomen who sought reelection to the House, 1 was defeated in the primary and 3, including Oakar, lost in the general election. Interestingly, this was the same number of female challengers who defeated male incumbents in the primary (2) and general election (2). Female incumbents actually had a somewhat lower rate of reelection to the House (85 percent) than did men (89 percent).

The use of the "outsider" label did not always refer to challenger versus incumbent. Most women ran as "outsiders," agents of change with the ability to "shake things up." In most cases, their ability was demonstrated in previous elective office or in other public positions. Of the women who ran for Congress in November, two-thirds had run for office before, and over half had held office. State legislatures continue to serve as the primary proving grounds for congresswomen. Eleven of the 24 women new to the House are former state legislators. Others had served in local legislative office (6), in another elected or appointed position in a public bureaucracy (4), or as a state party official (1). Peace activist Elizabeth Furse (D-Oreg.) and former television reporter (and wife of a former House member) Marjorie Margolies-Mezvinsky (D-Penn.) best fit the "outsider" label.[16]

Women's Issues

Past studies have indicated that only rarely are women's issues emphasized or even addressed by female candidates, for fear they will be perceived as concerned solely with the interests of women.[17] This was not true in 1992. Female candidates appealed directly to other women by running ads on afternoon television and campaigning in grocery stores and women-dominated workplaces like hospitals. Men, when facing a female opponent, sometimes adjusted their positions on work and family issues.

"[E]very new congresswoman elected in 1992 was pro-choice."

Dianne Feinstein, who in past campaigns had deemphasized gender, ran TV commercials about breast cancer, rape, and family leave. Patty Murray stressed workplace equity and family leave. Women's issues were discussed more often than civil rights in Braun's campaign. Only Lynn Yeakel was labeled a "single-issue" candidate "running as a woman." Yet her primary opponent, Lieutenant Governor Mark S. Singel, began his campaign by changing his long-held anti-abortion position (as did Braun's Republican opponent, Richard Williamson), and Senator Specter stressed his own strong record in support of abortion rights, child care, and women's health research. One of Boxer's ads showed her Republican opponent, Bruce Herschensohn, on film, stating, "What I want is the repeal of *Roe v. Wade*." More significantly, every new congresswoman elected in 1992 was pro-choice. These issues worked for women candidates (and for men, too).

Media Coverage

One study of news media coverage of Senate races, 1982–1986, found that more negative information was provided about women's campaign organizations and their viability than about men's.[18] Once again, at least in regard to the most highly publicized of the 11 Senate races involving women, this does not appear to hold true of the 1992 election. It was the opponents of Boxer, Braun, and Feinstein (Senator John Seymour) who were presented as weak and unimpressive campaigners. The two California women, in contrast, were described as brilliant strategists, good sound-bite stump speakers, and impressive fund-raisers. The campaign miscues of Braun, Yeakel, and Murray were noted, but the positive side of each campaign was also covered.

As for the six women whose campaigns were largely ignored by the national media, two were in the most lopsided races of the election: Mikulski's 71 percent to 29 percent victory over Alan Keyes, and the defeat of state senator Jean Lloyd-Jones, 72 percent to 28 percent, to incumbent Charles Grassley (R-Iowa). Three of the remaining four challengers had no history of office-holding: Gloria O'Dell ran after more than a dozen Democrats had declined to face Robert Dole (R-Kan.); the challenger to Tom Daschle (D-S.D.), Charlene Haar, as a pro-business, pro-life, pro–gun ownership Republican, did not fit "the year of the woman" script. Only St. Louis County councilwoman Geri Rothman-Serot may have been hurt by media underestimation of her campaign, described as plagued by low name recognition, funding problems, and lack of energy. Yet Kit Bond (R-Mo.) was only reelected by a margin of 54 percent to 46 percent, slightly below that of John Glenn (D-Ohio), whose vulnerability was reported.

Negative Advertising

Other bits of conventional wisdom were challenged. One is that women, as nurturers, should not engage in harshly negative advertising. Another is that "going negative" against a female opponent may backfire if the public becomes protective. Negative advertising in 1992 flew in both directions in congressional campaigns involving women. Even Arlen Specter, long-restrained by fears of reminding voters of Anita Hill, attacked Yeakel in the closing debates.

Some attacks were bizarre; Boxer's very conservative bachelor opponent, for example, was said to frequent a nude bar. Most of the charges were more conventional: racist and anti-Semitic ties (used against Yeakel and Braun); failure to pay city taxes (Yeakel); organized crime or gang connections (Braun and Geraldine Ferraro in the New York Senate primary); and abuse of office (Boxer and Braun).

There is little evidence that women were punished for using negative advertising, but it was often quite effective when directed against

women. Heavily favored Ferraro lost the Senate nomination by 11,254 votes, out of over 1.15 million cast. Charges of ethical and financial abuses took longer to penetrate, but voters may have been harsher toward Boxer, Yeakel, and Braun for failing to live up to higher standards. Although Braun received 53 percent of the vote, exit polls showed that 56 percent of voters (including close to one-third of her own supporters) doubted her honesty.[19]

THE ROLE OF WOMEN'S PACs

This was also "the year of women and their money." Research had already begun to dispel the myth that female candidates are greatly disadvantaged in fund-raising.[20] But press coverage in 1992 often gave the impression that women are now favored by political donors. Barbara Boxer raised more money in 1991–1992 than any other Senate candidate in the nation. The Federal Election Commission (FEC) found that for the first 15 months of the election cycle, 42 of the 47 female winners of House seats raised more money than their opponents.[21] But an analysis of FEC records through July 15 for the campaigns of Yeakel (challenger), Braun (open seat), and Mikulski (incumbent) concluded that: (1) women candidates, particularly challengers, are dependent on women donors; (2) women candidates are far more dependent upon small contributions than men; and (3) women candidates receive donations from men only as the odds of their election rise to near-certainty.[22]

The Democratic Senatorial Campaign Committee, finding that women candidates drew well in direct-mail appeals (particularly among first-time donors), created a fund in 1992 to allow donors to target women candidates. However, the so-called women's PACs, formed to promote female office-holding and women's issues, play the major role in tapping this source. Most experienced rapid growth in the wake of the Hill-Thomas hearings, at a minimum doubling the level of contributions raised in the last election. Among them:

- *ANA-PAC* (the American Nursing Association) contributed $330,000, over half to women candidates.
- *EMILY's List* (Early Money Is Like Yeast), described by television's "60 Minutes" as the most effective PAC in the country (and the largest congressional

117

PAC this year), is more properly "a donor network." Its 22,000 donors (10 percent men) contribute directly to the campaigns of Democratic women endorsed by the group, but send their checks to EMILY's List for "bundling" (thus avoiding limitations on PAC contributions). In 1992, $6 million was raised, a four-fold increase over 1990.

- *Hollywood Women's Political Committee* is a PAC and fundraiser for liberal candidates and issues, with a priority on women and federal office. Total contributions to women in 1992 were $543,671.
- *Leader PAC,* a new PAC for Republican women on both sides of the abortion issue, raised $100,000.
- *NARAL-PAC* (National Abortion Rights Action League) expected to contribute $3 to 4 million (triple that of 1990) to pro-choice candidates at all levels of government.
- *NOW-PAC* (National Organization for Women) and its state chapters raised $593,845.
- *NWPC-PAC* (National Women's Political Caucus) and its state affiliates quadrupled their donations to $500,000, evenly divided between federal and state/local candidates. The caucus also holds hundreds of training sessions annually, and in 1991–92 reached over a thousand women candidates.
- *WISH List* (Women in the Senate and House) is a donor network for pro-choice Republican women. It contributed approximately $250,000 to gubernatorial and House candidates.
- *Women's Campaign Fund* (WCF), the oldest women's PAC, raised $1.3 million, more than double its 1990 total.[23]

Winning the support of women's PACs is a requirement for female candidates, but each PAC has certain rules regarding partisan membership, policy stances, office sought, and viability. Although few PACs are restricted to members of one party, by virtue of their positions on screening issues (primarily abortion, but also the ERA, child care, family leave), more Democratic women are endorsed. Republican women are especially disadvantaged: if pro-choice, they must often forgo party funding; if pro-life, only the small Leader PAC is available to them as women. EMILY's List is most selective, focusing on federal office and governorships; the WCF is most inclusive and supports women seeking many types of office (including mayoral and county board positions).

One divisive issue among women's groups involves the use of electability in funding decisions. EMILY's List, WISH List, NWPC and WCF officially use this standard. NOW and the Fund for the Feminist Majority, a non-PAC group that recruits and endorses candidates, support "flooding the ticket" with numerous women candidates on the ground that winners cannot be predicted. The polling data and written strategy required by EMILY's List to gain consideration was estimated by one House candidate to cost $50,000. The feeling among some candidates and their managers is that women's PACs have become too exclusive in their endorsements and are much tougher to crack than men's networks. Yet an examination of congressional endorsements made by early fall, 1992, revealed only minor group differences. Leader PAC backed every Republican woman. The two partisan donor networks only rarely endorsed incumbents. The numbers of House candidates supported by WCF (50), NOW (55), and NWPC (68) were similar. And, with the exception of Leader PAC, each group's win-loss record in the House ranged between 50 percent (WISH List) and 68 percent (WCF).[24]

THE GENDER GAP AND GENDERCENTRIC VOTING

Exit polls showed moderate but consistent gender gaps in voting in all three presidential elections held during the 1980s. In each of these elections, 6 to 9 percent more women than men voted for the Democratic candidate. In 1992, that pattern remained intact, with 46 percent of women supporting Clinton, compared with 41 percent of men.[25] Clinton, who embraced such issues as child care, family leave, and abortion rights, often adopted women's own distinctive voice, based in relationships and caring. His memory of confronting an abusive stepfather no doubt resonated with many women.

More interesting is how the gender gap affected other races, in that, since 1982, the gap has been larger in subpresidential-level voting and has been responsible for the election of numerous senators and governors. The impact of the gender gap in congressional elections was the source of much speculation in 1992 because of the importance of the issues (that is, the environment, health care, unemployment, and some women's issues) on which former gender gaps had been based, and the particular appeal of women in elected office.

"A U.S. News & World Report poll found that 61 percent of those surveyed thought the country would be 'governed better' if more women held political office."

A Different and Better Voice

A *U.S. News & World Report* poll found that 61 percent of those surveyed thought the country would be "governed better" if more women held political office. In 1984, 28 percent had agreed.[26] In the Women's Voices Project poll, nearly three-quarters of women felt the country would be better off if *half* the leadership were women; men, too, agreed by a small majority.[27]

However, opinion polls on voter perceptions of male and female candidates and officials confirm that gender is linked with both strengths and weaknesses. In 1972, the public believed male officeholders were better on matters of foreign policy, defense, managing the economy, and dealing with civil disorder; women were favored on issues of education, health, social welfare, and children. By 1991, voters still preferred women on abortion, health care, education, and children's issues. Women continued to trail men on foreign policy, defense, and crime, but had pulled even on the economy and unemployment.[28] In the 1992 election women candidates were clearly advantaged on many of the most powerful issues of the campaign. This was reflected in polls that offered descriptions of hypothetical candidates; the female version was more attractive than the male version by up to 10 percentage points.[29]

Gender-Conscious and Gendercentric Voting

Despite these positive attitudes toward women in elective office, real choices appear on ballots.

One poll, taken in July, did suggest that women in unprecedented numbers might be voting for women candidates. In responding to the statement, "In a race between a man and a woman who had equal qualifications and skills, I would vote for the woman because the country needs more women in high public office," 57 percent of women surveyed agreed and 34 percent disagreed. Men disagreed 48 percent to 45 percent.[30] In the 11 races for the 1992 Senate that included a woman, the average gender gap was 10 percentage points, 10 times the average since 1980. The 15-point gender gap that elected Boxer was the greatest, but Feinstein (14 points), Mikulski and Yeakel (10 points), and Lloyd-Jones (12 points) also strongly benefited from gendercentric voting by women. In five other races the gender gap was 6 to 9 percentage points. Only in the race between Claire Sargent and John McCain (R-Ariz.) was there no significant difference.[31]

Some men no doubt also considered gender in favoring the female candidate over the man. Of those voters (40 to 43 percent) in California and Illinois who agreed that it was very important that more women serve in the Senate, between 75 and 84 percent supported the female candidate. In the California exit polls, both men and women reported that the two most critical factors in their vote were the gender of the candidate and the candidate's position on abortion.

Although exit-poll data for House and state office are less common and much less accurate, it is a fair assumption that gender-conscious voting occurred here too. In a study of congressional and gubernatorial primaries through June 1992, women candidates were 77 percent more successful than their male counterparts.[32]

"In 1992, a record number of women ran for public office and a record number won."

In congressional races, 40 percent of women seeking their party's nomination for the Senate and 48 percent of those filing in House races were successful, up from previous years.

Table 10.1

Women Candidates in 1992 for Federal and State Office

	State Legislature		Statewide Office		U.S. Senate		U.S. House	
	#	% Who Won	#	% Who Won	#	% Who Won	#	% Who Won
Nominated	2,373	—	37	—	11	—	106	—
Elected	1,374	58%	21	57%	5	45%	47	44%
Incumbent	867	92%	5	83%	1	100%	23	89%
Open Seat	425	55%	14	64%	3	100%	22	56%
Challenger	79	13%	2	20%	1	14%	2	5%

Source: Compiled from information provided by the Center for the American Woman and Politics, Eagleton Institute of Politics, Rutgers University. The percentages represent the rate of victory among those nominated and, among those elected, the rate of winning among different types of candidate (e.g., 91% of those running as incumbents were elected to the state legislature).

But in the general election, the proportion of female candidates who won their races was in line with figures from recent years, except in the Senate, where there was a dramatic increase. A key factor was the status of the candidate: female incumbents almost always won; challengers, only rarely; and more than half of those running in open seats were winners[33] (see Table 10.1).

CONCLUSION

In 1992, a record number of women ran for public office and a record number won. Women's groups, anticipating large numbers of open seats in a redistricting year, actively recruited female candidates, and women's PACs experienced exponential growth in supporting them. Women's issues were placed on the national agenda in ways largely defined by the feminist movement. Some veteran female officials felt that, for the first time, it was an advantage to be a women, and the appearance of gender-conscious and gendercentric voting confirmed this.

It was not an unqualified year of success for women in politics, however. No woman ran for president or was seriously considered as Clinton's running mate. And the setting of this election cycle may prove difficult to duplicate. Unless the trend toward imposing term limits expands and survives legal challenges, the number of open seats will not soon be matched. Of the 28 new women elected to both houses of Congress, only three are Republicans; in state legislatures, 61 percent are Democrats. In a Republican year, opportunities for women candidates could diminish. The major issues in the next campaign could shift. Gender stereotyping by the electorate continues and may not always favor women. The perception of female officials as speaking in a different voice risks setting higher expectations and standards for women and may prove a major burden in office-holding. Yet, the steady progress of women's numbers in elected office has been a constant over more than two decades and predictably will continue.

Chapter Eleven

American Ethnicities and the Politics of Inclusion

John A. Kromkowski

In our desire to understand and explain political events and processes, we must be careful not to minimize the complexity of the election of the president of the United States. Such elections have become even more complex in recent decades as the relatively new and elusive variable of ethnicity[1] has grown in importance. Ethnicity is a concept with no legal or constitutional lineage. Nevertheless, it is a social and cultural factor whose legitimacy in the American experience and scholarly endeavors is no longer marginal.[2] The persistence of ethnic phenomena and their importance for American politics have been documented.[3] The emerging role of ethnicity in regional cultural patterns, Congress, and electoral strategies has raised particularly acute concerns in American politics from 1968 to 1992. These developments suggest that the ethnic factor has become a potent variable, and one which marks a new phase of political articulation. In the election of 1992, the nation reached an unprecedented level of ethnic consciousness.

Bill Clinton's campaign adopted a theme of reinventing America. In particular, the notion underscored a growing contradiction: While espousing a vision of ethnic inclusiveness, the nation had increasingly found ways of avoiding ethnicity. A redefinition was necessary to reflect a new generation and a new direction for the first presidential election of the post–Cold War era.

In the 1992 campaign, more than in any earlier presidential election, Americans discovered that the political process of understanding pluralism is a part of citizenship in a democracy.

Immigration and migration of the last century and the demographic information developed by the U.S. Census since 1970 have widened our national horizons. This was the election about the era to come, an era that required agents of change who could lead and govern a country as pluralistic as America.[4] The election of 1992 also points to challenges incumbent on the practice and study of a polity that is more ethnically diverse than most imagined. Knowledge and understanding of this diversity are the first steps toward the political wisdom required of citizens and those of us who attempt to make clear observations about the great ritual of choice that occurs every four years. This ritual is more like an ethnic festival than we suspect.

MARGINALIZING ETHNICITY

That America is without ethnicity and politics without ethnic passion is an illusion, a hope for the future rather than a current reality.

Presidential campaigns dread the ethnic gaffe that will appear on the nightly news or the blunder that arouses scorn among opinion shapers and voters at the core of ethnic groups. When energized and impassioned, such voting groups determine the outcome in close elections. Even as the American population shifts and changes, the symbols that shape its consciousness of self also change; and so do ethnic patterns. In recent analyses of presidential campaigns, ethnicity has been regularly marginalized to accounts of ethnic faux pas: Jimmy

Carter saying "I"-talians in his acceptance speech; Jerry Ford eating the husk of a tamale at a Mexican-American campaign rally; George McGovern asking for milk to go with his kosher hot dog in Queens; Jesse Jackson referring to New York as Hymietown; George Bush enraging Ukrainian Americans by urging Ukraine to stick with Gorbachev and the New World Order. The rise of ethnic consciousness and the phrase "political correctness" prompt some to wonder if Tip O'Neill erred when he claimed "All

"*Ethnic politics is not local: it is a persistent and widespread habit.*"

politics is local." Perhaps he should have said, "All politics is ethnic." To this point, consider Jimmy Carter's recollection of what happened on the way to the inauguration of Ronald Reagan. Carter reports that he and Reagan really did not talk much to each other as they rode to Capitol Hill. Not only had President Carter gone without much sleep the prior three days as he continued to work on the release of the U.S. hostages from Iran, but Speaker of the House Tip O'Neill and the incoming president spent the trip exchanging Irish jokes. This tale illustrates Reagan's potential for successful relations with Congress, Carter's managerial ethos and impatience with superficialities, and Carter's underestimation of the role of the Irish-American factor in politics. Ethnic politics is not local: it is a persistent and widespread habit. Ethnicity is a modern American identity that echoes the many different ways in which the people of the United States are Americans.

Setting the Tone for Pluralism

In 1992 at Clinton's inauguration, the inaugural poet Maya Angelou read "On the Pulse of Morning," whose litany of Americans' numerous national and ethnic origins pays powerful tribute to this country's diversity. Addressing all past and recent immigrants, she concluded with these lines:

Lift up your eyes upon
This day breaking for you.
Give birth again
To the dream.

Thus the politics of 1992 in some respects was like the ancients' use of a poem or song to set the moral vision and guiding tone of the regime that is inaugurated when the president-elect takes the oath of office. The First Citizen thus accepts the choice of the people. On January 20 President Clinton proclaimed the mystery of renewal and the reinvention of America and symbolically affirmed the vision of America announced by Maya Angelou. Ethnic politics in America has never had such a time or place in public life. From the perspective of the poet, America could begin afresh: Good Morning! President Clinton would invite us to reinvent America. His remedy is hope, and his campaign theme song, "Don't Stop Thinking About Tomorrow," is the spirit of the regime.

A generation ago, amid significant ethnic turbulence and in the wake of disastrous showings by the Democratic Party, Mark Levy and Michael Kramer's *The Ethnic Factor: How America's Minorities Decide Elections*[5] attempted to disprove that ethnic group political behavior was disappearing in American politics. Levy and Kramer argued that fallacious claims about the decline of ethnic politics were based on the notion that ethnicity is divisive and unworthy of the American regime and its grounding in individual rights. American political science had fashioned and popularized this critique of the ethnicity and ethnic issues. In fact, it appears that all existing political orders must account for the persistence and ongoing malleability of ethnicity as a form of social experience and personal identity as well as a source of images and narratives that can be incorporated into political ideologies.

Levy and Kramer's pioneering work came at a time when few acknowledged the importance of the ethnic factor except among local politicians. Levy and Kramer applied commonsense perception as well as polling data to argue the following theses concerning national elections:

- a serious independent black presidential candidate would assure the defeat of any Democratic Party candidate;

- Italian Americans did not follow the Republican Party as strongly as conventional wisdom held;
- an Italian American on either party's ticket was good political sense;
- Jewish Americans were among the most liberal;
- myths of a backlash notwithstanding, Polish Americans continue to vote for the Democratic Party;
- Latino voters are at a political takeoff point that could determine the outcome of presidential elections in California and Texas; and
- Irish Americans are assimilated and middle class but vote 2 to 1 Democratic.[6]

The authors' findings about the persistence of the ethnic factor and its ongoing relevance were convincing, but they underestimated the resistance to developing the new language of political inclusiveness that was needed.[7]

THE DEMOCRATS AND INCLUSIVITY

Not until 20 years later did the Democratic Party, during the election of 1992, take giant steps toward ethnic inclusivity, diversity without exclusion, and the rhetoric of empathy with the concerns of all ethnic groups. The Clinton campaign was in regular communication with hundreds of ethnic media outlets. No Democratic campaign since 1960 was as gripped by outreach to ethnic constituencies. The ability of a campaign to build coalitions reflects its interest and competency in ethnic politics. The multiethnic coalition that was embraced by the Democratic Party and its standard-bearers, Bill Clinton and Al Gore was nurtured by party chair Ron Brown. Brown assiduously taught the National Democrats, who were excoriated throughout the Reagan era for their lack of traditional values, that the most important practice of Democratic politics is *addition,* and that the politics of fear and divisiveness which had been Democratic plagues for decades could be overcome. Clinton and Gore moved toward the world of local Democrats and took their campaign to grassroots ethnics throughout America. The campaign team included David Wilhelm, the son of an East German refugee, whose experience in Chicago with successful campaigns had honed his political senses to ethnic nuances and the importance of local organizing. The Democratic National Committee directed a program toward ethnic constituencies, and Christopher Hyland orchestrated relations between the Clinton campaign and ethnic media. Access to the campaign was amazingly fluid, and pluralistic coalitions abounded; George Stephanopoulos discovered the interest of Arab-American leaders through a call from Senator Joseph I. Leiberman, a Jewish Democrat from Connecticut.

The Republican Party and President George Bush and Vice President Dan Quayle failed to maintain their winning coalition of disaffected Democrats, the unaffiliated, those newly associated with the GOP, and, most importantly all, wings of the GOP. Thus came an end to the power that enabled Republicans to hold the presidency from 1969 to 1989 except for the Carter years—1977 to 1980. The Bush-Quayle defeat was signaled by the challenge from within the GOP led by Patrick Buchanan. Buchanan's strident, exlusionary, and nativistic rhetoric and his righteous crusade against the cultural elites that were foisting "political correctness" on America extended well beyond the life of his candidacy and into the prime time of the Republican Convention. Bush and Quayle were never able to transcend this narrow band of principled partisans and their image, nor could they tarnish their opponents with fears of radical feminism and treason. This crippled the capacity of President Bush and Vice President Quayle to seize the political and electoral ground beyond their firmly committed bases, which they had to do to ensure reelection.

"The differences in cultural-ethnic styles between the Clinton-Gore and Bush-Quayle teams were patently obvious from the outset of the campaign."

The differences in cultural-ethnic styles between the Clinton-Gore and Bush-Quayle teams were patently obvious from the outset of the campaign. Clinton and Gore "transvalued" a symbol of Democratic Party–induced change, busing, from a divisive emblem of racial-ethnic conflict into a populist, "down-home" and "working-class-friendly" sign of how close these new Democrats were to their southern origins. Their success resonated throughout the following states: Arkansas, Missouri, Louisiana, Tennessee, Georgia, Kentucky, West Virginia, and Ohio. State polling data[8] from September indicated the following percentages of support for Clinton and Gore: Arkansas, 58; Georgia, 43; Kentucky, 41; Missouri, 52; Ohio, 41; Tennessee, 46; West Virginia, 49.5. Only Louisiana at 36 percent was in doubt, but polls in October for Louisiana revealed a 10 percent surge that put it firmly in the Clinton-Gore win column. Thus Clinton and Gore established their base with a form of cultural affinity, an appeal to the ethno-cultural endowment that was part of the region where they launched their campaign. These Democratic candidates displayed a comfortable sense of identity and tradition. They projected this positive sense of identity from the very beginning; they were eager to go on busing the campaign "from our neighborhoods to yours." The election of 1992 was remarkable for the absence of divisive ethnic politics. The Clinton-Gore campaign appeared to proclaim its rootedness in a regional culture. From this ground the campaign reached out to the nation, conducting a high-tech and grass-roots campaign. The team of political operatives and an amazing network of "Friends of Bill," which took on some of the attributes of ethnic fraternities and sororities, came from a wide range of regional and ethnic backgrounds and included individuals who as volunteers had experienced the disasters of earlier Democratic presidential campaigns that had been unable to "speak American."[9] The Clinton-Gore campaign reached out to America with a message of empathy and hope, courage and change. The continuation of this style and the use of formats and techniques that emphasize sensitivity and empathy for dimensions and aspects of cultural variety and ethnic politics may well have implications for a new politics of inclusion and a new language of ethnic pluralism for America.

Although the Clinton-Gore campaign would sustain Levy and Kramer's findings, especially their point regarding the importance of disaggregating electoral data, a more current and targeted analysis with immediate correlation to the Clinton-Gore victory is the work by Joel Leiske on cultural issues and images in the 1988 presidential campaign. This article provides a most fruitful benchmark from which the campaign of 1992, its ethnic dimensions, and its outcome can be measured. Leiske outlines the ethnic and cultural configurations in American politics. He argues the following four points as causal aspects of the 1988 defeat of Michael S. Dukakis and the Democratic Party. The failure to acknowledge the following realities of America politics and to take strategic account of them caused the disaster of 1988:

1. The United States is a diverse, multicultural society composed of competing racial, ethnic, religious, and regional subcultures;
2. The Democratic New Deal Coalition is now sharply divided on most domestic policy issues, including a new set of racial and cultural life-style issues;
3. The 1988 Democratic Convention was an electoral and media disaster for the Democrats, comparable in effect to the 1968 and 1972 debacles;
4. The dominant cleavages in the presidential elections were not socioeconomic, but cultural; that is, they were divisions based on race-ethnicity, religion, and regional culture.[10]

From the perspective and experience of 1992, Leiske's first contention can be easily sustained. The 1990 U.S. Census as well as Weiss's[11] topology of America's differentiated neighborhoods indicate American pluralism. Detailed ethnic information from the U.S. Census suggests additional implications for electoral practice. However, the overriding concern about the economy articulated by Clinton, Gore, and Ross Perot, as well as the integration of national and international economic forces and the common lack of confidence in President Bush, appeared to weaken the force of regional diversity to some extent in the election of 1992. On the another level, that of ethnic patterns within states, the importance of a deeper structure will be taken up later in this chapter.

Leiske's third and fourth findings about the defeat of Dukakis and the Democratic Party now seem to be as appropriately applied to the Bush campaign and the GOP. If one were to write about why Bush and Quayle lost, the replication of Leiske's study with data and strategies used by the GOP in 1992 appears to confirm his findings about 1988. Thus three out of four aspects of how to lose a presidential campaign are now verified in two presidential elections.

BY LUCKOVICH FOR THE ATLANTA CONSTITUTION

THE IMPACT OF REAPPORTIONMENT

Data from the 1990 U.S. Census on the ethnic variety of states and regions of America reveal much about the context within which strategic and tactical elements of the election of 1992 occurred. Additional aspects of ethnic politics in the 1992 election are the immediate and long-term consequences of the decennial reapportionment of Congress. These features are just beginning to emerge into national view.

Of course, the impact of reapportionment and the ethnic factor could have had significant electoral implications if the strong surge of support for Clinton and Gore had not been maintained, and if the presidential election had been much closer. For example, the ethnic and electoral significance of Florida was accentuated in 1992 by the addition of 4 new electoral votes to the state after the 1990 reapportionment. Of the 10 newly elected members of Congress from Florida, 5 are Republican, thus increasing the number of Republicans to 13 out of 23 members

from the state.[12] Outside of Florida, Latino support for the Democratic Party is comprised of many groups, but Mexican-American and Puerto Rican populations are by far the largest. The highest concentration[13] of Latinos are found in California, Texas, Arizona, New Mexico, Colorado, Illinois, New York, Wyoming, and Kansas. One rough gauge of Latino political power in 1992 is the increase in Latino members of Congress. In 1990 there were 12 Latinos in Congress. In 1993, of the 19 Latino members, 3 are Republicans. New Republican members of Congress were elected from Texas and Florida. Not only did Bush and Quayle win these states, but each of these states gained new seats in Congress owing to reapportionment. Bush and Quayle also won Wyoming and Kansas, other states with large Latino populations.

To be sure, Texas gained two Democratic members of Congress, but the state that last voted for a Democratic president in 1976 and has voted for the victor in presidential elections ever since it joined the Union provided Bush with a victory by 3 percent over Clinton, with Perot

125

receiving 21 percent. Certainly the ethnic factor was not determinative, but it is a political dimension of Texas that Bush understood from his long association with Texas, including his previous service as a congressman from the state and an unsuccessful candidate for the Senate.

The longer-term implications of reapportionment are uncertain, and some aspects of ethnic group representation may become unsettling. Sectional realignment and severe ruptures in the fabric of American politics have become commonplace since 1930, when 21 states lost representatives prior to the emergence of the New Deal Coalition of the Democratic Party in 1932. The next two censuses initiated respective losses by 9 states. In 1960 16 states lost representatives. In 1970 9 states lost representatives. In 1980 10 states lost representatives, and in 1990 13 lost representatives. This steady, monotonous litany of diminishing electoral power for the older industrial states of the Northeast and Midwest intones the transformation of America. Those states with large concentrations of Eastern and Southern European populations are losing representation. The Voting Rights Act of 1982 and various Supreme Court decisions may exacerbate competition between ethnic groups in congressional elections.

In 1992 the following states gained representation in the U.S. House: California, Texas, Florida, North Carolina, Virginia, and Arizona. The following states lost members: New York, Pennsylvania, Illinois, Michigan, Ohio, New Jersey, Massachusetts, West Virginia, Iowa, Kansas, Montana, and Kentucky. Within this context of states that are gaining power and states that are losing it, particular new features of ethnic analysis and ethnic change in the U.S. House of Representatives intersected with the presidential election of 1992. The impact of Perot in this configuration poses an added matrix within which some measure of choice and orientation can be differentiated. The availability of new census data invites preliminary exploration of ethnic influence and the spillover of congressional and presidential appeals to voters. This relationship is especially interesting in the election of 1992 because the Clinton-Gore campaign, unlike many Democratic presidential campaigns of past decades, did not find local elected officials or senatorial and congressional candidates running away from the slippery coattails of their national ticket.

CENSUS BUREAU CATEGORIES DOMINATE

Other sources, such as exit polls, offer only glimpses into the ongoing intersection of ethnicity and elections.

In 1992 the *Los Angeles Times,* ABC News, CNN, and NBC News Consortium exit polling data did not provide detailed ethnic population data. As a result, the categories used in Tables 11.1 and 11.2 oversimplify and seem to stereotype the American reality.

These broad-brush sketches of the 1992 election, as well as comparable data for the prior four elections, are portaryed in a language of politics that collapses ethnicity into categories that reflect the history of the U.S. Census. These traditional categories were created by the U.S. Census and adopted by the scientific establishment, in part because census data are the largest data set, but also because these categories mirrored the cultural endowment and language of the English colonial experience that is the foundation of America. The continued use of this language of differentiation is institutionalized in the U.S. Census. The exit poll categories and the analysis they suggest are not the most indicative of the ethnic realities that are significant to a very large percentage of the American population. Nor do such data mesh easily with the political realities of the American electoral context and processes, which are essentially linked to the various states and their particularities. Moreover, such data distort differences and magnitudes of significance. For example, the use of percentages of the categories—Black, Latino, Asian, and White—does not lend itself to using this information in the quantitative perspective it deserves. In point of fact, these national tables

Table 11.1

1992 Exit Poll Data by Traditional Census Bureau Category

Voter Type	% Clinton/ Gore	% Bush/ Quayle	% Perot/ Stockdale
Black	83	10	7
Hispanic	61	25	14
Asian	31	55	15
White	39	40	20

Source: Voter Research & Surveys, November 3, 1992.

Table 11.2

Prior Elections' Exit Poll Data by Percentage of Traditional Census Bureau Category

Year	Candidates	Black	Hispanic	Asian	White
1988	Dukakis/Bentsen	89	70	na	40
	Bush/Quayle	11	30	na	60
1984	Mondale/Ferraro	91	66	na	34
	Reagan/Bush	9	34	na	66
1980	Carter/Mondale	83	56	na	36
	Reagan/Bush	14	37	na	56
	Anderson/Lucey	3	7	na	8
1976	Carter/Mondale	83	82	na	48
	Ford/Dole	17	18	na	52

Source: Public Opinion and Demographic Report, January/February 1993.

tell us something about four types of "quasi-ethnic" clusters or statistical constructs. Black, Latino, and Asian categories account for 13% of the voters in the election. Thus, this data format magnifies racial perceptions, grossly minimizes ethnic variety, and blurs political significance.

The exit poll data in Table 11.3 concerning issues provides information that is organized into national clusters of voters that approximate ethno-religious-regional differences.

The driving issue of the campaign—the economy—was more highly selected by populations that have ethnic affiliations distant from the southern, white, born-again tradition. Thus African-Americans, Latinos, and Eastern and Southern Europeans and other Catholics, as well as Jewish-Americans, were more concerned about and interested in the economy than the entire sample. They were least like those segments of the population that viewed family

Table 11.3

1992 Exit Poll Data Including Religious/Regional Categories
Which One or Two Issues Mattered Most in Deciding How You Voted?

Issue	All Respondents	Blacks	Hispanics	Southern White Protestants	White Catholics	Born Again	Jews (under 45)	Jews (over 45)
Economy	42	48	47	37	45	33	60	53
Federal Deficit	21	12	15	21	21	18	16	33
Health Care	20	28	23	17	20	16	18	34
Family Values	15	13	13	25	11	30	8	2
Taxes	14	11	12	14	17	13	9	9
Education	13	22	18	10	11	11	19	11
Abortion	12	5	9	15	9	22	25	10
Foreign Policy	8	2	2	11	10	7	8	4
Environment	5	3	4	4	5	2	7	4

Source: National Center for Urban Ethnic Affairs

Table 11.4

1984 Exit Poll Data by Percentage of Additional Ethnic Category

	German	Protes-tant	White	Irish	Italian	Catholic	Eastern Euro-pean	Jewish	Hispanic	Black
Presidential Election										
Reagan/Bush	70	67	66	62	61	56	54	35	32	9
Mondale/Ferraro	30	33	34	38	39	44	46	65	68	91
U.S. House Race (National Average)										
The Republican Candidate	59	54	53	48	48	45	43	26	26	8
The Democratic Candidate	37	42	42	47	47	50	50	67	71	86
Some other candidate	1	1	1	1	1	1	2	2	1	2
Didn't vote/not sure	3	3	4	4	4	4	5	5	2	4
Selected Senate Races										
Percy	59	56	53	47	53	46	47	na	na	8
Simon	38	42	45	50	46	52	52	na	na	91
Givot	3	2	2	3	1	2	1	na	na	1
Loisma	52	53	52	56	46	44	43	na	na	5
Levin	48	47	48	44	54	56	57	na	na	95

Source: National Center for Urban Ethnic Affairs Data File, derived from 1984 NBC News/*New York Times* exit polls.

values as the most important issue for the attention of the government. More detailed analysis about ethnic groups' support for candidates was provided in the exit poll data of 1984, found in Table 11.4.

Exit poll data in 1984 fostered finer-grain analysis and indicated greater ethnic specificity for national as well as Senate races in Illinois and Michigan. These data also enable us to assess the relationship between the presidential and congressional loyalties and the party affinities of various ethnic populations. At the state level, such information provides much more fruitful insight into the dynamics of electoral behavior. Thus the level of analysis that is nearest to the action yields the sort of specificity that truly improves our understanding of politics and the influences and contexts shaped by ethnocultural factors. Though the presidential election is national, it actually occurs in the states.

In this regard, the U.S. Census is a pivotal political and research source. In fact, U.S. Census data on political and ethnic culture determine our understanding of American pluralism.

FURTHER DETAILING ETHNICITY

Beginning in the mid-1970s, advocacy to change the data collection process of the U.S. Census was driven a multiethnic coalition headed by Monseigneur Geno C. Baroni.[14] In the 1980 Census and even more in the 1990 Census, the consequences of the new approach to measure ethnicity by self-identification supplement other forms of demographic data. The results are patently clear in Tables 11.5, 11.6, and 11.7. These data, as well as state-by-state disaggregations, provide the database from which an Index of Ethnic Variety was fashioned to explore the possibility of quantified analysis that could suggest some state-level as well as macro-level findings about ethnicity and the presidential election.

On the macro level, the political consequences of this ethnic pluralization of U.S. Census data by Congress and the prospect of widespread use of this new language of national political discourse are controversial and prob-

Table 11.5

Effects of the 1980 Census on the Measurement of Ethnicity in America

Group	1980 Census	1970 Census
English	49,598,035	2,465,050
German	49,224,146	3,622,035
Irish	40,165,702	1,450,220
French	12,892,246	343,367
Italian	12,183,246	4,240,779
Scottish	10,048,816	na
Polish	8,228,037	2,374,244
Mexican	7,692,619	na
American Indian	6,715,819	763,594
Dutch	6,304,499	na
Swedish	4,345,392	806,138
Norwegian	3,453,839	614,649
Czech	1,892,456	759,527
Hungarian	1,776,902	603,668
Welsh	1,664,598	na
Portuguese	1,024,351	na
Greek	959,856	434,571
French-Canadian	780,488	na
Slovak	776,806	na
Lithuanian	742,776	330,977
Ukrainian	730,056	na
Finnish	615,872	na
Canadian	456,212	3,034,556
Yugoslavian	360,174	447,271
Croatian	252,970	na
Armenian	212,621	na
Slovene	126,463	na
Serbian	100,941	na
Asian	3,726,440	
Black	26,482,349	
White	189,035,349	

Source: Data from U.S. Bureau of the Census.

lematic. The implications for the politics of ethnic pluralism may be the most important shift in the language of politics since the Founders struggled with the politics of numbers in Philadelphia at the Constitutional Convention. The U.S. Census data reveal the amplitude of American ethnic pluralism. These tables illustrate some of the regional patterns that emerge from aggregated state data that were used to develop the Indexes of Ethnic Variety. The census data indicate that nearly 85 percent of the total population self-identified an ethnicity. Only 6 percent of the U.S. population uses American (5 per-

cent), United States (0.3 percent) or White (0.7 percent) term as an ethnic identifier. The census data also included single and multiple ethnicities, so the overall population of ethnicities is approximately 50,000,000 more than the U.S. population of 248,000,000. The data on ethnic self-identification provides a fresh vista into the question of ethnic politics. Obviously this sort of self-identification radically changes the political discourse. Moreover, comparing 1980 and 1990 data suggests the malleability and mutability of ethnic identity. Like other social inventions, ethnicity is a form of choice, a political behavior that could command more scrutiny. Thus ethnic patterns and the resonance of some forms of political persuasion may be related to each other. At bottom the politicization of ethnicity should not be surprising. The massive increase in German Americans in the 1990 census is no doubt influenced by the remaking of attitudes regarding Germany and the remaking of the political order that the end of the Cold War has fostered. The passing of generations and the subsiding of ethnic trauma and denial may explain other shifts

"Like other social inventions, ethnicity is a form of choice. . . ."

in ethnic identity related to Eastern Europe and the changes in the USSR—notably a one-million-person increase in Slovak Americans evident in the 1990 data. Most interestingly, a proposal for an end to the dichotomous racialism of "Black" and "White" color-conscious language was incorporated into this report. This change from the language of divisiveness to the adoption of the term "African American" was initiated by the Rev. Jesse L. Jackson shortly after the disastrous defeat of the Democratic presidential ticket in 1988.[15] The introduction of African American into the language of American popular culture was desired because, as Jackson argued, African American possessed a "cultural integrity" that was absent in "Black." He emphasized that African Americans, like other ethnic groups, have reference to some land base, some historical and cultural base. Thus Jackson and other leaders of this ethnic group argue that to be

(continued on page 133)

Table 11.6

National Index of Ethnic Variety: Self-Identification of Census Respondents

1990 Rank	Ancestry Group	Number	Percent	1990 Rank	Ancestry Group	Number	Percent
	Total population	248,709,873	100.0				
1	German	57,947,374	23.3	51	Lebanese	394,180	0.2
2	Irish	38,735,539	15.6	52	Belgian	380,498	0.2
3	English	32,651,788	13.1	53	Romanian	365,544	0.1
4	Afro American	23,777,098	9.6	54	Spaniard	360,935	0.1
5	Italian	14,664,550	5.9	55	Colombian	351,717	0.1
6	American	12,395,999	5.0	56	Czechoslovakian	315,285	0.1
7	Mexican	11,586,983	4.7	57	Armenian	308,096	0.1
8	French	10,320,935	4.1	58	Pennsylvania German	305,841	0.1
9	Polish	9,366,106	3.8	59	Haitian	289,521	0.1
10	American Indian	8,708,220	3.5	60	Yugoslavian	257,994	0.1
11	Dutch	6,227,089	2.5	61	Hawaiian	256,081	0.1
12	Scotch-Irish	5,617,773	2.3	62	African	245,845	0.1
13	Scottish	5,393,581	2.2	63	Guatemalan	241,559	0.1
14	Swedish	4,680,863	1.9	64	Iranian	235,521	0.1
15	Norwegian	3,869,395	1.6	65	Ecuadorian	197,374	0.1
16	Russian	2,952,987	1.2	66	Taiwanese	192,973	0.1
17	French Canadian	2,167,127	0.9	67	Nicaraguan	177,077	0.1
18	Welsh	2,033,893	0.8	68	Peruvian	161,866	0.1
19	Spanish	2,024,004	0.8	69	West Indies	159,167	0.1
20	Puerto Rican	1,955,323	0.8	70	Laotian	146,930	0.1
21	Slovak	1,882,897	0.8	71	Cambodian	134,955	0.1
22	White	1,799,711	0.7	72	Syrian	129,606	0.1
23	Danish	1,634,669	0.7	73	Arab	127,364	0.1
24	Hungarian	1,582,302	0.6	74	Slovene	124,437	0.1
25	Chinese	1,505,245	0.6	75	Serbian	116,795	0.0
26	Filipino	1,450,512	0.6	76	Honduran	116,635	0.0
27	Czech	1,296,411	0.5	77	Thai	112,117	0.0
28	Portuguese	1,153,351	0.5	78	Asian	107,172	0.0
29	British	1,119,154	0.4	79	Latvian	100,331	0.0
30	Hispanic	1,113,259	0.4	80	Pakistani	99,974	0.0
31	Greek	1,110,373	0.4	81	Nigerian	91,688	0.0
32	Swiss	1,045,495	0.4	82	Panamanian	88,649	0.0
33	Japanese	1,04,645	0.4	83	Hmong	84,823	0.0
34	Austrian	864,783	0.3	84	Turkish	83,850	0.0
35	Cuban	859,739	0.3	85	Israeli	81,677	0.0
36	Korean	836,987	0.3	86	Guyanese	81,677	0.0
37	Lithuanian	811,865	0.3	87	Egyptian	78,574	0.0
38	Ukrainian	740,803	0.3	88	Slavic	76,931	0.0
39	Scandinavian	678,880	0.3	89	Trinidad & Tobagonian	76,270	0.0
40	Acadian/Cajun	668,271	0.3	90	Northern European	65,993	0.0
41	Finnish	658,870	0.3	91	Brazilian	65,875	0.0
42	United States	643,561	0.3	92	Argentinean	63,176	0.0
43	Asian Indian	570,322	0.2	93	Dutch West Indian	61,530	0.0
44	Canadian	549,990	0.2	94	Chilean	61,465	0.0
45	Croatian	544,270	0.2	95	Samoan	55,419	0.0
46	Vietnamese	535,825	0.2	96	Eskimo	52,920	0.0
47	Dominican	505,690	0.2	97	Australian	52,133	0.0
48	Salvadoran	499,153	0.2	98	Costa Rican	51,771	0.0
49	European	466,718	0.2	99	Assyrian	51,765	0.0
50	Jamaican	435,024	0.2	100	Cape Verdean	50,772	0.0

Table 11.6 (cont.)

1990 Rank	Ancestry Group	Number	Percent	1990 Rank	Ancestry Group	Number	Percent
101	Sicilian	50,389	0.0	151	New Zealand	7,742	0.0
102	Luxemburger	49,061	0.0	152	Soviet Union	7,729	0.0
103	Palestinian	48,019	0.0	153	Middle Eastern	7,656	0.0
104	Basque	47,956	0.0	154	US Virgin Islander	7,621	0.0
105	Albanian	47,710	0.0	155	Basque, Spanish	7,620	0.0
106	Indonesian	43,969	0.0	156	Carpath Russian	7,602	0.0
107	Latin American	43,521	0.0	157	Fijian	7,472	0.0
108	Western European	42,409	0.0	158	Antigua	7,364	0.0
109	Icelander	40,529	0.0	159	Manx	6,317	0.0
110	Venezuelan	40,331	0.0	160	Basque, French	6,001	0.0
111	Maltese	39,600	0.0	161	Hong Kong	5,774	0.0
112	Guamanian	39,237	0.0	162	Vincent/Grenadine Islander	5,773	0.0
113	British West Indian	37,819	0.0	163	Tirol	5,748	0.0
114	Barbadian	35,455	0.0	164	Rom	5,693	0.0
115	Bolivian	33,738	0.0	165	Central European	5,693	0.0
116	Afghanistan	31,301	0.0	166	Nova Scotian	5,489	0.0
117	Ethiopian	30,581	0.0	167	Paraguayan	5,415	0.0
118	Celtic	29,652	0.0	168	Newfoundland	5,412	0.0
119	Bulgarian	29,595	0.0	169	Bermudan	4,941	0.0
120	Malaysian	27,800	0.0	170	Cypriot	4,897	0.0
121	Estonian	26,762	0.0	171	Kenyan	4,639	0.0
122	Prussian	25,469	0.0	172	Sierra Leon	4,627	0.0
123	Cantonese	25,020	0.0	173	Saxon	4,519	0.0
124	Iraqi	23,212	0.0	174	Saudi Arabian	4,486	0.0
125	Belizean	22,922	0.0	175	Charnorro	4,427	0.0
126	Bahamian	21,081	0.0	176	Bavarian	4,348	0.0
127	Jordanian	20,656	0.0	177	Azorean	4,310	0.0
128	Macedonian	20,365	0.0	178	Belorussian	4,277	0.0
129	Ghanian	20,066	0.0	179	Eritrean	4,270	0.0
130	Moroccan	19,089	0.0	180	Yemeni	4,011	0.0
131	South African	17,992	0.0	181	Northern Irish	4,009	0.0
132	Alsatian	16,465	0.0	182	Cornish	3,991	0.0
133	Tongan	16,019	0.0	183	West German	3,885	0.0
134	Aleut	15,816	0.0	184	Moravian	3,781	0.0
135	Amerasian	15,523	0.0	185	Ruthenian	3,776	0.0
136	Uruguayan	14,641	0.0	186	Sudanese	3,623	0.0
137	Sri Lankan	14,448	0.0	187	Mongolian	3,507	0.0
138	Eurasian	14,177	0.0	188	St. Lucia	3,415	0.0
139	Flemish	14,157	0.0	189	Micronesian	3,406	0.0
140	North American	12,618	0.0	190	Algerian	3,215	0.0
141	Bangladeshi	12,486	0.0	191	Windish	3,189	0.0
142	Pacific Islander	11,330	0.0	192	Khmer	2,979	0.0
143	Grenadian	11,188	0.0	193	Kitts/Nevis Islander	2,811	0.0
144	South American	10,867	0.0	194	Ugandan	2,681	0.0
145	Polynesian	10,854	0.0	195	Nepali	2,516	0.0
146	Okinawan	10,554	0.0	196	Singaporean	2,419	0.0
147	Central American	10,310	0.0	197	Cypriot, Greek	2,197	0.0
148	German Russian	10,153	0.0				
149	Liberian	8,797	0.0				
150	Burmese	8,646	0.0				

Source: 1990 CP-S-1-2, Detailed Ancestry Groups for States.

Table 11.7

Regional Indexes of Ethnic Variety for 1980 and 1990 Censuses

1990 Rank	Ancestry group	Number	Percent	1980 Rank	Ancestry group	Number	Percent
	SOUTH	85,445,930	100.0		SOUTH	75,372,362	100.0
1	German	14,630,411	17.1	1	English	19,618,370	26.0
2	Irish	12,950,799	15.2	2	Irish	12,709,872	16.9
3	Afro American	12,936,066	15.1	3	Afro American	11,054,127	14.7
4	English	11,375,464	13.3	4	German	10,742,903	14.3
5	American	7,558,114	8.8	5	French	3,532,674	4.7
6	American Indian	4,086,342	4.8	6	Scottish	3,492,252	3.9
7	Mexican	3,774,379	4.4	7	American Indian	2,928,252	3.9
8	French	2,964,481	3.5	8	Mexican	2,663,868	3.5
9	Scotch-Irish	2,616,155	3.1	9	Dutch	1,651,125	2.2
10	Italian	2,473,371	2.9	10	Italian	1,555,340	2.1
11	Dutch	1,780,043	2.1	11	Polish	943,536	1.3
12	Scottish	1,768,494	2.1	12	Spanish	705,594	0.9
13	Polish	1,361,537	1.6	13	Swedish	511,426	0.7
14	White	946,103	1.1	14	Russian	441,287	0.6
15	Swedish	671,099	0.8	15	Cuban	373,695	0.5
16	Spanish	614,708	0.7	16	Welsh	360,272	0.5
17	Acadian/Cajun	609,427	0.7	17	Czech	348,110	0.5
18	Cuban	594,106	0.7	18	Norwegian	253,799	0.3
19	Russian	545,671	0.6	19	Hungarian	239,786	0.3
20	Welsh	545,082	0.5	20	Greek	167,926	0.2
21	British	440,352	0.5	21	Danish	147,029	0.2
22	French Canadian	423,497	0.5	22	Swiss	143,636	0.2
23	Norwegian	369,485	0.4	23	Austrian	140,666	0.2
24	Hispanic	347,411	0.4	24	Puerto Rican	120,394	0.2
25	United States	341,677	0.4	25	French Canadian	104,725	0.1

1990 Rank	Ancestry group	Number	Percent	1980 Rank	Ancestry group	Number	Percent
	WEST	52,786,082	100.0		WEST	43,172,490	100.0
1	German	10,910,791	20.7	1	English	10,266,505	23.8
2	English	8,109,565	15.4	2	German	8,876,940	20.6
3	Irish	6,721,361	12.7	3	Irish	7,129,413	16.5
4	Mexican	6,648,726	12.6	4	Mexican	4,261,286	9.9
5	Afro American	2,307,797	4.4	5	French	2,493,133	5.8
6	Italian	2,257,788	4.3	6	Scottish	2,375,842	5.5
7	French	2,078,259	3.9	7	Afro American	1,898,272	4.4
8	American Indian	1,960,826	3.7	8	Italian	1,703,052	3.9
9	Swedish	1,481,378	2.8	9	American Indian	1,628,926	3.8
10	Scottish	1,401,282	2.7	10	Swedish	1,326,916	3.1
11	American	1,357,965	2.6	11	Dutch	1,284,432	3.0
12	Dutch	1,303,040	2.5	12	Spanish	1,161,484	2.7
13	Norwegian	1,258,552	2.4	13	Norwegian	1,074,257	2.5
14	Scotch-Irish	1,150,485	2.2	14	Polish	788,081	1.8
15	Polish	1,036,235	2.0	15	Danish	657,792	1.5
16	Filipino	991,572	1.9	16	Japanese	607,630	1.4
17	Spanish	919,916	1.7	17	Filipino	540,680	1.3
18	Chinese	826,760	1.6	18	Russian	531,759	1.2
19	Danish	738,508	1.4	19	Chinese	487,530	1.1
20	Japanese	722,700	1.4	20	Welsh	447,446	1.0
21	Russian	641,256	1.2	21	Portuguese	419,844	1.0
22	Hispanic	555,029	1.1	22	Swiss	279,231	0.6
23	Welsh	548,974	1.0	23	Czech	276,119	0.6
24	White	501,934	1.0	24	Hungarian	248,994	0.6
25	Portuguese	468,812	0.9	25	Scandinavian	208,799	0.5

Source: 1990 CP-S-1-2, Detailed Ancestry Groups for States and PC 80-S1-10, Ancestry of the Population by State: 1980.

called black is baseless; moreover, that while "Black is beautiful" might have been appropriate when white meant to be fully American and black to be second class, the current situation requires the change to African American.[16] Thus the shift in the language of ethnicity that began in 1988 is evident not only in the census but in the politics that can be expected during the 1990s. The disaggregation found in the census data, unlike the exit polling data, only enables finer-grain analysis of contemporary ethnic diversity.

LEARNING FROM THE INDEXES OF ETHNIC VARIETY

The Index of Ethnic Variety scales the differences in various state population against the national data on ethnic variety. The assumption of the scale and resulting index is that some national pattern as well as some varieties of state patterns exist and that they are composed of population sizes of the following categories: foundational, older immigrant, recent immigrant, and Native Americans. The state Index of Ethnic Variety is a measure of context within which ethnic politics and the presidential elections occur. An Index of Ethnic Variety enables the quantitative measure of the ethnic demographic patterns of states, which can then be compared to the electoral outcomes of the 1992 presidential election.

Table 11.8 arrays Indexes of Ethnic Variety by region of the nation, by the states won by Clinton, and the states won by Bush, and includes the percentage of vote difference over Perot and the candidate that came in second in the respective states. Table 11.9 arrays Indexes of Ethnic Variety for the states that provided the highest total vote and the states that provided the highest percentage of state vote for Perot. These rudimentary measures of ethnic distance from or dissimilarity to the national population provide a very rough measure of variety. The National Index is scaled at 1.00; this is also exactly the Index of Tennessee, the home state of Vice President Gore. The Index for Arkansas, the home state of President Clinton, is 1.01, only a 1 percent variance from the National Index. Such preliminary and rudimentary indicators should not be overestimated, but even such gross findings enable us to see at glance that the Rhode Island Index of .44 is 56 percent unlike the composite of America. Except for their margin in Washington, D.C. (77 percent), Clinton and Gore had their highest margin of victory (19 percent) over Bush and Quayle in Rhode Island and New Hampshire. Such data may be very important for a regime that claims it wants to look like America. Even at this rudimentary level, it is clear that the states with considerable ethnic variety voted for Clinton and Gore. States with particularly high concentrations of voting-age ethnic populations may influence the outcomes in these states (see Table 11.10). The following patterns may reveal ethnic proclivities and dimensions related to the states that have particularly dense concentrations of various ethnic groups:

- States with high concentrations of Irish Americans, such as Massachusetts, Pennsylvania, New Jersey, and Illinois, all supported Clinton and Gore. However, members of Congress appearing on the letterhead of the Irish-American Caucus did not fare well. Of 61 congressmen listed, 20 failed to be reelected to the 103rd Congress for a variety of reasons.[17]
- States with high concentrations of Polish Americans, such as Michigan, Wisconsin, Illinois, Pennsylvania, New Jersey, New York, Massachusetts, and Connecticut, supported Clinton and Gore. In these same states, Perot's support was significantly lower than his national percentage, with the exception of Massachusetts (19 percent) and Wisconsin (28 percent).
- States with high concentrations of German Americans, such as Kansas, Indiana, North Dakota, and South Dakota, supported Bush and Quayle.
- States with high concentrations of Native Americans, such as Montana, Arizona, Oklahoma, Alaska, New Mexico, and North Carolina, narrowly supported Bush and Quayle. Bush and Quayle won South Dakota, North Carolina, and Oklahoma, by 4 percent, 1 percent, and 9 percent respectively. Perot won 24 percent of the Arizona vote, while Bush and Quayle beat Clinton and Gore by 2 percent.
- States with high concentrations of English Americans include Utah, South Carolina, Kentucky, and Maine. Bush and Quayle carried Utah, Idaho, and South Carolina. Clinton and Gore won in Kentucky and Maine. Perot won the support of 28 percent in Idaho, 29 percent in Utah, and 30 percent in Maine.

Table 11.8

Percentage of Vote Difference Between Candidates and Index of Ethnic Variety by State, 1992

STATE	Index of Ethnic Variety	CLINTON Bush	Perot	BUSH Clinton	Perot
AR	1.01	18	43	−18	25
DC	1.17	77	82	−77	5
GA	1.48	1	31	−1	30
KY	0.71	3	31	−3	32
LA	0.79	4	34	−4	30
MD	0.83	14	36	−14	22
TN	1	4	4	−4	37
WV	0.72	13	13	13	33
CA	0.81	15	26	−15	11
CO	0.7	6	17	−6	13
HI	0.24	12	35	−12	13
MT	0.5	2	12	−2	10
NV	0.76	3	11	−3	8
NM	0.72	8	30	−8	22
OR	0.72	11	18	−11	7
WA	0.92	13	20	−13	7
CT	0.5	6	20	−6	14
DE	0.61	8	23	−8	15
ME	0.79	8	9	−8	1
MA	0.64	19	25	−19	6
NH	0.75	1	16	−1	15
NJ	0.6	2	27	−2	25
NY	0.81	16	34	−16	18
RI	0.44	19	25	−19	6
VT	0.79	15	23	−15	8
IL	1.32	13	31	−13	18
IA	0.63	6	25	−6	19
MI	0.71	7	25	−7	18
MN	0.66	12	20	−12	8
MO	0.83	10	22	−10	12
OH	0.68	1	19	−1	18
PA	1.05	9	26	−9	18
WI	0.53	4	19	4	15

STATE	Index of Ethnic Variety	CLINTON Bush	Perot	BUSH Clinton	Perot
AL	1.08	−7	30	7	37
FL	1.12	−2	19	2	21
MS	1.04	−9	32	9	41
NC	1.13	−1	29	1	30
SC	1.06	−8	28	8	36
TX	0.63	−3	15	3	18
VA	1.06	−4	24	4	31
AK	0.61	−9	5	9	14
AR	0.53	−2	13	2	15
ID	0.89	−14	1	14	15
UT	0.87	−20	−3	20	17
WY	0.6	−6	8	6	14
IN	0.86	−6	17	6	13
KS	0.65	−5	7	5	12
NB	0.57	−17	6	17	23
ND	0.62	−12	9	12	21
OK	0.49	−9	11	9	20
SD	0.5	−4	15	4	19

Source: Data from 1990 Census and Federal Election Commission, 1992 voting totals.

- States with high concentrations of Asian Americans, such as California, Washington, Hawaii, and New York, were all carried by Clinton and Gore. Yet support for the Bush-Quayle ticket was strong among Asian Americans, and a Republican Korean American was elected to Congress from California.[18]

A basic premise of ethnic analysis is that ethnicity is a dimension of the American people and that to understand it is to diminish the distortions of this potentially volatile source of group passion and political interest. The United States of America is the world's most religiously, culturally, ethnically, demographically, socially, and economically diverse experiment in governance. In many respects, the success of this order has depended on commonly shared purposes that can be defended and the opportunity to participate in the rewards and recognition provided by this sort of regime. This was particularly true, as the polling data indicated in the 1992 election, of the economy. In 1992 both the Democratic Party and the GOP were forced by

"The United States of America is the world's most religiously, culturally, ethnically, demographically, socially, and economically diverse experiment in governance."

the Perot candidacy to stay riveted to the economic and budget issues. The Clinton-Gore campaign was attracted to the potential of deemphasizing polarization and thus celebrating the politics of diversity, inclusiveness, and pluralism. Bush and Quayle selected another path. The pattern of states which responded to these different approaches reflect their choices, as well as the ethnic endowments, context, and traditions that comprise the various states within which these choices were made (see Table 11.11). Perhaps the number of new members of Congress from these states also drove the message of change.

Concerns about culture, community, and other realms of ethnic values have been potent

Table 11.9

States With Highest 1992 Total Votes by Index of Ethnic Variety and Perot Support

Index	State	Percent Voting for Perot	Total Number Voting
0.61	AK	27	55,085
0.53	AZ	24	341,148
0.89	ID	28	129,897
0.65	KS	27	310,458
0.79	ME	30	205,076
0.66	MN	24	552,705
0.5	MT	26	106,869
0.57	NB	27	129,532
0.72	OR	25	307,860
0.87	UT	29	202,605
0.79	VT	31	85,512
0.6	WY	26	51,209
0.81	CA	21	2,147,409
1.12	FL	20	1,041,607
1.32	IL	17	832,484
0.64	MA	23	630,440
0.71	MI	19	820,855
0.66	MN	22	552,705
1.11	MO	22	518,250
0.81	NY	16	1,029,038
0.68	OH	21	1,024,598
0.83	PA	18	896,177
0.63	TX	22	1,349,947
0.53	WI	22	542,660

Source: Data from 1990 Census and Federal Election Commission, 1992 voting totals.

political forces in other types of situation and contexts. The future of ethnic politics may include attention to particularly focused ethnic residential clusters and the potential for a new ethnic politics in Congress, which has a substantially increased number of ethnic Americans (see Table 11.12). Political parties among immigrant groups may emerge in the wake of the election of 1992, in which the rhetoric of inclusiveness was espoused, proclaimed, and quite ably used to gain a plurality of voters and a majority in the Electoral College. In 1992, the constitutional structure and the capacity for coalition building prevailed over potential cleavages that can destroy large republics. The following account may forecast the approach to ethnic politics in the 1990s.

In Montana, a state carried by Clinton and Gore that had not voted for a Democratic presi-

(continued on page 137)

135

Table 11.10

Congressional Districts With Largest Ethnic Concentrations

District	City	% of Voting Age
Black Population		
1	Detroit, MI	66.1
13	Detroit, MI	67.4
7	Chicago, IL	59.8
2	Chicago, IL	66.4
1	Chicago, IL	90.1
5	Atlanta, GA	60.0
12	Brooklyn, NY	78.2
2	Philadelphia, PA	75.7
	Washington, DC	65.8
7	Baltimore, MD	69.6
Latino Population		
25	Los Angeles, CA	57.7
30	San Gabriel, CA	47.7
20	San Antonio, TX	55.8
34	Norwalk, CA	41.7
16	El Paso, TX	54.9
23	Laredo, TX	48.0
27	Corpus Christi, TX	55.4
15	McAllen, TX	66.1
18	Miami, FL	50.3
18	Bronx, NY	48.4
Asian Population		
7	Seattle, WA	7.3
3	Sacramento, CA	6.3
6	Marin Co., CA	12.3
5	San Francisco, CA	22.3
25	Los Angeles, CA	11.8
1	Honolulu, HI	64.9
2	Oahu-Outer Islands, HI	56.0
10	San Jose, CA	9.8
7	Queens, NY	6.9
15	Manhattan, NY	10.0
Irish Population		
7	Medford, MA	32.8
3	Philadelphia, PA	30.9
7	Haverford, PA	36.1
11	Boston, MA	37.7
3	Chicago, IL	28.9
3	Worcester, MA	27.8
8	Boston, MA	27.8
9	Boston, MA	28.9
3	Sandy Hook, NJ	26.8
16	Allegheny Co., PA	26.9
French Population		
2	Lewiston, ME	26.5
1	Manchester, NH	25.3
	Vermont	26.3
26	St. Lawrence Co., NY	27.6
2	Nashua, NH	26.2
2	Springfield, MA	27.0
1	Berkshire, MA	23.5
8	Alexandria, LA	27.0
3	Metairie, LA	38.1
7	Lake Charles, LA	39.1

District	City	% of Voting Age
Italian Population		
7	Medford, MA	27.2
2	Providence, RI	24.7
13	Brooklyn, NY	27.5
2	Babylon-Islip, NY	28.7
20	Westchester Co., NY	24.4
11	Essex Co., NJ	29.6
19	Bronx, NY	25.9
9	Bergen Co., NJ	25.3
14	Staten Island, NY	38.6
3	New Haven, CT	25.0
Native American Population		
2	Billings, MT	6.7
	South Dakota	6.5
	Sante Fe, NM	20.9
	Fayetteville, NC	7.6
2	Phoenix, AZ	5.2
3	Phoenix, AZ	5.1
4	Phoenix, AZ	15.4
3	Lawton, OK	7.6
2	Muskogee, OK	11.6
	Alaska	16.0
English Population		
1	Portland, ME	40.1
2	Lewiston, ME	40.6
2	Boise, ID	43.1
1	Ogden, UT	56.0
9	Blacksburg, VA	40.5
7	Ashland, KY	44.2
3	Provo, UT	55.3
2	Salt Lake City, UT	50.7
5	Boone Forest, KY	41.6
1	Charleston, SC	39.4
German Population		
19	York, PA	54.6
8	Green Bay, WI	51.9
2	Minnesota River, MN	55.0
6	Oshkosh, WI	64.0
1	Lincoln, NB	52.9
2	Cedar Rapids, IA	55.4
2	Madison, WI	51.6
9	Sheboygan, WI	63.4
5	Bowling Green, OH	53.6
16	Lancaster, PA	53.8
Polish Population		
33	Buffalo, NY	24.6
11	Wilkes-Barre, PA	20.0
6	Middlesex Co., NJ	15.2
14	Detroit, MI	21.9
12	Lake St. Clair, MI	15.3
4	Milwaukee, WI	25.7
5	Chicago, IL	20.5
11	Chicago, IL	18.7
8	Chicago, IL	18.0
32	Chicago, IL	16.5

Source: National Center for Urban Ethnic Affairs Data Files.

Table 11.11

Key States in the 1992 Election

| State | Index of Ethnic Variety | Percent Voting for | | | New Congressional Representatives |
		Clinton	Bush	Perot	
CA	0.81	47	32	21	17
NY	0.81	50	34	16	9
TX	0.63	37	40	22	4
FL	1.12	39	41	20	10
PA	0.83	45	36	18	5
IL	1.32	48	35	17	4
OH	0.68	40	39	21	6
MI	0.71	44	37	19	5
NJ	0.6	43	41	16	3
NC	1.13	43	44	14	2

Source: Data from 1990 Census and Federal Election Commission, 1992 election totals.

dential hopeful since 1964, a state that lost half of its delegation to the House of Representatives because of reapportionment, a state that cast 26 percent of its ballots for Perot, Clinton was the victor by a 2 percent margin.

This Montana result was explained by Alan Parker of the National Indian Policy Center, also a member of the Democratic National Committee's National Ethnic Council, at a DNC luncheon on Martin Luther King Day, January 18, 1993. Two days prior to the inauguration of Clinton and Gore, Parker claimed that 16,000 Native Americans were newly registered, that they had voted for Clinton and Gore, and that the margin of victory was thus attributable to Native Americans. It was ethnic politics at its best!

Parker went on to say that during the campaign of 1992, the Democratic Party, led by a national ticket that had the support of locally elected Democratic officials throughout the country, reminded him of the lessons that Native Americans were beginning to understand about their own variety of cultures, traditions, religions, and ethnicities. Parker said that Native Americans were not and are not a homogenous population, but that they had learned to respect each other, and, most important, that it was through cooperation and dialogue that our common good could be achieved. Just as Native Americans had learned that toleration and respect for diversity were necessary for survival, so must all Americans. Parker further argued that the vast array of ethnic groups that comprise

America could find a political home in the Democratic Party. His remarks were echoed and endorsed by the following ethnic group leaders who also spoke at the luncheon: Arthur Gajarsa, Italian-American Leadership Council; John Pikarski, United Polonia for Clinton-Gore; C. Dolores Tucker, National Political Congress of Black Women; Hyman Bookbinder, American Jewish Committee; Christine Warnke, Greek Liaison DNC Ethnic Council; Clara Apodaca, Public Liaison for the Presidential Inaugural Committee; and Stan Balzekas, Museum of Lithuanian Culture.[19]

> *"In some respects, all those involved in ethnic politics have learned something far more important than registration drives for new voters."*

Thus it appeared that in 1992 the DNC had adopted a new narrative that would be much more dramatically proclaimed by Maya Angelou at the inauguration two days later. In some respects, all those involved in ethnic politics

Table 11.12

Members of U.S. House of Representatives

Ethnic Group	1990	1992
African Americans	24	39
Latinos	12	19
Italian Americans	28	27
Polish Americans	13	12
Asian Americans	3	4

Source: Congressional Quarterly Special Report, January 16, 1993.

have learned something far more important than registration drives for new voters.

American ethnicity is a social invention and cultural identity with no legal and constitutional lineage and not much political currency in some circles. Ethnicity is a social and cultural phenomenon whose very legitimacy within the American experience and whose persistence and saliency for politics seem suspect. Ethnicity and

ethnic politics have existed in presidential elections since the meshing of political cultures that occurred when national and local social realities began to interact during the decades before world War II. It continued in new forms as immigration and migration influenced the development of an increasingly interdependent nation. This process of Americanization assumed that its purpose and goal included the eclipsing of those alien features and sensitivities deemed inappropriate to the core political and cultural mentalities of America. As the end of this century approaches, ethnicity and ethnic politics are re-emerging. This renaissance of ethnicity and its recent potency as a political force have had important political and electoral consequences. A generation ago, painful divisiveness erupted into national view in Little Rock, when national authority and the segregated dichotomous culture of Arkansas intersected. Following the election of 1992, Arkansas had another day in national view when its poet and its president moved to reinvent the language of concord among the peoples of the United States.

Chapter Twelve

The 1992 Horse Race in the Polls

Peter V. Miller

Public opinion polls were an interesting and complex facet of the 1992 election. After setting a historical context, this chapter will describe some prominent features of the polls, examine how media-sponsored polls were done and how they were reported, and evaluate the role of the polls in the election process.

HISTORICAL CONTEXT

Assessments of public opinion have been an integral part of journalism, and particularly election journalism, since the founding of the republic.[1] Prior to the introduction of the so-called "scientific" polls in the 1930s and 1940s, newspapers and magazines printed both unsolicited and solicited measures of the public opinion "horse race" during the course of election campaigns. Straw polls—oftentimes conducted by readers of a given publication while, for example, traveling by train—were a common feature of election reportage in the latter nineteenth century. (In this century, straw polls were centralized and conducted by news organizations themselves, soliciting mock votes at shopping centers and other public places during election campaigns.)[2]

Press interest in and sponsorship of various sorts of polls during election campaigns may be seen as part of a broader journalistic and commercial interest in public sentiment. Journalists see it as their responsibility to assess the state of "the public mind." Moreover, features that explore public opinion are seen by media executives as popular with their audiences (audience response choices), and thus as profitable for the media outlet. Whether we consider election polls, man-on-the-street interviews about the firing of a popular football coach, or 900 number call-in polls, assessments of public opinion appear to be a staple item in the journalistic repertoire.[3]

The legitimation of "scientific" public opinion polls during election campaigns was accomplished in large measure through the events of the election of 1936, which pitted George Gallup's poll of public sentiment against the better-known *Literary Digest* poll of its own readers. Gallup's poll relied on a form of sampling individuals geographically and seeking their opinions, rather than relying upon the readership of a publication to be representative of the views of people throughout the country. Gallup publicly wagered that his method would produce more accurate results than the *Literary Digest* poll, and even predicted the extent of the *Digest*'s likely error. He offered to return to newspaper editors the money they paid him for the right to publish his poll if he was wrong. His predictions, however, were more or less borne out, and the *Digest's* poll of its readership, along with similar efforts, were discredited.[4]

Gallup's success began the era of commercial election polling sponsored by media clients. This arrangement for measuring and reporting public opinion remains with us today, with a few modifications. Pollsters, including Gallup and his competitors Archibald Crossley and Elmo Roper, made reputations by conducting election

139

Polling organizations insist their methods of predicting elections are scientific.

MEDIA HOTLINE

TAROT

OUIJA

BY WRIGHT FOR THE PALM BEACH POST, FLA.

polls, and used their status to establish profitable research businesses outside of the political arena. This pattern, too, continues to the present time, as pollsters such as Richard Wirthlin and Patrick Caddell have leveraged their political polling experience to form commercial survey research ventures. Thus, election polling has evolved in part because of its commercial attraction both for media executives looking for audiences and for researchers looking to build or maintain a brand-name reputation.

Preelection polls are perennially controversial because of their fit or lack of fit to the election results, because of their possible effects on voters (for example, "bandwagon" or "underdog" effects), because of their potential effect on the ability of candidates to raise funds and run campaigns, and because of their importance as a focus of media attention—to the detriment of issue-based coverage.

Recent elections have witnessed examples of all of these concerns, including the famous "late shift" in 1980 that is said to have produced the disparity between the polls, which showed a "dead heat" between Jimmy Carter and Ronald Reagan, and the election outcome—a substantial Reagan victory. The "late shift" explanation has been a favorite defense of pollsters for erroneous predictions going back at least to the Thomas E.

Dewey–Harry S. Truman race of 1948, in which Truman was decidedly in second place in all the polls but won the election. In 1988, a favorite theme of election coverage was Michael S. Dukakis's vaunted 17-point lead following the Democratic Convention that was somehow frittered away in the subsequent months of the campaign. The horse-race focus was roundly criticized following that election (as it always is), along with the press's ineffectual efforts to analyze negative campaign advertising.[5]

> "*Coming into the campaign of 1992, then, polls were an established if not beloved aspect of presidential elections.*"

Coming into the campaign of 1992, then, polls were an established if not beloved aspect of presidential elections. With their accuracy always open to challenge and their effects undetermined but usually viewed as negative, the polls are often considered frivolous or pernicious.

Particularly after the 1988 campaign, which produced what many considered the worst in political discourse and vapid media coverage, one might have predicted a diminution of the role of polls in election coverage in 1992, along with other reforms. For a variety of reasons, however, the polls played an even bigger role in 1992 than they had heretofore.

A SYNOPSIS OF POLLING EVENTS IN 1992

If 1992 did not set a record for the greatest number of polls taken during the campaign, it certainly did offer plenty of polls to examine. A search of campaign coverage in major newspapers, wire services, and news magazines from the beginning of June (the time of the California primary when the major party candidates were officially determined) to Election Day reveals over 130 national polls published by news organizations.[6] This figure is almost certainly a low estimate of published national polls, and it greatly underestimates total polling activity, since it does not include the very numerous statewide public polls, or polls that did not focus on the presidential race, or any of the polls conducted privately for candidates or causes. The number of people interviewed for these various kinds of polls during the five-month period is easily in the hundreds of thousands.

The "horse race" story of the 1992 campaign told by the national presidential polls uncovered in the search is graphically depicted in Figure 12.1. To construct this diagram, the results of polls conducted in the same week were averaged. In total, some 124 polls were included in the analysis.

The three-time series depict several salient features of the campaign: (1) H. Ross Perot's position during his unofficial and official entries in the race, separated by a two-and-one-half-month hiatus; (2) William J. Clinton's unprecedented surge in July, around the Democratic Convention and Perot's initial decision not to run; (3) George Bush's narrow range of support throughout the entire period. Taken as a whole, Figure 12.1 captures the odd, volatile character of the campaign in which an independent candidate seemed to operate on an even footing with the major-party nominees early in the race, followed by a very large-scale shift of support to the Democrat, whose support then faded some-

what with the growth of backing for the Republican incumbent and for the independent, who finally entered the race officially at the beginning of October.

The Early Horse Race

In late May and early June, just before the California primary, press coverage of the campaign featured considerable attention to the potential Perot candidacy, and concomitant support in the polls for the Texas billionaire. Perot's support in these early soundings drove further press attention because of the allegedly unprecedented level of his backing in comparison to the major-party candidates.[7] In several polls published during this period, Perot led Bush, Clinton, or both (albeit by small and generally statistically insignificant margins), or ran roughly even with them.

> **"The "Perot factor," as it was called in many press accounts, presented considerable difficulty for those conducting polls and for those trying to figure out what they meant."**

The "Perot factor," as it was called in many press accounts, presented considerable difficulty for those conducting polls and for those trying to figure out what they meant. The indeterminate, unannounced quality of his candidacy posed the question of whether his support ought to be measured or not, and whether it should be interpreted in the same way as the backing for candidates who had come through the party primary process. Because the general election campaign was still in its early stages and because Perot's candidacy came on the scene so suddenly, it was reasonable to believe that his unprecedented support—and the backing measured in polls for Clinton and Bush, for that matter—was ephemeral and thus likely to vary considerably in different polls over time. The fact that Perot was described as leading in some

Figure 12.1

1992 Presidential Horse Race: Vote Intention Weekly Averages

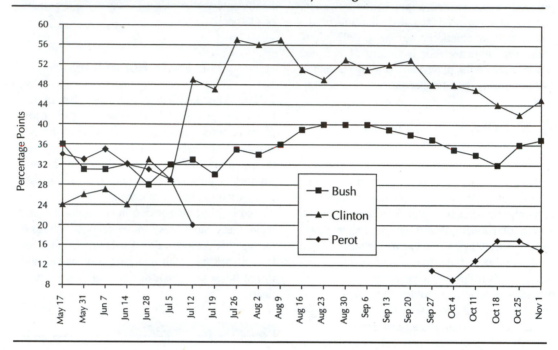

Note: Based on 124 polls, not including those whose dates couldn't be determined, with results averaged for each week. Estimates of likely voters were included; if a poll tallied both likely and registered voters, only the likely-voter estimate was used.

polls and trailing Bush and Clinton in others during May and June could be attributed to the notion that opinions about the three men had not crystallized and to methodological differences among the polls. In any case, the Perot factor, as it fed more and more polling activity and media speculation, also drew attention to the limitations of polls in picturing a horse race in which none of the participants were very popular or, in one case, even certain to be *in* the race.[8]

Convention "Bumps"

Late June and early July saw Perot's support peak and decline as Bill Clinton's rose. Press commentary on the race focused on the benefit Clinton had reaped from attacks and counterattacks between the Bush and Perot camps, which had driven up the negatives for both men. Further, attention was focused on reported disarray in the Perot organization concerning whether two campaign professionals—Ed Rollins and Hamilton Jordan—should have been involved in the effort, whether the campaign was going to

advertise or not, whether it was really a grassroots effort or simply another political campaign, and so forth. The approach of the Democratic Convention in mid-July and the selection of Senator Al Gore for the vice presidential slot produced considerable positive publicity for Clinton, as the news for Perot and Bush became increasingly bad.

The Democratic Convention   But Clinton's real gain in the polls came with the conclusion of the Democratic Convention and Perot's (later revoked) decision not to run. The confluence of publicity from the convention and Perot's announcement produced a "convention bump" for Clinton unlike any witnessed heretofore. Andrew Kohut, survey director of the Times Mirror Center for The People and The Press, noted that the center's studies in early June and after the convention had tracked a change in voting intention on the part of fully one-half of the electorate, an unrivaled movement in opinion based on his analysis of previous elections.[9] According to the Times Mirror survey, Clinton picked up two-thirds of former

Perot supporters, along with a large percentage of formerly undecided voters and even some Bush backers. The extent of the gain is easily observed in Figure 12.1, looking at the change in average poll horse-race numbers from the week of July 5 to July 12 and in the subsequent four weeks. On the other hand, the extent of Clinton's lead did not necessarily signal solid support, as many of those who shifted to him during this period were more opposed to Bush than they were for Clinton.

The Republican Convention Clinton's large lead provided the news frame for coverage of the Republican Convention in Houston in mid-August: Would George Bush be able to overcome the Democrat's advantage? Would the convention provide the kind of positive poll bump that Clinton had gotten? The answers to these questions were substantially more ambiguous than the changes observed in the polls after the Democratic Convention.

The immediate readings on the success of the Republicans' meeting to narrow the race were positive. The *Houston Chronicle* teamed up with The Hotline—a political information service—to sponsor a nightly "tracking" poll of national public sentiment during the convention, the results of which suggested that Bush had gained some support, particularly among previously undecided voters, on each night of the convention. Other polls, by Gallup, the *Los Angeles Times,* and the *Washington Post* supported the gap-narrowing thesis. Most dramatically, a single-night poll conducted by the *New York Times*/CBS News consortium at the end of the meeting found a virtual elimination of Clinton's lead, from double digits to a dead heat.[10]

But the findings of other polls called into question the extent of Bush's poll bump from the Republican Convention. In particular, the next polling effort by the *New York Times* and CBS News less than a week after the convention found that Clinton had apparently sprung back from a statistically nonsignificant 3-point margin to a 15-point lead. The *Times* story argued that Bush's convention gains had nearly "evaporated." Bush's pollster, Robert Teeter, was quoted as saying that the *Times* poll overestimated Clinton's lead, which he pegged at about 50 percent for Clinton and 40 percent for Bush. Stan Greenberg, Clinton's pollster, supported the thesis that Bush had lost much of his convention gain, beginning, he stated, with the nomina-

tion acceptance speech, which did not offer a convincing program for economic change.[11]

One story about the Republican Convention bump, then, was that Bush had gained on Clinton and then had slid back shortly after the convention. Another thesis also emerged during this period, however: Bush had not benefited from the convention, except perhaps marginally; instead, the polls taken during this time were unreliable. The CBS/*New York Times* one-night poll that had shown a statistical dead heat between Clinton and Bush near the end of the convention, for example, was part of a group of single-night efforts cited by Larry Hugick of the Gallup organization as producing less reliable information.[12] (The *Times* report on that poll itself had said in the second paragraph that "the results were considered somewhat less reliable than most polls that question more people and last several days."[13]) A Gallup *Newsweek* poll (another single-night effort) supported the "no significant bump" hypothesis, registering a statistically nonsignificant change of 3 points favorable to Bush after the convention.[14] Like the polls that had differed on the strength of support for Perot, Bush, and Clinton in May and June, the varying results around the time of the Republican Convention raised the question of whether poll information deserved credence. This question arose again with emphasis during the last week of the campaign, as we will see below.

Labor Day to Election Day

The official opening of the election campaign—Labor Day—found Clinton's average poll vote-intention number at around 50 and Bush's at around 40. From there, support for both candidates declined (gradually for Bush, somewhat jerkily for Clinton) until mid- to late October, rising again over the last two weeks of the campaign (see Figure 12.1). The decline for Bush and Clinton was associated with the reemergence of Ross Perot.

Perot officially entered the race at the beginning of October, but his level of support had begun to be reported again in anticipation of this event for a week or more. In the polls of the week of September 27, Perot can be seen pulling away from Clinton some of the backing that went to the Democrat at the time of Perot's decision not to run in July. The profoundly equivocal response to Perot's entry in the race at this time was signaled in a number of polls published prior to his candidacy announcement, all of which found significant opposition to his becoming a candidate. At the same time, Perot was shown in a Gannett News Service poll as garnering 20 percent of vote intentions in a hypothetical three-way race.[15] Perot's average standing in the polls increased until mid-October, concurrent with his performance in the presidential debates, and leveled off at around 15 percent.

After seeing his average support decline roughly in parallel with Clinton's until mid-October, Bush appeared to close the gap (to about 6 points) during the week of October 25. The final polls taken before the election, however, gave Clinton a slightly greater 8-point edge, 45 percent to 37 percent. On Election Day, Clinton received 43 percent of the popular vote to Bush's 38 percent and Perot's 19 percent. The extent of Bush's comeback in the final week, Clinton's rebound in the final polls, and the underestimation of Perot's support all were controversial polling and campaign issues.

"In the final week of the campaign, much press coverage was focused on polls that purported to show Bush and Clinton running neck and neck. . . ."

The Closing Gap   In the final week of the campaign, much press coverage was focused on polls that purported to show Bush and Clinton running neck and neck, with levels of support within the margin of sampling error. Perhaps the most prominent of these poll reports was one by CNN and *USA Today,* based on a tracking poll conducted October 26 and 27 and released October 28, that showed Clinton leading Bush by just 2 points—40 percent to 38 percent. The tracking poll, in which a sample of about 500 self-reported registered voters were interviewed each night and their aggregated responses were reported every two days, had shown an 11-point Clinton lead in the previous

day's report among all registered voters, and a 6-point lead among "likely" voters.

Likely voters are those who, by virtue of their answers to questions about previous voting and their likelihood of voting in the current election, are judged to be more apt to vote than others. Each polling organization has its own formula for determining voting likelihood. The CNN report on October 28 mentioned the fact that the 40 percent to 38 percent Clinton lead was based only on Gallup-estimated likely voters, but it did not mention that among registered voters in the samples, the spread was still more like 10 points. Thus, it could appear that, from October 27 to 28, Bush had gained enormous ground—from 11 points down to 2—if one were not careful to keep track of the base upon which percentages were calculated.

Even if one were clear on how the horse-race calculation was made, the Gallup method for determining likely voters also was a source of controversy. The procedure was questioned by the Clinton campaign and other news organizations, whose own estimates of vote intention from likely voters had shown a narrower race, but nothing so close as the Gallup figures. But these technical objections were lost in the loud advertisement of a neck-and-neck race picked up by print and broadcast editors from the initial CNN report.[16] This story set the frame for interpreting polls for the rest of the week, and probably helped to fuel the outrage of some Bush supporters who felt that the president would have pulled ahead if it had not been for new indictments brought against Caspar Weinberger on the Friday before the election as part of the Iran-Contra investigation by special prosecutor Lawrence Walsh.

For the remainder of the week, the Gallup likely-voter numbers continued to show a dead heat. Other polling organizations showed a narrower race than the week before, but none so close as the Gallup estimates. But the results of Gallup's two nightly polls on the weekend before the election showed a 44 percent figure for Clinton, 36 percent for Bush, and 14 percent for Perot. Gallup's final "election call"—somewhat surprisingly—estimated that 5 of the 6 percent of voters still undecided would vote for Clinton, with 1 percent going to Bush. Gallup's final estimate of 49 percent for Clinton, 37 percent for Bush, and 14 percent for Perot was the largest spread between the major-party candidates among all of the polls, ironically following a week in which its estimates showed the narrowest margin. This rather radical change in the polling numbers for one organization and the level of publicity they received because of CNN's prominent place in America's newsrooms gave ammunition to those who, like President Bush, thought that the pollsters were "nutty."

Final Polling Scorecard After the votes were tallied, it was time to see how well the final polls had done in judging the probable voting percentage for each of the three candidates. With the exception of the Gallup poll just discussed, the polls had come quite close to the actual vote in their predictions. Given the slippage one must allow for sampling error, all of the major news organizations' polls—with the exception of Gallup—gave reasonably accurate estimates of the vote for Clinton, Bush, and Perot. The Perot estimates were the least accurate, with all of the polls systematically underestimating by several points his 19-percent share of the vote.[17]

A LOOK INSIDE THE POLLS

Having tracked the polls' performance over the course of the general election campaign, it is useful to examine how these horse-race numbers were generated and to offer an evaluation.

Ways of Getting Polls Done

Unlike 1936, when George Gallup sold his poll information separately to interested newspapers, polls today involve exclusive contracts between polling firms and news organizations, or are carried out by employees of the news organizations themselves, sometimes with the assistance of outside firms who do sampling and interviewing. For example, we have seen that the Gallup organization in the 1992 campaign had a contract with CNN and *USA Today* to do polling throughout the campaign. Gallup also polled for *Newsweek*. In such arrangements, the news organization may have a survey expert on staff or a hired consultant who deals with the polling firm in designing questionnaires, supervising sampling and interviewing and analyzing the data. The in-house survey expert or consultant also deals with editors and other newsroom personnel to determine the timing and substance of polls.

Alternatively, some news organizations carry out the activities of polling entirely in-house (such as the CBS/*New York Times* operation), or mostly in-house (the ABC/*Washington Post* organization, for which Chilton Research, a survey firm owned by ABC, does the interviewing). It is difficult to say which kind of operation is better. In-house polling organizations offer the potential for better integration of polling activities with the newsroom, and the potential for more control over how polling information is used in news stories. Researchers at Gallup might have wished that their client, CNN, had not played the poll of October 26–27 as loudly and definitively as it did.

> **"[P]olls are often pictured as snapshots that freeze movement in public opinion for a closer look."**

At the same time, having a polling operation in-house is no guarantee that poll information will be reported accurately or with appropriate judgment. For example, the ABC/*Washington Post* poll of September 16–20 found Clinton with 58 percent and Bush with 37 percent. The large difference received page-one headline treatment in the *Post*. Other polls during the campaign had received less prominent treatment on an inside page. This particular poll's finding appeared on page one because the story of which it was to be a part was slotted for that place before the poll numbers were known. The headline was done by an editor, not a polling expert. The problem for the *Post* was that this particular poll's numbers were "outliers"—the estimates did not look like what other polls were getting, much like the Gallup poll that found the race neck and neck a month later. The *Post*'s next poll, conducted the following week, found the race much closer (in line with polls by other organizations), and the paper's polling expert had to explain how the prominently played poll could have shown the large lead. People who do polls for a living recognize that some readings of public opinion, because of the many errors that polls are subject to, are going to be quite far from the truth. In this case, the *Post* appeared to have conducted such a poll, and, due to a set of unrelated circumstances, given it very prominent display.[18]

Poll Design and Timing: Cross-Section Surveys

Polls that seek to measure the hypothetical national popular vote at various points in the campaign are mainly cross-section surveys: questions asked of a group of individuals sampled in order to represent the views of the relevant population group (for example, adults in the United States, registered voters, likely voters) at a single point in time. Oftentimes these surveys are done over a period of several days, so that the individuals not reached or who refuse to be interviewed at the initial call can be recontacted. The results obtained from such efforts depreciate in informational value over time as events reshape people's attitudes, so polls are often pictured as snapshots that freeze movement in public opinion for a closer look. Except for the final polls taken before Election Day, they are not predictions of how people will vote. Rather, they are representations of people's views at a given point in time, and should not be extrapolated beyond that point.

Some polling operations do these cross-section surveys at regular intervals, say, every week or month, depending on the budget. News organizations additionally often sponsor polls near major campaign events such as conventions or debates, in order to get a reading of their impact. In the 1992 campaign, as already noted, polls were also concentrated around the times that Ross Perot entered, left, and reentered the race.

Fast-Reaction Polls Polls that are timed to measure the impact of campaign events receive much attention and, for a variety of reasons, are apt to raise questions of reliability. For example, in the review of the 1992 polls—especially around the Republican Convention—we saw that poll estimates of the horse race were at variance with one another. Some polls recorded a convention bump for Bush, while others recorded no improvement. The differences among the polls can be attributed, in part, to attempts by news organizations to do polls that capture immediate public reaction to fast-breaking events.

The CBS/*New York Times* initial reading of public response to the Republican Convention, for example, was a one-night poll conducted near the end of the meeting.

As noted above, that poll showed Clinton's lead to have virtually vanished. Yet less than a week later, a separate poll by the same organization showed that Clinton's lead had reappeared. Had Bush lost his large convention bump so quickly? A plausible alternative explanation is that the initial one-night poll was wrong. In order to capture immediate public response, a poll must be completed quickly after the event in question. But the catch-22 is that doing a poll quickly creates greater risks of error. If a poll is done in one night, for example, there are many people in the sample who cannot be reached (not at homes, refusals, busy signals). This nonresponse error can make a big difference in poll accuracy; in the case of the one-night Republican Convention poll, the sample of people reached may have underrepresented Clinton supporters. The more general lesson is that fast-reaction polls are a risky business. Ironically, because they are associated with breaking news events, these chancy operations often receive more press attention than do polls that are conducted over several days and thus reduce the risks of nonresponse error.

Tracking Polls A special case of the one-night poll is the tracking poll. A tracking poll is a series of one-night polls whose findings are aggregated over two or more nights to produce a moving average of public opinion. For example, 500 interviews might be taken each night for several nights. The percentage of the sample supporting Clinton would be calculated for each night, and then the average support could be calculated for several nights. As interviewing proceeds, earlier nights can be dropped from the average as new ones are added. The tracking poll is an effort to combine the fast-reaction poll approach with the greater stability added by larger sample sizes gained through several nights' interviewing.

But tracking polls, because they draw a new sample for each night, are just as subject to nonresponse error as are one-night polls. The averages created by adding up the results of several nights' work may be more stable than the single night's estimate, but the combined samples still may over- or underrepresent particular kinds of voters. We saw that the CNN/*USA*

"Polling organizations do not disclose the way they question people about likelihood of voting, or analyze the answers, except in general terms."

Today/Gallup tracking polls of the final week of the campaign were controversial because they showed the race between Clinton and Bush essentially tied when others showed a Clinton lead. In part the Gallup estimates were probably due to their method for determining likely voters, but they may also have been affected by nonresponse error in each night's tracking poll, if Clinton supporters were underrepresented in the samples. Tracking polls, then, also need caution in their interpretation; ironically, however, like other one-night polls, they are more apt to get greater publicity and less careful treatment in the press because they purport to describe public opinion up to the minute.

Capturing Public Opinion: Telephones Are Essential

Polls rely on the telephone to gather information quickly. Nearly all households in the country have a telephone (estimates by the Bureau of the Census are 93–95 percent), though many telephones are not listed in phone directories. Polling organizations use a technique called random digit dialing to reach people who have listed or unlisted numbers. But telephone samples naturally exclude people who do not have phones or who do not live in households. Further, virtually every national sample excludes the opinions of people in Alaska and Hawaii, and so one must interpret the results of polls within these constraints. As telephones have come to be used more and more for solicitations of various kinds, interview requests compete with these other interruptions for people's cooperation. Many people refuse or are not available to answer poll questions. (Various press reports in 1992 estimated the nonresponse average at around 50 percent; it would probably be higher for one-night polls.) While the telephone has made it possible to conduct polls in several days or even one day, its advantages come with these drawbacks.

The Importance of Questionnaires
We noted earlier that polling organizations use different methods of determining which respondents are likely to vote. The methods can have a large impact on the horse-race estimates produced by polls, as seen by the disparity between the Gallup estimates and those of other organizations at the end of the campaign. But the likely-voter calculations are trade secrets. Polling organizations do not disclose the way they question people about likelihood of voting, or analyze the answers, except in general terms. Thus, one must be aware that there are different algorithms, and treat each method with caution.

Similarly, the questions used to estimate the horse race differ by organizations, as do the questionnaire contexts within which those items are asked. The average poll reader would not be aware of these differences, which can account for much of the variance in poll estimates. For example, the estimates of support for Clinton, Bush, and Perot in May and June varied among polls in part because of the way different polling organizations asked about the three-way contest. Further variance was produced by the questions that were asked prior to the vote-intention question that produced the horse-race estimates.[19]

REPORTING THE HORSE RACE

When headlines trumpet the latest poll results but news stories leave readers unaware of the limitations of polls due to the stage in the electoral process (for example, early in the campaign when opinions are not well grounded vs. the final week when most will have made up their minds), or due to the way polls are done, they give the illusory impression of a changing race. People must have a context for understanding what poll numbers mean, and why polls can differ in their estimates. News stories rarely provide that kind of information. As a result, faulty inferences can be drawn about which candidate can win (which affects contributions and volunteer support), or people can decide that poll numbers are meaningless.

For years, the polling profession has endeavored to teach the media how to report the polling story. Reporting practice actually has improved somewhat: there were many stories written in 1992 that attempted to disentangle differing poll estimates and the intricacies of methodology, in response to apparently disparate estimates coming from different polls.[20] Still, such efforts could not compete in number with the myriad of news accounts which simply reported new poll numbers. What is needed is a reporting approach that combines reporting of poll estimates with expert interpretation. Warren Mitofsky, head of Voter Research and Surveys, the organization that does all exit polling for the television networks, has suggested that polling experts write news releases themselves rather than relying on reporters to interpret the numbers. Others have advocated other approaches to making poll stories meaningful.[21]

SHOULD POLLS BE DONE AT ALL?

Recognizing the methodological pitfalls in polls, their potential for misinformation (particularly when opinion is not well crystallized), and the fact that they may deal with trivial matters, one could argue that they ought not to be published at all. The chief difficulty with this approach is the fact that candidates have access to private poll-ing data which they can selectively release to buttress claims about their support. They can also make up public opinion numbers. With no journalistic check, there would still be a horse race, but the information on it would be controlled by candidates.

It is clear, however, that there is no need for as many polls as are conducted, particularly those that attempt to track small changes in the race with crude techniques like tracking polls. If polls are done, they ought to be done carefully and reported within an appropriate context that gives a particular poll's findings in relation to others with differing methodologies. The breathless reporting of a poll that claims a majority of the public believe that a fictional television character (Murphy Brown) would make a better president than Dan Quayle does nothing for democracy and trivializes all polling efforts. Polls can teach us much about why people vote the way they do, and how they are reacting to the claims of candidates. Their value is decreased by the large number of polls, risky methodologies, and uninformed reporting. In 1992, horse-race reporting may well have been better than ever before. It still has a long way to go, however, before polls contribute most meaningfully to election campaigns.

Chapter Thirteen

The Presidential Election of 1992 in Historical Perspective

Peter F. Nardulli and Jon K. Dalager

Republics are different from other forms of government because they provide citizens with some input into the operations of the government, even if that input is largely indirect. Elections are the most important mechanism by which citizen input is registered, and presidential elections are the most influential of American elections, especially in recent times. How, and to what degree, the electorate responds to prevailing political, economic, and social conditions makes a difference for politicians and policymakers who have to make the American government work. These concerns are also important for students of American politics, who must attempt to make sense of how the various pieces of the political puzzle fit together. The role of this chapter in this ongoing effort is to interpret the results of the 1992 presidential election in light of historical electoral patterns. Our primary questions are: How does the 1992 presidential election differ from recent presidential elections? How do these differences compare with past patterns of change?

A focus on electoral change is appropriate here because, prior to William J. Clinton's 1992 victory, the Republican candidates had won five of the last six presidential elections, and seven of the last ten. The Democrats' only victories since 1948 have been John F. Kennedy's squeaker in 1960, Lyndon B. Johnson's landslide in 1964, and Jimmy Carter's victory in 1976. Because of this pattern of success, the Republicans were considered to have a "lock" on the White House, and few people expected, as late as early summer 1992, that George Bush would not be

reelected. In fact, many of the forecasting methods used by political scientists predicted that Bush would win.[1] Thus, Clinton's victory represented a break from the past, indicating that significant changes were occurring within the electorate.

Clinton's victory took many forecasters by surprise because there is much continuity in American politics, and its electoral arena is no exception. The reason for this electoral continuity is that, historically, voters have tended to develop strong partisan attachments to one of the two major parties. Angus Campbell wrote that partisan attachment can be described as "a degree of psychological attachment to one of the major parties. This partisan identification is remarkably resistant to passing political events. . . ." Campbell noted that the choice of the voter in any particular election "derives from the interaction of his political predispositions and the short-term forces generated by the current political situation."[2]

At the core of these attachments are symbols, values, and policies that voters, associate with the major parties. For many voters these associations outweigh the specific issues and personalities involved in a particular election campaign: people vote for the candidate nominated by *their* party.[3] There is some evidence that American voters are becoming increasingly discriminating, and that partisan attachments have less influence on electoral choices than in the past. Also, the impact of party images on voting seems to have varied across electoral offices in recent years, with many voters routinely supporting the Republican candidate for president and the Democratic candidate for Congress. This notwithstanding, if one were to focus just on the results of American *presidential* elections over the past two centuries, as we will shortly, long-term voting patterns are clearly discernible. Moreover, they usually determine the outcome of the election.

As clear as these long-term voting patterns are, however, they also make it evident that no election is a carbon copy of the previous election, or set of elections. But then again, there are different types of electoral change. Some change is little more than seemingly random fluctuations around a long-term voting trend line. These *short-term deviations* can sometimes be quite significant and can even result in an upset victory for a minority-party candidate. However, their long-term effect is limited. Electoral change of more consequence is that which reflects an abrupt, large, and enduring shift in electoral patterns. Such change is referred to in political science jargon as a *critical realignment.*

A third, more subtle type of electoral change could also account for the results of the 1992 election, one referred to as *dealignment* in political science jargon. Dealignment refers to long-term electoral change driven by the decreasing importance of partisan attachments to voting choices. In this view there is no majority or minority party at the presidential level. Electoral outcomes are determined largely on the basis of the issues, candidates, and campaigns.

To summarize, Clinton's 1992 victory is a clear change from recent electoral patterns and may have resulted from:

1. a short-term deviation from a long-term vote pattern that favors the Republicans at the presidential level;
2. a critical election marking the beginning of a new partisan era, one marked by unified Democratic control of the elected branches of the national government; or
3. a normal shift in electoral support in an era characterized by partisan dealignment.

This chapter will examine each of these possibilities by viewing the 1992 results from the perspective of American electoral history. Before we examine the data that bear on these different interpretations, we need to talk in more detail about short-term forces and deviating elections, critical elections and partisan realignments, and the notion of dealignment. Then we must discuss briefly the approach we used to measure electoral patterns, as well as changes in those patterns.

TYPES OF ELECTORAL CHANGE: SHORT-TERM ELECTORAL CHANGE AND DEVIATING ELECTIONS

The most common form of electoral change is that due to the effects of short-term factors. A wide variety of factors can lead to deviations of various magnitude from prevailing electoral margins. Examples would include exceptional economic conditions, international incidents, scandals, personalities, and third-party candidacies. Garden-variety occurrences of these developments during and before a presidential campaign are important enough to cause large groups of voters to depart from their traditional partisan allegiances, but they are not powerful enough to cause most voters to permanently shift their partisan attachments. The electoral impact of these short-term factors varies directly with the strength of the party system. Volatile voting patterns were somewhat common in the early nineteenth century, before the Whigs and Democrats firmed up their electoral support, as well as in the pre–Civil War years, when the party system was in crisis. But in the heyday of the American party system, the last quarter of the nineteenth century, the strength of local party organizations and the zealous partisan attachments of most voters minimized the impact of most such factors.

In the modern era, the decline in the organizational strength and vitality of the political parties and the emergence of a powerful, electronic mass media has enhanced the electoral role of short-term factors. The highly personable war hero, Dwight D. Eisenhower, generated extraordinary victory margins for the Republicans in the 1950s, while the troubled candidacy of George McGovern hurt the Democrats' showing in 1972. Nothing in the latter half of the nineteenth century can compare to the deviations from normal voting patterns that have occurred during the past 40 years.

However, as impressive as short-term deviations from a prevailing voting trend can be, they do not always affect the outcome of the elections. A majority party can benefit from good times and roll up even more impressive margins of victory. A minority party can capitalize on a scandal and come close to electoral victory, but still not prevail. Instances in which short-term effects lead to an isolated victory by a minority party are called *deviating elections.* Clear instances of deviating elections are a rarity in American electoral history, but some have occurred. The most dramatic examples are Woodrow Wilson's victory in 1912, Lyndon Johnson's victory in 1964, and Jimmy Carter's victory in 1976.

Wilson's victory, and his reelection in 1916, occurred in the midst of a strongly Republican era in presidential politics, the 1912 victory made possible by Theodore Roosevelt's third-party candidacy, which badly split the Republicans. Former president Roosevelt, who retired from politics in 1908, once again sought the Republican presidential nomination, even though the incumbent Republican president, William Howard Taft, was also seeking the nomination. Taft won the party's endorsement, inciting Roosevelt and his supporters to bolt from the Republican Party to the Progressive Party, which willingly nominated Roosevelt. Even though he was a third-party candidate, Roosevelt's popularity remained high. Unfortunately, most of his support came at the expense of his former friend and fellow Republican, President Taft. The three-way race changed the dynamics of the campaign, opening the door for the Democratic candidate, Woodrow Wilson. Wilson won the presidency with 42 percent of the popular vote, compared to 27 percent for Roosevelt and 23 percent for Taft. If Roosevelt had not run, it is quite possible that Taft would have been reelected. In 1920, the Republicans regained their position of electoral dominance and controlled the White House for the next 12 years.

In 1964, the Republicans failed to win the presidential election despite their advantage in the normal vote, a point that will be documented shortly. The short-term effects of this period were overwhelming, however, and it is clear that they had little hope of victory. Less than one year before Election Day, President John F. Kennedy was assassinated in Dallas, Texas. This tragedy and the ensuing drama shocked the nation and dominated its attention. Vice President Lyndon Johnson's campaign stressed the continuation of Kennedy's policies as a way to pay homage to the nation's fallen leader. Johnson also was able to widen his victory margin because of the poor campaign of conservative senator Barry Goldwater. The right wing of the Republican Party had gained strategic control of the national nominating convention and awarded the presidential nomination to Goldwater. The party platform represented the views of Goldwater and his supporters, but they were not shared by most Republicans, much less by a majority of voters. According to one historian, "disaffection developed on a scale unequaled since the Bull Moose split of 1912."[4] In the general election campaign, the Democrats took advantage of the Republicans' divisiveness and sought to portray Goldwater as a dangerous fanatic. As they succeeded in their efforts, Goldwater's support dwindled and Johnson won by a landslide. However, this was a short-lived victory, as the Republicans regained the presidency in 1968 and won every election until 1992, with the exception of Carter's victory in 1976.

Carter's success can be credited to the electorate's anger over the Watergate scandal that had dominated the media's political coverage for almost four years. The public was clearly upset with those in government, a fact taken advantage of by the Carter campaign. The Republican candidate, Gerald R. Ford, was helpless against this strong sentiment, as he campaigned as the incumbent president (having assumed the office after Richard M. Nixon resigned), had served in Congress for over two decades, and, perhaps worst of all, had granted a presidential pardon to Nixon. The voters' anger dissipated by 1980, when the Republicans' normal vote advantage reasserted itself.

Critical Elections and Critical Realignments

A far less common type of electoral change is a critical realignment. A critical realignment is a sudden, enduring change in partisan attachments that are initiated by a critical election. This concept was first set forth by V.O. Key in 1955.[5] In a seminal work, Key took note of

a category of elections in which voters are . . . unusually deeply concerned, in which the extent of electoral involvement is relatively quite high, and in which the decisive results of the voting reveal a sharp alteration of the preexisting cleavage within the electorate.

151

Moreover, and perhaps this is a truly differentiating characteristic of this sort of election, the realignment made manifest in the voting in such elections seems to persist for several succeeding elections.[6]

The occurrence of a critical partisan realignment in voting patterns is important because of the nature of the forces that lead to it, and because its consequences for the conduct of the government extend over a considerable time frame. Unlike the more transient factors that lead to short-term deviations from normal voting patterns, realigning forces affect the basic partisan attachment of the voter and signal the beginning of a new political era. Thus, a critical realignment will not be generated by such things as campaign commercials, candidate quality, or events at the party convention, but by a shift in the voter's basic outlook on political matters. This basic shift makes it possible, under certain conditions, to generate profound changes in the structures and/or policies of government.

> "[A] critical realignment will not be generated by such things as campaign commercials, candidate quality, or events at the party convention, but by a shift in the voter's basic outlook on political matters."

Despite the importance of critical partisan realignments for American politics, there has been a great deal of controversy as to when they occurred, where they occurred, and whether they still occur.[7] Much of this controversy stems from disagreements over how broad the geographic scope of an electoral shift must be before it qualifies as a realignment, when a voting shift is large or sudden enough to qualify as a "critical" realignment, and whether the shift has to be across all offices and levels of government. This notwithstanding, there is general consensus concerning at least three critical realignments in the history of U.S. presidential elections. One occurred around the Civil War, a second in 1896, and the third around the Great Depression. Each of these time periods evidenced a major shift in the level of support for each of the two major parties, and each new alignment continued for several elections after the critical election. While the New Deal realignment came close, none of these voting shifts were truly national in scope, even though they had national consequences.[8]

Prior to the pre–Civil War realignment of 1860, the two dominant political parties were the Jacksonian Democrats and the Whigs of Henry Clay and Daniel Webster. During the middle of the nineteenth century, America was increasingly divided over the issue of slavery. Both the Democratic and Whig Parties tried to straddle the issue, but in the 1850s, a new party evolved that adopted a firm antislavery stance. The electorate became polarized over the issue (mostly along geographical lines), and the Whig Party eventually disappeared. In the 1856 election, most of the Northeast swung sharply to the new Republican Party. Although the Republican candidate did not win in 1856, and Lincoln won the presidency in 1860 without a majority of the votes cast, the Republicans held the White House for the next 24 years.

In the 1896 realignment, the parties forged new coalitions, thereby changing the partisan structure that emerged in the Civil War era. The nation had suffered several economic crises in the 1880s and 1890s, during which time the farmers, small-town merchants, and rural residents formed a new coalition within the Democratic Party, joining the newly emergent "solid" South. The Republican Party appealed to the interests of the business community, city residents, and factory workers, thus completing the rural-urban division. In the election of 1896, Democratic candidate William Jennings Bryan led the rural interests in his pursuit of the presidency, but failed to overcome the strengths of William McKinley and his urban-industrial coalition. The Republican Party again dominated presidential elections until 1932, with the exception of the Wilson years.

Perhaps the best known of the critical elections occurred in 1932 when Democrat Franklin Delano Roosevelt defeated Republican Herbert Hoover in 1932. Roosevelt won by a significant margin as the voters sought relief from the severe economic depression. Roosevelt's tenure reinforced the Democratic Party's advantage in the presidential contest, which then continued for 30 years.

Partisan Dealignment

The notion of "partisan dealignment" refers to the reduced role of the political parties in the voters' electoral decisions. It developed as a response to the realignment literature in order to describe electoral change that was inconsistent with the basic tenets underlying Campbell's notion of voters' psychological attachment to the parties and Key's notion of a realignment of those attachments. Partisan dealignment reflects a gradual shift of the electorate away from a majority party, resulting in more competitive elections. In this environment, the outcome of any particular election may be determined by short-term factors that arise in the campaign. Evidence of dealignment can be found in survey results that show a declining number of voters identifying with either of the political parties, an increasing number of voters splitting their ballots, and more people than ever claiming that it is important to them to vote for the candidate without regard to the party.[9]

The subtle shift in significance from long-term partisan influences to short-term factors is attributable to several developments. One is clearly the increased role of the mass media, which have essentially replaced the parties as the voters' sources of political information. The significance of parties has declined in other ways as well. In the past, the political party organization was responsible for selecting the candidates, raising money, and spreading the campaign's message through newspaper editorials and brochures distributed throughout the country. In the modern era, the parties have little input on who the nominees will be because of the open primary, and the parties no longer need to "organize the troops" for the candidates. The nominees have the ability to rally their own supporters through extensive use of the electronic media.

MEASURING ELECTORAL CHANGE: CALCULATING THE NORMAL VOTE

To put the presidential election of 1992 into historical perspective, we must somehow derive an estimate of what was expected to happen in 1992, and then compare this estimate with what actually happened. The difference between the expected and the actual outcomes in 1992 must then be compared with expected and actual outcomes of past elections. Central to this analysis is the concept of a *normal vote,* first introduced by Converse in 1966. The normal vote concept emerged because analyses of survey results suggested that the vote cast by an electorate can be split into two components:

1. the normal or "baseline" vote division to be expected from a group, other things being equal; and
2. the current deviation from that norm, which occurs as a function of the immediate circumstances of the specific election. . . . The long-term component is a simple reflection of the distribution of underlying party loyalties, a distribution that is stable over substantial periods of time. In any specific election the population may be influenced by short-term forces associated with peculiarities of that election (for example, a candidate of extreme attractiveness or a recent failure of party representatives in government) to shift its vote.[10]

A very involved procedure was used to produce normal vote estimates for all U.S. presidential elections between 1828 and 1984, using aggregated voting records.[11] This effort required the integration and analysis of data on every presidential election during that period for every county and most major cities (3,136 counties and cities, 107,974 unit elections) in the U.S. A highly reliable procedure, based on cluster analysis, was developed to group contiguous counties into 215 electorally homogeneous, substate regions. These regions are aggregates of counties (and some major cities) that ebbed and flowed together over time. Examples of these regions include upstate New York, southern California, and the city of Chicago.

In an analysis guided by the realignment tradition, a procedure based upon interrupted time-series analysis was developed to chart the patterns of electoral change in these 215 homogeneous regions.

THE NORMAL VOTE IN PRESIDENTIAL ELECTIONS, 1828–1992

Based on this procedure, the national normal vote (expressed in terms of the expected margin

Figure 13.1

Distribution of Actual Margins of Victory Around Normal Vote Trend Lines for the Nation

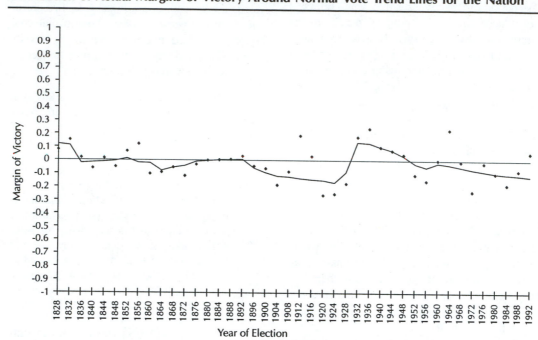

Note: Margin of victory = Democratic percentage of total vote minus Republican percentage of total vote.

of victory) for each presidential election from 1828 to 1992 is plotted in Figure 13.1, along with the actual margin of victory. Clearly, our normal vote estimate appears to be an adequate forecast of the actual vote. The significant deviation in 1992 is quite evident.

Eras in U.S. Presidential Elections

The electoral trends in Figure 13.1 reveal several distinct eras in American presidential elections. For the 60 years following Andrew Jackson's departure from the presidency (1836–1896), presidential elections were quite competitive. Neither major party enjoyed a marked advantage in the normal vote, with the exception of the period between 1860 and 1872. During that period the strife emanating from the issues that gave rise to the Civil War wreaked havoc with normal voting patterns. The national normal vote shifted toward the new Republican Party because many traditional southern voters who allied with the Confederacy could not vote in federal elections during this period (none did in 1864). Moreover, the newly enfranchised former slaves strongly embraced the Republicans.

The election of 1896, usually considered a critical election, brought an end to the competitive equilibrium that prevailed for most of the nineteenth century, and marked the beginning of a distinctly Republican era. The Republicans dominated presidential elections until 1932, with the exception of 1912 and 1916.

"Since the election of Eisenhower in 1952, the Republicans have slowly built a significant edge in national normal vote margins."

This Republican era was ended by the Great Depression that began in 1928, and the presidential election of 1932 stands as the prototypical critical election. The national normal vote shifted by almost 40 points, and the Democrats controlled the presidency for the next 20 years. In 1948, however, a massive and enduring shift away from the Democrats by the South signaled the beginning of what has become one of the most Republican presidential eras in American electoral history, second only to the post–1896 period. Since the election of Eisenhower in 1952, the Republicans have slowly built a significant edge in national normal vote margins. This normal advantage is, of course, what makes the Clinton victory in 1992 of such historic significance. Moreover, it was achieved without the calamitous events that preceded the Johnson and Carter victories.

An examination of Figure 13.1 reveals one other notable point concerning the most recent electoral era. There are more elections that depart further from the normal vote trend line after 1952 than in any period preceding 1952. Specifically, the elections of 1964, 1972, 1976, and now 1992 deviate from the expected vote by 10 to 20 points.

The 1992 Election

The 1992 normal vote, aggregated at the national level, predicted a Republican victory by a 12-point margin. If there had been only two candidates in the contest, this would have been translated into Bush's receiving 56 percent of the popular vote compared to Clinton's share of 44 percent.[12] When the final returns came in, however, Governor Clinton won the popular vote with 43.2 percent, compared to President Bush's total of 37.7 percent, a Democratic margin of 5.5 percent. This represented a deviation from the national normal vote of .175, almost triple the average deviation. H. Ross Perot did surprisingly well for an independent candidate, receiving 19 percent of the total vote, but because, on balance, his support appears to have come from each of the other candidates equally, his remarkable showing does not seem to have had an undue effect upon our analyses.

Although the aggregated national vote provides a quick summary of the election results, it can mask electoral trends at the state or regional level. Subnational trends are important in U.S. presidential elections because national returns do not always determine who wins. Under our unique system of choosing the president, the recipient of a majority of votes cast in the electoral college is elected—a procedure dependent on state-level returns.[13] In fact, three

times in our electoral history the winner of the popular vote has not been elected president.[14] Therefore, a state-by-state analysis will be useful in helping us understand the nature of electoral change embodied in the 1992 results.

This analysis will benefit greatly from the use of a benchmark in gauging the magnitude of the changes reflected in the 1992 returns. The election of 1988 will suffice as such a benchmark because, as indicated in Figure 13.1, it adheres quite closely to the normal vote projection at the national level.

The state-level results for 1988 are depicted in Figure 13.2. We list each of the 50 states and the District of Columbia according to their 1988 expected margin of victory, or normal vote, from the most Republican state to the least. Both the normal vote margin and the actual margin of victory are reported. For states that are normally Republican, the size of their advantage varies considerably—from a 50-point advantage in Utah to less than 1 point in Maryland. The Democrats have an overwhelming advantage in the District of Columbia, but for the handful of states in which they enjoyed an advantage, it was fairly small. Based on the state-level normal vote trend lines for 1988, it was expected that Michael S. Dukakis would win the popular vote in five states and the District of Columbia, totaling 45 electoral votes. Bush was expected to win all the other states and 493 electoral votes. As the election turned out, however, Dukakis did better than expected in six states, but failed to win Alabama, in which the Democrats' had a slight advantage. He won 112 electoral votes compared to Bush's 426 electoral votes.

It is apparent from Figure 13.2 that few states deviated significantly from their expected vote, with the exception of Iowa, Washington, and Oregon, where the Republicans fared more poorly than expected. In addition, in Alabama and several other of the more competitive states, Bush did better than expected. However, these isolated deviations are not unusual. Because of the political and cultural diversity among the states and between different sections of the country, short-term effects ordinarily generate some departures from the normal vote in any given election.

The 1992 election presents a far different picture from that of the 1988 election. Based on our state-level normal vote trend lines for 1992, Bush should have won 47 states consisting of 516 electoral votes. Clinton was expected to win

Figure 13.2

Distribution of Actual Margins of Victory Compared With Normal Vote Margins by State, 1988

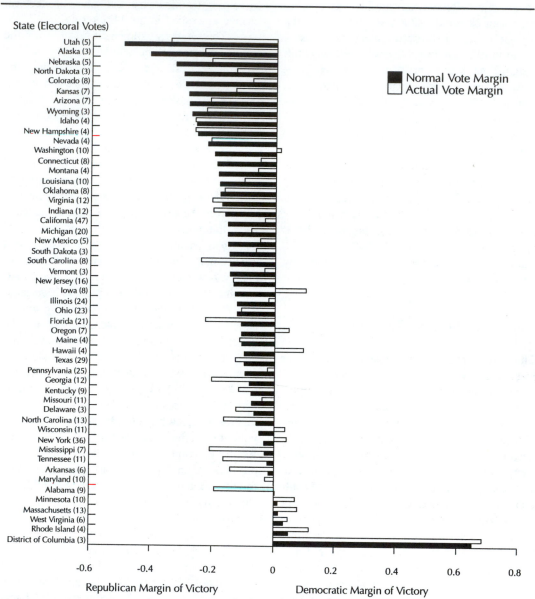

Note: Margin of victory = Democratic percentage of total vote minus Republican percentage of total vote.

three states and the District of Columbia, holding 22 electoral votes. Figure 13.3 presents the state-by-state normal vote and actual vote for 1992.

In the 1992 election, Clinton won 32 states and the District of Columbia, containing a total of 370 electoral votes; Bush won 18 states and 168 electoral votes; and Perot failed to win a majority in any state, thus receiving no electoral votes. Figure 13.3 reveals that although the Democrats were strongest in the District of Columbia, where they enjoyed an actual margin of victory over the Republicans of 75 points, they also did quite well in many states that were expected to vote Republican. Clinton won several very Republican states, such as Colorado and New Hampshire, which deviated from their normal vote by margins of .36 and .28 points,

Figure 13.3

Distribution of Actual Margins of Victory Compared With Normal Vote Margins by State, 1992

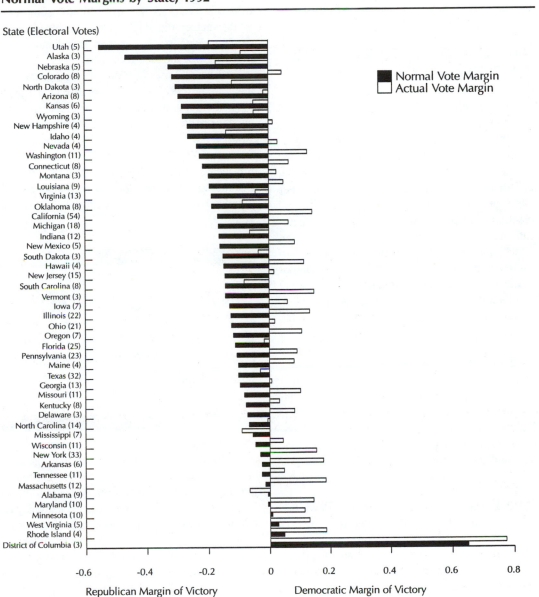

State (Electoral Votes)

Normal Vote Margin
Actual Vote Margin

Republican Margin of Victory

Democratic Margin of Victory

Note: Margin of victory = Democratic percentage of total vote minus Republican percentage of total vote.

respectively. In fact, the Democrats made substantial gains in almost every state, even if they failed to win the popular vote in some of the more Republican states. For example, Clinton came extremely close to winning Arizona, Florida, and North Carolina. This may indicate that in 1996, the Democratic candidate will have a better opportunity to win these states. Bush managed to avoid a Democratic landslide, but he did better than the normal vote projection in only two states, Mississippi and Alabama. The Democrats improved their standing in every other state.

The magnitude of the deviation in each state, as well as the size of the deviation at the national level, indicates that the 1992 election presented a considerable break from prevailing electoral trends. We now consider whether this result is merely a temporary divergence from these trends, the beginning of a new pattern of electoral trends, or further evidence that it is useless to talk about enduring electoral patterns.

THREE PERSPECTIVES ON THE 1992 PRESIDENTIAL ELECTION

The unexpected result of the 1992 presidential election may be accounted for by one of three possible explanations. The first is that it is simply a deviating election. This suggests that the Republicans may reassert their long-standing dominance in the presidential election of either 1996 or 2000. The second is that the 1992 election may be a critical election. The electorate may have abandoned their basic partisan attachment to the Republican Party in presidential elections, realigning in favor of the Democratic Party. The third explanation is that 1992 results are the normal consequences of an electoral era characterized by the dealignment of the electorate. The notion of a historical partisan attachment may not be relevant to contemporary electoral politics. Today's relatively well-educated electorate, inundated with political information from pervasive mass media, may no longer rely on party symbols when casting their ballots. We will examine each of these explanations, using historical comparisons to better understand the outcome of the 1992 election.

The Presidential Election of 1992 as a Deviating Election

Every presidential campaign consists of a number of factors that may affect the electorate's decision. These factors include the candidates' positions on a salient issue, the individual qualities and characteristics of the candidates, the presence or absence of political scandal, the effectiveness of political advertising, and so forth. Most of these short-term factors act to reinforce the voters' partisan predisposition, but occasionally they may persuade a segment of the electorate to reject their historical preference, causing the election outcome to deviate from the normal vote. On some occasions the deviation is of such a magnitude that it changes the outcome of the election, and the minority party wins the presidency. Figure 13.1 shows that most past elections have deviated to some degree from the

national normal vote, but only a handful can be considered deviating elections. In this century, the elections of 1912, 1964, and 1976 are all deviating elections that may provide some clue as to whether the 1992 election result is also a deviating election, rather than an indication of a more significant long-term shift.

The 1912 presidential campaign draws parallels to the 1992 campaign because of the presence of a popular, third-party candidate offering an alternative to the major parties. Theodore Roosevelt's 1912 campaign drew support away from the Republican nominee and incumbent president, William Howard Taft, thus allowing Democratic candidate Woodrow Wilson to win the election with only a plurality of the popular vote.

"[W]ith Perot as an alternative, voters who did not trust the Democratic candidate could cast their vote for someone other than Bush."

In 1992, George Bush did not have to contend with any former presidents, although, like Taft, he did face opposition to his renomination. Nevertheless, the independent candidacy of billionaire Ross Perot may have damaged Bush's chances of reelection, just as the candidacy of Roosevelt hurt Taft. As a third candidate, Perot reinforced Clinton's argument for change, he detracted from Bush's performance in the televised debates, and his attack on "Republican dirty tricks" undermined Bush's message that voters couldn't trust Clinton. In addition, with Perot as an alternative, voters who did not trust the Democratic candidate could cast their vote for someone other than Bush. The deviating election of 1964 has some similarities to the 1992 presidential election, but it also contained circumstances that were fortunately not replicated. Although the emotional response of the electorate to President Kennedy's death had no parallels in 1992, the conservative tone of Goldwater's campaign did find itself repeated in the Republican presidential campaign.

Figure 13.4

Scope and Magnitude of Electoral Shift: 1988–1992

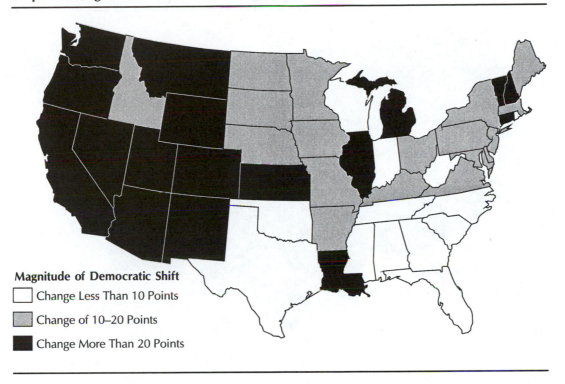

Magnitude of Democratic Shift

☐ Change Less Than 10 Points

▦ Change of 10–20 Points

■ Change More Than 20 Points

In 1992, the conservative wing of the Republican Party once again took control of the convention, and adopted a platform that espoused many right-wing views not generally shared within the Republican Party, much less by the public. Furthermore, many speakers at the Republican Convention (including Marilyn Quayle, former presidential candidate Patrick J. Buchanan, and television evangelist Pat Robertson) presented an image of intolerance and divisiveness in their remarks before a prime-time television audience. In contrast, the Democratic Party offered images of a unified party seeking to pull the nation together in order to solve its problems. Although George Bush did not personally share many of the extreme views of the conservative wing, he failed to separate himself sufficiently from this image, and many moderate voters were undoubtedly lost to the Democrats or to Perot.

The deviating election of 1976 was the first presidential election after the Watergate scandal, and the electorate's anger at the Republican Party was felt at all levels. Jimmy Carter, campaigning as a Washington outsider, benefited from this anger, taking full advantage of Gerald Ford's long tenure in Congress, as well as his presidential pardon of Richard Nixon.

Although the electorate showed some signs of anger at those in power in 1992, it did not reach the level of 1976, and there were no political scandals of a similar nature that aroused their ire. It should be noted, however, that the Republican campaign has blamed the late release of an indictment against former Secretary of Defense Caspar Weinberger as a crucial factor in Bush's loss. The indictment contained copies of Weinberger's notes that revealed that Bush was fully aware of the arms-for-hostages deal, even though he had consistently denied such knowledge.

Each of these previous deviating elections bears some resemblance to the 1992 election, but none can adequately explain the overwhelming shift toward the Democrats. Perot supporters came from each party equally, thus nullifying the "Teddy Roosevelt" hypothesis. Although the 1992 Republican convention and campaign appeared quite conservative, Bush was not seen to be as conservative as his party, and there was simply nothing that could compare with the impact of a presidential assassination. Lastly, the Watergate scandal had been thoroughly investi-

159

Figure 13.5

Scope and Magnitude of Electoral Shift: 1928–1932

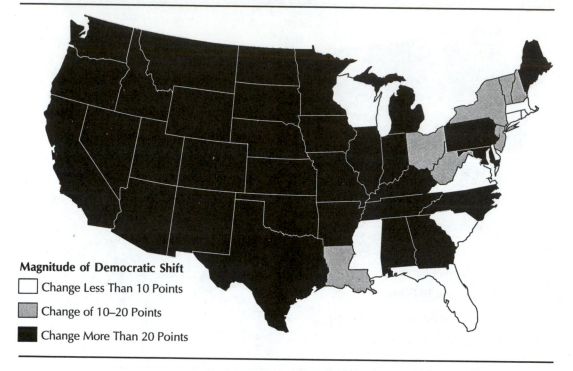

Magnitude of Democratic Shift

☐ Change Less Than 10 Points

▨ Change of 10–20 Points

■ Change More Than 20 Points

gated by 1976, revealing dishonesty and corruption at the highest levels of government. The minor scandals of Iran-Contra or Iraqgate, neither of which is yet well understood, did not have the media attention or shocking disclosures that would generate a similar effect on the electorate, although they no doubt were considered by some voters.

If none of these past deviating elections provides an adequate model for the 1992 election campaign, we might further ask if there were other short-term factors that may qualify 1992 as a deviating election. One additional factor to consider may be the economy. Although it hardly compared in severity to the Great Depression, the recession was unusually lengthy. The rate of growth was very slow, and the jobless rate remained steady at approximately 7 percent, although the number of businesses failing during Bush's presidency was greater than under any other president since World War II.[15]

It is also quite possible that a combination of several short-term factors gave the election to the Democrats. Although Perot's involvement did not appear to affect the outcome, his candidacy may have hurt Bush more than it affected Clinton because of Perot's persistent criticism of

"politics as usual" in Washington, a clear reference to the current administration. He also reinforced the Democrats' message of the need for change. The unanswered questions concerning the Iran-Contra scandal and the Administration's pre-war policies toward Iraq created additional dissatisfaction within the electorate. And perhaps the negative tone of the Bush campaign and the extreme conservatism of the Republican Convention, compared to that of the Democrats, persuaded others to change their vote. None of these factors was of such electoral significance as to cause a deviating election by itself, but the combined effect may indeed have generated a temporary Democratic majority. If that was indeed the case, the Republicans have an excellent chance of regaining the presidency in 1996 or 2000.

The 1992 Election as a Critical Realignment at the Presidential Level

A critical realignment, in its most basic sense, refers to a large, abrupt, and enduring shift in electoral patterns. It is best thought of, espe-

Figure 13.6

Scope and Magnitude of Electoral Shift: 1892–1896

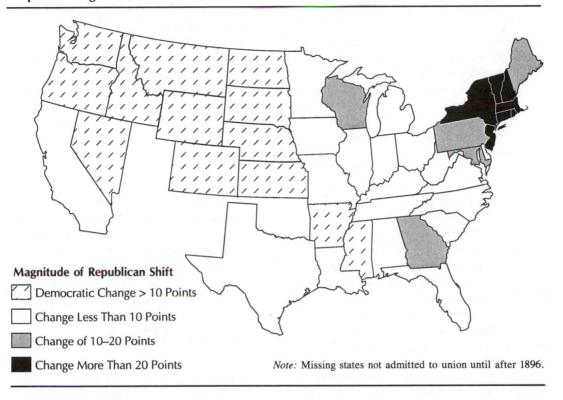

Magnitude of Republican Shift

- Democratic Change > 10 Points
- Change Less Than 10 Points
- Change of 10–20 Points
- Change More Than 20 Points

Note: Missing states not admitted to union until after 1896.

cially in modern times, as an office-specific phenomenon. Electoral trends across elective offices such as president, governor, senator, or representative have become disparate and disjointed in the twentieth century because they are driven by different expectations and forces. Thus, it is probably too much to expect a unified shift in electoral trends across offices that would be large and clear enough to qualify as a critical realignment. This type of unified movement may have happened during the nineteenth century, but voters have become more sophisticated, and the role of political parties has changed significantly throughout the twentieth century. To search for drastic breaks across elective offices today will only obscure our efforts to identify critical electoral change.

Not only should critical realignments be sought by examining office-specific electoral trends, but those electoral trends should be examined from a subnational perspective. The United States is simply too large and diverse to expect all of its constituent parts to react uniformly at the ballot box to a set of political stimuli. While the geographic scope of past critical realignments at the presidential level has

varied, there has never been one that was truly national in scope, a point that will be illustrated shortly.[16]

> *"The United States is simply too large and diverse to expect all of its constituent parts to react uniformly at the ballot box. . . ."*

These observations about the nature of critical realignments have important implications for our efforts to study them. They also suggest that our ability to say anything definitive about 1992 is severely limited. While we have adequate subnational electoral data on presidential returns to measure the magnitude of electoral change embodied in the 1992 results, we have no basis for knowing whether that change

161

will endure across a series of presidential elections.

As crippling as is our inability to see into the future, we can shed some light on the possibility that 1992 will prove to be a critical election. First, we can compare the magnitude and the scope of the electoral change embodied in the 1992 returns with two elections that history has shown to be critical elections, 1896 and 1932. If the magnitude and scope of the 1992 results do not compare with those registered in earlier realignments, we may be able to say that it was not a critical election. If these results match up favorably with those reflected in earlier critical elections, then it will prove useful to speculate as to the causes of the electoral shifts embodied in the 1992 results.

Enduring shifts in electoral patterns are due to the emergence of new and salient cross-cutting issues, or to significant alterations in the political landscape. The realignments that occurred before the Civil War, in 1896, and after the Great Depression were driven by the emergence of fundamental moral, cultural, and economic issues and developments. If subsequent elections show 1992 to be a critical election, we should be able to identify the issues or developments that contributed to the restructuring of prevailing electoral patterns. If we cannot point to anything that compares with historical critical elections, then the patterns that emerged in 1992 are not likely to endure.

To compare the magnitude and scope of the changes embodied in the 1992 presidential returns with those of 1896 and 1932, we compute a simple measure of change and then map the results by state. Our measure of change is the difference between the expected vote in the year preceding the critical election (1892, 1928, 1988) and the actual vote in the critical election year. Thus, if a state such as New York was expected to have favored the Republicans in 1928 by a margin of .10 points, but actually provided the Democrats with a .25 margin of victory in 1932, then its score on our measure of change is .35. To simplify the presentation of the results, we collapse this change variable into three groups. States that registered less than a 10-point shift were placed in one grouping; those that showed a 10- to 20-point shift were placed in a second grouping. States that displayed more than a 20-point change were put in a third category.

The results of this analysis are reported in Figures 13.4, 13.5, and 13.6. Although classify-ing change into only three categories is somewhat crude, the scope of the various alignments becomes clear in these maps. Figure 13.4 depicts the 1992 changes and makes it clear that most of the states outside the South, as well as a few in the South, registered significant electoral changes. The most dramatic changes are in the West, where the Democrats made dramatic gains in the most Republican section of the country. As impressive as are the changes depicted in Figure 13.4, they are dwarfed by those depicted in Figure 13.5, which reports the distribution of changes in 1932. The truly large Democratic shifts in 1932 extended further east and deeper into the South than the 1992 shifts. The scope and magnitude of the 1932 changes are not surprising, however, given the unprecedented economic and political situation at the time. These factors led to a shift in the national normal vote of almost 40 points in 1932, while the shift between 1988 and 1992 is just under 18 points.

"These results suggest that the magnitude and scope of electoral change, while not as great as that which occurred in 1932, compares favorably with the change that occurred in 1896."

The electoral shifts in 1932 are unparalleled in U.S. electoral history, and holding 1992 to such a standard is probably unreasonable. A more reasonable comparison may be with the critical election of 1896; its scope is depicted in Figure 13.6. The picture conveyed by this map is complicated by some massive, but short-term, Democratic gains in the West, generated by the populist appeal of William Jennings Bryan. The more enduring electoral change was that which benefited the Republicans. As is evident in Figure 13.6, this change was concentrated largely in the Northeast, joined by Wisconsin and Georgia. Comparisons between Figure 13.4 and Figure 13.6 must be tempered by the realization that the nation's population was much more concentrated in the East in 1896. This notwithstanding, the electoral changes embodied in the 1992 returns compare favorably with the critical election of 1896. The shift in the national normal vote in 1896 is 5. 1 points, compared to a jump of 17.5 points in 1992.

These results suggest that the magnitude and scope of electoral change, while not as great as that which occurred in 1932, compares favorably with the change that occurred in 1896. Thus, we turn to our second question: Is this change likely to endure? The answer to this question depends, in large part, on Clinton's performance in office as well as upon domestic and international developments beyond his control. But also important are the nature of the issues and political developments that contributed to his victory. To assess the durability of the electoral changes documented earlier, it is useful to consider Byron Shafer's insightful analysis of the post–World War II electoral order in the U.S.

By an "electoral order" Shafer means an array of preferences held by members of different social groups in the grand issue-areas of a political period. These issue preferences are manifested in a prevailing set of vote patterns for different elective offices. This set of vote patterns is likely to endure as long as the grand issue-areas remain stable and nothing occurs to upset the policy moods of important electoral groupings. The stability of the prevailing order is facilitated by the structure and alignment of two primary intermediary organizations, political parties and interest groups.[17]

Shafer argues that the most salient current political issues can be categorized within three main groupings: economic welfare, foreign affairs, and cultural values. There is, he contends, a national consensus that favors liberal economic welfare policies, a nationalist foreign policy, and the preservation of traditional cultural values. The distribution of preferences across these grand issue-areas explains the prevailing partisan makeup of the federal government. Simply put, because the House is primarily responsible for economic welfare policies, and the Democrats have an image of favoring welfare policies, it is a Democratic stronghold. The presidency is largely responsible for the conduct of foreign affairs and has the most central political role in setting the moral tone of the nation. Because the Republicans have an image of supporting a strong national defense and traditional cultural values, it has been a Republican stronghold. The institutional ambiguity and heterogeneity of the Senate mean that neither party has a "lock" on it.[18]

If we examine Shafer's analysis of the president's position within the current electoral order, the prospect for enduring change in the prevailing electoral patterns can be seen. First, consider the area of foreign policy. The unyielding stance of the Republican Party against the spread of communism and their advocacy of a strong defense has provided them with electoral dividends from many groups for several decades. But the end of the Cold War undermines the centrality of foreign affairs in the constellation of grand issue-areas, and introduces some ambiguity and uncertainty into the foreign policy preferences of important social groups that have lent support to Republican presidential candidates across a series of elections.

The globalization of economic matters, the existence of various "hot spots" throughout the world, and the United States' leadership role within the international community suggests that foreign affairs will remain a grand issue-area for the foreseeable future. But the demise of the Soviet Union removes an immediate threat to the security of the U.S. and neutralizes the electoral support that Republican presidential nominees have enjoyed by invoking the threat of the "red menace" and the spread of the "evil empire." Because of the end of the Cold War, the Republicans may find themselves in the same position as New Deal Democrats after their success in establishing the welfare state—without a constituency that responds electorally to established party themes and images. In any event, the end of the Cold War will provide the Clinton administration with the opportunity to influence the foreign policy views of important electoral groups, as these groups redefine their positions and reconsider the foreign policy stances of the major parties.

Similar change can be seen in the area of cultural values. Since at least the decade of the 1960s, cultural and moral issues have played a prominent role in presidential campaigns, and the Republicans' traditional image on these matters has generated a great deal of electoral support for them. But the social turbulence generated by such developments as the civil rights movement, the antiwar protests, the blatant use of drugs among middle-class youths, the crime epidemic, and other disruptions has dissipated to a large degree. Profound changes in the structure of the American family, the evolution of the abortion issue, the enhanced saliency of sexual harassment, the spread of the AIDS epidemic beyond the gay and drug subcultures, different perspectives on death and dying, and a host of other changes have clouded views on these cultural issues, thereby muting their effectiveness in political campaigns. The control of the 1992 Republican Convention by cultural extremists, and the intolerant image that they projected, could portend the eventual demise of the electoral dividends that have flowed from the Republicans' image as defenders of traditional values.

Because of the changes noted above, the Republicans were unable to draw sufficient electoral support from their issues stances on either foreign affairs or cultural values, stances that had worked well for them in the past. They had to rely on their stewardship of the economy and their domestic record because Clinton, Perot, and the media were able to keep these matters in the forefront of the campaign. The Republican administration's record might not have been a handicap had the economic situation been different at the time of the election. But it was not, and Bush was unable to articulate a domestic vision that captured the imagination of the people. Clinton had greater success at addressing the electorate's domestic concerns, and capitalized on the public's weariness of the paralysis caused by a divided government. His success in delivering on his campaign promises may well determine whether the changes evident in 1992 are sustainable.

"If partisan attachments have little hold on voters over time, there is no reason to expect that decisions made in 1992 will have any bearing on future electoral choices."

Dealignment of the Electorate and the 1992 Election

As noted earlier, the term "dealignment" most often refers to the weakening of party attach-

ments and the growth of voter independence.[19] If this phenomenon accounts for the outcome of the 1992 presidential election, then it would be incorrect to label it a deviating election. Dealignment means that partisan attachments no longer provide a firm basis for making projections about what is "normal." If short-term factors, not ingrained partisan loyalties, determine voting patterns, then electoral volatility is what is "normal." It also makes no sense to talk in terms of partisan realignment. If partisan attachments have little hold on voters over time, there is no reason to expect that decisions made in 1992 will have any bearing on future electoral choices. Candidates in future presidential campaigns will begin with a clean slate.

Empirical support for the dealignment thesis is derived largely from survey data on partisan identifications over time. Those data show a decline in the proportion of eligible voters who identified with a political party after 1968. This evidence seems consistent with the progressive decline of political parties as campaign organizations, and with the rise of the mass media in the political arena. The notion of dealignment also seems consistent with the increasingly disjointed electoral patterns across different offices throughout the twentieth century. Finally, the increasing magnitude of the post–World War II deviations from the expected vote (depicted in Figure 13.1) would appear to be consistent with the electoral volatility predicted by the dealignment thesis.

These observations notwithstanding, further scrutiny suggests that the evidence for the dealignment thesis is less than compelling. In a recent analysis of the survey data on partisan identifications over time, Warren Miller argues that earlier interpretations of the increase in political independents were misleading.[20] First, he argues, the increase in the number of respondents claiming to be independent was not due entirely to voter alienation from the party system, as advocates of the dealignment thesis would argue. Rather, much of this increase was due to the influx of baby-boomers just entering the electorate in the late 1960s. This group, coming of age in a time of civil and political unrest, did not immediately align with either of the political parties. They were merely "non-aligned" voters. The difference between non-aligned and dealigned voters is important because, as Miller shows, many of these young voters aligned later in life. Because many of these baby-boomers eventually identified with a political party, the proportion of voters who identify themselves as independents has dropped somewhat since the mid-1970s (from 34 percent to 30 percent), with recent polls showing as few as 20 percent of eligible voters claiming to be independent.[21]

Second, Miller argues that the apparent increase in the number of independents within the electorate has not had the destabilizing impact upon electoral patterns that it might have had because, over time, independents have become increasingly unlikely to vote. Thus, the larger proportion of partisans among actual voters enhances the stabilizing impact of long-term partisanship on voting patterns. This change in the composition of the voting population is evident from Miller's data showing the ratio between "strong partisans" and "independents" among actual voters. In the earliest period for which survey data are available (1952–1964), the ratio between strong partisans and independents among voters is 5.6 to 1. At the height of the electorate's most dealigned period (1968–1976), the ratio dropped to 3 to 1. For the most recent period (1980–1988), the ratio of strong partisans to independents has increased to 4.4 to 1.

Unlike the survey data on partisanship, the emergence of increasingly independent electoral trends across offices in the twentieth century is clear and irrefutable.[22] Election results for representative, governor, senator, and president do not follow one another as closely as they did in the nineteenth century, and this growing disparity can be used to bolster the dealignment thesis. However, upon closer scrutiny, this evidence is less compelling. While these increasingly disparate patterns may mean that political parties have lost their ability to integrate their followers across offices, it does not mean that parties no longer serve as important symbols that guide the voting decision. More sophisticated voters may simply be more discriminating in their use of party symbols in making their vote choice. These symbols may send messages to voters that lead to different voting norms for different offices, as Shafer's argument suggests. Thus, a voter may vote routinely Democratic in selecting his or her legislative representative, but routinely Republican in voting for president, because of the importance and clarity of the symbols the parties evoke.

If this argument is correct, however, we would expect to see little or no change over time

in the dispersion of actual votes around a normal vote trend line for a particular elective office (governor, president, senator, etc.). Yet in Figure 13.1 it is clear that the actual vote does not adhere as closely to the expected vote for president as it did during the apex of the American party system. Moreover, this greater dispersion around the normal vote trend line is undoubtedly caused by two factors that reflect the weakened role of parties in the electoral arena. The first is the enhanced role of the media in presidential campaigns. Their prominent role has had the effect of enhancing the relative importance of short-term factors. Related to this is the fact that, as Miller's data suggest, there is currently a rather sizable dormant pool of nonvoters with no ties to either party. These potential voters can be activated by a particularly intense campaign, and their activation can lead to the volatility evident in Figure 13.1.

In considering what this enhanced volatility means for the dealignment thesis, however, two factors should be kept in mind. First, while the correspondence between the normal vote and the actual vote has declined over time, this decline has not been so large as to suggest that partisan attachments are inconsequential for electoral patterns. Indeed, previous analyses showed that while the correlation between the normal vote and the actual vote is .90 for the last quarter of the nineteenth century, it is .72 for the period between 1952 and 1984.[23] This is only an 18 percent decline.

A second point is that the trend of the normal vote depicted in Figure 13.1 is inconsistent with the dealignment thesis. If party were not relevant to the vote choice in presidential elections, then the normal vote trend line would have converged to the midpoint in Figure 13.1, depicting a highly competitive electoral situation—one in which short-term effects would determine the outcome of the election. Instead, we have seen a virtually uninterrupted trend toward the Republicans dating back to 1932. The normal vote trend line has favored Republican candidates since 1952, and the 1980s were one of the most Republican eras in the history of American presidential elections, second only to the post-1896 era. Moreover, despite some of the largest departures from the expected vote in American electoral history, there have only been a handful of deviating elections since 1952. Thus, while the significance of party in electoral choices has undoubtedly declined somewhat

165

OUT OF THE WILDERNESS?

over the past century, to suggest that party has little relevance for electoral decisions is unwarranted.

CONCLUSION

If we reject the dealignment thesis as an explanation for the results embodied in the 1992 presidential election, we accept the possibility that this election may have enduring electoral consequences. While there are good reasons for thinking that an enduring shift may have occurred, we must await the analyses of the next generation of political analysts to answer this question definitively. What we can say now about the long-term electoral consequences of Clinton's victory is that they are dependent, in large measure, on perceptions of his success in office. These perceptions will depend on what he accomplishes, to be sure. But they will also be formed by what he is expected to accomplish. Clinton has promised much, and many groups who have been political outsiders during decades of Republican dominance are expecting much from him. In addition, expectations will be fueled by speculation that his victory, which is

sizable given the historical measures we have used, marks the beginning of a Democratic realignment.

Analysts who see Clinton's victory as a critical election, however, must be extremely cautious in projecting the frenzied type of policy activity associated with the prototypical American realignment, Roosevelt's New Deal. Three reasons lead us to be pessimistic about expecting high levels of policy activity from Clinton's victory.

> *"Clinton has promised much, and many groups who have been political outsiders during decades of Republican dominance are expecting much from him."*

The first is that while 1992 represents an abrupt departure from prevailing electoral trends at the presidential level, there is little evidence that parallel dramatic change occurred elsewhere. This, of course, would be consistent with the increasingly disjointed and independent electoral trends across offices noted earlier. But it means that Clinton will not have the benefit of a newly elected cadre of Democratic activists who are indebted to him electorally, who share a common vision of change, or who even see their political fate as tied to his. This will make it difficult to generate rapid policy change.

Compounding this difficulty are the institutional changes that have occurred in American government over the past half-century, changes that work against the achievement of swift and sweeping policy change. Chubb and Peterson[24] argue that American political institutions have developed in such a way as to insulate themselves from social and political change. There are more committees, more bureaucracies, more rules, and an increasingly complex web of institutional relationships across levels of government. Many of the internal changes in political institutions that have occurred have facilitated the maintenance of the status quo, thereby protecting the incumbents from external threats to their well-being. Reorienting this complex institutional network will be a task of monumental proportions.

Finally, even if the electoral and institutional handicaps noted above did not exist, there would be a third impediment to Clinton's chances of achieving sweeping policy changes: the federal deficit. Even before Clinton took office, projections of the deficit had skyrocketed far beyond what was discussed in the campaign. This will place severe limits on what Clinton can do, regardless of the electoral and institutional context within which he must operate.

None of these points is intended to imply that Clinton's administration will be a policy failure. What they do mean, however, is that he will have to manage expectations of his administration carefully, and he will have to choose his priorities and battles wisely.

The 1992 Presidential Vote, State by State

STATE	ELECTORAL VOTES	CLINTON VOTES	%	BUSH VOTES	%	PEROT VOTES	%
Alabama	9	686,571	41	798,439	48	180,514	11
Alaska	3	63,498	32	81,875	41	55,085	27
Arizona	8	525,031	37	548,148	39	341,148	24
Arkansas	6	498,548	54	333,909	36	98,215	11
California	54	4,815,039	47	3,341,726	32	2,147,409	21
Colorado	8	626,207	40	557,706	36	362,813	23
Connecticut	8	680,276	42	575,778	36	347,638	22
Delaware	3	125,997	44	102,436	36	59,061	21
District of Columbia	3	186,301	86	19,813	9	9,284	4
Florida	25	2,051,845	39	2,137,752	41	1,041,607	20
Georgia	13	1,005,889	44	989,804	43	307,857	13
Hawaii	4	178,893	49	136,430	37	52,863	14
Idaho	4	136,249	29	201,787	43	129,897	28
Illinois	22	2,379,510	48	1,718,190	35	832,484	17
Indiana	12	829,176	37	970,457	43	448,431	20
Iowa	7	583,669	44	503,077	38	251,795	19
Kansas	6	386,832	34	444,599	39	310,458	27
Kentucky	8	664,246	45	616,517	42	203,682	14
Louisiana	9	815,305	46	729,880	42	210,614	12
Maine	4	261,859	39	207,122	31	205,076	30
Maryland	10	941,979	50	671,609	36	271,198	14
Massachusetts	12	1,315,016	48	804,534	29	630,440	23
Michigan	18	1,858,275	44	1,587,105	37	820,855	19
Minnesota	10	998,552	44	737,649	32	552,705	24
Mississippi	7	392,929	41	481,583	50	84,496	9
Missouri	11	1,053,040	44	811,057	34	518,250	22
Montana	3	153,899	38	143,702	36	106,869	26
Nebraska	5	214,064	30	339,108	47	172,043	24
Nevada	4	185,401	38	171,378	35	129,532	26
New Hampshire	4	207,264	39	199,623	38	120,029	23
New Jersey	15	1,366,609	43	1,309,724	41	505,698	16
New Mexico	5	259,500	46	212,393	38	91,539	16
New York	33	3,246,787	50	2,241,283	34	1,029,038	16
North Carolina	14	1,103,716	43	1,122,608	44	353,845	14
North Dakota	3	98,927	32	135,498	44	70,806	23
Ohio	21	1,965,204	40	1,876,445	39	1,024,598	21
Oklahoma	8	473,066	34	592,929	43	319,978	23
Oregon	7	525,123	43	394,356	32	307,860	25
Pennsylvania	23	2,224,897	45	1,778,221	36	896,177	18
Rhode Island	4	198,924	48	121,916	29	94,757	23
South Carolina	8	476,626	40	573,231	48	138,140	12
South Dakota	3	124,861	37	136,671	41	73,297	22
Tennessee	11	933,620	47	840,899	43	199,787	10
Texas	32	2,279,269	37	2,460,334	40	1,349,947	22
Utah	5	182,850	26	320,559	45	202,605	29
Vermont	3	125,803	46	85,512	31	61,510	23
Virginia	13	1,034,781	41	1,147,226	45	344,852	14
Washington	11	855,710	44	609,912	32	470,239	24
West Virginia	5	326,936	49	239,103	36	106,367	16
Wisconsin	11	1,035,943	41	926,245	37	542,660	22
Wyoming	3	67,863	34	79,558	40	51,209	26
TOTAL		43,728,375	43	38,167,416	38	19,237,247	19
ELECTORAL VOTE		370		168		0	

Winners in 1992 State Gubernatorial Races

Winner is in boldface; * marks the incumbent, (D) denotes Democrat, (R) Republican.

Delaware	(D) **Thomas R. Carper*** (R) B. Gary Scott		Rhode Island	(D) **Bruce Sundlun*** (R) Elizabeth Ann Leonard
Indiana	(D) **Evan Bayh*** (R) Linley E. Pearson		Utah	(D) Stewart Hanson (R) **Mike Leavitt***
Missouri	(D) **Mel Carnahan*** (R) William L. Webster		Vermont	(D) **Howard Dean*** (R) John McClaughry
Montana	(D) Dorothy Bradley (R) **Marc Racicot***		Washington	(D) **Mike Lowry*** (R) Ken Eikenberry
New Hampshire	(D) Deborah Arnie Arnesen (R) **Steve Merrill***		W. Virginia	(D) **Gaston Caperton*** (R) Cleve Benedict
North Carolina	(D) **James B. Hunt, Jr.*** (R) Jim Gardner		**Louisiana	(D) **Edwin Edwards*** (R) David Duke
North Dakota	(D) Nicholas Spaeth (R) **Edward Schafer***			**Election on Nov. 16, 1991.

A
P
P
E
N
D
I
C
E
S

Winners in 1992 Races for the U.S. House of Representatives
Listed by congressional district.

Alabama
1. H. L. "Sonny" Callahan* (R)
2. Terry Everett (R)
3. Glen Browder* (D)
4. Tom Bevill* (D)
5. Bud Cramer* (D)
6. Spencer Bachus (R)
7. Earl F. Hilliard (D)

Alaska At Large
1. Don Young* (R)

Arizona
1. Sam Coppersmith (D)
2. Ed Pastor* (D)
3. Bob Stump* (R)
4. John Kyl* (R)
5. Jim Kolbe* (R)
6. Karen English (D)

Arkansas
1. Blanche Lambert (D)
2. Ray Thornton (D)
3. Tim Hutchinson (R)
4. Jay Dickey (R)

California
1. Dan Hamburg (D)
2. Wally Herger* (R)
3. Vic Fazio (D)
4. John T. Doolittle (R)
5. Robert T. Matsui (D)
6. Lynn Woolsey (D)
7. George Miller* (D)
8. Nancy Polosi (D)
9. Ronald V. Dellums (D)
10. Bill Baker (R)
11. Richard W. Pombo (R)
12. Tom Lantos (D)
13. Fotney "Pete" Stark (D)
14. Anna G. Eshoo (D)
15. Norm Mineta (D)
16. Don Edwards (D)
17. Leon E. Panetta (D)
18. Gary A. Condit (D)
19. Rick Lehman (D)
20. Calvin Dooley (D)
21. Bill Thomas (R)
22. Michael Huffington (R)
23. Elton Gallegly (R)
24. Anthony C. Beilenson (D)
25. Howard P. "Buck" McKeon (R)
26. Howard L. Berman* (D)
27. Carlos J. Moorhead (R)
28. David Dreier (R)
29. Henry A. Waxman (D)
30. Xavier Becerra (D)
31. Matthew G. Martinez (D)
32. Julian C. Dixon (D)
33. Lucille Roybal-Allard (D)
34. Esteban E. Torres* (D)
35. Maxine Waters (D)
36. Jane Harman (D)
37. Walter R. Tucker (D)
38. Steve Horn (R)
39. Ed Royce (R)
40. Jerry Lewis (R)
41. Jay C. Kim (R)
42. George E. Brown, Jr. (D)
43. Mark A. Takano (D)
44. Al McCandless (R)
45. Dana Rohrabacher (R)
46. Robert K. O. "Bob" Dornan (R)
47. Christopher Cox (R)
48. Ron Packard (R)
49. Lynn Schenk (D)
50. Bob Filner (D)
51. Randy "Duke" Cunningham (R)
52. Duncan Hunter (R)

Colorado
1. Patricia Schroeder* (D)
2. David E. Skaggs* (D)
3. Scott McInnis (R)
4. Wayne Allard* (R)
5. Joel Hefley* (R)
6. Daniel Schaefer* (R)

Connecticut
1. Barbara Bailey Kennelly* (D)
2. Samuel Gejdenson* (D)
3. Rosa L. De Lauro* (D)
4. Christopher Shays* (R)
5. Gary A. Franks* (R)
6. Nancy L. Johnson* (R)

Delaware At Large
1. Michael N. Castle (R)

Florida
1. Earl Hutto* (D)
2. Pete Peterson* (D)
3. Corrine Brown (D)
4. Tillie Fowler (R)
5. Karen L. Thurman (D)
6. Cliff Stearns* (R)
7. John L. Mica (R)

8. Bill McCollum (R)
9. Michael Bilirakis* (R)
10. C. W. Bill Young (R)
11. Sam M. Gibbons (D)
12. Charles T. Canady (R)
13. Dan Miller (R)
14. Porter J. Goss (R)
15. Jim Bacchus (D)
16. Tom Lewis (R)
17. Carrie Meek (D)
18. Ileana Ros-Lehtinen* (R)
19. Harry Johnston (D)
20. Peter Deutsch (D)
21. Lincoln Diaz-Balart (R)
22. E. Clay Shaw (R)
23. Alcee L. Hastings (D)

Georgia
1. Jack Kingston (R)
2. Sanford Bishop (D)
3. Mac Collins (R)
4. John Linder (R)
5. John Lewis* (D)
6. Newt Gingrich* (R)
7. George "Buddy" Darden* (D)
8. J. Roy Rowland* (D)
9. Nathan Deal (D)
10. Don Johnson (D)
11. Cynthia McKinney (D)

Hawaii
1. Neil Abercrombie* (D)
2. Patsy Takemoto Mink* (D)

Idaho
1. Larry LaRocco* (D)
2. Michael D. Crapo (R)

Illinois
1. Bobby L. Rush (D)
2. Mel Reynolds (D)
3. William O. Lipinski (D)
4. Luis V. Gutierrez (D)
5. Dan Rostenkowski (D)
6. Henry J. Hyde* (R)
7. Cardiss Collins* (D)
8. Philip M. Crane (R)
9. Sidney R. Yates* (D)
10. John E. Porter* (R)
11. George E. Sangmeister (D)
12. Jerry F. Costello (D)
13. Harris W. Fawell* (R)
14. J. Dennis Hastert* (R)
15. Thomas W. Ewing* (R)
16. Donald Manzullo (R)
17. Lane Evans* (D)
18. Robert H. Michel* (R)
19. Glenn Poshard (D)
20. Richard J. Durbin* (D)

Indiana
1. Peter J. Visclosky* (D)
2. Philip R. Sharp* (D)
3. Timothy J. Roemer* (D)
4. Jill L. Long* (D)
5. Steve Buyer (R)
6. Dan Burton* (R)
7. John T. Myers* (R)
8. Frank McCloskey* (D)
9. Lee H. Hamilton* (D)
10. Andrew Jacobs, Jr.* (D)

Iowa
1. Jim Leach* (R)
2. Jim Nussle* (R)
3. Jim Ross Lightfoot (R)
4. Neal Smith* (D)

Kansas
1. Pat Roberts* (R)
2. Jim Slattery* (D)
3. Jan Meyers* (R)
4. Dan Glickman* (D)

Kentucky
1. Tom Barlow (D)
2. William H. Natcher* (D)
3. Romano L. Mazzoli* (D)
4. Jim Bunning* (R)
5. Harold Rogers* (R)
6. Scotty Baesler (D)

Louisiana
1. Bob Livingston* (R)
2. William J. Jefferson* (D)
3. Billy Tauzin* (D)
4. Cleo Fields (D)
5. Jim McCrery (R)
6. Richard Baker* (R)
7. James A. "Jimmy" Hayes* (D)

Maine
1. Thomas H. Andrews* (D)
2. Olympia J. Snowe* (R)

Maryland
1. Wayne T. Gilchrest* (R)
2. Helen Delich Bentley* (R)
3. Benjamin L. Cardin* (D)
4. Albert R. Wynn* (D)

5. Steny H. Hoyer* (D)
6. Roscoe G. Bartlett (R)
7. Kweisi Mfume* (D)
8. Constance A. Morella* (R)

Massachusetts
1. John W. Olver* (D)
2. Richard E. Neal* (D)
3. Peter I. Blute (R)
4. Barney Frank* (D)
5. Martin T. Meehan (D)
6. Peter G. Torkildsen (R)
7. Edward J. Markey* (D)
8. Joseph P. Kennedy II* (D)
9. John Joseph Moakley* (D)
10. Gerry E. Studds* (D)

Michigan
1. Bart Stupak (D)
2. Peter Hoekstra (R)
3. Paul B. Henry (R)
4. Dave Camp (R)
5. James A. Barcia (D)
6. Fred Upton (R)
7. Nick Smith (R)
8. Bob Carr (D)
9. Dale E. Kildee (D)
10. David E. Bonior (D)
11. Joseph K. Knollenberg (R)
12. Sander Levin (D)
13. William D. Ford (D)
14. John Conyers, Jr. (D)
15. Barbara-Rose Collins (D)
16. John D. Dingell* (D)

Minnesota
1. Timothy J. "Tim" Penny* (D)
2. David Minge (D)
3. Jim Ramstad* (R)
4. Bruce F. Vento* (D)
5. Martin Olav Sabo* (D)
6. Rod Grams (R)
7. Collin C. Peterson* (D)
8. James L. Oberstar* (D)

Mississippi
1. Jamie L. Whitten* (D)
2. Mike Espy* (D)
3. G. V. "Sonny" Montgomery* (D)
4. Mike Parker* (D)
5. Gene Taylor* (D)

Missouri
1. William "Bill" Clay* (D)
2. James M. Talent (R)
3. Richard A. Gephardt* (D)
4. Ike Skelton* (D)
5. Alan Wheat* (D)
6. Patsy Ann "Pat" Danner (D)
7. Melton D. "Mel" Hancock* (R)
8. Bill Emerson* (R)
9. Harold L. Volkmer* (D)

Montana At Large
1. Pat Williams* (D)

Nebraska
1. Douglas K. Bereuter* (R)
2. Peter Hoagland* (D)
3. Bill Barrett* (R)

Nevada
1. James H. Bilbray* (D)
2. Barbara F. Vucanovich* (R)

New Hampshire
1. "Bill" Zeliff* (R)
2. "Dick" Swett* (D)

New Jersey
1. Robert E. Andrews* (D)
2. William J. Hughes* (D)
3. Jim Saxton (R)
4. Christopher H. Smith* (R)
5. Marge Roukema* (R)
6. Frank Pallone, Jr. (D)
7. Bob Franks (R)
8. Herbert C. Klein (D)
9. Robert G. Torricelli* (D)
10. Donald M. Payne* (D)
11. Dean A. Gallo* (R)
12. Dick Zimmer* (R)
13. Robert Mendenez (D)

New Mexico
1. Steven H. Schiff* (R)
2. Joe Skeen* (R)
3. Bill Richardson* (D)

New York
1. George J. Hochbrueckner* (D)
2. Rick A. Lazio (R)
3. Peter T. King (R)
4. David A. Levy (R)
5. Gary L. Ackerman (D)
6. Floyd H. Flake* (D)
7. Thomas J. Manton (D)
8. Jerrold L. Nadler (D)

9. Charles E. Schumer (D, L)
10. Edolphus Towns (D, L)
11. Major R. Owens (D, L)
12. Nydia M. Velazquez (D)
13. Susan Molinari (R)
14. Carolyn B. Maloney (D)
15. Charles B. Rangel (D, L)
16. Jose E. Serrano (D)
17. Eliot L. Engel (D)
18. Nita M. Lowey (D)
19. Hamilton Fish, Jr. (R)
20. Benjamin A. Gilman (R)
21. Michael R. McNulty (D)
22. Gerald B. H. Solomon (R)
23. Sherwood L. Boehlert (R)
24. John M. McHugh (R)
25. James T. Walsh (R)
26. Maurice D. Hinchey (D)
27. Bill Paxon (R)
28. Louise M. Slaughter (D)
29. John J. LaFalce (D)
30. Jack Quinn (R)
31. Amo Houghton (R)

North Carolina
1. Eva Clayton (D)
2. I. T. "Tim" Valentine, Jr.* (D)
3. Martin Lancaster* (D)
4. David E. Price* (D)
5. Stephen Neal* (D)
6. J. Howard Coble* (R)
7. Charles C. Rose III* (D)
8. W. G. "Bill" Hefner* (D)
9. J. Alex McMillan* (R)
10. T. Cass Ballenger* (R)
11. Charles H. Taylor* (R)
12. Melvin Watt (D)

North Dakota At Large
1. Earl Pomeroy (D)

Ohio
1. David Mann (D)
2. Willis D. Gradison, Jr.* (R)
3. Tony P. Hall* (D)
4. Michael G. Oxley* (R)
5. Paul E. Gillmor* (R)
6. Ted Strickland (D)
7. David L. Hobson (R)
8. John A. Boehner* (R)
9. Marcy Kaptur* (D)
10. Martin R. Hoke (R)
11. Louis Stokes (D)
12. John R. Kasich* (R)
13. Sherrod Brown (D)
14. Thomas C. Sawyer* (D)
15. Deborah Pryce (R)
16. Ralph Regula* (R)
17. James A. Traficant, Jr.* (D)
18. Douglas Applegate* (D)
19. Eric D. Fingerhut (D)

Oklahoma
1. James M. Inhofe* (R)
2. Mike Synar* (D)
3. Bill K. Brewster* (D)
4. Dave McCurdy* (D)
5. Ernest Jim Istook (R)
6. Glenn English* (D)

Oregon
1. Elizabeth Furse (D)
2. Bob Smith* (R)
3. Ron Wyden* (D)
4. Peter A. DeFazio* (D)
5. Mike Kopetski* (D)

Pennsylvania
1. Thomas M. Foglietta* (D)
2. Lucien E. Blackwell* (D)
3. Robert A. Borski* (D)
4. Ron Klink (D)
5. Bill Clinger (D)
6. Tim Holden (D)
7. Curt Weldon* (R)
8. Jim Greenwood (R)
9. Bud Shuster (R)
10. Joseph M. McDade* (R)
11. Paul E. Kanjorski* (D)
12. John P. Murtha* (D)
13. Marjorie Margolies Mezvinsky (D)
14. William J. Coyne* (D)
15. Paul McHale (D)
16. Robert S. Walker* (R)
17. George W. Gekas* (R)
18. Rick Santorum (R)
19. William F. Goodling* (R)
20. Austin J. Murphy (D)
21. Thomas J. Ridge* (R)

Rhode Island
1. Ronald K. Machtley* (R)
2. John F. Reed* (D)

South Carolina
1. Arthur Ravenel, Jr.* (R)
2. Floyd D. Spence* (R)
3. Butler Derrick* (D)

4. Bob Inglis* (R)
5. John Spratt* (D)
6. James R. Clyburn (D)

South Dakota At Large
1. Tim Johnson* (D)

Tennessee
1. James H. "Jimmy" Quillen* (R)
2. John J. Duncan, Jr.* (R)
3. Marilyn Lloyd* (D)
4. Jim Cooper* (D)
5. Bob Clement* (D)
6. Bart Gordon* (D)
7. Don Sundquist* (R)
8. John Tanner* (D)
9. Harold E. Ford* (D)

Texas
1. Jim Chapman* (D)
2. Charles Wilson* (D)
3. Sam Johnson* (R)
4. Ralph M. Hall* (D)
5. John Bryant* (D)
6. Joe Barton* (R)
7. Bill Archer* (R)
8. Jack Fields* (R)
9. Jack Brooks* (D)
10. J. J. "Jake" Pickle* (D)
11. Chet Edwards* (D)
12. Pete Geren* (D)
13. Bill Sarpalius* (D)
14. Greg Laughlin* (D)
15. E. "Kika" de la Garza* (D)
16. Ronald Coleman* (D)
17. Charles W. Stenholm* (D)
18. Craig A. Washington* (D)
19. Larry Combest* (R)
20. Henry B. Gonzalez* (D)
21. Lamar Smith* (R)
22. Tom DeLay* (R)
23. Henry Bonilla (R)
24. Martin Frost* (D)
25. Mike Andrews* (D)
26. Dick Armey* (R)
27. Solomon P. Ortiz* (D)
28. Frank Tejeda (D)
29. Gene Green (D)
30. Eddie Bernice Johnson (D)

Utah
1. James V. Hansen* (R)
2. Karen Shepherd (D)
3. Bill Orton* (D)

Vermont At Large
1. Bernie Sanders* (I)

Virginia
1. Herbert H. "Herb" Bateman* (R)
2. Owen B. Pickett* (D)
3. Robert C. "Bobby" Scott (D)
4. Norman Sisisky* (D)
5. L. F. Payne, Jr.* (D)
6. Robert W. "Bob" Goodlatte (R)
7. Thomas J. "Tom" Bliley, Jr.* (R)
8. James P. Moran, Jr.* (D)
9. Frederick C. "Rick" Boucher* (D)
10. Frank R. Wolf* (R)
11. Leslie L. Byrne (D)

Washington
1. Maria Cantwell (D)
2. Al Swift* (D)
3. Jolene Unsoeld* (D)
4. Jay Inslee (D)
5. Thomas S. Foley* (D)
6. Norman D. Dicks* (D)
7. Jim McDermott* (D)
8. Jennifer Dunn (R)
9. Mike Kreidler (D)

West Virginia
1. Alan B. Mollohan* (D)
2. Bob Wise (D)
3. Nick Joe Rahall, II (D)

Wisconsin
1. Les Aspin* (D)
2. Scott L. Klug* (R)
3. Steven C. Gunderson* (R)
4. Gerald D. Kleczka* (D)
5. Thomas M. Barrett (D)
6. Thomas E. Petri* (R)
7. David R. Obey* (D)
8. Toby Roth* (R)
9. F. James Sensenbrenner, Jr.* (R)

Wyoming At Large
1. Craig Thomas* (R)

Winners in 1992 Races for the U.S. Senate

Winner is in boldface; * marks the incumbent, (D) denotes Democrat, (R) Republican.

State	Term ends	Senator	State	Term ends	Senator
Ala.	1999	(D) **Richard C. Shelby***	Mo.	1999	(R) **Christopher "Kit" Bond***
		(R) Richard Sellers			(D) Geri Rothman-Serot
	1997	(D) Howell Heflin		1995	(R) John C. Danforth
Alaska	1999	(R) **Frank H. Murkowski***	Mont.	1995	(R) Conrad Burnes
		(R) Tony Smith		1997	(D) Max Baucus
	1977	(R) Ted Stevens	Neb.	1995	(D) J. Robert Kerrey
Ariz.	1999	(R) **John S. McCain***		1997	(D) J. James Exon
		(D) Claire Sargent	Nev.	1999	(D) **Harry M. Reid***
	1995	(D) Dennis DeConcini			(R) Demar Dahl
Ark.	1999	(D) **Dale Bumpers***		1995	(D) Richard H. Bryan
		(R) Mike Huckabee	N.H.	1999	(R) **Judd Gregg**
	1997	(D) David Pryor			(D) John Rauh
Calif.	1999	(D) **Barbara Boxer**		1997	(R) Robert Smith
		(R) Bruce Herschenshohn	N.J.	1995	(D) Frank R. Lautenberg
	1994	(D) **Dianne Feinstein**		1997	(D) Bill Bradley
		(R) John Seymour*	N.M.	1995	(D) Jeff Bingaman
Colo.	1999	(D) **Ben Nighthorse Campbell**		1977	(R) Pete V. Domenici
		(R) Terry Considine	N.Y.	1999	(R) **Alfonse M. D'Amato***
	1997	(R) Hank Brown			(D) Robert Abrams
Conn.	1999	(D) **Christopher J. Dodd***		1995	(D) Daniel Patrick Moynihan
		(R) Brook Johnson	N.C.	1999	(R) **Lauch Faircloth**
	1995	(D) Joe Lieberman			(D) Terry Sanford*
Del.	1995	(R) William V. Roth, Jr.		1997	(R) Jesse Helms
	1997	(D) Joseph R. Biden, Jr.	N.D.	1999	(D) **Byron L. Dorgan**
Fla.	1999	(D) **Bob Graham***			(R) Steve Sydness
		(R) Bill Grant		1995	(D) Kent Conrad
	1995	(R) Connie Mack	Ohio	1999	(D) **John Glenn***
Ga.	1999	(R) **Paul Coverdell**			(R) Michael DeWine
		(D) Wyche Fowler, Jr.*		1995	(D) Howard M. Metzenbaum
	1977	(D) Sam Nunn	Okla.	1999	(R) **Don Nickles***
Ha-waii	1999	(D) **Daniel K. Inouye***			(D) Steve Lewis
		(R) Rick Reed		1997	(D) David L. Boren
	1995	(D) Daniel K. Akaka	Ore.	1999	(R) **Bob Packwood***
Idaho	1999	(R) **Dirk Kempthorne**			(D) Les AuCoin
		(D) Richard H. Stallings		1997	(R) Mark O. Hatfield
	1997	(R) Larry E. Craig	Pa.	1999	(R) **Arlen Specter***
Ill.	1999	(D) **Carol Moseley Braun**			(D) Lynn Yeakel
		(R) Richard S. Williamson		1995	(D) Harris Wofford
	1977	(D) Paul Simon	R.I.	1995	(R) John H. Chafee
Ind.	1999	(R) **Daniel R. Coats***		1997	(D) Claiborne Pell
		(D) Joseph H. Hogsett	S.C.	1999	(D) **Fritz Hollings***
	1995	(R) Richard G. Lugar			(R) Thomas Hartnett
Iowa	1999	(R) **Charles E. Grassley***		1997	(R) Strom Thurmond
		(D) Jean Lloyd-Jones	S.D.	1999	(D) **Thomas A. Daschle***
	1997	(D) Tom Harkin			(R) Charlene Haar
Kans.	1999	(R) **Bob Dole***		1997	(R) Larry Pressler
		(D) Gloria O'Dell	Tenn.	1995	(D) James R. Sasser
	1997	(R) Nancy L. Kassebaum		1997	(D) Harlan Mathews
Ky.	1999	(D) **Wendell H. Ford***	Texas	1995	(D) Bob Krueger
		(R) David L. Williams		1997	(R) Phil Gramm
	1997	(R) Mitch McConnell	Utah	1999	(R) **Robert F. Bennett**
La.	1999	(D) **John B. Breaux***			(D) Wayne Owens
	1997	(D) J. Bennett Johnston		1995	(R) Orrin G. Hatch
Maine	1995	(D) George J. Mitchell	Vt.	1999	(D) **Patrick J. Leahy***
	1997	(R) William S. Cohen			(R) James H. Douglas
Md.	1999	(D) **Barbara A. Mikulski***		1995	(R) James M. Jeffords
		(R) Alan L. Keyes	Va.	1995	(D) Charles S. Robb
	1995	(D) Paul S. Sarbanes		1997	(R) John W. Warner
Mass.	1995	(D) Edward M. Kennedy	Wash.	1999	(D) **Patty Murray**
	1977	(D) John F. Kerry			(R) Rod Chandler
Mich.	1995	(D) Donald W. Riegle, Jr.*		1995	(R) Slade Gorton
	1997	(D) Carl Levin	W.V.	1995	(D) Robert C. Byrd
Minn.	1995	(R) David Durenberger		1997	(D) John D. Rockefeller IV
	1997	(D) Paul David Wellstone	Wis.	1999	(D) **Russell D. Feingold**
Miss.	1995	(R) Trent Lott			(R) Robert W. Kasten, Jr.*
	1997	(R) Thad Cochran		1995	(D) Herbert H. Kohl
			Wyo.	1995	(R) Malcolm Wallop
				1997	(R) Alan K. Simpson

Inaugural Address

President William Clinton, January 20, 1993

Following is a transcript of President Clinton's Inaugural Address, as recorded by The New York Times:

My fellow citizens, today we celebrate the mystery of American renewal. This ceremony is held in the depth of winter, but by the words we speak and the faces we show the world, we force the spring. A spring reborn in the world's oldest democracy that brings forth the vision and courage to reinvent America.

When our Founders boldly declared America's independence to the world and our purposes to the Almighty, they knew that America to endure would have to change. Not change for change sake but change to preserve America's ideals—life, liberty, the pursuit of happiness. Though we march to the music of our time, our mission is timeless. Each generation of Americans must define what it means to be an American.

Assuming the Mantle

On behalf of our nation, I salute my predecessor, President Bush, for his half-century of service to America.

And I thank the millions of men and women whose steadfastness and sacrifice triumphed over depression, fascism and communism. Today, a generation raised in the shadows of the cold war assumes new responsibilities in a world warmed by the sunshine of freedom but threatened still by ancient hatreds and new plagues.

Raised in unrivaled prosperity, we inherit an economy that is still the world's strongest but is weakened by business failures, stagnant wages, increasing inequality and deep divisions among our own people.

When George Washington first took the oath I have just sworn to uphold, news traveled slowly across the land by horseback and across the ocean by boat. Now the sights and sounds of this ceremony are broadcast instantaneously to billions around the world. Communications and commerce are global, investment is mobile, technology is almost magical, and ambition for a better life is now universal. We earn our livelihood in America today in peaceful competition with people all across the earth. Profound and powerful forces are shaking and remaking our world. And the urgent question of our time is whether we can make change our friend and not our enemy.

A Time for Vision, and Will

This new world has already enriched the lives of millions of Americans who are able to compete and win in it. But when most people are working harder for less, when others cannot work at all, when the cost of health care devastates families and threatens to bankrupt our enterprises great and small, when the fear of crime robs law-abiding citizens of their freedom, and when millions of poor children cannot even imagine the lives we are calling them to lead, we have not made change our friend. We know we have to face hard truths and take strong steps, but we have not done so. Instead, we have drifted, and that drifting has eroded our resources, fractured our economy and shaken our confidence.

Though our challenges are fearsome, so are our strengths. Americans have ever been a restless, questing, hopeful people, and we must bring to our task today the vision and will of those who came before us. From our Revolution to the Civil War, to the Great Depression, to the civil rights movement, our people have always mustered the determination to construct from these crises the pillars of our history.

Thomas Jefferson believed that to preserve the very foundations of our nation we would need dramatic change from time to time. Well my fellow Americans, this is our time. Let us embrace it.

Our democracy must be not only the envy of the world but the engine of our own renewal. There is nothing wrong with America that cannot be cured by what is right with America. And so today we pledge an end to the era of deadlock and drift, and a new season of American renewal has begun.

To renew America we must be bold. We must do what no generation has had to do before. We must invest more in our own people—in their jobs and in their future—and at the same time cut our massive debt. And we must do so in a world in which we must compete for every opportunity. It will not be easy. It will require sacrifice. But it can be done and done fairly. Not choosing sacrifice for its own sake, but for our own sake. We must provide for our nation the way a family provides for its children.

Our Founders saw themselves in the light of posterity. We can do no less. Anyone who has ever watched a child's eyes wander into sleep knows what posterity is. Posterity is the world to come. The world for whom we hold our ideals, from whom we have borrowed our planet and to whom we bear sacred responsibility. We must do what America does best: offer more opportunity to all and demand more responsibility from all.

It is time to break the bad habit of expecting something for nothing from our Government or from each other. Let us all take more responsibility not only for ourselves and our families but for our communities and our country.

To renew America we must revitalize our democracy. This beautiful capital, like every capital since the dawn of civilization, is often a place of intrigue and calculation. Powerful people maneuver for position and worry endlessly about who is in and who is out, who is up and who is down, forgetting those people whose toil and sweat sends us here and pays our way.

Americans deserve better, and in this city today there are people who want to do better.

And so I say to all of you here, let us resolve to reform our politics so that power and privilege no longer shout down the voice of the people. Let us put aside personal advantage so that we can feel the pain and see the promise of America. Let us resolve to make our Government a place for what Franklin Roosevelt called bold, persistent experimentation, a Government for our tomorrows, not our yesterdays. Let us give this capital back to the people to whom it belongs.

To renew America, we must meet challenges abroad as well as at home. There is no longer a clear division between what is foreign and what is domestic. The world economy, the world environment, the world AIDS crisis, the world arms race—they affect us all.

Today, as an old order passes, the new world is more free but less stable. Communism's collapse has called forth old animosities and new dangers. Clearly, America must continue to lead the world we did so much to make.

While America rebuilds at home, we will not shrink from the challenges nor fail to seize the opportunities of this new world. Together with our friends and allies we will work to shape change lest it engulf us. When our vital interests are challenged or the will and conscience of the international community is defied, we will act, with peaceful diplomacy whenever possible, with force when necessary.

The brave Americans serving our nation today in the Persian Gulf and Somalia, and wherever else they stand, are testament to our resolve.

But our greatest strength is the power of our ideas, which are still new in many lands. Across the world we see them embraced and we rejoice. Our hopes, our hearts, our hands are those on every continent who are building democracy and freedom. Their cause is America's cause.

The American people have summoned the change we celebrate today. You have raised your voices in an unmistakable chorus, you have cast your votes in historic numbers, and you have changed the face of Congress, the Presidency and the political process itself. Yes, you, my fellow Americans, have forced the spring.

Now we must do the work the season demands. To that work I now turn with all the authority of my office. I ask the Congress to join with me. But no President, no Congress, no government can undertake this mission alone.

My fellow Americans, you, too, must play your part in our renewal.

The Trumpets' Call

I challenge a new generation of young Americans to a season of service; to act on your idealism by helping troubled children, keeping company with those in need, reconnecting our torn communities. There is so much to be done. Enough, indeed, for millions of others who are still young in spirit to give of themselves in service, too.

In serving, we recognize a simple but powerful truth: We need each other and we must care for one another. Today we do more than celebrate America, we rededicate ourselves to the very idea of America: An idea born in revolution and renewed through two centuries of challenge; an idea tempered by the knowledge that but for fate we, the fortunate and the unfortunate, might have been each other; an idea ennobled by the faith that our nation can summon from its myriad diversity the deepest measure of unity; an idea infused with the conviction that America's long, heroic journey must go forever upward.

And so, my fellow Americans, as we stand at the edge of the 21st century, let us begin anew with energy and hope, with faith and discipline. And let us work until our work is done. The Scripture says, "And let us not be weary in well-doing, for in due season we shall reap if we faint not."

From this joyful mountaintop of celebration we hear a call to service in the valley. We have heard the trumpets, we have changed the guard. And now each in our own way, and with God's help, we must answer the call.

Thank you, and God bless you all.

State of the Union Address

President William Clinton, February 17, 1993

Special to The New York Times
WASHINGTON, Feb. 17—Following is the prepared text of President Clinton's economic address to a joint session of Congress, as provided by the White House:

Mr. President, Mr. Speaker:

When Presidents speak to the Congress and the nation from this podium, they typically comment on the full range of challenges and opportunities that face us. But these are not ordinary times. For all the many tasks that require our attention, one calls on us to focus, unite and act. Together, we must make our economy thrive once again.

It has been too long—at least three decades—since a President has challenged Americans to join him on our great national journey, not merely to consume the bounty of today but to invest for a much greater one tomorrow.

Nations, like individuals, must ultimately decide how they wish to conduct themselves—how they wish to be thought of by those with whom they live, and, later, how they wish to be judged by history. Like every man and woman, they must decide whether they are prepared to rise to the occasions history presents them.

We have always been a people of youthful energy and daring spirit. And at this historic moment, as Communism has fallen, as freedom is spreading around the world, as a global economy is taking shape before our eyes, Americans have called for change—and now it is up to those of us in this room to deliver.

Our nation needs a new direction. Tonight, I present to you our comprehensive plan to set our nation on that new course.

I believe we will find our new direction in the basic values that brought us here: opportunity, individual responsibility, community, work, family and faith. We need to break the old habits of both political parties in Washington. We must say that there can be no more something for nothing, and we are all in this together.

The conditions which brought us to this point are well known. Two decades of low productivity and stagnant wages; persistent unemployment and underemployment; years of huge Government deficits and declining investment in our future; exploding health care costs, and lack of coverage; legions of poor children; educational and job training opportunities inadequate to the demands of a high wage, high growth economy. For too long we drifted without a strong sense of purpose, responsibility or community, and our political system too often was paralyzed by special interest groups, partisan bickering and the sheer complexity of our problems.

I know we can do better, because ours remains the greatest nation on earth, the world's strongest economy and the world's only military superpower. If we have the vision, the will and the heart to make the changes we must, we will enter the 21st century with possibilities our parents could not even have imagined, having secured the American dream for ourselves and future generations.

I well remember, 12 years ago Ronald Reagan stood at this podium and told the American people that if our debt were stacked in dollar bills, the stack would reach 67 miles into space. Today, that stack would reach 267 miles.

I tell you this not to assign blame for this problem. There is plenty of blame to go around—in both branches of the Government and both parties. The time for blame has come to an end. I came here to accept responsibility; I want you to accept responsibility for the future of this country, and if we do it right, I don't care who gets the credit for it.

Our plan has four fundamental components:

Jump-Starting Economy

First, it reverses our economic decline, by jump-starting the economy in the short term and investing in our people, their jobs and their incomes in the long term.

Second, it changes the rhetoric of the past into the actions of the present, by honoring work and families in every part of our lives.

Third, it substantially reduces the Federal deficit, honestly and credibly.

Finally, it earns the trust of the American people by paying for these plans first with cuts in Government waste and inefficiency—cuts, not gimmicks, in Government spending—and by fairness, for a change, in the way the burden is borne.

Creating Jobs

Tonight, I want to talk about what government can do, because I believe our government must do more for the hard-working people who pay its way. But let me say first: government cannot do this alone. The private sector is the engine of economic growth in America. And every one of us can be an engine of change in our own lives. We've got to give people more opportunity, but we must also demand more responsibility in return.

Our immediate priority is to create jobs, now. Some say we're in a recovery. Well, we all hope so. But we're simply not creating jobs. And there is no recovery worth its salt that does not begin with new jobs.

To create jobs and guarantee a strong recovery, I call on Congress to enact an immediate jobs package of over $30 billion. We will put people to work right now and create half a million jobs: jobs that will rebuild our highways and airports, renovate housing, bring new life to our rural towns and spread hope and opportunity among our nation's youth with almost 700,000 jobs for them this summer alone. And I invite America's business leaders to join us in this effort, so that together we can create a million summer jobs in cities and poor rural areas for our young people.

Second, our plan looks beyond today's business cycle, because our aspirations extend into the next century. The heart of our plan deals with the long term. It has an investment program designed to increase public and private investment in areas critical to our economic future. And it has a deficit reduction program that will increase savings available for private sector investment, lower interest rates, decrease the percentage of the Federal budget claimed by interest payments, and decrease the risk of financial market disruptions that could adversely affect the economy.

Over the long run, all this should result in a higher rate of economic growth, improved productivity, higher wages, more high-quality jobs and an improved economic competitive position in the global economy.

In order to accomplish public investment and deficit reduction, Government spending is being cut and taxes are being increased. Our spending cuts were carefully thought through to try to minimize any economic impact, to capture the peace dividend for investment purposes and to switch the balance in the budget from consumption to investment. The tax increases and spending cuts were both designed to assure that the cost of this historic program to face and deal with our problems is borne by those who could most readily afford that cost.

Our plan is designed to improve the health of American business through lower interest rates, improved infrastructure, better trained workers, and a stronger middle class. Because small businesses generate most of our nation's jobs, our plan includes the boldest targeted incentives for small business in history. We propose a permanent investment tax credit for small business, and new rewards for entrepreneurs who take risks. We will give small business access to the brilliant technologies of our time and to the credit they need to prosper and flourish.

With a new network of community development banks, and one billion dollars to make the dream of enterprise zones real, we will being to bring new hope and new jobs to storefronts and factories from South Boston to South Texas to South-Central Los Angeles.

Our plan invests in our roads, bridges, transit facilities; in high-speed railways and high-tech information systems; and in the most ambitious environmental clean-up of our time.

Opening New Markets

On the edge of the new century, economic growth depends as never before on opening up new markets overseas. And so we will insist on fair trade rules in international markets.

A part of our national economic strategy must be to expand trade on fair terms, including successful completion of the latest round of world trade talks. A North American Free Trade Agreement with appropriate safeguards for workers and the environment. At the same time, we need an aggressive attempt to create the hi-tech jobs of the future; special attention to troubled industries like aerospace and airlines, and special assistance to displaced workers like those in our defense industry.

I pledge that business, government and labor will work together in a partnership to strengthen America for a change.

But all of our efforts to strengthen the economy will fail unless we take bold steps to reform our health care system. America's businesses will never be strong; America's families will never be secure; and America's government will never be solvent until we tackle our health care crisis.

Reforming Health Care

The rising costs and the lack of care are endangering both our economy and our lives. Reducing health care costs will liberate hundreds of billions of dollars for investment and growth and new jobs. Over the long run, reforming health care is essential to reducing our deficit and expanding investment.

Later this spring, I will deliver to Congress a comprehensive plan for health care reform that will finally get costs under control. We will provide security to all our families, so that no one will be denied the coverage they need. We will root out fraud and outrageous charges and make sure that paperwork no longer chokes you or your doctor. And we will maintain American standards—the highest quality medical care in the world and the choices we demand and deserve. The American people expect us to deal with health care. And we must deal with it now.

Perhaps the most fundamental change our new direction offers is its focus on the future and the investments we seek in our children.

Each day we delay carries a dear cost. Half our two-year-olds don't receive immunizations against deadly diseases. Our plan will provide them for every eligible child. And we'll save ten dollars for every one we'll spend by eliminating preventable childhood diseases.

The Women, Infants, and Children nutrition program will be expanded so that every expectant mother who needs our help receives it.

Asking More of Students

Head Start—a program that prepares children for school—is a success story. It saves money, but today it reaches only one-third of all eligible children. Under our plan, we will cover every eligible child. Investing in Head Start and WIC is not only the right thing, it's the smart thing. For every dollar we invest today, we save three tomorrow.

America must ask more of our students, our teachers, and our schools. And we must give them the resources they need to meet high standards.

We will bring together business and schools to establish new apprenticeships, and give young people the skills they need today to find productive jobs tomorrow.

Lifelong learning will benefit workers throughout their careers. We must create a new unified worker training system, so that workers receive training regardless of why they lost their jobs.

College Loan Program

Our national service program will make college loans available to all Americans, and challenge them to give something back to their country—as teachers, police officers, community service workers. This will be an historic change on a scale with the creation of the Land Grant Colleges and the G.I. Bill. A hundred years from now, historians who owe their education to our plan for national service will salute your vision.

We believe in jobs, we believe in learning, and we believe in rewarding work. We believe in restoring the values that make America special.

There is dignity in all work, and there must be dignity for all workers. To those who heal our sick, care for our children, and do our most tiring and difficult jobs, our new direction makes this solemn commitment:

By expanding the Earned Income Tax Credit, we will make history: We will help reward work for millions of working poor Americans. Our new direction aims to realize a principle as powerful as it is simple: If you work full time, you should not be poor.

Plan to End Welfare

Later this year, we will offer a plan to end welfare as we know it. No one wants to change the welfare system as much as those who are trapped by the welfare system.

We will offer people on welfare the education, training, child care and health care they need to get back on their feet. Then, after two years, they must get back to work—in private business if possible; in public service, if necessary. It's time to end welfare as a way of life.

Our next great goal is to strengthen American families.

We'll ask fathers and mothers to take more responsibility for their children. And we'll crack down on deadbeat parents who won't pay their child support.

We want to protect our families against violent crime which terrorizes our people and tears apart our communities. We must pass a tough crime bill. We need to put 100,000 more police on the street, provide boot camps for first-time non-violent offenders, and put hardened criminals behind bars. We have a duty to keep guns out of the hands of criminals, If you pass the Brady Bill, I'll sign it.

To make government work for middle-class taxpayers and not the special interests, we must reform our political system.

I'm asking Congress to enact real campaign finance reform. Let's reduce the power of special interests and increase the participation of the people. We should end the tax deduction for special interest lobbying and use the money to help clean up the political system. And we should quickly enact legislation to force lobbyists to disclose their activities.

But to revolutionize government we have to insure that it lives within its means. And that starts at the top—with the White House. In the last few weeks, I have cut the White House staff by twenty-five percent, saving ten million dollars. I ordered administrative cuts in the budgets of agencies and departments, I cut the federal bureaucracy by 100,000 positions, for combined savings of nine billion dollars. It's time for government to be as frugal as any household in America. That's why I congratulate the Congress for taking similar steps to cut its costs today. Together, we can show the American people that we have heard their call for change.

But we can go further. Tonight, I call for an across-the-board freeze in federal government salaries for one year. Thereafter, federal salaries will rise at a rate lower than the rate of inflation.

We must reinvent government to make it work again. We'll push innovative education reform to improve learning, not just spend more money. We'll use the Superfund to clean up pollution, not just increase lawyers' incomes. We'll use federal banking regulators, not just to protect the security and safety of our financial institutions, but to break the credit crunch. And we'll change the whole focus of our poverty programs from entitlement to empowerment.

For years, there has been a lot of talk about the deficit, but very few credible efforts to deal with it. This plan does. Our plan tackles the budget deficit—seriously and over the long term. We will put in place one of the biggest deficit reductions and the biggest change of federal priorities in our history at the same time.

We are not cutting the deficit because the experts tell us to do so. We are cutting the deficit so that your family can afford a college education for your children. We are cutting the deficit so that your children will someday be able to buy a home of their own. We are cutting the deficit so that your company can invest in retraining its workers and retooling its factories. We are cutting the deficit so that government can make the investments that help us become stronger and smarter and safer.

If we do not act now, we will not recognize this country ten years from now. Ten years from now, the deficit will have grown to 635 billion dollars a year; the national debt will be almost 80 percent of our gross domestic product. Paying the interest on that debt will be the costliest government program of all, and we will continue to be the world's largest debtor, depending on foreign funds for a large part of our nation's investments.

Our budget will, by 1997, cut 140 billion dollars from the deficit—one of the greatest real spending cuts by an American president. We are making more than 150 difficult, painful reductions which will cut federal spending by 246 billion dollars. We are eliminating programs that are no longer needed, such as nuclear power research and development. We are slashing subsidies and cancelling wasteful projects. Many of these programs were justified in their time. But if we're going to start new plans, we must eliminate old ones. Government has been good at building programs, now we must show that we can limit them.

Reducing Military Spending

As we restructure American military forces to meet the new threats of the post–Cold War world, we can responsibly reduce our defense budget. But let no one be in any doubt: The men and women who serve under the American flag will be the best trained, best equipped, best prepared fighting force in the world, so long as I am President.

Backed by a leaner and more effective national defense and a stronger economy, our nation will be prepared to lead a world challenged by ethnic conflict, the proliferation of weapons of mass destruction, the global democratic revolution, and the health of our environment.

Our economic plan is ambitious, but it is necessary for the continued greatness of our country. And it will be paid for fairly—by cutting government, by asking the most of those who benefitted most in the past—by asking more Americans to contribute today so that all Americans can do better tomorrow.

For the wealthiest—those earning more than 180,000 dollars per year, I ask you to raise the top rate for federal income taxes from 31 percent to 36 percent. Our plan recommends a ten percent surtax on incomes over 250,000 dollars a year. And we will close the loopholes that let some get away without paying any tax at all.

For businesses with taxable incomes over ten million dollars, we will raise the corporate tax rate to 36 percent. And we will cut the deduction for business entertainment.

Our plan attacks tax subsidies that reward companies that ship jobs overseas. And we will ensure that, through effective tax enforcement, foreign corporations who make money in America pay the taxes they owe to America.

Middle-class Americans should know: You're not going alone any more; you're not going first; and you're no longer going to pay more and get less. Ninety-eight point eight percent of America's families will have no increase in their income tax rates. Only the wealthiest one point two percent will see their rates rise.

Let me be clear: There will be no new cuts in benefits from Medicare for beneficiaries. There will be cuts in payments to providers: doctors, hospitals, and labs, as a way of controlling health care costs. These cuts are only a stop-gap until we reform the whole health care system. Let me repeat that, because it matters to me, as I know it matters to you: This plan will not make new cuts in Medicare benefits for any beneficiary.

The only change we are making in Social Security is to ask those older Americans with higher incomes, who do not rely solely on Social Security to get by, to contribute more. This change will not affect eighty percent of Social Security recipients. If you do not pay taxes on Social Security now, you will not pay taxes on Social Security under this plan.

Our plan includes a tax on energy as the best way to provide us with new revenue to lower the deficit and invest in our people. Moreover, unlike other taxes, this one reduces pollution, increases energy efficiency, and eases our dependence on oil from unstable regions of the world.

Taken together, these measures will cost an American family earning 40 thousand dollars a year less than 17 dollars a month. And because of other programs we will propose, families earning less than 30,000 dollars a year will pay virtually no additional tax at all. Because of our publicly stated determination to reduce the deficit, interest rates have fallen since the election. That means that, for the middle class, the increases in energy costs will be more than offset by lower interest costs for mortgages, consumer loans and credit cards. This is a wise investment for you and for your country.

I ask all Americans to consider the cost of not changing, of not choosing a new direction. Unless we have the courage to start building our future and stop borrowing from it, we are condemning ourselves to years of stagnation, interrupted only by recession; to slow growth in jobs, no growth in incomes, and more debt and disappointment.

Worse yet—unless we change, unless we reduce the deficit, increase investment, and raise productivity so we can generate jobs—we will condemn our children and our children's children to a lesser life and a diminished destiny.

Tonight, the American people know we must change. But they are also likely to ask whether we have the fortitude to make those changes happen.

They know that, as soon as we leave this Chamber, the special interests will be out in force, trying to stop the changes we seek. The forces of conventional wisdom will offer a thousand reasons why it can't be done. And our people will be watching and wondering to see if it's going to be business as usual again.

So we must scale the walls of their skepticism, not with our words but by our deeds. After so many years of gridlock and indecision, after so many hopeful beginnings and so few promising results, Americans will be harsh in their judgments of us if we fail to seize this moment.

This economic plan cannot please everybody. If this package is picked apart, there will be something that will anger each of us. But, if it is taken as a whole, it will help all of us.

Resist the temptation to focus only on a spending cut you don't like or some investment not made. And nobody likes tax increases. But let's face facts: For 20 years incomes have stalled. For years, debt has exploded. We can no longer afford to deny reality. We must play the hand we were dealt.

The test of our program cannot simply be: What's in it for me? The question must be: What's in it for us?

If we work hard—and work together—if we rededicate ourselves to strengthening families, creating jobs, rewarding work, and reinventing government, we can lift America's fortunes once again.

Tonight I ask everyone in this Chamber—and every American—to look into their hearts, spark their hopes, and fire their imaginations. There is so much good, so much possibility, so much excitement in our nation. If we act boldly, as leaders should, our legacy will be one of progress and prosperity. This, then, is America's new direction. Let us summon the courage to seize the day.

Thank you very much. Good night. And may God bless America.

Preamble from the 1992 Democratic Platform, "A New Covenant with the American People"

Two hundred summers ago, this Democratic Party was founded by the man whose burning pen fired the spirit of the American Revolution—who once argued we should overthrow our own government every 20 years to renew our freedom and keep pace with a changing world. In 1992, the party Thomas Jefferson founded invokes his spirit of revolution anew.

Our land reverberates with a battle cry of frustration that emanates from America's very soul—from the families in our bedrock neighborhoods, from the unsung, workaday heroes of the world's greatest democracy and economy. America is on the wrong track. The American people are hurting. The American Dream of expanding opportunity has faded. Middle class families are working hard, playing by the rules, but still falling behind. Poverty has exploded. Our people are torn by divisions.

The last 12 years have been a nightmare of Republican irresponsibility and neglect. America's leadership is indifferent at home and uncertain in the world. Republican mismanagement has disarmed government as an instrument to make our economy work and support the people's most basic values, needs and hopes. The Republicans brought America a false and fragile prosperity based on borrowing, not income, and so will leave behind a mountain of public debt and a backbreaking annual burden in interest. It is wrong to borrow to spend on ourselves, leaving our children to pay our debts.

We hear the anguish and the anger of the American people. We know it is directed not just at the Republican administrations that have had power, but at government itself.

Their anger is justified. We can no longer afford business as usual—neither the policies of the last 12 years of tax breaks for the rich, mismanagement, lack of leadership and cuts in services for the middle class and the poor, nor the adoption of new programs and new spending without new thinking. It is time to listen to the grassroots of America, time to renew the spirit of citizen activism that has always been the touchstone of a free and democratic society.

Therefore we call for *a revolution in government*—to take power away from entrenched bureaucracies and narrow interests in Washington and put it back in the hands of ordinary people. We vow to make government more decentralized, more flexible, and more accountable—to reform public institutions and replace public officials who aren't leading with ones who will.

The Revolution of 1992 is about restoring America's economic greatness. We need to rebuild America by abandoning the something-for-nothing ethic of the last decade and putting people first for a change. Only a thriving economy, a strong manufacturing base, and growth in creative new enterprise can generate the resources to meet the nation's pressing human and social needs. An expanding, entrepreneurial economy of high-skill, high-wage jobs is the most important family policy, urban policy, labor policy, minority policy and foreign policy America can have.

The Revolution of 1992 is about putting government back on the side of working men and women—to help those who work hard, pay their bills, play by the rules, don't lobby for tax breaks, do their best to give their kids a good education and to keep them away from drugs, who want a safe neighborhood for their families, the security of decent, productive jobs for themselves, and a dignified life for their parents.

The Revolution of 1992 is about a radical change in the way government operates—not the Republican proposition that government has no role, nor the old notion that there's a program for every problem, but a shift to a more efficient, flexible and results-oriented government that improves services, expands choices, and empowers citizens and communities to change our country from the bottom up. We believe in an activist government, but it must work in a different, more responsive way.

The Revolution of 1992 is about facing up to tough choices. There is no relief for America's frustration in the politics of diversion and evasion, of false choices or of no choices at all. Instead of everyone in Washington blaming one another for inaction, we will act decisively—and ask to be held accountable if we don't.

Above all the Revolution of 1992 is about restoring the basic American values that built this country and will always make it great: personal responsibility, individual liberty, toler-ance, faith, family and hard work. We offer the American people not only new ideas, a new course, and a new President, but a return to the enduring principles that set our nation apart: the promise of opportunity, the strength of community, the dignity of work, and a decent life for senior citizens.

To make this revolution, we seek a *New Covenant* to repair the damaged bond between the American people and their government, that will expand *opportunity*, insist upon greater individual *responsibility* in return, restore *community*, and ensure *national security* in a profoundly new era.

We welcome the close scrutiny of the American people, including Americans who may have thought the Democratic Party had forgotten its way, as well as all who know us as the champions of those who have been denied a chance. With this platform we take our case for change to the American people.

Preamble from the 1992 Republican Platform, "The Vision Shared: Uniting Our Family, Our Country, Our World"

Abraham Lincoln, our first Republican President, expressed the philosophy that inspires Republicans to this day: "The legitimate object of Government is to do for a community of people whatever they need to have done, but cannot do at all, or cannot so well do, for themselves in their separate and individual capacities. But in all that people can individually do as well for themselves, Government ought not to interfere."

We believe that most problems of human making are within the capacity of human ingenuity to solve.

For good reason, millions of new Americans have flocked to our shores: America has always been an opportunity society. Republicans have always believed that economic prosperity comes from individual enterprise, not government programs. We have defended our core principles for 138 years; but never has this country, and the world, been so receptive to our message.

The Fall of the Berlin Wall symbolizes an epochal change in the way people live. More important, it liberates the way people think. We see with new clarity that centralized government bureaucracies created in this century are not the wave of the future. Never again will people trust planners and paper shufflers more than they trust themselves. We all watched as the statue of Soviet hangman Feliks Dzherzhinsky was toppled in front of Moscow's KGB headquarters by the very people his evil empire sought to enslave. Its sightless eyes symbolized the moral blindness of totalitarians around the world. They could never see the indomitable spirit of people determined to be free from government control—free to build a better future with their own heads, hands, and hearts.

We Republicans saw clearly the dangers of collectivism: not only the military threat, but the deeper threat to the souls of people bound in dependence. Here at home, we warned against Big Government, because we knew concentrated decisionmaking, no matter how well-intentioned, was a danger to liberty and prosperity. Republicans stood at the rampart of freedom, defending the individual against the domineering state. While we did not always prevail, we always stood our ground, faithful to our principles and confident of history's ultimate verdict.

Our opponents declared that the dogmas of the Left were the final and victorious faith. From kremlins and ivory towers, their planners proclaimed the bureaucratic millennium. But in a tragic century of illusion, Five Year Plans and Great Leaps Forward failed to summon a Brave New World. One hundred and fifty years of slogans and manifestos came crashing down in an ironic cascade of unintended consequences. All that is left are the ruins of a failed scoundrel ideology.

As May Day lapses back into just another spring festival, the Fourth of July emerges as the common holiday of free men and women. Yet, in 1992, when the self-governing individual has overcome the paternalistic state, liberals here at home simply do not get it. Indeed, their party seeks to turn the clock back. But their ideas are old and tired. Like planets still orbiting a dying star, the believers in state power turn their faces to a distant and diminishing light.

The Democrats would revise history to rationalize a return to bigger government, higher taxes, and moral relativism. The Democrat Party has forgotten its origins as a party of work, thrift, and self-reliance. But they have not forgotten their art for dissembling and distortion. The Democrats are trapped in their compact with the ideology of trickle-down government, but they are clever enough to know that the voters would shun them if their true markings were revealed.

America had its rendezvous with destiny in 1980. Faced with crisis at home and abroad, Americans turned to Republican leadership in the White House. Presidents Reagan and Bush turned our Nation away from the path of over-taxation, hyper-regulation, and mega-government. Instead, we moved in a new direction. We cut taxes, reduced red tape, put people above bureaucracy. And so we vanquished the idea of the almighty state as the supervisor of our daily lives. In choosing hope over fear, Americans raised a beacon, reminding the world that we are a shining city on a hill, the last best hope for man on earth.

Contrary to statist Democrat propaganda, the American people know that the 1980s were a rising tide, a magnificent decade for freedom and entrepreneurial creativity. We are confident that, knowing this, they will never consciously retreat to the bad old days of tax and spend. Our Platform will clarify the choice before our fellow citizens.

We have learned that ideas do indeed have consequences. Thus, our words are important not for their prose but for what they reveal about the thinking of our President and our Party.

Two years ago, President Bush described the key elements of what he called "our new paradigm," a fresh approach that aims to put new ideas to work in the service of enduring principles—principles we upheld throughout the long twilight struggle, principles George Bush has acted decisively to advance. Thus we honor the Founders and their vision.

Unlike our opponents, we are inspired by a commitment to profound change. Our mission combines timeless beliefs with a positive vision of a vigorous America: prosperous and tolerant, just and compassionate. We believe that individual freedom, hard work, and personal responsibility—basic to free society—are also basic to effective government. We believe in the fundamental goodness of the American people. We believe in traditional family values and in the Judeo-Christian heritage that informs our culture. We believe in the Constitution and its guarantee of color-blind equal opportunity. We believe in free markets. We believe in constructive change, in both true conservatism and true reform. We believe government has a legitimate role to play in our national life but government must never dominate that life.

While our goals are constant, we are willing to innovate, experiment, and learn. We have learned that bigger is not better, that quantity and quality are different things, that more money does not guarantee better outcomes. We have learned the importance of individual choice—in education, health care, child care—and that bureaucracy is the enemy of initiative and self-reliance. We believe in empowerment, including home ownership for as many as possible. We believe in decentralized authority, and a bottom-line, principled commitment to what works for people.

We believe in the American people: free men and women with faith in God working for themselves and their families, believing in the value of every human being from the very young to the very old.

We believe the Founders intended Congress to be responsive, flexible, and foresighted. After decades of Democrat misrule, the Congress is none of these things. Dominated by reactionaries, obsessed with the failed policies and structures of the past, the Democratic majority displays a "do-nothing" doggedness: they intend to learn nothing and forget nothing. Seeking to build a better America, we seek to elect a better Congress.

Finally, we believe in a President who represents the national interest, not just the aggregation of well-connected special interests; a President who brings unity to the American purpose.

America faces many challenges. Republicans, under the strong leadership of President Bush, are responding with this bold Platform of new ideas that infuses our commitment to individual freedom and market forces with an equal commitment to a decent, just way of life for every American.

With a firm faith that the American people will always choose hope over fear, we Republicans dedicate ourselves to this forward-looking agenda for America in the 1990s, transcending old, static ideas with a shared vision of hope, optimism, and opportunity.

NOTES

Chapter 1

1. The figures are from the Committee for the Study of the American Electorate, Curtis Gans, Director. They are reported in Robert Pear, "55 Percent Voting Rate Reverses 30-Year Decline," *New York Times,* November 5, 1992, p. B4. For comparative assessments of turnout in other nations, see Raymond E. Wolfinger, David P. Glass, and Peverill Squire, "Predictors of Electoral Turnout; An International Comparison," *Policy Studies Review,* vol. 9, no. 3 (Spring 1990), pp. 551–574. For an assessment of the implications, see William Crotty, "Setting Forth Premises: The Politically Invisible," *Policy Studies Review,* vol. 9, no. 3 (Spring 1990), pp. 505–515.

2. Unless otherwise indicated, the data and the poll figures used in this chapter are taken from the *New York Times*/CBS News poll as reported in "Portrait of the Electorate," *New York Times,* November 5, 1992, pp. B9–B10.

3. Rhodes Cook, "Democratic Clout Is Growing As the Gender Gap Widens," *Congressional Quarterly Weekly Report,* October 17, 1992, pp. 3265–3268; Jeffrey L. Katz and Ceci Connolly, "Women, Minorities Rock Records, But Ideology Will Barely Budge," *Congressional Quarterly Weekly Report,* November 7, 1992, pp. 3557–3564; John R. Cranford, "The New Class: More Diverse, Less Lawyerly, Younger," *Congressional Quarterly Weekly Report,* November 7, 1992, pp. 7–10.

4. Cranford, "The New Class: More Diverse, Less Lawyerly, Younger."

5. Rhodes Cook, "Perot Positioned to Defy a Past Seemingly Carved in Stone," *Congressional Quarterly Weekly Report,* June 13, 1992, pp. 1721–1729; Ronald D. Elving, "Return of Perot, Debates Energize Final Weeks," *Congressional Quarterly Weekly Report,* October 3, 1992, pp. 3086; and Steven A. Holmes, "An Eccentric But No Joke," *New York Times,* November 5, 1992, p. 1.

6. "Perot Decides Against Forming Third Party," *Chicago Tribune,* December 19, 1992, p. 10; and Richard L. Berke, "Perot Re-Enters the Limelight as a Watchdog," *New York Times,* January 12, 1993, p. 1.

7. "Bush Appeals for Public Support," *Congressional Quarterly Almanac* (Washington, DC: Congressional Quarterly, Inc., 1990), p. 135.

8. Maureen Dowd, "Bush: As the Loss Sinks In, Some Begin Pointing Fingers," *New York Times,* November 5, 1992, p. B5.

9. "Thomas Confirmation," *Congressional Quarterly Almanac* (Washington, DC: Congressional Quarterly, Inc., 1991), p. 47B. Initially, the Senate Judicial Committee deadlocked 7–7 on the Thomas nomination and by a 13–1 margin decided to send the nomination without a recommendation to the full Senate for a vote. This was before the Hill testimony. After the Hill accusations and televised hearings, which had a major impact on the 1992 election, the committee decided to forward the nomination, appearing to accept Thomas's account or, at least, believing it had insufficient evidence to repudiate it.

   The Senate vote to confirm Thomas, then a Federal Appeals Court judge, for the Supreme Court took place on October 15, 1991. The Senate voted 52–48 in favor of Thomas, the closest confirmation vote in the Senate in the twentieth century. Republicans voted 41–2 in favor of Thomas and Democrats 46–11 against.

10. Rhodes Cook, "New Hampshire Win May Hold Recipe for Movable Feast," *Congressional Quarterly Weekly Report,* February 22, 1992, pp. 423–427.

11. The demands of the Republican right wing, and the manner in which he responded to these, have been a constant problem for George Bush throughout his public career. See Gary Wills, "The Hostage," *New York Review of Books,* August 13, 1992, pp. 21–27.

12. "Rocky Road to Houston," *Newsweek,* Special Election Issue, November/December, 1992, pp. 65–69.

13. "U.S. Dismisses Official Over Passport Search," *Chicago Tribune,* November 11, 1992, p. 5; and Robert Pear, "Appointee Encouraged Requests on Clinton File, Investigators Say," *New York Times,* November 17, 1992, p. 1.

14. "White House Implicated in Passport Probe," *Chicago Tribune,* December 22, 1992, p. 2; and David Johnston, "Independent Prosecutor to Open Inquiry on Search of Clinton File," *New York Times,* December 18, 1992, p. 1.

15. Charles M. Madigan, "Grand Old Problems: GOP Rethinking Fundamentals of Party Spectrum," *Chicago Tribune,* November 29, 1992, Section 4, p. 1; and "GOP Needs New Image, Pollster Says," *Chicago Tribune,* December 3, 1992, p. 21.

16. Ronald D. Elving and Beth Donovan, "Candidates Spread Their Bets in Presidential Gamble," *Congressional Quarterly Weekly Report,* February 22, 1992, pp. 419–422.

17. "Tsongas Hospitalized for Cancer Treatment," *New York Times,* January 7, 1993, p. A9; and "Tsongas Leaves Cancer Institute," *Chicago Tribune,* January 10, 1993, p. 24.

18. The nickname was coined by columnist Mike Royko, who later said he regretted having done it. Nonetheless, it stayed with Brown. See Ronald D. Elving, "Brown Is Unlikely Carrier of a Timely Message," *Congressional Quarterly Weekly Report,* January 18, 1992, pp. 126–132.

19. See "Six Men and a Donkey," *Newsweek*, Special Election Issue, November/ December, 1992, pp. 24–30; and Ronald D. Elving, "Kerrey Quits Race," *Congressional Quarterly Weekly Report*, March 7, 1992, p. 556. In dropping out, Kerrey indicated he intended to be a candidate for the presidency in the future.

20. Beth Donovan, "Harkin Signs Out of Race," *Congressional Quarterly Weekly Report*, March 14, 1992, p. 633.

21. Rhodes Cook, "Wilder's Exit From Race Leaves Questions About Black Vote," *Congressional Quarterly Weekly Report*, January 11, 1992, p. 66.

22. Rhodes Cook, "Arkansan Travels Well Nationally As Campaign Heads for Test," *Congressional Quarterly Weekly Report*, January 11, 1992, pp. 58–60; Rhodes Cook, "Allegations of Clinton Affairs May Recast Democrats' Race," *Congressional Quarterly Weekly Report*, February 8, 1992, p. 326; and "State of Union Rallies GOP; Polls Stand by Clinton," *Congressional Quarterly Weekly Report*, February, 1, 1992, p. 258.

23. Tsongas, while not formally withdrawing, "suspended" his campaign on March 19, 1992, shortly after Kerrey and Harkin had withdrawn. "Tsongas Suspends Campaign," *Congressional Quarterly Weekly Report*, March 21, 1992, p. 749.

24. David Broder, "Hits, Misses and Selected Errata From a Year's Worth of Columns," *Chicago Tribune*, December 31, 1992, p. 25. See also: Rhodes Cook and Ronald D. Elving, "Clinton Can't Shake Doubters Despite Strong Performance," *Congressional Quarterly Weekly Report*, April 11, 1992, pp. 965–966; and Rhodes Cook, "November Race Crystallizing; Bush, Clinton in Command," *Congressional Quarterly Weekly Report*, March 21, 1992, pp. 746–748.

25. See Jeffrey Schmalz, "Voting Scared: Americans Are Sadder and Wiser, But Not Apathetic," *New York Times*, November 1, 1992, Section 4, p. 1.

26. Thomas B. Edsall, "Bloc Busting: The Demise of the GOP Majority," *Washington Post*, October 11, 1992, p. C-1.

27. Thomas B. Edsall, *The Politics of Inequality* (New York: W. W. Norton, 1984); *Power and Money* (New York: W. W. Norton, 1988); and with Mary D. Edsall, *Chain Reaction* (New York: W. W. Norton, 1992).

28. Schmalz, "Voting Scared: Americans Are Sadder and Wiser, But Not Apathetic."

29. Dowd, "Bush: As the Loss Sinks In, Some Begin Pointing Fingers." See also: "Key to Bush's Survival Strategy . . . Is His Character, Not His Ideas," *National Journal*, July 7, 1992, pp. 1592–1593; and William Schneider, "Wrong Year for Negative Campaigning," *National Journal*, October 17, 1992, p. 2042.

30. Bernard Weinraub, "Ex-President Is of Two Minds About Bush's Loss," *New York Times*, November 5, 1992, p. B4.

31. Schmalz, "Voting Scared: Americans Are Sadder and Wiser, But Not Apathetic." For a similar expression of views, see "Why Voters Are Worried: Read Our Lips, They Tell Candidates," *Chicago Sun-Times*, October 28, 1992, p. 1.

32. Schmalz, "Voting Scared: Americans Are Sadder and Wiser, But Not Apathetic."

33. Schmalz, "Voting Scared: Americans Are Sadder and Wiser, But Not Apathetic."

34. "Portrait of the Electorate," *New York Times*, November 5, 1992, pp. B9–B10. For a statement of the Clinton-Gore issue views, see Governor Bill Clinton and Senator Al Gore, *Putting People First: How We Can Change America* (New York: Times Books, 1992).

35. Schmalz, "Voting Scared: Americans Are Sadder and Wiser, But Not Apathetic."

36. "Bulls-Eye: Targeting Helped Clinton Use Resources Wisely," *Milwaukee Journal*, November 6, 1992, p. 10. I appreciate the help of Lawrence D. Longley in bringing this to my attention. See also Gwen Ifill, "Clinton: Forging Discipline, Vision and Luck Into Victory," *New York Times*, November 5, 1992, p. 1; and the series of analyses in *Newsweek*, Special Election Issue, November/December, 1992, and *Time* (Election Special), November 16, 1992.

37. Steve Daley, "TV's 'New News' Shook Some Old Political Notions," *Chicago Tribune*, November 1, 1992, Section 4, p. 1.

38. "Bull's-Eye: Targeting Helped Clinton Use Resources Wisely."

39. "Face to Face In Prime Time," *Newsweek*, Special Election Issue, November/December, 1992, pp. 88–91.

40. The figures are from the *New York Times*/CBS News poll results; see "The 1992 Elections," *New York Times*, November 9, 1992, p. B9.

41. Lawrence I. Barrett, "A New Coalition for the 1990s," *Time*, November 16, 1992, pp. 47–48. See also Howard Fineman, "The Torch Passes." *Newsweek*, Special Election Issue, November/ December, 1992, pp. 4–10; Kevin Phillips, "Down and Out: Can the Middle Class Rise Again?" *New York Times Magazine*, January 10, 1993, pp. 16 ff.; and Robin Toner, "Dawn of a New Politics," *New York Times*, November 5, 1992, p. 1.

42. On Perot, see: Tom Morganthau, "Citizen Perot," *Newsweek*, November 9, 1992, pp. 23–28; Jim Squires, "A Collision Made in Heaven," *Newsweek*, November 9, 1992, p. 29; Stanley W. Cloud, "The Lessons of Perot," *Time*, November 16, 1992, pp. 69–70; "Superhero," *Newsweek*, Special Election Issue, November/December, 1992, pp. 70–77; Steve Daley, "Perot Seems Unlikely to Go Away," *Chicago Tribune*, November 5, 1992, p. 1; and

Steven A. Holmes, "An Eccentric But No Joke," *New York Times,* November 5, 1992, p. 1.

43. This estimate is by Dr. Herbert E. Alexander, director of the Citizens Research Foundation. All of the receipts and expenditures normally take months to tabulate in the post-election period. On 1988, see: Herbert E. Alexander and Monica Bauer, *Financing the 1988 Election* (Boulder, CO: Westview Press, 1991). On congressional costs and proposals for reform, see: David B. Magleby and Candice J. Nelson, *The Money Chase* (Washington, DC: The Brookings Institution, 1990).

44. The data are from the Federal Election Commission. See: Federal Election Commission, "Spending Jumped to $504 Million by '92 Congressional Candidates," December 30, 1992.

Chapter 2

1. For an elaboration on the factors that led voters away from the Democratic Party and toward the Republicans, see Francis E. Rourke and John T. Tierney, "The Setting: Changing Patterns of Presidential Politics, 1960 and 1988," in Michael Nelson, ed., *The Elections of 1988* (Washington, DC: CQ Press, 1989), pp. 13–19.

2. See the President's State of the Union Message, text reprinted in *New York Times,* January 29, 1992, p. A16.

3. Gillian Peele, "The Constrained Presidency of George Bush," *Current History 91* (April 1992), p. 154.

4. Peggy Noonan, "Why Bush Failed," *New York Times,* November 5, 1992, p. A35.

5. On the gathering storm clouds in 1991 that threatened Bush's political future, see James A. Barnes, "Blown Off Course," *National Journal,* October 31, 1992, pp. 2742–2746.

6. Paul J. Quirk, "Domestic Policy: Divided Government and Cooperative Presidential Leadership," in Colin Campbell, S.J., and Bert Rockman, eds., *The Bush Presidency: First Appraisals,* (Chatham, NJ: Chatham House Publishers, 1991), p. 77.

7. Quirk, pp. 80–82.

8. For a good account of conservatives' dissatisfaction with Bush, see Richard Brookhiser, "Gravedigger of the Revolution," *The Atlantic,* October 1992, pp. 70–78.

9. Jonathan Rauch, "The Long Good-Bye," *The National Journal,* February 22, 1992, p. 438.

10. E. J. Dionne, Jr., "A New Act in America's Political Drama," *Washington Post National Weekly Edition,* November 9–15, 1992, p. 14.

11. Voters weren't just imagining these economic disparities; by 1992, studies would confirm what the people had known instinctively. See, for example, John D. McClain, "Study Shows Rich Got Richer in the 1980s—Much Richer," *Boston Globe,* October 30, 1992, p. 67.

12. See Robin Toner, "Casting Doubts: Economy Stinging Bush," *New York Times,* November 26, 1991, p. A1.

13. Gary Jacobson, *The Politics of Congressional Elections,* 2nd ed. (Boston: Little, Brown, 1987), pp. 7–24.

14. Richard Cohen, "Lame-Duck Congress," *National Journal,* January 19, 1991, p. 123.

15. Cohen, p. 125.

16. Another factor making voluntary retirement from the House particularly attractive in 1992 was the fact that for House members who had been there in January 1980 (166 of them), 1992 would be the last chance to keep any surplus money in their campaign treasuries. See Cohen, "Lame-Duck Congress."

17. See Rhodes Cook, "Democratic Clout is Growing As the Gender Gap Widens," *Congressional Quarterly Weekly Report,* October 17, 1992, pp. 3265–3273.

18. Robert Guskind, "Airborne Attacks," *National Journal,* October 31, 1992, p. 2479.

Chapter 3

1. The polling data supporting this conclusion were drawn from *American Enterprise* (July–August 1992, pp. 84–85, and September–October 1992, pp. 82–83); *Public Perspective* (September–October 1992), pp. 14, 14a; compilations provided by Jen Baggette of the American Enterprise Institute; and various issues of the *New York Times* and *The Gallup Poll Monthly.*

2. The Republican announcements to run were State Representative David Duke (Louisiana, December 4, 1991), Patrick J. Buchanan (Virginia, December 10), and President Bush (Texas, February 12, 1992). "The Ins and Outs of '92," *Congressional Quarterly Weekly Report,* December 21, 1991, p. 3735, and February 15, 1992, p. 361.

3. "Bush Approval at 89 Percent, Highest in Polling History," *Gallup Poll Monthly,* March 1991, pp. 2–3.

4. These percentages were in response to the question, "Now let me ask you about some specific problems facing the country. As I read off each one, would you tell me whether you approve or disapprove of the way President Bush is handling that problem?" as reported in "Bush After the War," *Gallup Poll Monthly,* March 1991, pp. 5–13, especially, pp. 7, 12–13. The order in which issues were presented was rotated by poll takers to minimize bias in respondents.

5. George Bush, Republican National Convention acceptance speech, August 18, 1988.

6. When Bush sought to raise questions about Clinton's trustworthiness, Clinton hit back with comments that underscored Bush's dismal economic record, claiming that Bush was "personally untrustworthy" because he broke his pledge

not to raise taxes and failed to create the promised 15 million new jobs. Gwen Ifill, "The Democrats: Clinton Says Bush Is Untrustworthy on Jobs and Taxes," *New York Times*, August 22, 1992, p. A1.

7. Rhodes Cook, "Wilder's Exit From Race Leaves Questions About Black Vote," *Congressional Quarterly Weekly Report*, January 11, 1992, p. 66.

8. "President and Six Other Candidates Qualify for Matching Funds," *FEC Record*, January 1992, 19; "Buchanan, Eight Other Candidates Receive Matching Funds," *FEC Record*, March 1992, p. 15.

9. See Charles D. Hadley and Harold W. Stanley, "Super Tuesday 1988: Regional Results and National Implications," *Publius* 19 (Summer 1989): 19–37.

10. Rhodes Cook, "Allegations of Clinton Affairs May Recast Democrats' Race," *Congressional Quarterly Weekly Report*, January 25, 1992, p. 187.

11. "Contenders' Ranks Steady in Week Before Voting," *Congressional Quarterly Weekly Report*, February 8, 1992, p. 326.

12. Quoted in Richard L. Berke, "The Media: Why Candidates Like Public's Questions," *New York Times*, August 15, 1992, p. A7.

13. Cook, "Allegations," p. 187. The delegate percentages were calculated from "Nominating Season at a Glance," *Congressional Quarterly Weekly Report*, February 1, 1992, p. 259.

14. Larry Hugick, "1992 Presidential Campaign: Poll Shows Good News, Bad News for Bush and Clinton," *Gallup Poll Monthly*, February 1992, pp. 25–27.

15. Rhodes Cook, "Iowa Caucuses Lose Limelight As Nominating Season Opens," *Congressional Quarterly Weekly Report*, February 1, 1992; Rhodes Cook, "Tsongas Passes Clinton in N.H.; Harkin Wins in Iowa Caucuses," *Congressional Quarterly Weekly Report*, February 15, 1992, p. 372.

16. Rhodes Cook, "New Hampshire May Hold Recipe for Moveable Feast," *Congressional Quarterly Weekly Report*, February 22, 1992, pp. 423–27; and Ronald D. Elving and Beth Donovan, "Candidates Spread Their Bets in Presidential Gamble," *Congressional Quarterly Weekly Report*, February 22, 1992, pp. 419–422. Even if Cuomo's write-in bid had been successful, filing deadlines remained open in only 9 states and Washington, DC, with a mere 751 delegates (19 percent of the convention total).

17. Cook, "New Hampshire," pp. 423–27; and Elving and Donovan, "Candidates," pp. 419–422.

18. Rhodes Cook, "Super Tuesday Tone to Be Set in Early Southern Face-Offs," *Congressional Quarterly Weekly Report*, February 29, 1992, pp. 482–486.

19. Rhodes Cook, "Clinton, Brown Taste First Wins; Bush-Buchanan Duel Rolls On," *Congressional Quarterly Weekly Report*, March 7, 1992, p. 554–562.

20. Rhodes Cook, " 'Super' Kick Propels Front-Runners Onto Fast Track to Nomination," *Congressional Quarterly Weekly Report*, March 14, 1992, p. 634; and Beth Donovan, "Harkin Signs Out of Race," *Congressional Quarterly Weekly Report*, March 14, 1992, p. 633.

21. Cook, " 'Super' Kick," pp. 631–632, 634; Jeffrey L. Katz, "Clinton Sweep Shows Strength, Justifies Regional Primary," *Congressional Quarterly Weekly Report*, March 14, 1992, pp. 641–642; Dave Kaplan, "Bush, Clinton Win Overwhelmingly in Central, South States," *Congressional Quarterly Weekly Report*, March 14, 1992, 643–644; and Ines Pinto Alicea, "Low-Turnout Victories Go to North's Favored Sons," *Congressional Quarterly Weekly Report*, March 14, 1992, pp. 645–646.

22. Hadley and Stanley, "Super Tuesday 1988," p. 22; Cook, " 'Super' Kick," pp. 631–632, 635, 638–640. Duke finally abandoned his futile challenge to President Bush on April 22; see Rhodes Cook, "Duke Out of Race: 'My Role Is Over,' " *Congressional Quarterly Weekly Report*, April 25, 1992, p. 1086.

23. Rhodes Cook, "November Race Crystallizing: Bush, Clinton in Command," *Congressional Quarterly Weekly Report*, March 21, 1992, pp. 746–752.

24. Rhodes Cook, "Connecticut Calls Into Doubt Clinton's Air of Inevitability," *Congressional Quarterly Weekly Report*, March 28, 1992, pp. 818–824; Harkin quoted on p. 822.

25. Gwen Ifill, "Keeper of the Democratic Flame Applies Heat as Necessary," *New York Times*, April 19, 1992, p. D3.

26. "Democrats' Dilemma: Falling Turnout," *Congressional Quarterly Weekly Report*, May 16, 1992, p. 1376.

27. "Primary Turnout: Ups and Downs," *Congressional Quarterly Weekly Report: Guide to the 1992 Democratic National Convention*, July 4, 1992, p. 71.

28. R.W. Apple, Jr., "Yearning for Fresh Faces Shows in Tiny Turnout and Newcomer's Victory," *New York Times*, April 29, 1992, p. A18.

29. "1992 Republican Primary Turnout," *Congressional Quarterly Weekly Report: Guide to the 1992 Republican National Convention*, August 8, 1992, p. 67.

30. Rhodes Cook, "Arkansan Travels Well Nationally As Campaign Heads for Test," *Congressional Quarterly Weekly Report*, January 11, 1992, pp. 59–60; Cook, " 'Super' Kick," pp. 641–642; Kaplan, "Bush, Clinton Wins," p. 643; "Democratic Endorsements," *Congressional Quarterly Weekly Report*, March 28, 1992, p. 824.

31. Michael deCourcy Hinds, "Pennsylvania Governor Criticizes Process That's Turning to Clinton," *New York Times,* April 24, 1992, p. A1.

32. " 'Manhattan Project,' 1992," *Newsweek,* Special Election Issue, November/December 1992, pp. 40–41.

33. "Democratic Endorsements," *Congressional Quarterly Weekly Report,* February 29, 1992, p. 485; Beth Donovan with Janet Hook, "Clinton and Democrats Plan to Touch Bases—Gingerly," *Congressional Quarterly Weekly Report,* April 25, 1992, pp. 1082–1086.

34. Members of Congress quoted in Donovan with Hook, "Clinton;" Rhodes Cook and Ronald D. Elving, "Pennsylvania Primary Signals Breakthrough for Clinton," *Congressional Quarterly Weekly Report,* May 2, 1992, pp. 1185–1186.

35. Cook, "November Race Crystallizing," p. 748; "Clinton Is Closer to Nomination," *Congressional Quarterly Weekly Report,* April 18, 1992, p. 1034.

36. " 'Manhattan Project,' 1992," *Newsweek,* Special Election Issue, November/December 1992, p. 55; and Phil Duncan, "Female Candidates, Perot Grab June 2 Spotlight," *Congressional Quarterly Weekly Report,* June 6, 1992, p. 1620.

37. Ronald D. Elving, "Perot Seeks a Bigger Stage . . . For His Political Theories," *Congressional Quarterly Weekly Report,* March 28, 1992, pp. 820–821.

38. Robin Toner, "Primaries: Clinton Wins a Majority for Nomination but Perot's Appeal is Strong in Two Parties," *New York Times,* June 3, 1992, p. A1.

39. Between 10 and 15 percent of the voters participating in the Oregon primary wrote in Perot's name in both the Democratic and Republican contests. In the first ever (but low turnout) Washington primary, Perot garnered 20 percent of the vote, which under Washington Republican Party rules would have entitled him to about seven delegates; he also drew about 20 percent of the vote in the Washington Democratic Party "beauty contest." Ronald D. Elving, "Perot Seeks," pp. 820–821; Rhodes Cook, "Perot Steps on Leaders' Toes in Oregon, Washington," *Congressional Quarterly Weekly Report,* May 23, 1992, pp. 1493–1495; Rhodes Cook, "Perot Steals Show Amid Bush, Clinton Primary Victories," *Congressional Quarterly Weekly Report,* June 6, 1992, pp. 1643–1647; Dr. Frank Newport and Alec Gallup, "1992 Presidential Campaign: July," *Gallup Poll Monthly,* July 1992, pp. 15, 20, 31; and, Larry Hugick, "1992 Presidential Campaign: August," *Gallup Poll Monthly,* August 1992, pp. 11, 21.

40. *American Enterprise,* July/August, 1992, pp. 84, 86.

41. "[As] of now, Perot and Bush are dividing the large bulk of electoral votes, and . . . Clinton is getting so few that he is currently not a factor." Quoted in R.W. Apple, Jr., "Close 3-Way Race Holds Opportunities for Clinton," *New York Times,* June 23, 1992, p. A18.

42. Quoted in Gwen Ifill, "Strategy: Discipline, Message, and Good Luck: How Clinton's Campaign Came Back," *New York Times,* September 5, 1992, p. A7.

43. For a review of such retrospective voting, see Myron A. Levine, *Presidential Campaigns, and Elections: Issues, Images, and Partisanship* (Itasca, IL: F. E. Peacock Publishers, 1992).

44. *Congressional Quarterly Weekly Report,* May 16, 1992, p. 1377, and *Congressional Quarterly Weekly Report: Guide to the 1992 Democratic National Convention,* July 4, 1992, supplement, p. 71.

45. R. W. Apple, Jr. "Close 3-Way Race Holds Opportunities for Clinton," *New York Times,* June 23, 1992, p. A18.

46. Robin Toner, "Anxious Days for Bush's Campaign as GOP Heads into a 3-Way Race," *New York Times,* May 21, 1992, p. A22.

47. Stanley Greenberg in Robin Toner, "Perot Makes Major Parties Do Some Major Rethinking," *New York Times,* June 4, 1992, p. A19.

48. Kevin Sack, "Minority Voters: Jackson Waits for Plan from Clinton," *New York Times,* July 18, 1992, p. A9. Clinton's criticism of Sister Souljah and disagreements with labor suggested he would not shy from confrontations, a suggestion helpful in addressing the "slick Willie" problem discussed later.

49. Elizabeth Kolbert, "Test-Marketing a President," *New York Times,* August 30, 1992, p. F18.

50. " 'Manhattan Project,' 1992," *Newsweek,* Special Election Issue, November/December 1992, p. 56.

51. Ifill, "Strategy."

52. Ifill, "Strategy"; and Ronald D. Elving, "Clinton Sets Out to Recast Personal, Party Images," *Congressional Quarterly Weekly Report,* July 18, 1992, p. 2075.

53. Kolbert, "Test-Marketing."

54. *New York Times*/CBS News poll releases. Bush's favorable-unfavorable-undecided ratings were essentially unchanged, about 29–44–27 in May and June and 31–46–23 in late August.

55. Robin Toner, "The Republicans: Bush Needs Convention to Get Campaign Going," *New York Times,* August 16, 1992, p. A24.

56. Robin Toner, "Anxious Days for Bush's Campaign as GOP Heads into a 3-Way Race," *New York Times,* May 21, 1992, p. A22.

57. "Unhappy Warrior," *Newsweek,* Special Election Issue, November/December 1992, pp. 58–61.

58. Robin Toner, "Pressure Builds on President as Anxiety Mounts in Party," *New York Times,* July 26, 1992, p. A1.

59. Kolbert, "Test-Marketing."

60. Robin Toner, "Anxious Days for Bush's Campaign as GOP Heads into a 3-Way Race," *New York Times,* May 21, 1992, p. A22; Robin Toner, "Pressure Builds on President as Anxiety Mounts in Party," *New York Times,* July 26, 1992, p. A1.

61. Robin Toner, "Pressure Builds on President as Anxiety Mounts in Party," *New York Times,* July 26, 1992, p. A1.

62. Approval ratings are all from Gallup polls as reported in *Gallup Poll Monthly,* August 1992, p. 33. Bush's approval rating had dipped to 29 percent in a July 31–August 1 Gallup poll.

63. Robin Toner, "The 1992 Campaign: Political Memo," *New York Times,* September 7, 1992, p. A1. On the recent acquisition of the South as part of the Republican presidential political base, see Earl Black and Merle Black, *The Vital South* (Cambridge, MA: Harvard University Press, 1992).

64. Greenberg, quoted in Ifill, "Strategy."

Chapter 4

1. The fourth incumbent defeated for reelection in this century is the Republican William Howard Taft, whose 1912 popular vote total was 55 percent below that of his 1908 numbers and whose electoral vote dropped from 312 to 8. Both are records that seem as secure as Cy Young's record of 511 career wins in the major leagues.

2. Dan Balz and Richard Morin, "An Electorate Ready to Revolt," *Washington Post National Weekly Edition,* November 11–17, 1991, p. 6.

3. See William Schneider, "The Suburban Century Begins," *The Atlantic Monthly,* July 1992, pp. 33–44.

4. *The Polling Report,* January 27, 1992 (Washington, DC: The Polling Report, Inc.), pp. 1, 2, & 8.

5. See John Kenneth White, *The New Politics of Old Values,* 2nd ed. (Hanover: University Press of New England, 1990).

6. See Alexander P. Lamis, *The Two-Party South* (New York: Oxford University Press, 1984) and Earl Black and Merle Black, *The Vital South* (Cambridge: Harvard University Press, 1992).

7. See Thomas Byrne Edsall, *The New Politics of Inequality* (New York: W. W. Norton, 1984), chaps. 2 & 3.

8. See James A. Barnes, "Blown Off Course," *National Journal,* October 31, 1992, pp. 2472–2476, for an excellent summary of the Bush campaign and its problems.

9. *The Polling Report,* December 23, 1991, p. 2, and February 10, 1992, p. 3.

10. David S. Broder, "We Deserve Better," *Washington Post National Weekly Edition,* February 10–17, 1992, p. 4.

11. *The Polling Report,* April 27, 1992, p. 1.

12. Miniscandals in the House of Representatives bank and post office fueled the anti-incumbency mood and made members feel even more exposed to voter scrutiny than usual.

13. *Congressional Quarterly Weekly Report,* February 1, 1992, p. 217.

14. E. J. Dionne, Jr., and Dan Balz, "Reworking Clinton's Batting Stance," *Washington Post National Weekly Edition,* May 25–31, 1992, p. 13.

15. A number of liberal Democrats in the Congress, weary of losing the presidency, signaled a readiness to abandon political purity for pragmatism in their party's 1992 nomination. See Barney Frank, *Speaking Frankly: What's Wrong with the Democrats and How to Fix It* (New York: Times Books, 1992).

16. The most dramatic example was Clinton's criticism of rap singer Sister Souljah at the national convention of Jesse Jackson's Rainbow Coalition. It angered an already estranged Jackson, but did not alienate African Americans in general and did make Clinton look like a different kind of Democrat to many whites.

17. Rhodes Cook, "Clinton Aims for New Image: Young, Moderate, Southern," *Congressional Quarterly Weekly Report,* July 11, 1992, pp. 2017–2020.

18. Thomas B. Edsall, "The Democrats Pick a New Centerpiece," *Washington Post National Weekly Edition,* July 20–26, 1992, p. 14.

19. *Congressional Quarterly Weekly Report,* July 18, 1992, p. 2128.

20. See Kevin P. Phillips, *The Emerging Republican Majority* (New Rochelle, NY: Arlington House, 1969).

21. See Everett Carll Ladd, *Where Have All the Voters Gone?* 2nd ed. (New York: W. W. Norton, 1982).

22. See Jerome M. Mileur, "Dump Dixie—West is Best: The Geography of a Progressive Democracy," in *The Democrats Must Lead,* James MacGregor Burns, William Crotty, Lois Lovelace Duke, and Lawrence D. Longley, eds. (Boulder, CO: Westview, 1992), pp. 97–111.

23. *USA Today,* November 5, 1992, p. 6A.

24. The discipline of the Clinton campaign is further illustrated by media consultant Mandy Grunwald's post-election comment that it had resisted the temptation to increase spending in Massachusetts and California in the final weeks when polls showed a 30-point Clinton lead cut in half. See *USA Today,* November 5, 1992, p. 6A.

25. *USA Today,* November 5, 1992, p. 1.

26. Robert Neuman, former communications director at the Democratic National Committee (DNC), quoted by Curtis Wilkie, "Inside Job," *Boston Globe Magazine,* January 17, 1993, p. 32. Clinton had been a kind of at-large ambassador for the DNC in the early 1980s, meeting with state chairs. Wilkie observes, "Some poli-

ticians, upon obtaining high office, disdain the party foot soldiers—the local chairmen and party activists. Clinton cultivated them across the country for the next decade . . ." (p. 31).

27. David Nyhan, "Why Clinton's Ohio Win Was So Sweet," *The Boston* Sunday Globe, November 8, 1992, p. A25.

28. Nyhan, "Why Clinton's Ohio Win Was so Sweet."

29. *USA Today,* November 5, 1992, p. 1A.

30. *The Polling Report,* June 8, 1992, p. 5, and June 22, 1992, p. 4.

31. Rhodes Cook, "Perot Steals Show Amid Bush, Clinton Primary Victories," *Congressional Quarterly Weekly Report,* June 6, 1992, p. 1643.

32. President Bush won all 27 Republican primaries, but captured just over 70 percent of the votes cast, which was the lowest share for any incumbent Republican since World War II, except for Gerald R. Ford in 1976.

33. Tom Morganthau, "The Quitter: Why Perot Bowed Out," *Newsweek,* July 27, 1992, pp. 28–30, and John Mintz and David Von Drehle, "The Day Perot Pulled the Plug," *Washington Post National Weekly Edition,* July 27–August 2, 1992, pp. 9–10.

34. *The Polling Report* September 7, 1992, supplement.

35. Burt Solomon, "What's the Mission?" *National Journal,* August 15, 1992, pp. 1880–1884. Solomon comments: "Nothing in his life has prepared Bush for a contest in which vision may count more than values" (p. 1881).

36. E. J. Dionne, Jr., "A Little Erosion Over on the Right," *Washington Post National Weekly Edition,* August 10–16, 1992, p. 14.

37. Dan Balz, "The GOP Reckoning," *Washington Post National Weekly Edition,* August 17–23, 1992, pp. 6–7.

38. *The Polling Report.*

39. George F. Will, "The Republicans' Graceless Rhetoric," *Boston Sunday Globe*, August 23, 1992, p. 79.

40. Robin Toner, "President Stresses Experience as Leader on the World Stage," *New York Times,* August 21, 1992, p. A15.

41. David S. Broder, "Which Way Will the Votes Swing?" *Washington Post National Weekly Edition,* September 14–10, 1992, p. 4.

42. Howard Kurtz, "The Candidates' Ad Campaigns Go Their Separate Ways," *Washington Post National Weekly Edition,* September 28–October 4, 1992, p. 13; Martin F. Nolan, "Electoral College Bowl," *Boston Sunday Globe,* October 25, 1992, p. 71.

43. The Bush campaign did poorly in its battleground states. It lost all but 1 of its 12 states in category #3, 8 of 13 in category #2, and even 3 of the 15 in category #1. It won none of the states in category #4.

44. William Schneider, "A Loud Vote for Change," *National Journal,* November 7, 1992, pp. 2542–2544.

45. Burt Solomon, "Boomers Take Charge," *National Journal,* November 7, 1992, pp. 2532–2536.

46. E. J. Dionne, Jr., "Perot Seen Not Affecting Vote Outcome," *Washington Post,* November 8, 1992, p. A36.

47. Ann Devroy, "The Low Road That Went Nowhere," *Washington Post National Weekly Edition,* November 9–15, p. 7, and Christopher Connell, "Quayle Sees Flaws in Bush Campaign," *Boston Globe,* November 6, 1992, p. 19.

48. Michael Kranish, "Roots of Bush Defeat Showed Long Before Campaign Began," *Boston Globe,* November 6, 1992, p. 19.

Chapter 5

1. Albert Gore, Jr., acceptance speech, Democratic National Convention, New York, July 16, 1992.

2. Walter Lippmann, *The Phantom Public* (New York: Harcourt, Brace, 1925), pp. 56–57.

3. In 1984, 49 percent said they were "better off" financially than they were in 1980; just 20 percent said they were "worse off." Of those who thought their wallets had grown fatter, 84 percent backed Reagan. Of those whose wallets were slimmer, 85 percent supported Mondale. Source: CBS/*New York Times* poll, November 8–14, 1984.

4. Gallup Organization poll for *Newsweek,* September 10–11, 1992.

5. Voter Research and Surveys, exit poll, November 3, 1992.

6. Voter Research and Surveys.

7. Voter Research and Surveys.

8. David S. Broder, "Politicians on Probation," *Washington Post,* December 6, 1992, p. C7.

9. Voter Research and Surveys.

10. The figures were 8 and 2 percent respectively. Source: Voter Research and Surveys.

11. "Transcript of the Second Debate Between the Presidential Candidates," *New York Times,* October 17, 1992, p. A10.

12. Gilbert K. Chesterton, *What I Saw in America* (New York: Dodd, Mead, 1922), p. 8.

13. Quoted in Terry W. Hartle, "Dream Jobs?" *Public Opinion* (September/October 1986), p. 11.

14. Garry Wills, *Inventing America* (New York: Vintage Books, 1978), p. xxii.

15. Ronald Reagan, acceptance speech, Republican National Convention, Detroit, July 17, 1980.

16. See John Kenneth White, *The New Politics of Old Values* (Hanover, New Hampshire, 1990), especially pp. 37–55.

17. Quoted in Fred Barnes, "Campaign '88: Bush's Mandate," *New Republic,* November 14, 1988, p. 12.

18. Quoted in the MacNeill/Lehrer "NewsHour," PBS broadcast, September 25, 1992.

19. Richard B. Wirthlin, lecture, Catholic University of America, September 29, 1992.

20. "The Family and 'Family Values' in American Politics: An Interview with Richard B. Wirthlin," *The Public Perspective* (September/October 1992), p. 25.

21. "Rocky Road to Houston," *Newsweek,* November/December, 1992, p. 66.

22. E. J. Dionne, Jr., "Buchanan Heaps Scorn on Democrats," *Washington Post,* August 18, 1992, p. A18.

23. Dionne, "Buchanan Heaps Scorn."

24. William Schneider, "A Loud Vote for Change," *National Journal,* November 7, 1992, p. 2542. There were some interesting differences among supporters of the three candidates on this question. Eighty-seven percent of Bush backers and 75 percent of Perot supporters said government should "encourage traditional family values"; just 9 and 19 percent respectively said that government should "encourage tolerance of nontraditional families." Clinton voters were more evenly split, with 53 percent saying government should "encourage traditional values" and 42 percent arguing for tolerance. Source: Voter Research and Surveys.

25. Peter Hart and Vince Breglio for NBC News poll, September 3–5, 1992.

26. CBS News/*New York Times* poll, September 9–13, 1992.

27. CBS News/*New York Times* poll.

28. Emil Reich, *Success among the Nations* (New York: Harper and Brothers, 1904), pp. 265–66.

29. Reich, *Success among the Nations.*

30. Quoted in Daniel Bell, "The End of American Exceptionalism," *The Public Interest,* Fall 1975, p. 203.

31. George Bush, CNN interview, June 15, 1992.

32. Charles Witt, Jr., "Sunday Today" interview, NBC broadcast, March 29, 1992.

33. Ross Perot, "National Town Meeting" interview, CBS broadcast, June 2, 1992.

34. David Kusnet, *Speaking American: How The Democrats Can Win in the Nineties* (New York: Thunder's Mouth Press, 1992).

35. "Best Lines Slung from Tongues in '88," *Providence Journal,* January 3, 1989, p. B4.

36. Bill Clinton, acceptance speech, Democratic National Convention, New York, July 16, 1992.

37. Quoted in Kusnet, *Speaking American,* p. 40.

38. Clinton, acceptance speech.

39. Clinton, acceptance speech.

40. Kusnet, *Speaking American,* pp. 40–41.

41. Bill Clinton, election eve address, NBC broadcast, November 2, 1992.

42. Gallup/CNN/*USA Today* poll, November 10–11, 1992.

43. Clinton, election eve address.

Chapter 6

1. Jarol B. Manheim, *All of the People, All the Time: Strategic Communication and American Politics* (Armonk, NY: M. E. Sharpe, 1991), pp. 30–47. For a case study that illustrates these points, see Gwenda Blair, *Almost Golden: Jessica Savitch and the Selling of Television News* (New York: Simon & Schuster, 1988).

2. Larry J. Sabato, *Feeding Frenzy: How Attack Journalism Has Transformed American Politics* (New York: Free Press, 1991).

3. L. Patrick Devlin, "Contrasts in Presidential Campaign Commercials of 1988," *American Behavioral Scientist* (1989), pp. 389–414. For a characterization of the types of negative advertising, see Montague Kern, *30-Second Politics: Political Advertising in the Eighties* (New York: Praeger, 1989), pp. 93–112.

4. Manheim, p. 55.

5. Manheim, p. 57.

6. David Broder, "Five Ways to Put Some Sanity Back in Elections," *Washington Post,* January 14, 1990, pp. B1, B4.

7. Howard Kurtz, "Media Alter Approach to Campaign Coverage," *Washington Post,* September 11, 1992, p. A10.

8. Howard Kurtz, "The Talk Show Campaign," *Washington Post,* October 28, 1992, pp. A1, A14.

9. Elizabeth Kolbert, "Test-Marketing a President: How Focus Groups Pervade Campaign Politics," *New York Times Magazine,* August 30, 1992, pp. 18 ff.

10. Michael Kelly, "The Making of a First Family: A Blueprint," *New York Times,* November 14, 1992, pp. 1, 9.

Chapter 7

1. Clinton Rossiter, *Parties and Politics in America* (Ithaca, NY: Cornell University Press, 1960), pp. 4–5.

2. See the "authorized" version of this, Ken Follett, *On the Wings of Eagles* (New York: Morrow, 1983).

3. Ed Bark, "Perot Treated to Free Appearances on Interview Talk Shows," *Dallas Morning News,* September 30, 1992, p. 10A.

4. Contributing to this, perhaps, was the reported refusal of President Bush to have one-on-one interviews with a list that included five network reporters and anchors. These included Dan Rather (CBS), Peter Jennings (ABC), and

Bryant Gumbel (NBC), according to CBS reporter Lesley Stahl, *Dallas Morning News*, September 29, 1992, p. 12A.

5. Kevin Sack, "In Debut of His Revived Campaign Perot Is Tangled in Contradictions," *New York Times*, October 6, 1992, p. 15A.

6. Ed Bark, "Perot, Media Trade Negative Reviews," *Dallas Morning News*, September 29, 1992, p. 12A.

7. Kevin Sack, "Perot Scores in 3d Debate, Then Opens Fire on the Press," *New York Times*, October 21, 1992, p. A12.

8. "Vote for Ross Perot?" *New York Times*, November 2, 1992, p. A14.

9. See "The American Enterprise Public Opinion and Demographic Report" in *The Public Perspective* 4 (November/December 1992), p. 100.

10. Joseph Schlesinger, "Political Party Organization," in James March (ed.), *Handbook of Organizations* (Chicago: Rand McNally and Co., 1965), pp. 77 ff.

11. Edward J. Rollins, "Perot Deserves No Second Chance," *New York Times*, September 28, 1992, p. A18.

12. Kevin Sack, "Perot Scores in 3d Debate, Then Opens Fire on the Press."

13. "Transcript of First TV Debate Among Bush, Clinton and Perot," *New York Times*, October 12, 1992, pp. A12–A15.

14. Rhodes Cook, "Clinton Picks the GOP Lock on the Electoral College," *Congressional Quarterly Weekly Report*, November 12, 1992, p. 3553.

15. Admittedly, this is based on preliminary figures, aggregated at the state level, and excluding the District of Columbia. If D.C., where Perot did quite poorly, is included, the Perot effect is even less. The statistic computed is Pearson's correlation coefficient r.

16. "If there is a common thread running through [these states], it is a history of fiercely independent and often contrarian politics. People everywhere talk about not putting up with politics as usual, but in these states they seem to mean it." Kevin Sack, "Why Perot Thrived in Fertile Kansas," *New York Times*, November 6, 1992, p. A12.

17. These conclusions are drawn from a *New York Times* poll, November 1, 1992, p. A16.

Chapter 8

1. Gary C. Jacobson, *The Politics of Congressional Elections*, 3rd ed. (Boston: Little, Brown, Inc., 1992), chapter 3.

2. Frank J. Sorauf, *Money in Elections* (New York: HarperCollins Publishers, 1988).

3. Jacobson, *The Politics of Congressional Elections*, p. 121.

4. Morris Fiorini, *Congress: Keystone of the Washington Establishment* (New Haven: Yale University Press, 1977).

5. Jacobson, *The Politics of Congressional Elections*, chapter 3.

6. Kenneth Prewitt, *The Recruitment of Political Leaders: A Study of Citizen-Politicians* (Indianapolis: Bobbs-Merrill Company, 1970), chapter 1.

7. Information on the results of the 1992 election was assembled from a wide variety of national and local news sources and especially from: *Congressional Quarterly Weekly Report: Special Report*, "The New Class: More Diverse, Less Lawyers, Younger," *Congressional Quarterly*, November 7, 1992, pp. 7–10; also: Jeffrey L. Katz and Ceci Connolly, "Women, Minorities, Rock Records, But Ideology Will Barely Budge," *Congressional Quarterly Weekly Report*, November 7, 1992, pp. 3557–3563.

8. Hanna F. Pitkin, *The Concept of Representation* (Berkeley: University of California Press, 1967), chapters 4–6.

9. *Congressional Quarterly*, "The New Class," pp. 8–9.

10. Thomas E. Mann, *Unsafe at Any Margin: Interpreting Congressional Elections* (Washington, DC: American Enterprise Institute, 1977); David R. Mayhew, *Congress: The Electoral Election* (New Haven: Yale University Press, 1974).

11. Karlyn H. Keene and Everett Carl Ladd, eds., "Congress' Ratings at an All-Time Low," *The American Enterprise* (Washington, DC: November/December, 1992), pp. 86–87; and "How Different Groups View Congress Term Limits," pp. 88–89.

12. The information on these Arkansas races was extracted from various articles in the *Arkansas Times* and the *Arkansas Democrat-Gazette* as well as the *Congressional Quarterly Weekly Report*, November 7, 1992, p. 22.

13. For more on the story of politics in Bill Clinton's home state see: Diane R. Blair, *Arkansas Politics and Government: Do the People Rule?* (Lincoln: University of Nebraska Press, 1988).

14. Philip Converse, "The Nature of Belief Systems in Mass Publics," in *Ideology and Discontent*, David E. Apter, ed. (New York, Macmillan, 1964), chapter 6.

15. Keene and Ladd, "Congress' Ratings," p. 87.

16. "U.S. House Margins Shrink." *USA Today*, November 6, 1992, p. 7A.

17. *USA Today*, "U.S. House Margins Shrink"; also see, Katz and Connolly, "Women, Minorities, Rock Records," pp. 3557–3563.

18. David R. Mayhew, "Congressional Elections: The Case of the Vanishing Marginals," *Polity* (Spring 1974), pp. 295–319.

19. Mitchell Levin, "A Presidential Style Emerges," *Chicago Tribune*, December 17, 1992, Section 1, p. 5.

Chapter 9

1. Janet Hook, "Voters Will Render Judgements on Members' Checking Habits," *Congressional*

Quarterly Weekly Report, April 18, 1992, p. 991.

2. "Congressional Departures," *Congressional Quarterly Weekly Report,* September 26, 1992, p. 2916.

3. David B. Magleby and Candice J. Nelson, *The Money Chase* (Washington, DC: The Brookings Institution, 1990), p. 28; and "1990 Congressional Spending Drops to Low Point," Federal Election Commission press release, February 22, 1991.

4. Herbert E. Alexander, *The Case for PACs* (Washington, DC: Public Affairs Council), p. 9; and "1990 Congressional Spending Drops to Low Point."

5. "FEC Announces 1992 Presidential Spending Limits," Federal Election Commission press release, February 12, 1992.

6. "FEC Approves Matching Funds for 1992 Presidential Candidates," Federal Election Commission press release, October 30, 1992.

7. "FEC Announces 1992 Presidential Spending Limits."

8. "FEC Approves Matching Funds for 1992 Presidential Candidates."

9. "FEC Announces 1992 Presidential Spending Limits."

10. Herbert E. Alexander, *Financing Politics: Money, Elections and Political Reform,* 4th ed. (Washington, DC: Congressional Quarterly Press, 1992), p. 72.

11. "FEC Finds Congressional Campaign Spending Up $75 Million as 1992 General Election Approaches," Federal Election Commission press release, October 30, 1992.

12. Charles R. Babcock, "Democrats Outrun GOP in Recent Fund-raising," *Washington Post,* October 30, 1992, p. 25.

13. "Independent Expenditures of $21 Million Reported in '88, FEC Study Shows," Federal Election Commission press release, May 19, 1989.

14. Maralee Schwartz and Charles R. Babcock, "Candidates Reach for Wallets to Give Themselves Late Boost," *Washington Post,* November 3, 1992, p. A9.

15. "FEC Approves Matching Funds for 1992 Presidential Candidates."

16. Peter Stone, "Return of the Fat Cats," *National Journal,* October 17, 1992, p. 2351.

17. Carol Matlock, "Fat Cats Slightly Slimmer Now," *National Journal Convention Special,* August 22, 1992.

18. "Fat Cats Slightly Slimmer Now."

19. Charles R. Babcock, "GOP Donors Open Wallets for Democrats," *Washington Post,* October 24, 1992, p. A10.

20. "GOP Donors Open Wallets for Democrats."

21. Beth Donovan, "Bush's Soft Touch," *Congressional Quarterly Weekly Report,* May 2, 1992, p. 1134.

22. "Return of the Fat Cats."

23. "Return of the Fat Cats."

24. John R. Cranford, "New Clinton Economic Team Veers Towards the Center," *Congressional Quarterly Weekly Report,* December 12, 1992, pp. 3799, 3824.

25. Brett D. Fromson and Charles R. Babcock, "Politicians Mine a Rich Vein at Wall Street Firm," *Washington Post,* October 5, 1992, p. A1.

26. Alexander, *Financing Politics: Money, Elections and Political Reform,* 4th ed., p. 115.

27. *Federal Election Commission Record,* vol. 18, no. 12 (December 1992), p. 4.

28. *Federal Election Commission Record* (December 1992), p. 5.

29. *Federal Election Commission Record* (December 1992), p. 5.

30. Michael Abramowitz and Charles R. Babcock, "DNC Leads Again in Fund-raising," *Washington Post,* October 5, 1992, p. A7.

31. Herbert E. Alexander, *Financing Politics: Money, Elections and Political Reform,* 3rd ed. (Washington, DC: Congressional Quarterly, 1984), pp. 130–131.

32. Alexander, *Financing Politics: Money, Elections and Political Reform,* 3rd ed., p. 125.

33. Babcock, "Democrats Outrun GOP in Recent Fund-raising."

34. Schwartz and Babcock, "Candidates Reach for Wallets to Give Themselves Late Boost."

35. "Congressional Departures," *Congressional Quarterly Weekly Report,* September 26, 1992, p. 2916.

36. "Congressional Departures."

37. Michael Barone and Grant Ujifusa, *The Almanac of American Politics 1992* (Washington, DC: National Journal, 1991), p. 375.

38. "Financial Activity of 1992 Congressional Campaigns Soars," Federal Election Commission press release, August 9, 1992; and Bob Benenson, "Incumbent Tremors in Illinois: Democrat Dixon Dumped," *Congressional Quarterly Weekly Report,* March 21, 1992, p. 743.

39. Figures are based on financial disclosure reports through October 14, 1992. "FEC Finds Congressional Spending Up $75 Million as 1992 General Election Approaches."

40. "FEC Finds Congressional Spending Up $75 Million as 1992 General Election Approaches."

41. Kenneth Cooper, Charles R. Babcock, and Gary Lee, "Money: A Ticket to Victory," *Washington Post,* November 6, 1992, p. A18.

42. Cooper, Babcock, and Lee, "Money: A Ticket to Victory."

43. Glenn R. Simpson, "Why Did So Few Incumbents Lose Nov. 3rd?" *Roll Call,* November 9, 1992, p. 2.

44. Simpson, "Why Did So Few Incumbents Lose Nov. 3rd?" and "FEC Finds Congressional

Spending Up $75 Million as 1992 General Election Approaches."

45. Magleby and Nelson, *The Money Chase,* p. 37.

46. Calculated from "FEC Finds Congressional Campaign Spending Up $75 Million as 1992 General Election Approaches."

47. Charles R. Babcock, "In Donating $230 Million, Interests Favored Bush, Hill Democrats," *Washington Post,* October 23, 1992, p. A19.

48. Babcock, "In Donating $230 Million, Interests Favored Bush, Hill Democrats."

49. Babcock, "In Donating $230 Million, Interests Favored Bush, Hill Democrats."

50. Calculated from "FEC Finds Congressional Campaign Spending Up $75 Million as 1992 General Election Approaches."

51. Magleby and Nelson, *The Money Chase,* p. 26.

52. "Campaign Finance Bill Moves to Conference," *Congressional Quarterly Weekly Report,* September 29, 1990, p. 3092.

53. "Veto of Campaign Finance Bill," *Congressional Quarterly Weekly Report,* May 16, 1992, p. 1384.

54. Beth Donovan, "Campaign Finance Highlights," *Congressional Quarterly Weekly Report,* April 4, 1992, p. 862.

55. Beth Donovan, "Smooth Sailing Isn't in Forecast for Election Law Revisions," *Congressional Quarterly Weekly Report,* November 21, 1992, p. 3666.

56. Donovan, "Campaign Finance Highlights," p. 863.

Chapter 10

1. Center for the American Woman and Politics (CAWP), National Information Bank on Women in Public Office, Eagleton Institute of Politics, Rutgers University, Fact Sheets issued periodically throughout 1992.

2. CAWP Fact Sheets.

3. CAWP Fact Sheets.

4. The survey data may be found in Neil A. Lewis, "Anita Hill Says She Is Skeptical About Specter," *New York Times,* October 7, 1992, p. A14.

5. When the 103rd Congress organized, both Dianne Feinstein and Carol Moseley Braun were appointed to the Senate Judiciary Committee.

6. Quoted in Richard E. Cohen, "California Gold Rush," *National Journal,* September 26, 1992, 2182.

7. CBS-*Times* polls quoted in "Opinion Outlook," *National Journal,* July 11, 1992, p. 1653, and October 24, 1992, p. 2453.

8. *Gallup Poll Monthly,* January 1992, p. 6; "Opinion Outlook," *National Journal,* November 7, 1992, p. 2544.

9. "Opinion Outlook," *National Journal,* July 11, 1992, p. 1656.

10. Others were Nancy Reagan (4), Jacqueline Kennedy Onassis (6), and Betty Ford (10). "Religious Figures are Prominent on List of 'Most Admired'," *Emerging Trends,* January 1992, p. 5.

11. Daniel Wattenberg, "The Lady Macbeth of Little Rock," *The American Spectator,* August 1992, p. 25.

12. Wattenberg, "The Lady Macbeth of Little Rock," pp. 25–32; Margaret O'Brien Steinfels, "Rights 'R' Us: Kids, Hillary, and the Law," *Commonweal,* May 8, 1992, pp. 4–5; Christopher Lasch, "Hillary Clinton, Child Saver," *Harper's Magazine,* October, 1992, pp. 74–82.

13. The irony here is that Marilyn Quayle, another lawyer, had formerly been portrayed as a combative, power-mad spouse; her "outmoded" flip hairstyle quietly disappeared during this campaign. Also forgotten was the controversy in 1990 when Barbara Bush was invited to address Wellesley graduates; students there charged that as a college drop-out wife and mother, she was only invited because of her husband's status. But see the small critical literature on Barbara Bush: Andrew Sullivan, "Sacred Cow," *New Republic,* June 22, 1992, p. 42; Ann McDaniel, "Barbara Bush: The Steel Behind the Smile," *Newsweek,* June 22, 1992, pp. 34–36; Marjorie Perloff, "Mommy Dearest," *New Republic,* October 5, 1992, pp. 13–16.

14. Polls on Hillary Clinton appear in: "Opinion Outlook," *National Journal,* April 18, 1992, p. 960; August 15, 1992, p. 1920; November 28, 1992, p. 2746; "Will Hillary Hurt or Help?" *Newsweek,* March 30, 1992, p. 30; Eleanor Clift, "Hillary Then and Now," *Newsweek,* July 20, 1992, p. 39; Eleanor Clift and Mark Miller, "Hillary: Behind the Scenes," *Newsweek,* December 28, 1992, p. 23; Patricia O'Brien, "The First Lady With a Career?" *Working Woman,* August 1992, pp. 46–47; Matthew Cooper, "The Hillary Factor," *U.S. News & World Report,* April 27, 1992, pp. 30–37.

15. E. J. Dionne, Jr., "Survey Finds Rift to GOP Coalition," *Washington Post,* December 4, 1991, p. A20. Some caution should be applied here in that preference for an "insider" or an "outsider" may also be related to party identification. A CBS-*Times* poll taken in March 1992 showed that 34 percent of Republicans and 50 percent of Democrats favored an "outsider" in the White House. In contrast, 45 percent of Democrats and 49 percent of Republicans preferred an "outsider" as their representative in Congress. See "Opinion Outlook," *National Journal,* April 18, 1992, p. 960.

16. Figures compiled from information in *CAWP News & Notes* 8 (Fall 1992), pp. 5–14.

17. Susan J. Carroll, *Women as Candidates in American Politics* (Bloomington: Indiana University Press, 1985), pp. 101–102.

18. Kim Fridkin Kahn and Edie N. Goldenberg, "The Media: Obstacle or Ally of Feminists?" *The Annals* 515 (May 1991), pp. 109–112.

19. Thomas Hardy, "Honestly, Braun's Overwhelming Success in Race for Senate Defies Belief," *Chicago Tribune,* November 8, 1992, p. 4:4.

20. Lucy Baruch, Katheryne McCormick, and Kris Ronan, "Women Congressional Candidates: 1992 Campaign Receipts," *CAWP News & Notes* 9 (Winter 1993), pp. 22–23.

21. Barbara C. Burrell, "Women's and Men's Campaigns for the U.S. House of Representatives, 1972–1982: A Finance Gap?" *American Politics Quarterly* 13 (July 1985), pp. 251–272; Carol J. Uhlaner and Kay L. Schlozman, "Candidate Gender and Congressional Campaign Receipts," *Journal of Politics* 48 (February 1986), pp. 30–50; John Theilmann and Al Wilhite, *Discrimination and Congressional Campaign Contributions* (New York: Praeger, 1991).

22. "Women's Campaigns Fueled Mostly By Women's Checks," *Congressional Quarterly Weekly Report,* October 17, 1992, p. 3269.

23. Figures were taken from "Women Raising Money for Women Candidates," *CAWP News & Notes* 8 (Fall 1992), p. 2, and from the groups' own materials.

24. Figures compiled from information in *CAWP News & Notes* 8 (Fall 1992), pp. 5–14.

25. Bush did receive the "homemakers' vote," about 8 percent of all voters, by a margin of 45 percent to Clinton's 36 percent and Perot's 19 percent.

26. Steven V. Roberts, "Will 1992 be the Year of the Woman?" *U.S. News & World Report,* April 27, 1992, p. 37. See also Dionne, "Survey Finds Rift to GOP Coalition."

27. *A Polling Report, Women's Voices '92* (New York and Washington, DC: Ms. Foundation for Women and Center for Policy Alternatives, 1992), pp. 28–29.

28. Louis Harris, *The 1972 Virginia Slims American Women's Opinion Poll* (New York: 1972); *Winning With Women* (New York: 1991).

29. See Dionne, "Survey Finds Rift to GOP Coalition"; Harris, *Winning With Women.*

30. "Opinion Outlook," *National Journal,* August 15, 1992, p. 1920.

31. Richard Morin, "Putting Women in Their Place," *Washington Post National Weekly Edition,* November 30–December 6, 1992, p. 36.

32. Sandra Musumeci, "Primaries Herald La Belle Epoque," *Campaign,* August 1992, pp. 1, 7–8. This figure is in contrast with earlier studies that indicated that women were 10 percent less successful in 1986, equal with men in 1988, and 58 percent more successful in 1990.

33. CAWP, Fact Sheets.

Chapter 11

1. Lawrence H. Fuchs, *American Ethnic Politics* (New York: Harper & Row, 1968); Otto Feinstein, ed., *Ethnic Groups in the City* (Lexington, MA: Heath Lexington Books, 1971); Michael Parenti, "Ethnic Politics and the Persistence of Ethnic Identification," *American Political Science Review* 6 (1967), pp. 717–726; Raymond Wolfinger, "The Development and Persistence of Ethnic Voting," *American Political Science Review,* 59 (1965), pp. 896–908; Thomas J. Pavlak, "Social Class, Ethnicity and Racial Prejudice," *Public Opinion Quarterly,* 37 (1973), pp. 225–231; Edward O. Laumann, *Bonds of Pluralism: The Form and Substance of Urban Social Networks* (New York: Wiley, 1973); Donald E. Pienkos, "Foreign Affairs Perceptions of Ethnic Politics," *Ethnicity,* 3 (1974), pp. 19–33; Andrew M. Greeley, *Ethnicity in the United States: A Preliminary Reconnaissance* (New York: Wiley, 1974); Stanley Lieberson, *A Piece of the Pie: Black and White Immigrants Since 1880* (Berkeley: University of California Press, 1980); Nathan Glazer and Daniel P. Moynihan, *Beyond the Melting Pot* (Cambridge, MA: MIT Press, 1964); Rudolf J. Vecoli, "Ethnicity: A Neglected Dimension of American History," in *The State of American History* (Chicago: Quadrangle Books, 1970); Wayne Charles Miller et al., *A Comprehensive Bibliography for the Study of American Minorities* (New York: New York University Press, 1976).

2. See thematic essays in Stephen Thernstrom, ed., *The Harvard Encyclopedia of Ethnic Groups in America* (Cambridge: The Belknap Press of Harvard University Press, 1980), esp. Philip Gleason, "American Identity and Americanization."

3. Lee Benson, *The Concept of Jacksonian Democracy: New York as a Test Case* (Princeton, 1961); Samuel T. McSeveney, "Ethnic Groups, Ethnic Conflict and Recent Quantitative Research in American Political History," *International Migration Reviews* 7 (Spring 1973), pp. 14–33; Peter James and Melvin G. Holli, eds., *The Ethnic Frontier* (Grand Rapids, 1977); John Higham, ed., *Ethnic Leadership in America* (Baltimore, 1977).

4. See Milton Gordon, *Assimilation in American Life* (New York: Oxford University Press, 1964) and Arthur Mann, *The One and the Many: Reflections on the American Identity* (Chicago: Chicago University Press, 1979).

5. See Mark R. Levy and Michael S. Kramer, *The Ethnic Factor: How America's Minorities Decide Elections* (New York: Simon & Shuster, 1972).

6. Levy and Kramer.

7. For a contemporaneous account of this problem, see Murray S. Friedman, ed., *Overcoming Middle Class Rage* (Philadelphia: Westminster

Press, 1971), especially Chapter V articles and speeches of Kevin P. Phillips, Spiro Agnew, Edmund S. Muskie, Andrew Greeley, and Bayard Rustin. See Geno Baroni, Sylvano Tomasi and Michael Wenk, *Pieces of a Dream* (New York: Migration Studies, 1972).

8. State Polling Data Batch, National Center for Urban Ethnic Affairs, 1992.

9. The message of speechwriter David Kuznets, author of *Speaking American: How the Democrats Can Win in the Nineties* (New York: Thunder Mouth Press, 1992) resonated throughout the effort. A pluralistic, catholic theme of compassion and firmness pervaded the entire campaign.

10. Joel Leiske, "Cultural Issues and Images in the 1988 Presidential Campaign: Why the Democrats Lost—Again," *PS*, 24 (June 1991), pp. 180–87.

11. Michael J. Weiss, *The Clustering of America* (New York: Harper & Row, 1988).

12. *Congressional Quarterly*, Special Report, January 16, 1993.

13. Congressional District Ethnic Concentrations for Selected Ancestry Groups, U.S. Census 1980, NCUEA Data File.

14. For George Bush's attempt to derail this multi-ethnic coalition, see Chapter 10 "George Bush Attacks," in Lawrence M. O'Rourke, *Geno: The Life and Mission of Msgr. Geno Baroni* (New York: Paulist Press, 1991).

15. Editorial, the *New York Times*, December 28, 1988.

16. For an exceptionally insightful social history of the forces that created the Southern mentalities of race consciousness, see Joel Williamson, *A Rage for Order: White-Black Relations in the American South Since Emancipation* (New York: Oxford Press, 1986).

17. NCUEA Data File, Washington, DC, 1993.

18. *Congressional Quarterly*, Special Report, January 16, 1993.

19. Democratic National Committee, Ethnic Council, Luncheon Program, January 18, 1993, and interview with Chuck Santangelo.

Chapter 12

1. See Susan Herbst, *Numbered Voices* (Chicago: University of Chicago Press, 1993).

2. The Chicago *Sun Times* conducted a straw poll in this manner as recently as 1978.

3. See Peter Prichard, *The Making of McPaper* (Kansas City, MO: Andrews, McMeel, and Parker, 1987). Al Neuharth, former Gannett chairman, the driving force behind the introduction of *USA Today*, made photographic man-on-the-street features a prominent part of the first newspaper he published, *SoDak Sports*. Later, *USA Today* would contain such a feature on its editorial page.

4. See J. Converse, *Survey Research in the United States* (Berkeley: University of California Press, 1987) for a thorough discussion of the 1936 election and the growth of commercial polling.

5. Following the 1988 election there were numerous conferences which offered criticism of press performance. One such conference was sponsored by the Annenberg Washington Program of Northwestern University, a portion of which focused on poll coverage.

6. The newspapers in which poll coverage was examined include the *New York Times*, the *Washington Post*, the *Los Angeles Times*, the *Atlanta Constitution*, the *Chicago Tribune*, the *Boston Globe*, the *Minneapolis Star-Tribune*, the *Houston Chronicle*, New York *Newsday*, and the *Washington Times*. The wire services include Associated Press, United Press International, Gannett, Reuters, and Agence France Presse. The news magazines include *Newsweek*, *Time*, and *U.S. News & World Report*. These print outlets also carried news of broadcast news-sponsored polls, including those sponsored by CNN, CBS, ABC, and NBC.

7. For example, a press conference was held in early June to announce the findings of an unusual poll, sponsored by a New York businessman, which purported to document the unparalleled voter discontent nationwide that fueled Perot's unannounced candidacy. The poll's findings, presented by Gordon Black, a sometime pollster for media clients, were supplemented by an analysis by Theodore Lowi, president of the American Political Science Association. Lowi argued that Perot's candidacy was unprecedented, resting on a base of support much broader than that of any independent candidate in modern times—and that American dissatisfaction was equally unprecedented.

8. In a June 27 op-ed piece in the *New York Times*, Kathleen Frankovic, director of the CBS survey research unit, argued that the conflicting pictures of Perot's support in various polls were, at least in part, due to question order effects. She argued, further, that concentration on the horse race was inappropriate at that point in the campaign, when many citizens were unfamiliar with the candidates. The effects of methodological differences among polls could be heightened by the fact that expressed voter preferences were not based on a firm knowledge base.

9. The Times Mirror Center's report was issued on August 6. Kohut's commentary was reported in the *Los Angeles Times*, August 7, 1992.

10. The CBS/*New York Times* poll is discussed further below. A summary of the results from several polls was given in the *New York Times*, August 25, 1992, p. A19.

11. See Adam Clymer, "Bush's Gains from Convention Nearly Evaporate in Latest Poll," *New York Times*, August 26, 1992, p. A1.

12. Clay Richards, "For Whom the Bounce Polls," *Newsday*, August 28, 1992, p. 15.

13. Andrew Rosenthal, "The 1992 Campaign: The Overview; Bush Pulls Close in Poll, but Not with Women," *New York Times*, August 22, 1992, p. 1.

14. Howard Fineman and Ann McDaniel, "Bush: What Bounce?" *Newsweek*, August 31, 1992, p. 26.

15. "Series of Polls Shows Perot's Support Fading," *Chicago Tribune*, September 30, 1992, p. 4; Chuck Raasch, "Poll Shows Difficulty Gauging Impact If Perot Decides to Run," Gannett News Service, September 29, 1992.

16. "Poll Says Bush Now Nearly Even With Clinton," Reuters, October 28, 1992; Irwin Arieff, "Polls Can Vary Widely, Depending on Survey Methods," Reuters, October 29, 1992; Martin Schram, "How the Latest Polling Story Faded," *Newsday*, October 30, 1992, p. 113.

17. "The 1992 Campaign; The Poll Findings Converge," *New York Times*, November 3, 1992, p. A13; Richard Morin, "Pollsters' 'Nutty' Calculations Added Up on Day That Counted; In Academia, However, One Well-Known Political Crystal Ball Lies Shattered," *Washington Post*, November 5, 1992, p. A37.

18. Richard Morin, "Clinton Slide in Survey Shows Perils of Polling," *Washington Post*, September 29, 1992, p. A6; Joann Byrd, "Poll Play," *Washington Post*, October 4, 1992, p. C6.

19. See Note 8. For example, polls that asked, prior to the horse-race question, an item tapping the respondent's view of "how things in the country are going these days" measured more support for Perot, presumably because the question elicited thoughts about the negative state of the economy, gridlock in Washington, and so forth.

20. My search produced over 30 such stories produced by major publications and wire services. In addition, the *New York Times* had a regular feature that compared the findings of recent polls from other news organizations.

21. Warren Mitofsky, "A Challenge for Campaign '92: Training Reporters and Informing the Public," Invited Paper, Annual Meeting of the American Statistical Association, August, 1992; Peter V. Miller, Daniel M. Merkle, and Paul Wang, "Journalism with Footnotes: Reporting the Technical Details of Polls," in Paul Lavrakas and Jack Holley, eds., *Polls and Presidential Election Coverage* (Beverly Hills, CA: Sage, 1990).

Chapter 13

1. For an example of such a model, see Michael Lewis-Beck and Tom W. Rice, *Forecasting Elections* (Washington, DC: Congressional Quarterly Press, 1992), pp. 133–141. For a general discussion and assessment of election forecasts, see Richard Morin, "The Proof is in the Polling," *Washington Post National Weekly Edition*, September 14–20, 1992, p. 14; Elizabeth Kolbert, "As for All That Lore About Sure-Thing Election Prophecies, Forget About It," *New York Times*, November 5, 1992, p. B1; and Richard Morin, "Surviving the Ups and Downs of Election '92," *Washington Post National Weekly Edition*, November 9–15, 1992, p. 37.

2. Angus Campbell, "Voters and Elections: Past and Present," *Journal of Politics* 26 (November 1964), p. 747, quoted in James L. Sundquist, *Dynamics of the Party System: Alignment and Realignment of Political Parties in the United States*, rev. ed. (Washington, DC: Brookings Institution, 1983), p. 5.

3. Angus Campbell, Philip E. Converse, Warren E. Miller, and Donald E. Stokes, *The American Voter*, (New York: John Wiley, 1960).

4. Eugene H. Roseboom, *A History of Presidential Elections: From George Washington to Richard M. Nixon* (New York: Macmillan, 1970), p. 577.

5. V. O. Key, Jr., "A Theory of Critical Elections," *Journal of Politics* 17 (February 1955): pp. 3–18.

6. Key, p. 4.

7. For a very thorough bibliography of realignment literature, see Harold F. Bass, Jr., "Background to Debate: A Reader's Guide and Bibliography" in *The End of Realignment? Interpreting American Electoral Eras*, Byron E. Shafer, ed. (Madison, WI: University of Wisconsin Press, 1991), pp. 141–178.

8. See Peter F. Nardulli, "Beyond the 'End of Realignment': The Concept of a Critical Realignment and Presidential Elections, 1828–1984." (Paper delivered at the annual meeting of the American Political Science Association, Chicago, IL, September 3–6, 1992.)

9. See Martin P. Wattenberg, *The Rise of the Candidate-Centered Politics: Presidential Elections of the 1980s* (Cambridge, MA: Harvard University Press, 1991), pp. 31–46.

10. Philip E. Converse, "The Concept of a Normal Vote," in *Elections and the Political Order*, Angus Campbell, Philip E. Converse, Warren E. Miller, and Donald E. Stokes, eds. (New York: John Wiley, 1966), pp. 9–39.

11. Peter F. Nardulli, "A Normal Vote Approach to the Study of Electoral Change: Presidential Elections, 1828–1984," *Working Paper #26*, James H. Kuklinski, ed. (Urbana, IL: Institute of Government and Public Affairs, 1993).

12. Because our normal vote estimates are based on longitudinal trends in the differences between the vote percentages of the two major parties, they cannot predict the portion of the national vote given to minor-party candidates. Most often the minor candidates receive very few votes, or, as in the case of Ross Perot, they draw their support equally from the major parties. In a post-election survey, "How the Nation Voted," *New York Times*, November 5, 1992, p. B4, Perot voters were asked which candidate they would have voted for had Perot not been a candidate. Clinton was named by 38 percent,

Bush was named by 38 percent, and 14 percent said they would not have voted. Thus, the existence of third-party candidates has caused few problems for our efforts to map the contours of the normal vote, with the exception of 1912 when Roosevelt drew disproportionately from the Republican Party.

13. Each state is allocated a number of electoral votes equal to the number of representatives it has in Congress (House and Senate). The District of Columbia has also been given three electoral votes, even though it does not have any official congressional representation. In nearly every state (with the exception of Maine and Nebraska), the candidate who wins the popular vote, regardless of the margin of victory, is awarded all of that state's electoral votes.

14. Although Andrew Jackson won the popular vote in 1824, the House of Representatives decided the election, choosing second-place finisher John Quincy Adams, because none of the four candidates received a majority of the electoral vote. In 1876, Rutherford B. Hayes received one more electoral vote than did Samuel Tilden, although Tilden received 250,000 more popular votes in a disputed election. In 1888, Benjamin Harrison received 65 more electoral votes than did Grover Cleveland, even though Cleveland won the popular vote.

15. "How the Economy Has Fared Under 9 Presidents," *New York Times,* November 4, 1992, p. B11.

16. For a more complete discussion of the view of critical realignments embodied in this section, as well as an empirical examination of past realignments, see Nardulli, 1992.

17. Byron E. Shafer, "The Notion of an Electoral Order," in *The End of Realignment? Interpreting American Electoral Eras,* Byron E. Shafer, ed. (Madison, WI: University of Wisconsin Press, 1991), pp. 37–84.

18. Shafer.

19. See Wattenberg, *The Rise of Candidate-Centered Politics,* and Martin A. Wattenberg, *The Decline of the American Political Parties, 1956–1988* (Cambridge, MA: Harvard University Press, 1989).

20. Warren E. Miller, "The Electorate's View of the Parties," in *The Parties Respond: Changes in the American Party System,* L. Sandy Maisel, ed. (Boulder, CO: Westview Press, 1990), pp. 97–115.

21. Miller, p. 108. Two recent polls are cited by David S. Broder, "Parties on Probation," *Washington Post National Weekly Edition,* December 14–20, 1992, p. 4.

22. See Walter Dean Burnham, "Critical Realignment: Dead or Alive?" in *The End of Realignment? Interpreting American Electoral Eras,* Byron E. Shafer, ed. (Madison, WI: University of Wisconsin Press, 1991), pp. 101–139.

23. Nardulli, 1993, p. 19.

24. John E. Chubb and Paul E. Peterson, "Realignment and Institutionalization," in *The New Direction in American Politics,* John E. Chubb and Paul E. Peterson, eds. (Washington, DC: Brookings Institution, 1985), pp. 1–30.

CONTRIBUTORS

Janet K. Boles is an associate professor of political science at Marquette University. She specializes in studying women in politics, the women's movement, and feminist public policy. She is the author of *The Politics of the Equal Rights Amendment* and the editor of *The Egalitarian City* and *American Feminism*. Recently she participated in a study of the impact of women in public office, sponsored by the Center for the American Woman and Politics, Rutgers University.

William Crotty is a professor of political science at Northwestern University. He is the author of a number of books on political parties and elections, including *The Party Game, Party Reform*, and *Decision for the Democrats*, and editor and coeditor of several other works, including the four-volume *Political Science: Looking to the Future*. He has served as president of the Midwest Political Science Association, the Policy Studies Organization, and the Political Organizations and Parties Section of the American Political Science Association, from which he received the Samuel J. Eldersveld Lifetime Achievement Award.

Jon K. Dalager received a J.D. from the University of Minnesota, and is currently a doctoral candidate in political science at the University of Illinois at Urbana-Champaign. His dissertation research concerns the long-term effect of the development of the mass media on electoral behavior.

Frank B. Feigert is Regents Professor of Political Science at the University of North Texas. He has authored or coauthored three books on American political parties, and has published articles on parties and voting behavior in such journals as the *American Political Science Review, Western Political Quarterly, Electoral Studies, Legislative Studies Quarterly, Public Opinion Quarterly, Publius*, and *American Politics Quarterly*, as well as in several anthologies.

Charles D. Hadley is a research professor of political science at the University of New Orleans and president of the Southern Political Science Association. Among his published books, articles, and chapters are studies of partisan change, nomination rules reform, presidential campaigns, and political party activists.

He is coauthor of *Transformations of the American Party System*.

John S. Jackson III is dean of the College of Liberal Arts and a professor of political science at Southern Illinois University at Carbondale. His teaching and research specialties are in political parties, party leadership, presidential elections, and Congress. He is coauthor, with William Crotty, of *Presidential Primaries and Elections*. His work has appeared in the *Journal of Politics, American Politics Quarterly, Polity, Midwest Journal of Political Science, Western Political Quarterly*, and *Legislative Studies Quarterly*.

John A. Kromkowski is assistant dean of the College of Arts and Sciences at the Catholic University of America and president of The National Center for Urban Ethnic Affairs in Washington, D.C. In addition, he coordinates international seminars and internship programs in four countries, and is conducting research projects on domestic institutions and political representation in the United States and the development of pluralism in Eastern Europe.

Jarol B. Manheim earned a Ph.D. from Northwestern University and is a professor of political communication and director of the National Center for Communication Studies at George Washington University. His research appears in the leading journals of political science, journalism, and communication. His most recent book, *All of the People, All the Time*, examines the techniques of strategic political communication as used in campaigns, lobbying, and public relations, whether for candidates, corporations, special interests, or foreign governments.

Jerome M. Mileur is a professor of political science at the University of Massachusetts at Amherst. He is coauthor with George T. Sulzner of *Campaigning for the Massachusetts Senate*, editor of *The Liberal Tradition in Crisis*, and coeditor with John K. White of *Challenges to Party Government*. He is a former executive director of the Committee for Party Renewal, a former member of the Massachusetts Democratic State Committee, and presently a director of the Center for Party Development.

Peter V. Miller is an associate professor of communication studies, an associate professor of journalism, and director of the Institute for

Modern Communications at Northwestern University. He holds A.B. and Ph.D. degrees from the University of Michigan. He has served on the faculties of Purdue University, the University of Illinois at Urbana-Champaign, and the University of Michigan. While at Michigan, he served as Study Director in the Survey Research Center of the Institute for Social Research, as well as an assistant professor of communication and sociology and director of the Detroit Area Study. Miller is past chair of the Standards Committee of the American Association for Public Opinion Research. He is currently editor of the Poll Review Section of *Public Opinion Quarterly* and chair of the Faculty Advisory Committee of the Northwestern University Survey Laboratory.

Peter F. Nardulli is a professor and department head of political science at the University of Illinois at Urbana-Champaign. Most of his past work has been in the area of law and politics, and his recent works include *The Tenor of Justice* and *The Constitution and American Political Development: An Institutional Perspective*. Most of his research over the past six years has been devoted to the study of electoral patterns in U.S. presidential elections, 1828–1984, for all counties and major cities.

Candice J. Nelson is an assistant professor of government at The American University and director of the University's Campaign Management Institute. Prior to coming to The American University, she was a visiting fellow at the Brookings Institution, where she wrote, with David B. Magleby, *The Money Chase*. She has also been an American Political Science Association Congressional Fellow and a special assistant to Senator Alan Cranston. She is a coauthor of *The Myth of the Independent Voter*, as well as

numerous articles on congressional elections and campaign finance. Her fields of expertise include the U.S. Congress, electoral behavior, interest groups, and campaign finance.

Harold W. Stanley is an associate professor of political science at the University of Rochester. Among his published articles and books are studies of partisan change, nomination rules reform, presidential campaigns, party activists, coalition building, and voter mobilization. He is also an editor of *Vital Statistics on American Politics*.

John Tierney is a member of the political science faculty at Boston College. With widely varying interests in American national politics, he is the author of several books, including *Organized Interests and American Democracy*, coauthored with Kay Lehman Schlozman. He has contributed articles to many scholarly journals and edited volumes on topics including the politics of government corporations, health-care policy-making, American foreign policy, and the ties that bind lobbyists and legislators. He is currently at work on a book about the intensifying political and cultural conflict surrounding federal land management policy in the western states.

John Kenneth White is an associate professor of politics at the Catholic University of America. He is author of *The Fractured Electorate*, *The New Politics of Old Values*, coeditor with Peter W. Colby of *New York State Today*, and coeditor with Jerome M. Mileur of *Challenges to Party Government*. He is a former executive director of the Committee for Party Renewal and currently vice president of the Center for Party Development.